The Kumiuta and Danmono

Traditions of Japanese Koto Music

Published under the auspices of the Institute of Ethnomusicology,

University of California, Los Angeles

The Kumiuta and Danmono Traditions of Japanese Koto Music

By

Willem Adriaansz

UNIVERSITY OF CALIFORNIA PRESS

Berkeley · Los Angeles · London

University of California Press
Berkeley and Los Angeles, California

University of California Press, Ltd.
London, England

ISBN: 0-520-01785-4
Library of Congress Catalog Card Number: 79-126026

Printed in the United States of America

To the memory of Jaap Kunst

Of the various genres of Japanese music, that for the *koto* is perhaps the easiest of access by the Westerner. He may be attracted to the pleasing, harplike timbre, and the somewhat formal and elegant quality of the music may remind him of chamber music of the Baroque in his own culture. A complete understanding of this music, however, requires musical reorientation, because the aesthetic underlying it is characteristically Japanese. And here, moreover, the student of Japanese music is at a disadvantage compared with the student of art, to whom numerous books and reproductions are available. Outside Japan, scores and records, as well as performances of Japanese music, are scarce, and include only the most popular items of the standard repertoire. There are, for example, practically no opportunities to hear a *kumiuta* (a song cycle with koto accompaniment) outside Japan.

And, indeed, the opportunity is hardly better in Japan itself. Although fifty-three kumiuta are known, they are rarely performed. Since the Meiji reformation in the second half of the nineteenth century Japanese musicians have become increasingly interested in musical Westernization, especially in koto music. Today many koto musicians and amateurs are strongly involved in *shinkyoku* ("New Music," i.e. Westernized music), often at the expense of older and more specifically Japanese forms. The old kumiuta, which flourished in the seventeenth and the first half of the eighteenth centuries, as the oldest form of their repertoire, is as highly regarded as it is rarely performed by the professional; to the amateur it is usually unknown. It is mainly the concern of a few specialists.

Danmono, a purely instrumental form of koto music, contemporary with kumiuta, has fared somewhat better. Two pieces, *Rokudan* and *Midare,* belong to the standard repertoire of every koto musician. Other compositions in this form, however, are rarely or never performed.

In the course of time both the kumiuta and danmono repertoires have been subjected to several revisions. The first version of a prominent kumiuta, *Fuki,* for example, is the one performed in Tsukushi-goto, the oldest school of koto music. Yatsuhashi Kengyō made a new arrangement of this composition, which was incorporated into the repertoire of the second school of koto music, named after him the Yatsuhashi-ryū. (Today both Tsukushi-goto and the Yatsuhashi-ryū are practically extinct.) Yatsuhashi's *Fuki* again was revised by one of his students, Kitajima Kengyō, whose version was incorporated into the repertoire of the oldest of the two great modern schools, the Ikuta-ryū. The version of the Ikuta school, finally,

vii

was adapted to the performance style of the second modern school, the Yamada-ryū. The purpose of the present study was a musicological investigation of the final stage of the kumiuta and danmono repertoires, rather than one devoted to their historic development. The older versions as contained in the repertoires of Tsukushi-goto and the Yatsuhashi-ryū have been touched upon only slightly. Because of the two modern schools, the Ikuta-ryū and the Yamada-ryū, only the Ikuta-ryū includes the complete repertoire of kumiuta and danmono, it was logical to base this study on the versions of this specific school. One exception, *Hatsune no Kyoku*, which is exclusively performed in the Yamada-ryū, had to be studied under the guidance of a Yamada musician.

In 1963 and 1964 I spent a year in Japan to collect and study the complete repertoires of danmono and kumiuta. All the danmono and most of the kumiuta were taught to me by Miss Hagiwara Seigin, and a few of the secret kumiuta by Miss Kikuzuki Shūei. Both musicians belong to the Ikuta School in Kyōto. Valuable information concerning Yamada School practice was obtained from Miss Torii Namino of Tōkyo. The collection of the repertoires was time-consuming but relatively easy. Because modern printed collections are practically non-existent, I worked from an eighteenth-century collection, the *Sōkyoku Taiishō*, which, however, like most koto notations does not include a notation of the voice part. In daily meetings with Miss Hagiwara first the koto part was checked, then the vocal melody was added, Miss Hagiwara singing the melody in fragments that I notated and later checked. I used Western notation —first, because the pitches used in koto music are in general very similar to those used in the West; second, because Japanese notation would present a serious stumbling block to the Western reader. During a second visit in 1969 I had an opportunity to make a study of the repertoire and performance practice of the Yatsuhashi-ryū with Mrs. Sanada Shin. Although the results of this later study have not been completely incorporated in this book (they are published separately), part was used in order to provide some historic perspective.

Like the kumiuta and danmono repertoires, this book has suffered several revisions. Its oldest version served as a doctoral dissertation (1965). The first revision was ready for the press in the summer of 1966, when, after an initial start, its publication was suspended until the spring of 1970. In the meantime I had conducted more research, some of the results of which had to be incorporated into what I hope will be the final version of this book. Its organization is partly determined by the needs of the Western reader, for whom, because of their unavailability in Western languages, an historic introduction as well as a discussion of the instrument have been included. Because of the topic of the book the historic section is strongly slanted toward kumiuta and danmono, that is, the repertoire until about the middle of the eighteenth century. On the other hand, a good deal of information concerning other forms of koto composition is included in order to place danmono and kumiuta in their proper historic perspective. A rather extensive discussion of instrumental techniques was considered necessary because knowledge of these techniques provides better than anything else an insight into the idiomatic style of koto composition. The fact that danmono have been discussed before kumiuta, notwithstanding the fact that the latter historically as well as quantitatively are the most important, was a matter of convenience: of the two forms, danmono provides the better introductory material because of the absence of complicating factors caused by the inclusion of the voice, the more limited number of tunings employed in danmono, and the small number of compositions, which makes danmono more easily accessible as a group.

A study of this kind is impossible without the active interest and help of Japanese musicians and musicologists. I received these without reserve. I am grateful above all to Miss Hagiwara, who spent countless hours with me, carefully and patiently singing phrase after phrase, over and over. Her astonishing knowledge of the koto repertoire was available to me at any time and, trying as our work must have been to her, her kind interest and patience never faltered. I am also indebted to Miss Kikuzuki, my second informant, and Miss Tsuda Michiko, with whom I had many fruitful discussions. Aside from these three musicians in Kyōto, I am grateful to Mrs. Sanada Shin and Dr. Kishibe Shigeo in Tōkyo for providing me with much valuable information. After the completion of my research in Japan I received further help in Los Angeles from Mr. Sam Hileman and Mrs. Nakako Memon, in Sydney from Dr. Geoffrey Sargent. Finally, I owe gratitude to Dr. Mantle Hood, Director of the Institute of Ethnomusicology of the University of California at Los Angeles, whose help in obtaining a Rockefeller grant made my research in Japan possible, and to the American Council of Learned Societies for a grant enabling me to study the Yatsuhashi-ryū.

CONTENTS

PART I: INTRODUCTION

I   The Sources of Koto Music   3
II   The Instrument   22
III   Scales and Tunings   31
IV   Notation   41
V   Playing Techniques   50

PART II: DANMONO

VI   The First Dan   63
VII   The Later Dan   86
VIII   Other Considerations (I)   109
IX   Other Considerations (II)   133

PART III: KUMIUTA

X   Fuki, the First Kumiuta   147
XI   Kumiuta in Hira-Jōshi   176
XII   Kumiuta in Other Chōshi   213
XIII   The Vocal Part in Kumiuta   226
XIV   Conclusion   258

PART IV: AN ANTHOLOGY OF KUMIUTA AND DANMONO

Introduction 265
Fuki 268
Kumoi no Kyoku 284
Sue no Matsu 302
Tamakazura 316
Shiki no Koi 330
Hien no Kyoku 342
Haru no Miya 358
Ōtsu no Kyoku 372
Hatsune no Kyoku 386
Akikaze 400
Godan 426
Kumoi Kudan 431
Midare 440
Yamada-Ryū Shirabe 451

APPENDIXES

A The Danmono Repertoire 454
B The Kumiuta Repertoire 455
C Kakezume Charts of Kumiuta in Tunings other than
                                        Hira-Jōshi   458
D Classification of the Repertoire 466

NOTES 468

BIBLIOGRAPHY 478

INDEX 484

PART I

INTRODUCTION

CHAPTER I

THE SOURCES OF KOTO MUSIC

Traditional Japanese art music is the product of a long assimilation and thorough Japan-
ization of a music that, as part of a larger cultural complex, was imported from China.
According to ancient Chinese histories, direct contacts between China and Japan existed as
early as the first century A.D.[1] Initially these contacts were rare and, because of the dan-
gers of the voyage across the East China Sea, occurred mainly by way of Korea. Gradually,
however, they increased in frequency and were made directly. Cultural borrowing, including
elements so diverse as political organization, Buddhist religion and art, and the writing system, as well as music, increased until a height of cultural intercourse was reached between
the beginning of the seventh and the end of the ninth centuries.

The earliest Japanese record of importation of foreign music mentions the arrival of eighty
musicians from the Korean state of Silla (Japanese: Shiragi) to attend to the funeral of
Emperor Ingyō in 453 A.D. (Aston 1956: 326). Later exposure to music from Korea, including that from the states of Paikche (Japanese: Kudara) and Kokuli (Japanese: Koma),
continued until at least the beginning of the seventh century. This music was strongly under
the influence of that from China, using not only Chinese instruments but also Chinese compositions. Direct musical influence from China itself increased gradually and in 702, when
the Gagaku-Ryō, the Department of Music, was established at the Japanese court, it included
not only Japanese and Korean but also Chinese musicians.[2] During the Nara and the early
Heian period (710-794 and 794-1185, respectively) many Chinese compositions of the T'ang
dynasty (618-907) were imported, and during the later Heian period they were thoroughly
adapted to the quite different Japanese taste.

Among the instruments that were imported from China was the *koto* (Chinese: *cheng*).
The function of this instrument in China had been twofold: it was part of the orchestras maintained by the T'ang nobility, and in socially less elevated classes it was used as a solo instrument. The T'ang orchestral music was taken over by the Japanese court in Kyōto where
it was to have, as *gagaku*, an important place in the ceremonial and social life of Japan's
aristocracy. The *gakusō*, as the koto in gagaku is called, plays a modest although indis-
pensable part in gagaku, a part consisting mainly of standardized patterns. In the *nokorigaku* version (an ornamented treatment) of some of the orchestral compositions as also
in the accompaniment of two genres of vocal gagaku music, *saibara* and *imayō*, its function
is somewhat more elaborate, but these forms still cannot be strictly regarded as *sōkyoku*
(solo koto music) and fall, therefore, outside the scope of this study. Nevertheless, gakusō

3

techniques had a strong influence on those of Tsukushi-goto—a koto school named after a region in the northwest of the island of Kyūshū—the results of which will be discussed in some detail in Chapter IV.[3]

According to legend, koto solo music was imported directly from China into the island of Kyūshū in the ninth century (Tanabe 1954: 249), where, eventually, it was to become one of the bases of Tsukushi-goto; this cannot be documented, however. The introduction of sōkyoku into Japan is often attributed to Fujiwara no Sadatoshi, a blind *biwa* player who lived in the ninth century and who could have learned koto solo music from his Chinese wife, the daughter of a famous biwa player. Although there is no doubt about Sadatoshi's connection with certain compositions for the biwa, nothing is known of a similar relationship with sōkyoku (Tanabe 1962: 168). Gagaku, because of its function in the elaborate court ceremonial, has survived until today; koto music in Kyūshū, having no such external support, did not survive, and we know of it only through legends. The best known of these tells how Ishikawa Iroko, a virgin of the Naikyobo shrine in Kyūshū, learned from a mysterious Chinese stranger koto pieces which she played for Emperor Uda (r. 887-897) when he visited the Hikoyamagongen shrine (*ibid.*: 169).

By the middle of the Heian period, a solo literature for the koto had developed at the court in Kyōto. None of this music has survived, and our knowledge of it depends entirely on literary sources of the late Heian and early Kamakura (1185-1336) periods such as the *Genji Monogatari* by Murasaki Shikibu and the *Heike Monogatari*, which is attributed to Nakayama Yukinaga. The *Genji Monogatari* contains numerous descriptions of more or less formal concerts in all available combinations of instruments, and among these, performances on the koto were especially frequent.[4] The *Heike Monogatari* contains a well-known story of a lady of the court, Kogō no Tsubone, who at the end of the Heian period played a composition called *Sōfukoi* on her koto in her hermitage at Sagano. This specific mention of the name of a composition has intrigued Japanese musicologists, several of whom have tried to identify the work with a gagaku composition, *Sōfuren*. Tanabe, however, pointing out that it is senseless to try to play a gagaku composition on the koto alone, proposes that the name *Sōfukoi* is probably a product of the imagination of the author of the *Heike Monogatari*.[5]

Artistic life among the aristocracy of the Heian court was of a high level, and the loss of the music for koto solo is probably a serious one. Several reasons can be given why this music did not survive. First, koto performance was in the hands not of professional musicians but of the noblemen and ladies, for whom it was a fashionable as well as pleasant social entertainment. Always interested in the newest and latest modes, they rarely bothered to try to conserve older music. The following quotation from the *Genji Monogatori* in the translation by Arthur Waley may illustrate their typically critical attitude toward anything not quite up to date:

> He spoke with so much enthusiasm and discernment that Genji was charmed with him and insisted upon his playing something on the large zithern. The old man's skill was astonishing. True, his handling of the instrument was such as is now considered very old-fashioned, and his fingering was all entirely in the discarded "Chinese" style with the left hand notes heavily accentuated (Murasaki 1960: 410).

Another, more important explanation for the loss of this music is provided by the social up-heavals at the end of the Heian period, which seriously disrupted Kyōto court life and caused many of the established court aristocracy, especially the ladies, to flee. Some of the refugees found safety on Kyūshū and may have introduced Heian sōkyoku there.

Tsukushi-goto

Tsukushi-goto derives its name from Tsukushi, the name of a region in the northwestern part of the island of Kyūshū. It may seem strange that an important new school of koto music could develop in a place so far removed from Kyōto, the center of musical activity, indeed, of culture in general. We have mentioned two of the hypotheses that have been adduced to explain the presence of sōkyoku in Kyūshū. The hypothesis of an introduction directly from China is supported only by legends. The possibility of introduction from Kyōto is supported by the occurrence in Tsukushi-goto of several compositions the titles of which are identical to those of pieces that are known to have been played in Kyōto at an earlier date; for example: *Rōei, Otome no Kyoku, Fuyu Nagauta,* and *Ogura no Kyoku* (Tanabe 1962:169). A third hypo-thesis suggests that Heian sōkyoku may have been introduced by Sugawara no Michizane (d. 903), a renowned scholar, during his provisional governorship of Dazaifu (901-903). There is no clear evidence, however, that an independent sōkyoku had developed in Kyūshū before the sixteenth century. Most doubtful of all is the story about Taira no Kiyomori (1118-1181), who is said to have consoled himself during his exile from Kyōto by playing the koto, thus introducing Heian sōkyoku to Kyūshū. Kiyomori's exile was in point of fact in Bizen (the present Okayama prefecture), not on Kyūshū (Tanabe 1954: 259).

Although how and when sōkyoku came to Kyūshū cannot be stated with confidence, we are on more solid ground, probably, in accepting *zokkyoku* (popular songs) as one of the sources from which Tsukushi-goto drew. This music, which included *kouta* and *odori-uta* (folk songs and dances) and which could be accompanied by the koto, was very popular on Kyūshū in the region around Hakata during the time when foreign trade still was allowed (from the middle of the sixteenth century to the middle of the seventeenth). For a while zokkyoku spread widely. It did not, however, penetrate the Kinki area (Kyōto and Ōsaka), which at that time was disturbed by warfare. Zokkyoku was exported to the Ryūkyū islands where part of it survives in what today sometimes is called the Okinawan Yatsuhashi-ryū. The occurrence on Okinawa of a body of compositions called Yatsuhashi-ryū is intriguing, for this music does not seem to have any direct connection with the Japanese composer and creator of modern sōkyoku, Yatsuhashi Kengyō.[6] The oldest printed source of sōkyoku, the *Shichiku Shoshinshū* (pub-lished in 1664), contains several examples of zokkyoku, among which two compositions for koto solo. One of these two instrumental compositions, *Rinzetsu*, shows a striking simi-larity to both *Rinzetsu* of Tsukushi-goto and *Takiotoshi Sugagaki* also called *Ichidan* of the Okinawan koto repertoire, while the other, *Sugagaki*, has been shown to be prototype of the Japanese and Okinawan danmono repertoires.[7] In Japan zokkyoku, accompanied by the koto, flourished for only a short while.

The music of the island of Kyūshū discussed above might have disappeared completely had not the priest-musician Kenjun (1547-1636) selected and organized into a group a number of pieces. These, together with ten of his own vocal-instrumental compositions, *kumiuta,*[8] were to form the repertoire of what came to be called Tsukushi-goto or, later, *Tsukushi-ryū.*[9] Kenjun was a priest at the Zendōji at Kurume where at a young age he learned to play the gagaku compositions which were performed in the temple. Kenjun's knowledge of gagaku was highly significant for his own compositions —especially his first kumiuta, *Fuki*— which took a strong imprint from the older art. Construction, instrumental techniques, and tunings were derived directly from gagaku. In addition to the music performed in the temple (*Zendōjigaku*), Kenjun studied the *shichigenkin* (the Chinese "*ch'in*") under the guidance of Teikajō, a master of *Mingaku* (Chinese music of the Ming dynasty). Chinese influence is obvious in the texts of two of Kenjun's compositions, *Yōkan no Kyoku*, which is sung in Chinese with the pronunciation of the Ming dynasty, and *Kigan no Kyoku*, sung in T'ang Chinese.

Tsukushi-goto, performed by Buddhist priests, Confucian scholars, and noblemen, was not a popular art. Its teaching to blind men (the carriers of the more popular traditions) was forbidden and from the time of Kenjun's student Genjo (d. 1662), women were also excluded. Usually performed in temples, Tsukushi-goto had a pensive, retired mood, aloof from the world. Under no condition was it played purely for entertainment.

Kenjun's training in gagaku and shichigenkin probably accounts for this non-popular, esoteric character of Tsukushi-goto. Traditional Tsukushi-goto tunings are related to those of the gakusō; that is, the octave is divided into five steps consisting of major seconds and minor thirds. The most characteristic tuning in Tsukushi-goto is as follows:[10]

Example 1.

About a hundred years following Kenjun's death, in the middle of the Edo period (1600-1868), a few Tsukushi-goto pieces were composed for a tuning with half steps, *kamimu-chō*, which is identical to the tuning *kumoi-jōshi* in the later zokusō.[11] These compositions were not considered to be representative of the school, however, and were classified as minor works (*ōgi*).

Gagaku influence is also evident in the instrument and instrumental techniques. The koto is similar to the gakusō, and the *tsume*, the finger plectra, somewhat resemble those used in gagaku. As for the instrumental techniques, like those in the older genre, they consist in large part of standard patterns and are closely related to the stereotyped gagaku patterns *shizugaki* and *hayagaki*. The connections between the patterns in Tsukushi-goto, however, are more elaborate and complex than their gagaku counterparts.[12]

The restrictions on the performance of Tsukushi-goto, as well as the characteristic mood of the music, proved fatal for its survival. When, after the Meiji reforms, the school lost its traditional patronage by the Saga clan, its aloofness made competition with the younger Ikuta and Yamada-ryū impossible and there followed a rapid decline that reached its nadir during the Taishō period (1912-1926). The last head of the school, Noda Chōshō, in a desperate attempt to save Tsukushi-goto from oblivion, violated one of the oldest rules by accepting four female students. When the attention of Japanese musicologists was drawn to

Tsukushi-goto about thirty years ago, they found that the school was all but extinct. There was no living performer of professional quality; only two aged female players remained to carry on the old tradition. Professional guidance is necessary for a complete understanding of Tsukushi-goto, for the scores are incomplete, and this could no longer be provided for the entire repertoire because neither of the two musicians knew all the pieces. At present the situation seems quite hopeless; one of the two players (Murai Reiko) is now dead, the other (Inoue Mina) has no students.

From Kenjun's time on, classification of the repertoire became a matter of concern for all founders of new schools of koto music. The purpose of classification was twofold: it grouped pieces of the same kind together, and it also provided a fixed order by which the students were guided through the repertoire. A classification of representative works, according to Tanabe (1956: 52), is as follows:[13]

1. *Tsukushi-ei,* comprised of the group of Kenjun's ten kumiuta: *Fuki* (also called *Etenraku, Harukaze, Karakami, Umegae, Shiki no Midare, Rankyoku, Shūka no Kyoku, Kanya no Kyoku, Hana no En, Aki no Yama,* and *Shiki.*

2. *Tsukushi-hiei,* comprised of *hikyoku,* "secret pieces": *Otome no Kyoku* (also called *Takiochi), Yōkan no Kyoku, Shūfū no Ji, Ogura no Kyoku, Fuyu Nagauta, Rōei, Kigan no Kyoku,* and *Ukigomo.*

3. *Ōgi,* comprised of *Uya no Kyoku, Saikiku, Hakke no Kyoku,* and *Isshi no Kyoku.*

4. *Dengai-hikyoku* ("most secret pieces"), consisting of only one composition: *Kaikyū no Kyoku.*[14]

Yatsuhashi Kengyō and Zokusō Kumiuta

A visit to Kyōto by Genjo,[15] the second head of the Tsukushi-ryū, had unexpected and far-reaching consequences for the development of sōkyoku. Highly appreciated by the court aristocracy, he was requested to send a skillful player back to them when he returned to Kyūshū. Genjo sent his student Hosui, whose performance for some reason or other was received unfavorably by his demanding audience.[16] Hosui thereupon went to Edo, where he accepted a blind shamisen player, Yamazumi Kōtō, whose original name had been Johide, as his student in sōkyoku. This violation of the rule forbidding instruction in Tsukushi-goto to the blind caused Hosui's exclusion from the Tsukushi-ryū. We shall see later that there are reasons for assuming that Hosui taught only a limited number of pieces to his gifted student. The often repeated story that Yamazumi afterwards went to Kyūshū to study with Genjo seems very unlikely: there is no evidence to support the story and one would hardly expect that Genjo, after condemning Hosui for teaching a blind man, would himself violate the same rule immediately afterwards (Tanabe 1962: 177). Yamazumi settled down in Kyōto where he changed his name to Kaminaga Kengyō,[17] and later again to Yatsuhashi Kengyō.

In his compositions, thirteen kumiuta, Yatsuhashi made a revolutionary innovation by using the popular *in* scale, rather than the scales of gagaku or of the Tsukushi and Okinawan koto schools. This seven-tone scale is distinguished by the presence of half steps between the first and the second, and between the fifth and the sixth degrees. These half steps reappear in what was to become, for several centuries, the most important koto tuning, *hira-jōshi*.[18] Yatsuhashi used this tuning in all but two of his compositions, *Kumoi no Kyoku* and *Kumoi Rōsai*; in the latter he used *Hon-kumoi-jōshi* which is also based on the *in* scale (see Ex. 2).

Example 2.

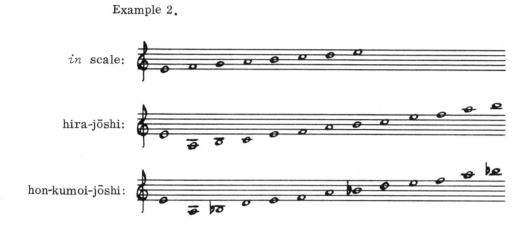

in scale:

hira-jōshi:

hon-kumoi-jōshi:

Some of Yatsuhashi's compositions are no more than arrangements of kumiuta from Tsukushi-goto. These arrangements consist of an adaptation of the original composition to the new tuning, hira-jōshi, and the use of more elaborate connections between the patterns than those in the originals. It is likely that the tempo was increased; this is not certain, however, for sōkyoku notations contain no tempo indications, and the tradition is unreliable in this respect, having shown a development toward faster tempi, especially during recent generations.

These changes contributed to the creation in Yatsuhashi's kumiuta of a spirit and mood rather different from those in Tsukushi-goto. He deliberately avoided the devotional, religious feeling that characterizes the music of Tsukushi-goto, and this undoubtedly should be interpreted as a movement toward   popularization. It is not without reason that the term *zokusō* was applied to this new music. Zokusō can be translated as "popular koto," or "vulgar koto."[19]   But there is no trace of vulgarity in this elegant and refined music which never really became popular, although it was accepted by the professional musicians. The application of the term zokusō must be explained as a result of a shift in the social milieu of the music (see pages 12-13).

Yatsuhashi's kumiuta became the model for this genre and, for a time, for all compositions of koto music in general. A kumiuta, it may be repeated, is a song cycle, the texts of which have the remarkable characteristic that, being taken from different sources, they are not necessarily related to one another. Since Yatsuhashi's time, kumiuta normally consists of six songs, each of thirty-two measures of 4/4 or 2/2. The form is very regular, strict, severe, and balanced, with an intimate, somewhat subdued, refined quality; it has characteristics, in short, that appealed more to aristocrats whose rearing traditionally included thorough education in aesthetic fields, than to developing bourgeosie just beginning to bring art into the constantly widening circle of their interests. In retrospect, it seems inevitable that kumiuta had to be replaced, eventually, by livelier, lighter, and less severe forms.

Kumiuta were composed not only for the koto but for the shamisen as well. Yatsuhashi during his years as a shamisen virtuoso undoubtedly was familiar with the shamisen kumiuta. The instrument itself, having been imported around 1562 from Ryūkū, was at that time still rather a novelty in Japan and its literature was practically limited to kumiuta. It is not sure when the first shamisen kumiuta were composed. Fujita Tonan (1930: 11) dates them during the Genna-Kanei period (1615-1630); Kikkawa Eishi (1961: 7 and 1965: 167) sets them farther back, in the Keichō period (1596-1615). Whatever the date, the first known shamisen kumiuta are said to have been composed by Ishimura Kengyō (d. 1642) and Torazawa Kengyō (d. 1654). Later the form was developed by Yanagawa Kengyō in Kyōto and by Nogawa Kengyō in Ōsaka. These latter two musicians were founders of their own schools of kumiuta, the Yanagawa-ryū and Nogawa-ryū, which survive today.

Like the texts of kumiuta for the koto, the texts of shamisen kumiuta were a combination of several, normally unrelated poems. The sources for koto kumiuta texts were usually standard, esteemed works of serious literature; such sources were not drawn on for shamisen kumiuta texts, which mostly were taken from various types of popular songs such as kouta, odori-uta, and *kabuki-uta*. The music, however, was sophisticated and, although simple during its early stages, quite formal and elegant and the technique required of the accompanying shamisen became highly developed.

It is said that Yatsuhashi's compositions for the koto are influenced somewhat by shamisen kumiuta. It is very likely, indeed, that Yatsuhashi's introduction of the *in* scale in sōkyoku represents an adaptation of a practice already existing in shamisen music. The secularization of sōkyoku and also the development of the instrumental technique may well have been influenced by the shamisen example, which at that time had been developed to a high artistic and technical level by Yatsuhashi's contemporary, Yanagawa Kengyō. The influence does not, however, extend to formal elements: the shamisen kumiuta is loosely constructed, while that for the koto is tightly controlled with a fixed number of beats (128) of quarter-note duration for each uta. Melodic patterns that typically characterize koto kumiuta are absent in those composed for the shamisen. Koto kumiuta texts are on an artistic level that is considerably higher than shamisen texts, and more care is devoted to the combination of poems that make up a kumiuta. The stylistic development of shamisen kumiuta was so swift and so radical that the form had practically dissolved itself into later forms of *jiuta* by the end of the seventeenth century. Koto kumiuta, on the other hand, maintained throughout their entire history a strong stylistic homogeneity. The following chart summarizes the differences between shamisen and koto kumiuta:[20]

	Shamisen Kumiuta	Koto Kumiuta
Origin	Popular genres of beginning 17th century	Tsukushi-goto
Text	Derived from popular material	Carefully selected from artistic sources
Number of uta	Varying between one and fifteen, with a certain preference for six	Normally, six
Form of uta	Free	Very strict, each uta containing a fixed number of measures
Instrumental interlude	In earlier stages absent, frequent and often extensive in later types	Practically absent, very short
Stylistic evolution	Considerable	Slight

The complete repertoire of koto kumiuta, including, of course, those composed by Yatsuhashi Kengyō, is listed in Appendix B. Two compositions *Kumoi Rōsai* [21] and *Shin Kumoi Rōsai* are included in the list because they are usually classified as kumiuta, although structurally they do not belong to this form, being related to the shamisen kouta. Traditionally a number of purely instrumental pieces, such as *Rokudan* and *Hachidan,* are classified as kumiuta, probably because they used to be published in kumiuta collections. Structurally, there is not the slightest reason for this classification, although, like kumiuta, these pieces consist of several movements (called *dan*) that are very strict in form and contain a fixed number of beats. These instrumental pieces are usually referred to as *danmono* or *shirabemono*.

To Yatsuhashi Kengyō is usually attributed the authorship of *Rokudan, Hachidan,* and *Midare*. This attribution is far from certain, especially in respect to the first (see page 5, note 7). In his book *Shin Kinkyokushū,* Kisegawa Kōtō at the end of the Edo period suggested the possibility that *Rokudan* in its present form may be attributed to Yatsuhashi's student, Kitajima Kengyō (Tanabe, 1962: 171). [22]

Tanabe has investigated the relationship between the texts of Yatsuhashi's kumiuta and those of Tsukushi-goto. He concluded that only the texts of *Kokoro Zukushi, Yuki no Ashita, Usugoromo, Kiritsubo, Ōgi no Kyoku,* and *Kumoi no Kyoku* had not been borrowed from the older school. Tanabe's findings concerning the derivation of the texts of the other kumiuta are as follows:

Yatsuhashi's Compositions		*Tsukushi-goto*	
Fuki		*Fuki*	(with the omission of two uta)
Umegae	: uta 1	*Umegae*	(uta 1)
	: uta 2	*Rankyoku*	(uta 1)
	: uta 3, first part	*Umegae*	(uta 3, first part)
Tenka Taihei	: uta 5	*Hana no En*	(uta 3)
	: uta 6	*Aki no Yama*	(uta 4)
Usuyuki	: uta 2	*Hana no En*	(uta 1)
Kumo no Ue	: uta 1	*Hana no En*	(uta 3)
	: uta 2	*Rankyoku*	(uta 2)
Suma	: uta 2	*Hana no En*	(uta 1)
	: uta 5	*Shūka no Kyoku*	(uta 1)
Shiki no Kyoku	: uta 1	*Aki no Yama*	(uta 1)
	: uta 2, 3, 4 and 5	*Shiki*	

The above chart makes clear which pieces Yamazumi learned from Hosui. Tanabe's suggestion (1962: 178), that they might have been taught incorrectly, is probably influenced by Hosui's reputation as a mediocrity and sounds somewhat malicious.

Takano Tatsuyuki (1926: 739-752) has shown that the origin of some kumiuta texts dates from before Tsukushi-goto.[23] A collection of koto music of the Kamakura period, the *Shinsōgochō*, which is preserved in the Sampōin in Daigo, near Kyōto, contains texts that are very similar to the texts of *Fuki, Umegae, Kiritsubo,* and *Kokoro Zukushi.*

Yatsuhashi's kumiuta normally contains six uta; exceptions are *Fuki* and *Shiki no Kyoku,* the former containing seven (the addition is an introductory uta), the latter consisting of an introductory uta, followed by four uta, each of which represents a season of the year. Yatsuhashi's thirteen kumiuta are known as *Yatsuhashi no jūsan-gumi.* Three of the most famous, *Shiki no Kyoku, Ōgi no Kyoku,* and *Kumoi no Kyoku,* form a group referred to as the *Yatsuhashi no san-kyoku.*[24]

With the creation of zokusō, a new shift in social milieu of the music can be noticed. Heian sōkyoku had been the privilege of the aristocracy, Tsukushi-goto that of priests and Confucianists. Zokusō came to be composed and performed mostly by blind professional musicians, while its amateurs were found among the bourgeosie. To learn Tsukushi-goto was a privilege, granted a student; as for zokusō, its instruction to members of well-to-do families, especially young girls, became a main source of income for the musicians in whose hands it had passed. These blind musicians were organized as the *Shoku-yashiki,* a professional organization comparable to a guild, which bestowed ranks upon and protected the professional and material interests of its members. Women were excluded. Four ranks existed: *kengyō, bettō,*[25] *kōtō,* and *zatō.* The highest, kengyō, was regarded as equal to *Jūmango ku-daimyō.*

The position of a kengyō in the organization was powerful and therefore the rank was much desired. Normally it was attained by merit, not by purchase, although a few cases of its being bought are known. It is interesting to note that, while playing kumiuta, a kengyō used to wear a special headdress, somewhat similar to that of a Buddhist priest. This he would not wear while playing other forms. Herein we may see a sign of special respect for the kumiuta, which was the oldest and most highly respected zokusō form, although definitely not, in later times at least, the one most often performed. The Shoku-yashiki was disbanded at the beginning of the Meiji period (1868-1912). For a while afterwards the kengyō rank continued to be given to outstanding blind musicians, but this custom has been abandoned. One of the last musicians to be addressed as kengyō was Tsuda Kengyō (Tsuda Seikan), who died shortly after World War II.

With the activities of Yatsuhashi Kengyō a new school of sōkyoku, the Yatsuhashi-ryū, may be considered to have begun. The official establishment of the school—by Kagawa Kengyō and his pupil Kamejima Kengyō—did not take place before the late Edo period, however, when it became necessary to distinguish it from new developments, represented mainly by the Ikuta-ryū (Tanabe, 1955-1957: 52). Like the Tsukushi-ryū, the Yatsuhashi-ryū today is almost extinct, being represented by only one performer, Sanada Shin. [26]

Yatsuhashi Kengyō was succeeded by his student Kitajima Kengyō (d. 1690), an excellent composer whose kumiuta *Akashi*, *Sue no Matsu*, and *Utsumemi* are in no respect inferior to those of his master. Kitajima's most important students were Kurahashi Kengyō (d. 1690) and Ikuta Kengyō (1656-1715). As composers, this third generation was not very important. Kurahashi composed *Shin Kumoi Rōsai*, a kind of restatement of Yatsuhashi's *Kumoi Rōsai* that is not an improvement upon the older piece. As the founder of Ikuta-ryū, a new school of sōkyoku that opened urgently needed new vistas, Ikuta's importance is not easily overestimated; as a composer, however, he is almost negligible: his name is mentioned only in connection with two kumiuta, *Omoigawa* and *Kagami no Kyoku*, and one danmono, *Godan*, and that he was actually the composer of these pieces is uncertain.

Until the end of the seventeenth century kumiuta and danmono were the only forms of sōkyoku, and the Japanese, as always keenly reacting to changing situations, had begun to condemn the form as old-fashioned and unable to meet the demands of the time. The shamisen, generally a more popular instrument than the somewhat more formal koto, and therefore responding more quickly to new demands, already had developed new styles that had replaced the old shamisen kumiuta. Sōkyoku also had to renew itself in order to survive. Ikuta Kengyō, a musician in Kyōto, recognized this situation and opened the way toward development by founding in 1695 a new school, the Ikuta-ryū.

In his quest for a rejuvenation of koto music, Ikuta Kengyō turned his attention to the new forms in shamisen music, which collectively were known as jiuta. Literally, jiuta means regional songs, the region referred to being the Kyōto-Ōsaka area, which is also known as Kamigata. Sometimes the term *Kamigata-uta* was used to distinguish jiuta from shamisen music from the Edo region. In its widest sense, the term jiuta includes all shamisen music of a lyrical and non-narrative character and therefore concerns kumiuta as well as later forms such as *hauta*, *kouta*, and *nagauta*, which during the Jōkyō (1684-1688) and Genroku

(1688-1704) periods succeeded kumiuta.[27] Terminology in Japanese music is not always consistent, and in this case, for example, it is not possible to draw a clear line between hauta and nagauta. Kamigata-nagauta should not be confused with Edo-nagauta, which were composed in close relationship to the Kabuki theater; and so also the hauta of around 1700 should be distinguished from hauta, short shamisen songs, of the late Edo period (first half of the nineteenth century).

In jiuta, the strict structural limitations of the koto kumiuta are abandoned in favor of freer forms. The result is more variety of atmosphere than in the homogeneous kumiuta. Texts begin to be taken from contemporary sources or to be written especially, and the relationship of text to the music is more direct. The instrumental technique developed to constantly higher levels. Concerned as the musicians were with the production of a beautiful tone, the tempo tended to remain rather slow, and the mood, although livelier and more sensual than in kumiuta, remained formal. Unlike kumiuta, the form of a jiuta was not predetermined, but followed the requirements of the text. Short works, for example, consist of one or two parts; longer ones follow the *jo-ha-kyū* concept.[28] In general, jiuta begin slowly, speed up gradually until, near the end, the tempo suddenly slows down to the initial speed.

Ikuta Kengyō rightly perceived that the future of sōkyoku lay in an association with these newly developed shamisen forms. Shamisen jiuta were now played on the koto also, mostly in ensemble with the shamisen. In the beginning, the koto part was practically the same as that of the shamisen and this meant sacrificing the independence of the koto. This break with older tradition was a serious one and could not be made so long as the creator of that tradition, Yatsuhashi Kengyō, still lived. In 1695, however, there was no longer any obstacle: ten years had passed since the death of Yatsuhashi Kengyō and five years since that of Ikuta's teacher, Kitajima Kengyō.

As several tunings were in use for the shamisen, new tunings had to be devised for the koto if the two instruments were to be played together. Among these new tunings were *nakazora, han-nakazora, han-kumoi,* and *akebono.*[29] Another innovation was the introduction of square tsume *(kakuzume* or *kadozume),* which were more suitable to the now rather frequently-occurring alternation of down and upstrokes *(sukuizume),* that imitated a similar practice of the shamisen *(sukuibachi).* It is assumed that the square tsume was devised by Kitajima Kengyō who, however, did not make his innovation public out of respect for his teacher, Yatsuhashi Kengyō, who was still alive. The playing position was also changed, and from now on the player knelt at an angle at the right end of the instrument.

The association of the koto with jiuta did not mean that kumiuta performance and composition were abolished. The Shoku-yashiki would not accept the Ikuta-ryū as a new school unless kumiuta were classified as the main work of the school; the other, later forms were considered as less important *(gekyoku).* Ikuta Kengyō arranged kumiuta according to difficulty into four classes: *omote-gumi, ura-gumi, naka-yurushi,* and *oku-yurushi.* The popularity of kumiuta, however, declined and the form became more and more a concern of specialists.

The most important later composer of kumiuta was Mitsuhashi Kengyō (d. 1760), the relatively prolific composer of eight works. *Miya no Uguisu, Shiki no Fuji, Jichō, Setsu-gekka, Mutamagawa, Tamakazura, Ukifune,* and *Shiki no Koi.* The traditional Japanese composer, unlike his Western colleague, usually will not attempt to make important changes in a form once its model has been set by a composer whose authority has been accepted. The technique may be refined but not changed to such a degree that its original character might be obscured, let alone lost. Thus, regarded as a body, kumiuta show a strong homogeneity that sometimes, with minor composers, degenerates into uniformity. Mitsuhashi's kumiuta, although by no means violating the established form, reflect to a certain degree the developments that had taken place in the Ikuta-ryū. The most obvious of his innovations was the introduction of new tunings, such as nakazora, han-nakazora, and han-kumoi, and the change of tuning within a single kumiuta. Moreover, his *ai-no-te*—short instrumental interludes that in the kumiuta of his predecessors had been of minuscule length—tended to become a little longer, while his use of standard melodic patterns was subordinated somewhat in favor of free sections.

Mitsuhashi's best student was Yasumura Kengyō (d. 1779), the composer of a single kumiuta, *Hien no Kyoku*. In his function as *Sō-kengyō*, President of the Shoku-yashiki, Yasumura prohibited the composition of more kumiuta, considering their number to have grown too large and, apparently, not expecting new contributions of value. The form had by this time largely lost its capacity to reflect the changing musical tide, and Yasumura showed good insight. It would have been well if his order had been obeyed. A number of kumiuta composed by Hisamura Kengyō *(Shiki no Tomo* and *Tomo Chidori)*, Ishizuka Kengyō *(Hana no En*, and *Haru no Miya*, which is also called *Mitsu no Shirabe)*, and some anonymi did not contribute anything that had not been done better before, except to add a tuning, akebono, that until then had not appeared in kumiuta. Moreover, Yasumura's excellent *Hien no Kyoku* would have been a worthy conclusion to the kumiuta repertoire. His prohibition probably caused a number of later kumiuta to be published anonymously, their authors not wanting to violate it openly.

At about the same time as the founding of the Ikuta-ryū, other new schools came into being which, like the Ikuta-ryū, combined the koto with the jiuta shamisen. These were the Sumiyama-ryū, founded by Sumiyama Kengyō who was, like Ikuta Kengyō, a student of Kitajima Kengyō; the Shin Yatsuhashi-ryū, founded by Shin Yatsuhashi Kengyō; and the Tsugiyama-ryū, founded by Tsugiyama Kengyō (d. 1697) as a branch of the Sumiyama-ryū. Tsugiyama Kengyō, a student of Sumiyama Kengyō, originally was a physician in Kyōto and it was there that he established his school. Through one of his female students, Osuma, the Tsugiyama-ryū found many followers in Ōsaka, where one of Osuma's students named Kikuike Kengyō founded a new school, the Kikuike-ryū, that was to remain limited to the Ōsaka region. Later still other schools, such as the Fujiike-ryū and the Shin Ikuta-ryū, appeared. All of these schools, most of which have today disappeared almost entirely, can be considered to be Ikuta-ryū in a wider sense.

A number of kumiuta belonging to these smaller schools are classified as "secret" and "most secret" pieces *(hikyoku* and *goku-hikyoku*, respectively). The Shin Yatsuhashi-ryū possessed two kumiuta, *Yaegaki* and *Tobiume*, which were both classified as hikyoku. Tsugiyama Kengyō was the composer of *Otsu no Kyoku, Kan no Kyoku, Kasumi no Kyoku,* and *Kō Genji,* the first two of which are hikyoku, the other two, goku-hikyoku. When the prohibition against free distribution of the secret pieces was lifted in the Meiji period, kumiuta by then had become so limited to only specialists that in effect not much was changed: the secret pieces remained practically unknown.

As already stated, the bulk of the kumiuta repertoire was complete by the time of Yasumura Kengyō, that is, by the last quarter of the eighteenth century. The few compositions written soon after Yasumura have been mentioned; the last of these that can be dated confidently were composed not later than the early nineteenth century. It is possible that a few kumiuta were anonymously composed early in the nineteenth century; however, during most of the century, kumiuta were performed very seldom and were considered thoroughly out of date. Toward the middle of the century, to be sure, there was a slight quickening of interest in kumiuta, though nothing so important as a revival, and at least one composition was composed that can be classified as a kumiuta, while others were influenced by the form. Before discussing these, it is well to follow the development of other forms of koto music, in order to establish the context in which the last compositions appeared.

Jiuta composers were strongly interested in instrumental technique and this, eventually, led to new forms in their compositions as the length of the instrumental interludes, the ai-no-te, were gradually extended until they frequently were longer than the sung parts. These long ai-no-te were called *tegoto*, and the form in which they occurred, *tegoto-mono*. This development began in the Genroku period (1688-1703) with the compositions *Sandan-jishi* by Sayama Kengyō and *Sarashi* by Fukakusa Kengyō[30] and reached its definite shape in Ōsaka around the Kansei period (1789-1800) with the works of Minezaki Kōto (a. o. *Azuma-jishi*, *Zangetsu*, and *Echigo-jishi*) and Mitsuhashi Kōtō (*Sho-chiku-bai* and *Nebiki no Matsu*). Basically, the tegoto form consists of three parts: *mae-uta* (fore-song), tegoto and *ato-uta* (after-song). The mae-uta is sung slowly; the tempo of the tegoto is rather fast and its technique is difficult; the ato-uta is slow again, although usually somewhat faster than the mae-uta. Keeping this basic three-part structure in mind, it is easy to understand how more complicated forms were derived from it. For example, the mae-uta could be preceded by a short instrumental introduction, the *mae-biki*, and followed by a passage of transitional character, a *tsunagi*, to connect it with the tegoto. The tegoto could be preceded by a *makura* (also called *jo*), a rather extensive section of introductory character. The tegoto itself could consist of several sections, *dan*, and be concluded by a finale-like part, the *chirashi*. The ato-uta, finally, could be followed by an instrumental postlude, *ato-biki*. Further subdivisions could be made without essentially changing the basic structure. A chirashi could occur twice, the first time as a temporary climax, *naka-chirashi*, in the middle of the tegoto, the second time as the real climax at the end, the *hon-chirashi*. Occasionally another song, *naka-uta*, could be inserted in the middle of the tegoto. The following scheme may illustrate the simple and complex tegoto mono structures.

I.	MAE-UTA (Foresong)	I.	1.	Mae-biki (Introduction)
			2.	MAE-UTA
			3.	Tsunagi (Connection)
			4.	Makura (Introduction)
			5.	TEGOTO (consisting of several dan)
II.	TEGOTO (Interlude)	II.	6.	Naka-chirashi (Temporary climax)
			7.	TEGOTO (continued)
			8.	Hon-chirashi (Climax)
III.	ATO-UTA (Aftersong)	III.	9.	ATO-UTA
			10.	Ato-biki (Postlude)

The relationship between the shamisen and the koto also gradually changed from an almost complete dependence of the koto on the shamisen in the earlier jiuta, to increasing independence of both instruments. We have seen that in the beginning, the koto played the same part as the shamisen. Soon the koto part would be developed into an ornamental version of the basic shamisen melody adapted to the special technical possibilities of the instrument. This development took place mainly in Ōsaka during the Bunka period (1804-1817), in the compositions of Ichiura Kengyō *(Kamakura Hakkei, Tsukimi, Konkai, Ko Dōjōji, Hōkasō, Tamagawa,* and *Okina)*.   When koto and shamisen play equally important, interdependent parts, one speaks of *kaete-shiki sōkyoku*. "Kaete" refers to the ornamental version, added to the original part, called *honte*. Usually the kaete is played in a higher register than the honte. Two remarkable performance practices developed at this same time: *uchiawase* and *dangaeshi*. In uchiawase, two pieces, normally one already existing and one newly composed, are played simultaneously. Two types of "uchiawase-mono" exist: (a) a combination of two complete compositions (e.g. *Yachiyo-jishi* and *Bansei-jishi; Uchiban* and *Yokozuchi; Suribachi* and *Rengi)*; (b) a combination of parts of two compositions (e.g. the chirashi from the tegoto of *Hagi no Tsuyu* and *Isochidori)*. In dangaeshi two players perform simultaneously two dan of a tegoto —a possibility that exists only when the dan are equal in length — after which they switch parts. Thus the listener hears the same music twice. Obviously dangaeshi is of more interest to the players than to their audience.

Although begun in Ōsaka, kaete-shiki sōkyoku reached its highest development in Kyōto, especially in the works of Yaezaki Kengyō (d. 1848), where such compositions were called *kyōmono*. Yaezaki's strength lay in his arrangements as kaete-shiki sōkyoku of shamisen compositions by other composers. Specialization of this kind in composition may seem strange to Westerners, but is common practice in Japan.[31] Several of the most famous sōkyoku found their final shape under Yaezaki's hands —among others, *Tama no Utena, Sue no Chigiri, Shiki no Nagame, Uji Meguri, Yotsu no Tami, Shinya no Tsuki, Wakana* and *Shin Ukifune,* all composed by Matsuura Kengyō (d. 1822); *Isochidori, Fune no Yume, Imakomachi, Cha no Yū Ondo (Chaondo), Sasa no Tsuyu* (also called *Sake)*, *Yūgao, Miyama-jishi, Kaji Makura, Keshi no Hana,* and *Nagara no Haru,* composed by Kikuoka Kengyō (d. 1847); and *Yaegoromo* by Ishikawa Kōto.

According to Satō (1941, Text Volume: 10), Yaezaki may be the composer of four kumiuta usually considered anonymous: *Wakana, Tachibana, Tanabata,* and *Sakaki-ba.* Although certain stylistic features indicate a rather late date of composition, Yaezaki's authorship cannot be definitely proved.

During the Tempō period (1830-1843), when kyōmono had reached its highest development, a remarkable reaction set in against this form and attempts were made to free the koto from the hegemony of the shamisen, which still largely dominated in sōkyoku. Mitsuzaki Kengyō (d. 1853), partly in cooperation with Yaezaki Kengyō had composed a number of masterpieces in kyōmono (a.o. *Yoyo no Hoshi, Nanakomachi, Chio no Uguisu,* and *Sakuragawa)* before writing *Godan-Ginuta,* a highly original composition for two koto without shamisen. Notwithstanding its originality, however, *Godan Ginuta* in its instrumental brilliance, as well as its construction and mood, is still close to kyōmono. In a later composition, *Akikaze no Kyoku,* Mitsuzaki revived the simplicity of the old, pure sōkyoku, the clearest example of which had been kumiuta. *Akikaze* combines the danmono form in the long introduction for solo koto with that of kumiuta for the following six songs. The introduction, consisting of six dan, is often played simultaneously with *Rokudan*. The text, arranged by Makita Unsho, is taken in its entirety from the famous Chinese poem *Chōkonka*, and in this respect, therefore, deviates from the standard kumiuta text compiled from multiple sources. The tuning is a unique one, used exclusively for this composition (see page 37).

Mitsuzaki's interest in older styles was not an isolated phenomenon but reflected a widespread tendency among the intellectuals of his time. A classical scholar like Motoori Nobunaga, for example, attempted to guide the attention of the Japanese back to their ancient culture and its literary masterpieces. It is not surprising, therefore, that Mitsuzaki's example, although unappreciated by his elders (it is said that he had to leave Kyōto because of his unorthodox activity), was followed by others. Only a few isolated *shin-kumiuta* ("new-kumiuta") were composed, however.

One of those composers who followed Mitsuzaki's example was Yoshizawa Kengyō (1800-1872), of Nagoya. Yoshizawa selected texts from an old collection of poems, the *Kokinshū* ("Ancient and Modern Collection," compiled A.D. 922) and used them in five compositions for voice and koto which, collectively, are known as *kokingumi*. Like Mitsuzaki, he strove for simplicity, but he did not return to the old forms of danmono and kumiuta. Only the first of the kokingyumi, *Chidori no Kyoku*, contains a tegoto; in the other four (*Haru no Kyoku, Natsu no Kyoku, Aki no Kyoku,* and *Fuyu no Kyoku,* collectively representing the four seasons, a subject matter traditionally favored) the tegoto is omitted, leaving a simple, elegant melody with unobtrusive accompaniment by the koto. The tuning for all of the kokingumi, *kokin-chōshi*, is related to a gagaku tuning, *banshiki-chō*, from which it differs only in the tuning of strings 6 and 11; in banshiki-chō, these strings are a minor second higher than in kokin-chōshi. Both kokin-chōshi and banshiki-chō share the characteristic ascending fourth followed by a descending seventh:

Example 3. (a) kokin-chōshi; (b) banshiki-chō.

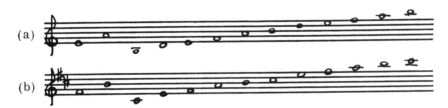

It is typical of the period in which they were written that the kokingumi gained popularity only after tegoto for them had been composed by Matsuzaka Harue (1854-1920) in Kyōto; even today they are normally performed in the altered versions. In Nagoya, however, they are still played in their original form, without tegoto. Yoshizawa later composed four more pieces, *shin-kokingumi* (*Yamazakura, Karagoromo, Hatsusegawa,* and *Shin Setsugekka)* which did not gain the same popularity as the earlier works. In contrast to Mitsuzaki's *Akikaze no Kyoku*, the kokingumi and shin-kokingumi are related only in spirit, not in form, to the old kumiuta.

Brief mention must be made of a special performance practice, *sankyoku* (literally: "music for three"), in which a third instrument is added to the usual jiuta ensemble of shamisen and koto. The first time that the term sankyoku is known to have been used was in 1785 in reference to an occasion when a jiuta was performed by shamisen, koto and *kokyū,* a small, three-or four-stringed bowed lute.[32] This performance was an isolated case, however, and it was not until the end of the Edo period that sankyoku became a regular practice. Initially, the third instrument was the kokyū but gradually its place was taken by the *shakuhachi,* an endblown bamboo flute. Until the Meiji reforms, the shakuhachi had been the privilege of the *komusō,* the itinerant priests of the Fuke sect, but when in 1871 that privilege was withdrawn, the instrument became available for nonreligious music. In Kyōto a famous shakuhachi player, Kondō Sōetsu, frequently joined the shamisen and koto in jiuta performances; in Tōkyo the introduction of the shakuhachi in sankyoku was mainly the result of the activities of Yoshida Itchō and Araki Chikuō. At present, the sankyoku ensemble normally includes the shakuhachi, the use of the kokyū having become exceptional.

The kumiuta repertoire in all consists of fifty-three compositions. All of these except one are performed in the Ikuta-ryū. The exception, *Hatsune no Kyoku,* is played only by the Yamada-ryū, a school of koto music that began toward the end of the eighteenth century and developed alongside the Ikuta-ryū to become the most important school in the Kantō district. The Ikuta-ryū was popular in the Kansai area, but although it occasionally had reached Edo, mainly through students of Mitsuhashi Kengyō travelling from Kyōto, it had never gained a foothold in the Kantō district. The only koto music existing in Edo was Tsukushi-goto, which by its nature did not enjoy popularity. In an attempt to spread the Ikuta-ryū, Yasumura Kengyō sent Hasetomi Kengyō to Edo. Just as in the seventeenth century the important result of Hosui's teaching in Edo had been the Yatsuhashi-ryū, so now Hasetomi's teaching led to the founding of the Yamada-ryū.

The music of the Ikuta-ryū, still largely consisting of kumiuta, did not appeal to the population of Edo, who preferred their livelier local shamisen music, and consequently Hasetomi acquired only a small number of students. One of these was Yamada Shōkoku, a physician and an accomplished koto player, who in 1779 published the results of his studies with Hasetomi in the form of an important collection of kumiuta, the *Sōkyoku Taiishō.* Yamada Shōkoku met a youthful, musically-gifted masseur whom he took under his protection and had study with Hasetomi. This child, whose original name was Toyoichi, was given the name of his protector, and later became known as Yamada Kengyō (1757-1817), the founder of the new school, the Yamada-ryū.

Although he fulfilled his obligation to the past by composing one kumiuta, *Hatsune no Kyoku* Yamada Kengyō soon discovered that this form never would be popular among the people of Edo and therefore looked for inspiration among the local shamisen styles, *Katōbushi, Itchūbushi,* and *Tomimotobushi,* all of which belonged to the category of *katarimono,* narrative pieces. Thus, although both Ikuta-ryū and Yamada-ryū sought inspiration in existing shamisen forms, the former devoted itself, with few exceptions, to lyrical forms, while the latter was concerned with narrative styles. Yamada went beyond shamisen music in his search for inspiration and made use of *yōkyoku,* the music for the Nō theatre, and *heikyoku,* epic poetry with biwa accompaniment, both genres more narrative than purely musical. A consequence of this narrative orientation is that primary attention is given to the vocal part, rather than, as in the Ikuta-ryū, to the instrumental tegoto. Tegoto-mono is foreign to the original style of the Yamada-ryū, and when one is performed, the composition is usually one taken over from the repertoire of the Ikuta-ryū. Another important difference between the Ikuta-ryū and Yamada-ryū is the relative importance of the performing instruments. In the Ikuta-ryū the shamisen is the main instrument and is played by the leading musician of the group. In the Yamada-ryū, the main function is assigned to the koto, the shamisen being given no more than an obligato part.

In collaboration with his younger brother, Shigemoto Fusakichi, Yamada Kengyō made some slight changes to the instrument, mainly striving for larger volume of sound. The tsume, unlike those of the Ikuta-ryū, are oval in shape. The player kneels at a right angle at the right end of the instrument.

The repertoire of the Yamada-ryū consists of:

1. Kumiuta and danmono: Yamada Kengyō selected twenty-seven kumiuta from those in the Ikuta school and added one of his own compositions, *Hatsune no Kyoku,* the only kumiuta that is played exclusively in the Yamada-ryū.

2. Saku-uta: This category includes Yamada Kengyō's own compositions, of which the best known are *Yuya, Kogō no Kyoku, Aoi no Kyoku,* and *Chōkonka.* Collectively these four pieces are known as *Yotsumono.*

3. Shin saku-uta: All works other than kumiuta, saku-uta, tegoto-mono, and shin-sōkyoku.

4. Tegoto-mono: Very few tegoto-mono have been composed in the Yamada-ryū, the best known of these being *Miyako no Haru* by Yamase Shōin (1845-1908), the third Yamase Kengyō. When tegoto-mono were taken over from the Ikuta-ryū to be adapted to the Yamada-ryū style, slight changes were made, the most conspicuous of which was the transposition from hira-jōshi to kumoi-jōshi, resulting in a higher register.

5. Joruri-mono: This group includes arrangements from the narrative shamisen literature, such as Katōbushi and Tomimotobushi.

The Yamada-ryū spread rapidly over the Kantō area, mainly under the leadership of three of Yamada Kengyō's students: Yamato Kengyō, Yamaki Kengyō, and Yamase Kengyō. Although today the schools have penetrated somewhat into one another's regions (especially in Tōkyo), the Yamada-ryū is found mainly in the Kantō area, the Ikuta-ryū in the Kansai.

Musical Changes in the Meiji Period

As a living genre that attracted composers and was regularly performed, the kumiuta ceased after the middle of the nineteenth century. The modern history that follows here is given, therefore, only to show the extension through the nineteenth century into the present of developments in style and taste that had resulted in the earlier decline of the kumiuta genre. To be sure, kumiuta have continued to be highly esteemed—almost, indeed, revered. But the chief characteristic of the Meiji period (1868-1912) was a thorough cultural reorientation that led to various attempts to renovate and Westernize Japanese music, a music in which kumiuta by now found a place of honor, but also one of near silence.

Meiji shinkyoku. The opening of Japan after almost three centuries of isolation altered most facets of Japanese life. Music also was affected. With energy typical of the period Western music was imported: military bands were organized and instructors hired from England, France, and Germany, and the newly reorganized court musicians followed the Emperor to his new residence in Tōkyo and were instructed in Western classic music. Music education in the public schools was organized along strictly Western lines, employing music in Western style. At the same time, the ancient Japanese professional musical organizations such as the Shoku-yashiki and the Fukeshu were dissolved, compelling many musicians to reorient themselves socially and professionally (Komiya 1956: 329). Although the koto proved to be a favorite instrument for experimentation in combining traditional Japanese and Western music, changes were introduced very gradually. Despite Westernization, the forms of the late Edo period continued to be used, especially in Kyōto, where kyōmono remained very fashionable.

The first indications of revision of musical values and aesthetics following the Meiji restoration occurred in Ōsaka shortly before 1880 (Kikkawa 1961: 26). Pioneers in that revision considered that the new, positive trends of the time should be reflected in new music ("shinkyoku"), and the traditional preoccupation with love and nature should be abandoned. The most representative composition in this new style, *Mikuni no Homare* ("Glory of the Nation") by Kikudaka Kengyō does not use the shamisen, an instrument that could be too easily associated with the amusement quarter of the city. Instead, the voice is accompanied by high and low koto, as in *Godan-Ginuta*. The tuning of the koto does not use half steps and could, therefore, be considered more "positive." The text is a song of praise to Emperor and country. Nevertheless, and this is characteristic of the Meiji shinkyoku of Ōsaka, these innovations hardly went beyond the limitations of the traditional musical idiom.

An increasing use of left-hand plucking, creating harmony-like effects, may have been a more direct result of the influence of Western music. The technique was not new, but it had been rarely used (examples may be found in the late Edo period, for example, in *Fune no Yume* by Kikuoka-Yaezaki. During the Meiji period, however, it rapidly became a standard technique. It was developed mainly in Ōsaka by composers such as Kikuzaka Kengyō (1846-1910). Kikuyoshi Kengyō, and Tateyama Noboru. Representative compositions are Kikuzaka's *Meiji Sho-chiku-bai* and *Mitsu no Keshiki*, Kikuyoshi's *Gyosei no Kyoku* and *Yoshino Shizuka*, and Tateyama's *Hototogisu no Kyoku* and *Kongōseki*.

The Kyōgoku school. Around 1900 a personal response to his confrontation with Western music was given by Suzuki Koson (1875-1931) in a number of works that have been characterized as a combination of romantic feeling with classic form. The texts for his compositions were taken from contemporary poets. He composed for voice with koto accompaniment, never shamisen. Structurally, and also in his use of modes, Suzuki shows a conscious return to the classic practices of the Heian period. He founded a new school that for a short time commanded attention, but nowadays its works are rarely performed.

Shin Nihon Ongaku. Westernization of sōkyoku had been slight, hesitating, and superficial before the activities of Miyagi Michio (1894-1956), whose conscious goal in music could be characterized as the combination of *hōgaku* (Japanese traditional music) and *yōgaku* (Western music). Although his first composition, *Mizu no Hentai* (1909), still follows the traditional tegoto form, in feeling and in certain stylistic elements it shows Western influence. Its melody closely follows the content and emotion of the text, with supple changes of tempo. Later compositions show increasing Westernization. For example, *Kara Kinuta* is a quartet for kotos and shamisens, somewhat comparable to the Western string quartet. Canonic imitations appear in *Aki no Shirabe.* Miyagi's life may be divided into three periods. In the first he composed chamber music for Japanese instruments. To the second belong orchestral works for Japanese instruments, while in the third he combined Japanese and Western instruments *(Concerto for Koto and Orchestra).*[33]

Miyagi's influence has been and still is very strong. Not in all respects has this been fortunate for sōkyoku. Although historically Miyagi's importance is undeniable, as a composer he was no more than mediocre. Moreover, the value of some of his ideas can be doubted, as, for example, the orchestral use of Japanese instruments. The koto especially is by nature a solo instrument, a good deal of the charm of which consists in subtle microtonal ornamentation by the left hand. This is regrettably lost in large ensembles, which suffer also the common problem of all ensembles of plucked instruments: a disturbing lack of exactness. Miyagi's orchestral experiment, therefore, must be regarded as a misstep, rather than an advance, and although he has still much influence, there are suggestions among younger composers— for example, Mamiya Michio—of a renewed interest in solistic music. This can probably be taken as an indication that the Western influence that to Miyagi was a powerful but superficial one has been deepened and by some absorbed.

CHAPTER II

THE INSTRUMENT

Originally, in the Nara and Heian periods, the term "koto" referred to many types of stringed instruments, like the term "vina" in India. One spoke of the *kin-no-koto (shichigenkin* or *kin,* the Chinese *ch'in),* for example; of the *sō-no-koto (sō* or *koto);* of the *hitsu - no-koto (hitsu,* Chinese *se);* of the *biwa-no-koto (biwa);* of the *Yamato-goto* (wagon); of the *kudara-goto* (the harp, *kugo);* and of the *Shiragi-goto* (the modern Korean *kayakeum*). Later the term came to be applied exclusively to the *sō-no-koto*. *Hitsu-no-koto, Kudara-goto,* and *Shiragi-goto* ceased to be used in Japan, while the other instruments lost the suffix "no-koto," and were referred to simply as kin, biwa, wagon, and so on (Tanabe 1962: 244). A certain inconsistency in the use of words "koto" and "kin" remained throughout the Edo period and even later. At times the word "kin" was used when the instrument koto was meant. This usage explains, for example, the title of an important collection of sōkyoku, *Kinkyoku Shifu;* *Sōkyoku Shifu* would have been more correct. Some confusion in writing results nowadays from the circumstance that the *kanji* for "koto" (箏) is not included in the *Tōyō Kanji,*[1] that for "kin" (琴) standing in its place.

The origin of the word koto is obscure. One theory explains the word as a corruption of *oto* ("sound") (Tanabe 1954: 244); another holds that it is derived from *Amenonori-goto,* which is mentioned in the *Kojiki* ("Record of Ancient Matters," A.D. 712) as being used by the Gods (*ibid.*: 245). We know that the Amenonori-goto was a stringed instrument, but have no details about its construction. A third hypothesis calls attention to the suffix "ko" in the names of the Korean long zithers *kayako* (kayakeum) and *komunko* (hyenkeum). According to Andreas Eckardt (1930: 43), "ko" may have been the old word for "keum," which was preserved in the Japanese word "koto."

The koto belongs to the family of long zithers with movable frets that is found in several East Asiatic countries. The best known representatives of the family are the cheng and the se in China, the kayakeum and komunko in Korea, the *dàn tranh* in Vietnam, and the wagon and the koto in Japan. All of these instruments probably were imported at some time or other from China, with the possible exception of the wagon, which has been claimed to be indigenously Japanese (Garfias 1965: pp. 7-10). The origin of long zithers in China has been placed as far back as the first beginnings of the Empire, the two principal Chinese instruments in the family, the unfretted ch'in with seven strings and the se with movable bridges and a varying number of strings (originally about fifty, reduced later to about twenty-five) having existed, according to literary sources, at the beginning or even before the Chou dynasty (1122-256 B.C.)

22

(Reinhard 1956: 14). The Chinese version of the koto, the cheng, seems to have developed during the Ch'in dynasty (221-206 B.C.) (Tanabe 1954: 247). The invention of this instrument, which is referred to by the Japanese as "Shin-sō," is often attributed to the Chinese general, Mōten (Chinese: Meng Tien, d. 209 B.C.), who fought along the western frontier (Yamada 1779: Vol. 6; Van Gulik 1951: 13). Although this attribution is speculative, if it may be granted credence, it may point to a Western origin for the instrument. The proto-cheng so hypothesized may, it has been suggested, have been further developed in China, taking over elements from the already existing ch'in and se.

Where facts are absent, fiction appears, eager to account for intriguing unexplained relationships. An amusing legend explains the origin of the cheng as follows: Two sisters quarreled for possession of a se made of bamboo. In a solution worthy of Solomon, if not David, they split the instrument in two, thus obtaining two cheng, one with twelve and the other with thirteen strings. The presence of the twelve-stringed instrument in Korea (the kayakeum) is explained by adding that one of the two sisters emigrated to Korea, while the other remained in China. This legend also explains the origin of the kanji for koto (箏) as the combination of those for bamboo (竹) and quarrel (爭).[2]

During the Han dynasty (206 B.C. - 220 A.D.) the twelve- and the thirteen-stringed cheng existed side by side. Initially a solo instrument for popular use, the cheng later was included in the orchestras of the Chinese ruling classes, a practice that continued through the Sui (581-618) and T'ang (618-907) dynasties, when the instrument was introduced into Japan. There, only the thirteen-stringed koto survived. Three different playing techniques of the Han fretted long zithers existed: *sūsō*, *dansō*, and *assō*, in which the instrument was plucked with the fingers, plucked with finger plectra, or bowed with a resined stick without hair, respectively. Both sūsō and assō survive in Korea today, as kayakeum and *a-chaing*, but only dansō is known in Japan.

It is remarkable that in the country of origin, China, the long zithers continued to evolve, while in Japan as well as in Korea, the ancient forms were maintained, refined somewhat, but intrinsically unchanged. There is no essential difference between the oldest Japanese representative of the family, the gakusō, and the youngest, the Yamada koto. Later Chinese innovations, such as the introduction by the end of the seventeenth century, of tuning pegs and brass or steel (rather than silk) strings, were never adopted in Japan and Korea.

Although we know that the koto was introduced into Japan at the beginning of or, shortly before, the Nara period (710-794), the exact date is uncertain. The earliest evidence for the presence of the instrument is a koto teaching system known to have existed at the time when the Gagaku-Ryō, the Department of Music, was established as part of the administrative organization of the central government in 702 (Garfias 1965: pp. 32-33). The earliest remnants of koto relics are found among the personal belongings of Emperor Shōmu (r. 724-749) which after his death were dedicated to the Buddha of the Tōdaiji in Nara and in 756 were stored there in a specially constructed repository, the Shōsōin. This unique collection consists of manuscripts, paintings, ornaments, gigaku masks, weapons, utensils, and several musical instruments, among the last the fragments of several kotos (Hayashi 1964: 86 ff.).

The types of koto can be classified by use into four groups: (1) gakusō, used in gagaku; (2) tsukusō, the instrument of the Tsukushi-ryū; (3) zokusō, used in zokuso; and (4) shinsō, the group of new koto types, most of them invented by Miyagi Michio during the Shōwa period (1926-) and used in specially composed music. Shinsō include such instruments as the *jushichigenkin* (the seventeen-stringed bass koto) and the *tansō* (a small koto, the strings of which are tightened by pegs, and which in performance is put on a table and played by a player sitting on a chair rather than kneeling on the floor).

The first three types are closely related. Gakusō and tsukusō are practically identical, differing only in details. Within the zokusō group, the most important variants are the Ikuta and Yamada koto. At present the Yamada koto, probably because of its somewhat larger volume of sound, enjoys a growing popularity at the expense of the Ikuta koto, which is rapidly losing ground, even in the Ikuta-ryū.

The koto consists of a long (about 180-190 cm.), slender (about 24 cm. at the midpoint), rectangular wooden body that has a slight convex curve longitudinally and larger convex curve laterally (see Fig. 1, d and b). Thirteen strings of equal length are stretched under equal tension the length of the body over fixed bridges, from insertion points about 10 cm. from the right end (as the instrument is placed before the player) and about twice that distance to the other end. The strings are permanently fixed—within, of course, the limitations of the material. The length of the vibrating part of the strings is determined by the placement of movable bridges (*ji*) (Fig. 1, f), each string being supplied with one bridge. Different placements of the bridges provide different tunings of the instrument. The ji are made of wood or ivory, or, nowadays, plastic. The strings are plucked with bamboo, bone, or ivory finger plectra (tsume), which vary in shape from school to school.

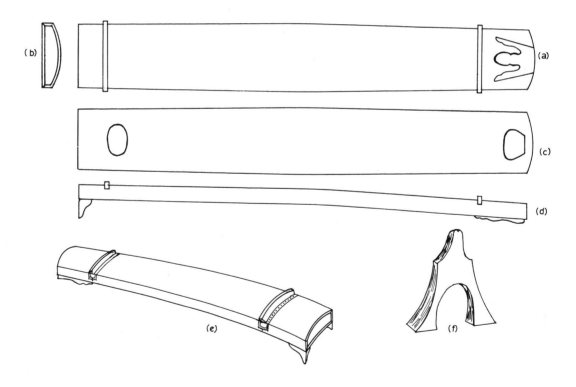

Figure 1. Yamada koto.

The body of the koto is made of kiri wood (Paulownia imperialis). The *yamawari*, a woodsman who is a specialist in the selection of the right quality of wood, locates suitable trees in the mountains. The best wood is from trees in cold regions such as Aizu, Yuwate, Echigo, and Hida in the Kantō area, and Fukui and Ishikawa in Kansai. A suitable tree must be at least twenty years old; the best wood comes from trees two hundred years old or older.

The koto is constructed essentially of two pieces of wood, a thick plank for the top, hollowed out on the underside in such a way that the long sides are formed also, and a second, thinner plank from which the bottom is made. In kotos of better quality, the left end (as the instrument is placed before the performer) is also integral with the top, and only the right end is set in. Ribs across the open underside of the top piece stiffen the sides and provide support for both top and bottom.

The grain of the wood, so noticeable a feature in the appearance of the instrument, is determined by the location within the log of the plank that is used for the top. Either the grain runs the length of the plank (Fig. 2a), or it shows a complicated pattern (Fig. 2b). Planks such as that illustrated in Figure 2a are cut from the log as shown in the figure and usually are used in instruments of better quality. Complicated grain patterns, however, are found in instruments of high quality as well as in cheaper ones. Preference seems largely a matter of taste. The quality of the sound is not dependent on the grain pattern, except that wood taken from the core of the log, and showing, therefore, a rather open grain, is softer than wood from the outer part of the log, and hence produces a sound not so bright as the latter.

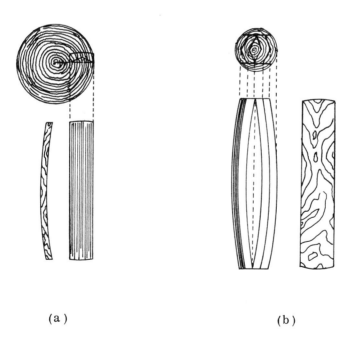

(a)   (b)

Figure 2. Grain patterns of koto.

After the rough planks are sawed from the log, they are carefully dried for about a year. The top is then formed, the instrumentmaker chiseling out the wood from the underside and giving the piece the correct curvature. One end of the top is left solid, the other is made open. The undersurface of the top is chiseled in a pattern of longitudinal grooves; in superior instruments the pattern is herringbone. Six ribs, *sekiban,* are now fitted in position. The bottom, which like the top is slightly curved, is formed (of one plank in superior instruments, of two or three in cheaper ones), and the two sound holes, which serve also to provide access into the body when stringing the instrument, are cut. The shape of these holes *(marukuchi)* varies somewhat, as does the length of the instrument, from school to school. The Ikuta koto has holes in the shape shown in Figure 3a, and the Yamada koto, the shape in Figure 3b. Figure 3a also shows the typical pattern of grooves to be found in all schools in instruments of moderate cost, while the herringbone pattern *(ayasugi)* that is found only in more expensive instruments is shown in Figure 3b.

(a)   (b)

Figure 3. Sound holes of (a) Ikuta koto and (b) Yamada koto.

The quality of the instrument also depends on the method by which the bottom is glued to the top: in instruments of better quality it is bevelled and set in, but not in cheaper ones (Fig. 4, a and b).

(a)   (b)

Figure 4. Cross section of koto.

The two fixed bridges, *ryūkaku*, are next set into the top. Usually these bridges are made of cherrywood, and they may or may not be decorated with ivory. Bridges of solid ivory are sometimes found. Each bridge is protected from the friction of the strings by an *itomakura*, a strip made of ivory, antler, or metal. At the left end the *kashiwaba*, a leaf-shaped ornament of cherrywood, ivory, or a combination of both, is attached (see Fig. 1a). The kashiwaba, partly covered by the *ogire*, consisting of several layers of brocade or deerskin (Fig. 1a), protects the body from the strings. The ogire prevents the strings from slipping. Into the right end is fitted the *zetsu*, a tongue-shaped piece of wood carrying the name of the instrument, a family crest, or a lacquer ornament. Finally, the legs are attached. The legs at the left end are permanent, those at the right are detachable. Nowadays, presumably because the Japanese seem to be growing taller, a separate stand *(makura)*, which is somewhat higher than the legs, may be used to support the right end. The legs of the instrument vary from school to school and, like the *marukuchi*, provide an easy identification as to which school the instrument belongs.

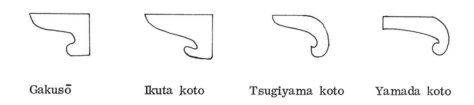

Gakusō   Ikuta koto   Tsugiyama koto   Yamada koto

Figure 5. Legs of the koto.

Decoration is usually quite restrained, the visual beauty of an instrument being judged in terms of the quality of the wood and the craftsmanship; the ultimate refinement of simple lines is preferred to the superficial appeal of decoration. If decoration does occur, it consists of no more than discreet strips of ivory on the fixed bridges and legs. In the past, however, the sides of the Ikuta koto tended to be ornamented in gold lacquer or by a thin covering of a different kind of wood.[3]

The thirteen strings of the koto traditionally are made of silk. Nowadays, however, nylon and tetron are often used. The quality of the sound of the latter two materials is less delicate than that of silk; on the other hand, nylon and tetron are considerably stronger than silk—an advantage that anyone who has had to replace strings on the koto can appreciate. The strings are secured by tying to the instrument and a special deftness, combined with strength, is required to tighten and secure them. The tension on the strings has increased gradually over the centuries, especially during recent decades.

The names of the strings are: *ichi* ("one"), *ni* ("two"), *san* ("three"), *shi* ("four"), *go* ("five"), *roku* ("six"), *shichi* ("seven"), *hachi* ("eight"), *kyū* or *ku* ("nine"), *jū* ("ten"), *tō* ("unit of measure," string 11), *i* ("to do," string 12), and *kin* ("cloth," string

13). We notice an inconsistency in the system: only the first ten strings have numerals as their names. The last three have survived from an older nomenclature: *jin* ("benevolence"), *chi* ("wisdom"), *rei* ("ritual"), *gi* ("righteousness"), *shin* ("sincerity"), *bun* ("military skill"), *hi* ("elegance"), *ran* ("door"), *sho* ("commerce"), *tō* ("a unit of measure"), *i* ("to do"), and *kin* ("cloth").[4]

The Ikuta-ryū uses thinner strings than the Yamada-ryū (Ikuta-ryū: 19 momme[5] for practice, 17-18 momme for concert; Yamada-ryū: 20 and 19 momme, respectively). The height and thickness of the movable bridges has changed in the course of time. Those used with the Yamada koto are largest. The ji not only determine the length of the vibrating portion of the strings, they also transmit the vibrations of the strings to the body, where the volume of sound is strengthened by resonance.

The strings are plucked with plectra, tsume, that are attached to the palmar surface of the terminal phalanx of thumb, index, and middle fingers of the right hand. A tsume consists of an *atama* ("head," the plectrum itself) and an *obi* ("belt") that fits around the finger and holds the plectrum securely in position. Size and shape vary from school to school (see Fig. 6). The gakusō tsume are made of bamboo or bone, glued to a wide belt of cat skin. The atama of Tsukushi-goto is longer, the belt narrower. The tsume of the Ikuta-ryū and Yamada-ryū are made of ivory with a narrow belt of leather, cloth, or paper.

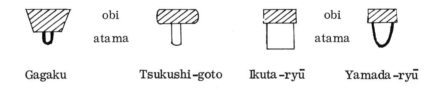

obi		obi	
atama		atama	
Gagaku	Tsukushi-goto	Ikuta-ryū	Yamada-ryū

Figure 6. Tsume.

Notice the conspicuous difference between the square tsume *(kakuzume)* of the Ikuta-ryū and the round *(maruzume)* tsume of the Yamada-ryū.

The following table shows some of the differences in dimensions between gakusō, Ikuta, and Yamada koto. Although dimensions are standardized for each type, it should be pointed out that kotos are made in several sizes. The measures in the table refer to the largest, standard, size of each type.

	Gakusō	Ikuta Koto (modern)	Ikuta Koto [6]	Yamada Koto
Length*	188.5	189.5	177.0	182.0
Width at right end	24.4	25.0	24.0	24.6
Width at left end	22.7	22.9	22.6	23.1
Thickness at side, right end	4.3	4.6	4.0	4.0
Thickness at middle, right end	8.0	8.4	7.2	7.6
Thickness at side, left end	4.4	4.6	4.0	4.0
Thickness at middle, left end	7.0	7.8	6.0	7.0
Height of ji	5.1	5.5		5.5
Width of ji	5.6	5.1		5.1
Distance between strings	2.0	2.0	2.0	2.0
Distance between ryūkaku	153.6	156.7	151.6	149.0

*Measurements are in centimeters.

As part of the heritage from China, extramusical connotations of a philosophical, cosmo-logical, or poetic nature surround the koto, though they are known to only a few. We have already seen an example of philosophical connotations in the older names for the strings. In addition, the curved surface of the instrument corresponds to the vault of heaven, the bottom to the earth, while the interior is as empty as the universe. The number of strings corres-ponds to the thirteen months of the leap year (lunar calendar). Therefore, the koto embodies the four quadrants: heaven, earth, universe, and year. When the instrument is played, the *go-on,* literally the "five sounds" of the pentatonic scale, are heard; they correspond to the five cardinal points, elements, colors, and tastes. The koto, therefore, is the instrument of human wisdom (Fujita and Kikkawa 1955-57: 37). All this has a strong Confucian flavor and we may safely assume that knowledge of these connotations was originally limited to Confucianist players.

A poetic likening of the koto to a dragon lying on a beach is known to most koto players. The names of several parts of the instrument derive from this image. For example, the top of the koto is called kō (shell); the bottom, hara (belly); the sides are the iso (the beach on which the dragon is supposed to be lying). At the right end are the ryūkaku (forehead), the ryūbi (nose), the ryūken (elbow), the ryūhō (cheek), the ryūshin (lips), the ryūzetsu (tongue), and the ryūkaku (horns). The left end is called the ryūbi (tail). The two legs under the "head" are called ryūshu (hands), those at the "tail," ryūshi (legs).

Investigations of the acoustical properties of the koto have been made by the Japanese physi-cists Obata Jūichi and Sugita Eizi (1931). They inform us that a basic characteristic of koto timbre results from the phenomenon that after the string has been plucked, a certain amount of time is required before maximum volume is reached. This phenomenon must be ascribed to the large size of the body and the volume of air enclosed. In general, instruments with large reso-nating bodies share this phenomenon, and in this respect the koto is comparable, for example, to the piano.

Also characteristic of the tone quality is a relatively simple overtone structure with promi-nence of low partials in general, the second partial in particular. A slight shift in partial structure is shown when the registers are compared. For example, the third partial and partly also the fourth determine the quality of the lower tones; the second that of the strings in the middle register; from string 10 upward, the fundamental is the determinant.   The dominance of relatively high partials in the lower tones may be accounted for by the fact that these tones are produced by long vibrating lengths, plucked near their end.

Another phenomenon that must be taken into consideration is the sympathetic vibration of unplucked strings.   Vibrations are easily transmitted from string to string, through the air as well as through the ji and body.   In this respect the koto is like other stringed instruments with undampened strings, the harp, for example.   Sympathetic vibration of higher strings in general strengthens higher partials; lower strings, however, may be excited also when higher ones are played.

Finally, it should be mentioned that at the moment of attack of a string, a very weak, high-pitched sound is heard which is caused by the tsume.   This is of short duration and is of little importance in the tone of the instrument.

CHAPTER III

SCALES AND TUNINGS

Koto tunings are characteristic of the genres (gagaku, etc.) in which the instrument has been used, with each genre requiring adaptation to its scale system. The tunings are alike, however, in that they all contain only five tones to the octave, the most important degrees of the scale to which the instrument is tuned. In order to understand the development of kumiuta tunings, therefore, it is necessary to devote some attention to the history of scales in Japanese music. Japanese music theory, like its art music, has roots in T'ang China, and although since the Nara period musical developments in Japan have required important changes in the original theory, the original Chinese impetus was so strong that the scale structure of even seventeenth- and eighteenth-century sōkyoku cannot be clearly understood without some reference to Chinese theory.

The Chinese tone system recognized twelve tones in the octave. Scales were explained as generated by superimposing perfect fifths (702 cents) one upon the other, and the first five tones so obtained were the most important in the music. The names of these five tones and the intervals between them were as follows:

Degree name:	kung	shang	chiao	chih	yu	(kung)
Interval (in cents):	204	204	294	204	294	

The series consisted therefore of major seconds and minor thirds, with the thirds between tones chiao and chih and tones yu and kung. Two more tones, pien-chih and pien-kung, were added to the basic five, filling in the "gaps" of the minor thirds. The names of these tones indicate that they were regarded as being related to their upper neighbors, and in the music they had an auxiliary function:

I	II	III	IV	V	VI	VII	VIII
kung	shang	chiao	pien-chih	chih	yu	pien-kung	(kung)
204	204	204	90	204	204	90	

Five modes could be constructed by using each of the five basic tones as first (and last) tone of the scale (the pien tones never served as such tonal centers). Since transposition permitted any of the twelve tones in the system to serve as first degree of a mode, there could be sixty combinations, that is, twelve transpositions of the five modes. Many further intricacies in the Chinese modal theory, not being essential for an understanding of Japanese musical theory, will not be pursued here.

Japan imported from China both the twelve-tone system and the principle of seven-tone scales in which five tones were considered basic and the remaining two auxiliary. The Japanese names of the series of twelve tones are given below. As ōshiki (the Japanese equivalent of *huang-chung*, the generating tone in China) in present practice equals the Western tone a' of 440 cycles, it is possible to give the corresponding tone names in the Western system:

ichikotsu	d	fūsho	g♯
tangin	d♯	ōshiki	a
hyōjō	e	rankei	a♯
shōsetsu	f	banshiki	b
shimomu	f♯	shinsen	c
sōjo	g	kamimu	c♯

However, the actual tonal material of Tōgaku, that part of the court music which is considered to be of Chinese origin, consists of only nine tones:

		fūsho	g♯
ichikotsu	d	ōshiki	a
hyōjō	e	banshiki	b
shimomu	f♯	shinsen	c
sōjo	g	kamimu	c♯

Seven modes existed in Tōgaku, which may be divided into three groups according to their number of accidentals: modes in Group I have one accidental, f♯; those in Group II have two, f♯ and c♯; those in Group III require f♯, c♯, and g♯.

			I	II	III	IV	V	VI	VII	(I)
I	ichikotsu-chō	:	d	e	f♯	(g)	a	b	(c)	d
	sōjō	:	g	a	b	(c)	d	e	(f♯)	g
	ōshiki-chō	:	a	b	(c)	d	e	f♯	(g)	a
II	suichō	:	a	b	c♯	(d)	e	f♯	(g)	a
	hyōjō	:	e	f♯	(g)	a	b	c♯	(d)	e
III	taishiki-chō (ryō)	:	e	f♯	g♯	(a)	b	c♯	(d)	e
	taishiki-chō (ritsu)	:	e	f♯	(g♯)	a	b	(c♯)	d	e
	banshiki-chō	:	b	c♯	(d)	e	f♯	g♯	(a)	b

The Japanese names for the degrees of the seven-tone scales are Japanizations of the original Chinese terms:

Chinese :	kung	shang	chiao	pien-chih	chih	yu	pien-kung
Japanese :	kyū	shō	kaku	hen-chi	chi	ū	hen-kyū

These seven-tone modes contain, like their Chinese counterparts, five basic tones and two additional tones that function as auxiliary or exchange tones. Here, however, we meet an essential change from the Chinese system: in Japanese music the positions of the exchange tones are not limited to degrees IV and VII, but may also be degrees III and VII. Two structural types therefore exist: the *ryō* type, which corresponds to the Chinese system and has degrees IV and VII as exchange tones, and the *ritsu* type with degrees III and VII as exchange tones. In the chart on page 32 the exchange tones are indicated by parentheses. The occurrence of suichō and the ritsu version of taishiki-chō are very rare. Ritsu taishiki-chō, moreover, is distinguished from all the other modes by having degree VI as an exchange tone instead of VII.

It is noteworthy that the Chinese modal system provides more modes than the Japanese chose to use. The ritsu structural type may be considered a Japanese contribution to the system. The Japanese preference for this type is shown by the larger number of gagaku compositions in ritsu than in ryō.

Tsukushi-goto used gagaku scales; the first real innovation in scales in the field of sōkyoku was not made before the first half of the seventeenth century when Yatsuhashi Kengyō introduced the *in-sen,* or *in* scale, thereby creating modern "popular" sōkyoku: zokusō. It was mentioned earlier that the *in* scale was used in shamisen music and that Yatsuhashi as a former shamisen virtuoso was very probably familiar with it. The *in* scale in its seven-tone form is:

Example 4.

kyū   shō   ei-shō   kaku   chi   ū   ei-ū   (kyū)

The nomenclature of the notes clearly shows the five tones that are basic and the two additional tones. The exchange tones are *ei-shō* and *ei-ū,* meaning sharpened *shō* and sharpened *ū.* The "ei" versions usually appear in ascending, and the "original" forms, *shō* and *ū,* in descending order. Since *ei-shō* does not appear frequently, it is possible to give two forms of the ascending pattern of the scale with either *shō* or *ei-shō,* the descending form being the same in both cases:

Example 5.

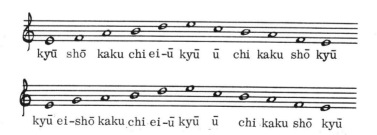

kyū shō kaku chi ei-ū kyū ū chi kaku shō kyū

kyū ei-shō kaku chi ei-ū kyū ū chi kaku shō kyū

Turning to the practice, we find that in the matter of koto tuning Yatsuhashi's innovations did not cause very considerable changes:

Example 6.

Tsukushi-goto:

Zokusō (hira-jōshi):

Three tones, e, a, and b, with their octaves, remained unaltered. In theory, these tones were considered the most important of the basic five because they are the first three in the cycle of fifths. The changes involve only the fourth and sixth tones with their octaves, tones that even today are not very stable (see page 39).

Comparing the hira-jōshi tuning with the *in* scale, we notice that the koto is tuned to the descending form of the scale, a practical arrangement because it is possible to raise the pitch of the strings a minor or a major second (with difficulty, even a minor third), but practically impossible to lower them. A string is raised by pressing down to the left of the movable bridge, thus increasing tension on the sounding part and raising the tone. (For example, by pressing down the f string, it is possible to produce tone f♯ as well as tone g.) The range of the koto in hira-jōshi spans an octave of the *in* scale (from e' to e''), flanked by a fifth on both sides. The fundamental, e', is doubled on the first string. Hira-jōshi has always been the most popular zokusō tuning; this may perhaps be explained by the very balanced mid-position of the basic octave, plus the fact that the first string doubles the fundamental. When we compare the four tunings that occur in kumiuta, arranging them in order of their frequency of occurrence, we notice immediately that they are not much more than transpositions of the original hira-jōshi, to subdominant, dominant, and dominant of the dominant respectively[1] (see Example 7; brackets indicate the five tones of the descending *in* scale in each chōshi). In view of the frequent occurrence of descending cadences from dominant to tonic and from tonic to dominant, it is clear that no tuning lends itself so well as hira-jōshi to use of the entire range of the instrument. More important than this, however, is the degree to which the tuning of the first two strings, which is the same for all four tunings, agrees with the scale itself. In hira-jōshi this agreement is as favorable as possible: both tones "e" and "a" occur as two basic tones in the scale, as fundamental and subdominant, respectively. Kumoi-jōshi has almost equally favorable agreement, the first two strings representing fundamental and dominant. String 1 of hira-jōshi, however, doubles the fundamental; that of kumoi-jōshi doubles the dominant. In nakazora, string 1 agrees with the subdominant of the scale, while string 2 is a strange element the presence of which can be explained only by assuming that the tuning of the first two strings to tones e' and a is conventional. The first two strings in akebono, finally, have no relation to the tones of the scale.

Example 7.

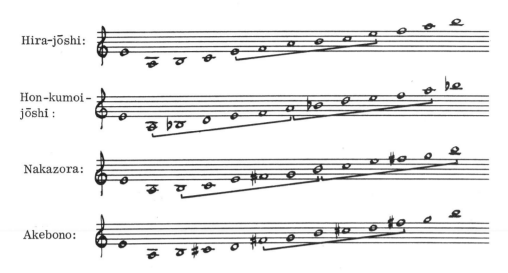

Hira-jōshi:

Hon-kumoi-jōshi:

Nakazora:

Akebono:

The open strings of the koto tuned in hira-jōshi (or, for that matter, as they are transpositions of the hira-jōshi, any of the other important tunings) give the most representative form of the *in* scale which, especially in this descending form, strongly reminds one of the older ritsu scale structures. Since the left-hand technique presents special difficulties, the beginning koto student is at first given material that uses open strings only. This presents no problems to the teacher, however, for numerous simple songs (among them several very popular ones) exist that can be played completely on the open strings of a koto tuned in hira-jōshi. Yatsuhashi used no more than two tunings: hira-jōshi and hon-kumoi-jōshi.[2] Although in the course of time other tunings were developed, hira-jōshi continued to be regarded as the basic tuning from which the others were derived. Hon-kumoi-jōshi, for example, is explained as starting from hira-jōshi with strings 3, 8, and 13 tuned a half tone down and 4 and 9 a whole tone up. Other tunings are similarly explained in relation to hira-jōshi and, frequently, similarly executed as well.

Example 8 contains all tunings that occur in kumiuta and danmono.[3] The selection of tone e' for the first string permits a minimum of accidentals.[4] The seemingly large number of tunings becomes considerably less impressive when one recognizes that several are no more than variants of others. Compare, for example, kumoi, hon-kumoi, shimo-chidori, and han-kumoi. Disregarding an occasional displacement to the lower octave of string 1, and excluding the unique Akikaze-chōshi, there are essentially no more than four basic tunings:

1. *hira-jōshi,* with one variant, *kin-uwajōshi.*
2. *hon-kumoi,* with three variants, *kumoi, shimo-chidori,* and *han-kumoi.*
3. *nakazora,* with two variants, *ura-chidori* and *han-nakazora.*
4. *akebono,* with one variant, *karigane.*

Example 8.

hira-jōshi

hira-jōshi
sometimes:
shimo-chidori

kin-uwa-jōshi

hon-kumoi-jōshi

hon-kumoi-jōshi

shimo-chidori

kumoi-jōshi

han-kumoi-jōshi

Example 8 (continued).

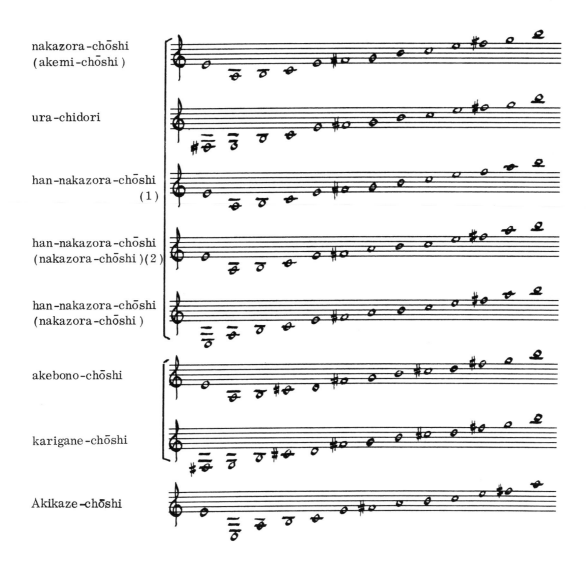

It could be objected that the lower parts of han-kumoi and han-nakazora are similar to hira-jōshi and that, therefore, these tunings could be as easily classified as variants of hira-jōshi as of hon-kumoi and nakazora, respectively. However, these chōshi occur only in the course of a composition, mostly following hira-jōshi (once only, in *Tamakazura,* han-kumoi precedes hira-jōshi), and the player will ordinarily use the kumoi or nakazora part of the tuning. The advantage of these "han" tunings is that with them the player has fewer bridges to move in changing from one chōshi to another.

In Appendix B, in which the kumiuta are arranged chronologically by composer, the title of each composition is followed by the tuning(s) in which it was composed. The following chart shows the distribution of the tunings and the number of their occurrences in the total of fifty-two kumiuta.[5]

hira-jōshi	31 example(s)
kin-uwa-jōshi	1 "
hira-jōshi—han-kumoi	2 "
hira-jōshi—han-nakazora	2 "
hira-jōshi—han-nakazora—nakazora	1 "
hira-jōshi—nakazora—akebono	1 "
hon-kumoi	6 "
shimo-chidori	2 "
han-kumoi—hira-jōshi	1 "
ura-chidori	2 "
ura-chidori—karigane	1 "
karigane	2 "
Total	52 examples

The seven danmono give the following distribution of chōshi:

hira-jōshi	6 example(s)
hon-kumoi-jōshi	1 "
Total	7 examples

It is immediately obvious that hira-jōshi is rightfully considered the basic tuning in zokusō. The kumoi group, second in importance, follows far behind, while nakazora and especially akebono occur rarely. The change of chōshi in the course of a kumiuta, mainly in compositions by Mitsuhashi Kengyō, represents modulation to dominant or subdominant. For example, the tuning sequence hira-jōshi—nakazora—akebono *(Haru no Miya)* shows a modulation twice to the dominant. Hira-jōshi to han-kumoi *(Shiki no Fuji)* is a modulation to the subdominant. The fact that a return to the original chōshi is not considered necessary differentiates koto modulation from that practiced in Western music.[6]

Turning to Appendix B again, we may expect the chronological arrangement of the material to give an insight into the evolution of the use of chōshi. Yatsuhashi and two student generations following him (Kitajima, Makino, Ikuta, and Kurahashi) use only hira-jōshi and hon-kumoi-jōshi. It is significant that two of the three compositions, the authorship of which is uncertain, are not in hira-jōshi, and one of these is the first to change chōshi in the course of the composition *(Wakaba)*. By the end of the seventeenth century there appears a tendency to move away from the hegemony of hira-jōshi, in the process of which kumoi-jōshi receives more attention. Yet no really new tunings have been introduced at this time. Nakazora and its related forms do not occur in kumiuta before Tsugiyama Kengyō and Mitsuhashi Kengyō; akebono is not met in kumiuta before the sixth generation following Yatsuhashi, Ishizuka Kengyō. Mitsuhashi Kengyō, besides being the most productive kumiuta composer since Yatsuhashi, also is one of the most adventurous in his selection of chōshi and their combination within a piece. By this time, modulation has become common in kumiuta. Ishizuka Kengyō is the only composer besides Mitsuhashi to combine three chōshi in the course of one kumiuta, *Haru no Miya,* which for this reason received a second name, *Mitsu no Shirabe* (Investigation of Three Chōshi).

The classification in omote, ura, naka, and oku also takes chōshi into consideration. The lower classes, omote and uragumi, include compositions exclusively in hira-jōshi; naka-yurushi adds kumoi-jōshi; while han-kumoi, nakazora, han-nakazora, and akebono are found only in the highest class, oku-yurushi. The secret pieces (hikyoku and goku-hikyoku) are distinguished by the use of a number of chōshi that are variants of hira-jōshi, kumoi-jōshi, nakazora, and akebono. These variants are used only in these pieces and it becomes clear that their use constituted one of the properties of the secret repertoire.

Having established the historical priority of hira-jōshi and its numerical dominance over the other chōshi, we shall now consider the method by which the koto is tuned. Example 9 shows that the strings are tuned strictly in order from one through thirteen.[7] Each new tone is followed by a "check" consisting of an interval or a melodic sequence of two tones, or sometimes an octave followed by a short melodic succession in octaves, that tests the accuracy of the tuning:

Example 9.

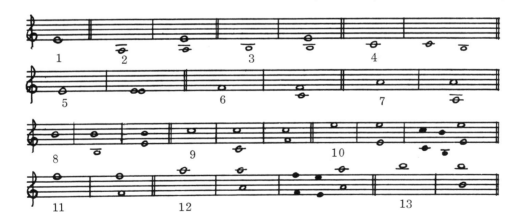

Thus, the accuracy of pitch is checked in two different ways:

1. Harmonically, by striking simultaneously two strings, producing intervals of perfect fifth, fourth, unison, and octave. This harmonic control is used for strings 2, 3, 5, and 6 through 13. The double check in fifths for strings 8 and 9 is not always made.

2. Melodically, by comparing the pitch of a newly tuned string with that of the next lower one, judging the correctness by "melodic intuition" (Ellis 1885: 522). The melodic sequences in octaves after strings 10 and 12 are usually made but are not obligatory. In theory at least, the check using octaves is sufficient.

It is apparent that on a well-tuned koto the pitches produced on nine of thirteen strings correspond to those of Western music, with the understanding, of course, that perfect and not tempered fifths and fourths are used. In hira-jōshi, these tones will be e, b, and a with their octaves —three tones, therefore, in a fifth relationship of fundamental, dominant, and subdominant. There is a certain functional correspondence to Western music that makes the use of these terms not too awkward. Tone e in hira-jōshi indeed is the fundamental, and b and a can be safely compared to dominant and subdominant. The reader is requested to keep in mind this fifth relationship as well as the specific way in which these three tones are tuned, since in practical use these tones appear to constitute the basic tones of the scale.

The tuning of the tones discussed so far, that is, e, b, and a, is the same, no matter which player is tuning the instrument. This is not true for the remaining four strings, tones c and f with their octaves —here the pitches will be slightly different with each tuner. Apparently melodic intuition provides less uniform results than checking by means of perfect intervals. Every traditionally educated musician, however, will tune his fourth string (and consequently, string 6 as well) somewhat lower than the corresponding tone in Western tempered tuning. [8] There is a tendency nowadays to tune the koto to the Western tempered scale. The results of measurements made by Obata and Sugita (1931: 59-60) of tunings by three outstanding koto musicians show the difference between the size of the semitones produced by the two more traditional musicians and the practically equal-tempered tuning of the third, a musician very much interested in the Westernization of Japanese music. The half-tones produced by one of the more traditional musicians varied between 72 and 80 cents, with an average of 75 cents; those of the other were slightly larger, moving between 78 and 89 cents with an average of 85 cents. The shinkyoku musician tuned in his half-steps between 96 and 103 cents, and his average of 99.5 cents is indistinguishable from the semitones of a piano.

Despite the difference in size between the minor seconds (and consequently the neighboring intervals, the major thirds) of the koto and those resulting from the Western tuning system, koto music may be notated in Western notation —if these differences are kept in mind.

CHAPTER IV

NOTATION

Until quite recently written music was not used in the instruction of sōkyoku, which was almost exclusively taught by rote. A teacher would play a fragment, the student would repeat it with him over and over until the teacher was convinced that the part had been memorized, whereafter a new fragment would be added. This procedure required time and almost daily lessons, but it had advantages that should not be underestimated. Retention and perception were developed to a degree rarely found in Western practice, which is oriented toward printed music. Learning by rote is general in most Oriental cultures. In the specific case of the Japanese koto musicians it was a practical necessity, for many of the professional musicians were blind.

The koto student is aided in his memorization by the use of a mnemonic system consisting of onomatopoeic syllables which is called *shōfu* or —it would seem inappropriately, since the word refers to the shamisen rather than the koto—*kuchi-jamisen*.[1] The use of mnemonic syllables in Japan is old and was known to the gagaku musicians of the Heian court, whose system was called *shōka*. The term kuchi-jamisen suggests that the koto mnemonic system is an adaptation of that used for the shamisen. The principle in both systems is the simultaneous memorization of a melody and a series of syllables that indicate the type of stroke to be used, the register of the instrument, sometimes a choice of a limited number of pitches to be played, and the rests. As the syllables in shōfu may refer to a choice of pitches, the system may not be equated with solmization. In addition, certain techniques and some more or less standardized melodic patterns are represented by their own combinations of syllables. Most of the syllables used in the system for the shamisen also occur in that for the koto. Exceptions concern techniques specific to only one of the two instruments —for example, syllables indicating left-hand pizzicati on the shamisen or lengthwise "scraping" of the strings on the koto.

A table published by William P. Malm (1963: 63) shows that the shamisen system uses a total of nine syllables, the choice of which is determined by the string to be plucked (first, second, or third), the type of stroke to be applied (downstroke, upstroke, or left-hand pizzicato), and whether the string is to be open or stopped. The most important syllables are *ton, ten, tsun,* and *chin.* These syllables, which are all taken from the t-column of the Japanese syllabary, represent the normal downstrokes on the shamisen. *Ton* and *ten* refer to open strings, *tsun* and *chin* to stopped strings. The syllables *ton* and *tsun* are used for both strings 1 and 2, *ten* and *chin* for string 3 only. Onomatopoeically, the system admirably fits the sounds produced: the attack of the *bachi* (plectrum) plucking the shamisen strings is reproduced by the initial "t" of the syllables; the darker vowels, "o" and "u," represent the lower tones and the lighter vowels, "e" and "i," represent the higher ones. Upstrokes and left-hand pizzicati are met less frequently, and the syllables representing them all begin with "r." Again, use of r-sounds for the representation of these specific techniques is appropriate to the almost gentle quality of upstrokes and left-hand pizzicati. This second group also consistently distinguishes between open and stopped strings.

Because there are thirteen strings on the koto and only three on the shamisen, playing techniques are very different. In order to make a comparison between the two syllable-systems it is necessary to replace string numbers by a denominator shared by both instruments: pitches. The most common shamisen tuning, called *hon-chōshi* (the three strings are tuned to b, e', and b'), corresponds to hira-jōshi for the koto; the pitches in the following table are in reference to these two tunings. The numbers in the "string" column refer to string numbers on the shamisen.

Syllable	Instrument	Stroke	String	Pitch
Ton	Shamisen	Down	Open (1, 2)	b, e'
	Koto	Down	Open	Mainly b and e'
Ten	Shamisen	Down	Open (3)	b'
	Koto	Down	Open	Mainly e', b', e'', b''
Tsun	Shamisen	Down	Stopped (1, 2)	All tones that can be produced on these stopped strings (b cannot)
	Koto	Down	Open **or** pressed	Generally, lower register tones other than e and b
Chin	Shamisen	Down	Stopped (3)	Tones higher than b'
	Koto	Down	Open	Generally, upper register tones other than e'' and b''
Ren	Shamisen	Upstroke left-hand	Open (1, 2, 3)	b, e' and b'
	Koto	Upstroke*	Open	Mainly e'
Rin	Shamisen	Upstroke left-hand	Stopped (1, 2, 3)	All tones that can be produced by stopping (b cannot)
	Koto	Upstroke	Open	Mainly f''

*The content of the koto part of this table is based on the kumiuta-danmono repertoire, and in the period of the composition of this repertoire upstrokes were rarely used. Basically, however, the information here given is valid for later periods also.

The table contains only those syllables that are common to both shamisen and koto systems. It should be noted that the koto system is based on scale degrees and thus the pitch references of its syllables change from mode to mode, while the shamisen system is based on string numbers. This explains, in terms of consistency, the superiority of the shamisen system. Since the koto system is looser than that for the shamisen, only those pitches that are normally connected with the syllable under discussion have been included in the table. Occasionally, however, one encounters other pitches used with the same syllable.

The general similarity between kuchi-jamisen and koto shōfu may be noticed. For example, for both the koto and the shamisen, normally *ton* refers to tones b and e in the lower register and *ten* to the same tones in the higher register; thus, in general, *ton* and *ten* signify the fundamental and dominant of the mode. Occasionally, however, *ton* and *ten* in the koto system may indicate tone a (the "subdominant"), or even other tones. In the koto system *tsun* refers to the tones produced on the remaining open strings mainly in the lower register and *chin* to those in the higher. In addition, *tsun* is used to indicate tones produced on pressed-down strings (in hira-jōshi mainly d', g', c♯", d", f♯", and g"). R-sounds appear in the koto system only in reference to upstrokes, *ren* being used for basic tones and *rin* for other tones. Especially in later music, upstrokes often appear in rapid succession with downstrokes, in which case the vowels of both strokes agree, while the final "n" is dropped from both syllables; for example *tsu-ru, tsu-ru; te-re, te-re; chi-ri, chi-ri*. The presence or absence of the final "n" seems in general to be a matter of euphony as much as of time values and tempo. When pronunciation must be rapid, or when a combination of syllables is difficult to pronounce, the "n" is dropped.

In addition to the syllables contained in the table, shamisen and koto share three more mnemonics: *shan*, indicating a plucking of two neighboring strings in such rapid succession the result is practically a single sound; *i-ya* and *yo-i*, both indicating rests. The idiomatic koto techniques in which the strings are scraped lengthwise *(chirashizume* and *waren)* are referred to as *shu*. Scraping from right to left and back to right *(surizume)* is called *shū-shū*. *Ryan*, which is sometimes used instead of *shan*, refers to *oshiawase* (two neighboring strings sounding the same pitch and plucked in unison).

The relative inconsistency of the koto system strengthens the hypothesis that it is an adaptation of that for the shamisen rather than an original development. Two examples of consistent use of the koto shōfu are given below:

Example 10. (a) *Midare*, mm. 4-6; (b) *Midare*, mm. 11-13.[2]

Combinations of several notes offer special problems, because often in these cases the use of the syllables becomes less consistent and the choice of the mnemonics will be determined partly by the actual pitches, partly by euphonic considerations. Certain techniques, such as *uraren*, *nagashizume*, *warizume*, etc., have their own specific syllables *(sararin*, *kararin*, *sha-sha-ten)* and so do a limited number of melodic patterns. The shōfu syllables of the best known of these last are *koririn*, referring to a group of three descending notes, played on consecutive strings, usually degrees I-VI-V or V-IV-II:

Example 11. *Rokudan*, mm. 2-3.

sha-sha ko-ro-rin chi   ton

The *kakezume* pattern which occurs almost exclusively in kumiuta, also has its own special shōfu syllables. However, different syllables are used in different schools as well as in different parts of the country to refer to this pattern. In the following example the first syllabization is typical for Kyōto, the second is taken from Satō's *Kumiuta Zenshū* (published in Nagoya), while the third occurs in the *Yamada-ryū Koto no Kagami* (a Tokyo publication).

Example 12. *Fuki*, mm. 1-2.

ton	ren	ton	ren	ten
ton	ten	ton	ten	ten
ton	ten	ton	tsun	chin

Example 13, finally, shows a longer sequence with atypical syllabization for the sake of euphony. The use of *chi* for e" may be explained as a subsidiary function, which appears only in combinations with another syllable to indicate the higher of the two tones.

Example 13. *Rokudan*, mm. 25-27.

tsun   chi-te chi-tsu-te-chi tsu-te-tsu-te   ko-ro-ri chi   ton

Although not—or hardly—necessary for propagation of the music, a notation for the solo koto developed early, derived from the notation for the koto in gagaku. The *Shichiku Shoshinshū* of Nakamura Sōsan, which is dated 1664 and is an important source of information on seventeenth-century music for shamisen, koto, and shakuhachi, contains a number of notations of zokkyoku for the koto.[3] This seventeenth-century notation shares the main characteristic of the gakusō notation: the indication of string numbers rather than pitches, which therefore is a tablature. Never abandoned, this principle was maintained in important eighteenth-century collections such as the *Kinkyoku Shifu* (1772) and *Sōkyoku Taiishō* (1779) and is the basis of notation today. The first ten strings of the koto, as we have seen, are numbered *ichi* through *jū*, while the remaining three are called *to*, *i*, and *kin*. The kanji by which these string-names are represented are as follows:

一　　二　　三　　四　　五　　六　　七　　八　　九　　十　斗　為　巾

ichi,   ni,   san,   shi,   go,   roku,   shichi, hachi, ku,   jū, to,   i,   kin.[4]

These kanji, written or printed in vertical columns (Ikuta-ryū) or horizontal lines (Yamada-ryū), combined with rhythmic and certain technical indications, form the scores of zokusō.

Example 14 shows four different notations of the beginning of the same composition, *Rokudan*. The *Sōkyoku Taiishō* and present-day Ikuta-ryū notation both are written in vertical columns. The Yamada-ryū uses the most recently developed type of notation, which, like the Western, is written horizontally. The three types of notation show a gradual development toward greater precision, chiefly in rhythmic but also in some melodic aspects. The later notations being the simpler, it seems best to begin our considerations with one of these, the Ikuta notation. In this notation, the music is written in vertical columns, which are divided into rectangles, each of which represents one time-unit (see Ex. 14b). The kanji, which indicate strings to be plucked, are written or printed in the rectangles or spaces, about equidistant from the two sides. To the left of the kanji, very close to the left side of the spaces, are the shōfu syllables, written in *katakana*. To the right of the kanji sometimes (but by no means always), appear Arabic numerals that indicate fingerings. If no numeral appears, it is understood that the first finger (thumb) is to be used. In the kanji area of the spaces, i.e., their central portion, also appear special indications for left-hand techniques, for certain right-hand techniques, and for rests. The tuning of the koto is given at the very beginning of the piece.

Example 14.   The beginning of the first dan of *Rokudan* in different notations:
(a) *Sōkyoku Taiishō*,(b) Ikuta notation, (c) Yamada notation,
(d) a transcription in Western notation. In order to facilitate
comparison, (c) and (d) have been turned 90 degrees.

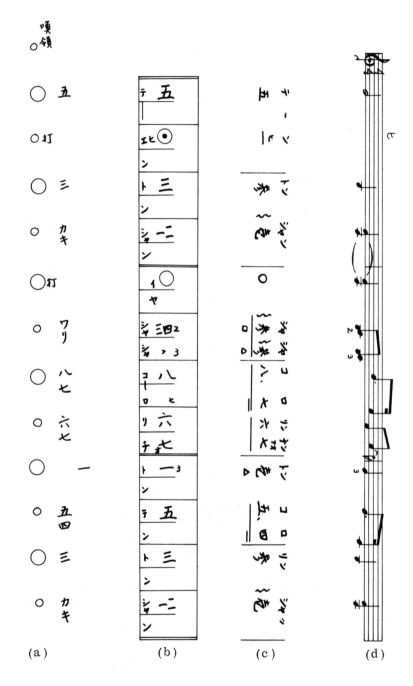

(a)   (b)   (c)   (d)

Each rectangle in the column is divided into two equal parts, an upper half and a lower half, the division being indicated by a horizontal line that extends from the left-hand side of the rectangle about two-thirds of the distance to the right-hand side. The time-value of a note is determined by the distance between one kanji and the next. For example, a kanji written in a half space and immediately followed by another kanji in the following half space will receive a value of a half time-unit; when a kanji is followed by an unoccupied half space, its time-value will be a whole unit; and so on. When transcribed into Western notation, a whole time-unit corresponds to a quarter-note, a half time-unit to an eighth, etc. Full spaces not used for the indication of kanji usually are occupied by a circle (◯) or a circle with a dot in the center (⊙). Although a dotted circle refers to a prolongation of the previous note and an open circle to a rest, in practice no difference between the two exists, because normally the tones of a koto are not damped and continue sounding. When a time-value shorter than a half-unit (eighth) is required the kanji is written in a reduced size and placed somewhat to the right in the space. Normally this notation will represent a quarter of a time-unit (sixteenth) but sometimes values shorter. It is at this point that the Ikuta notation ceases to be accurate, but one may question whether exact metric accuracy in the notation of these shorter note values is desirable. A koto player tends to play whole notes down to eighth-note values with metric precision. With shorter values a certain interpretative freedom exists, and often the actual value of notes shorter than eighths depends on the tempo: in slow movements the tendency is to play these notes quite short, as thirty-seconds, for example; in fast movements they are played longer, approaching an eighth-note triplet. Full spaces are combined in groups of four by means of a double line. One will look in vain for groups of three spaces, for Japanese koto music (with the exception of some shinkyoku) uses duple, not triple, meter.

Notwithstanding its superficially very different appearance, Yamada notation is quite similar to that of the Ikuta-ryū.[5] Western influence shows in the horizontal arrangement and in the indication of metric values for notes shorter than a quarter. These values are shown by underlining the kanji once, twice, three, or (very rarely) four times, to convey values of eighths, sixteenths, thirty-seconds, or sixty-fourths, respectively.[6] The vertical "barlines" show that the Yamada-ryū tends to interpret the same music metrically in a way different from the Ikuta-ryū, that is, in 2/4, rather than 4/4. The importance of this difference should not be exaggerated, however, for metric accents (in the Western sense) are either weak or absent in the music, and the notation does not automatically imply strong and weak beats of the 1, 2, 1, 2, or the 1, 2, 3, 4 type.   There are some other slight differences between the two systems; for example, different kanji are used for the lowest three strings (see footnote 4, page 44). In the Yamada-ryū the use of two neighboring strings simultaneously is shown by notation of only the lower one plus a wavy line to the left, and small squares and triangles rather than Arabic numerals indicate the use of second or third finger.

We turn finally to the oldest notation in Example 14, that of the *Sōkyoku Taiishō*. A general similarity to the notation of the Ikuta-ryū may be observed in the use of vertical columns. In general, however, there is less precision in the older notation, both rhythmically and melodically. Meter is indicated by an alternation of small and large circles, the space in between each two representing one time-unit.[7] Unlike the Ikuta system, no subdivision of the time-unit is provided in the notation and values shorter than the time-unit are shown by placing the kanji between two circles. Whether such placement represents eighths, sixteenths, or thirty-seconds, however, cannot be determined from the notation alone; the student must depend on oral instruction or upon his grasp of the style. The *Sōkyoku Taiishō* usually does not give the tuning

of the instrument. Where specific indication of the tuning is absent, hira-jōshi is assumed.
Nor does the *Taiishō* consistently represent all strings by their kanji; rather, it also uses
abbreviations, mostly in katakana for some of the well-known techniques. We have previously
noted the partial survival of this practice in present-day notation, in which its use is limited
and all sources for misinterpretation are eliminated. The older notation uses many more
technique-indications, the realization of which sometimes may be differently interpreted. The
example from *Rokudan* contains two such abbreviations: 丿 キ which stands for *kakite* and
フ リ representing *warizume*. In both Ikuta and Yamada notations kakite and warizume are
interpreted by strings 1 and 2, and 3 and 4, respectively. Neither the interpretation of kakite
nor that of warizume in this instance presents cause for confusion, but not infrequently it
occurs that one is not sure which two lower neighboring strings to select for kakite: the lowest
pair on the instrument, or the two just one octave below the next tone in the notation. In the
following example, taken from the eighth dan of *Hachidan,* three measures are shown in the
notation of *Sōkyoku Taiishō,* Ikuta-ryū, and Yamada-ryū. It may be observed that in the
Ikuta notation kakite is consistently interpreted as strings 1 and 2. The Yamada notation
gives 1 and 2 only the first times the kakite occurs; thereafter, kakite is consistently one
octave below the following note. Similar differences in interpretation, although less frequent,
can be encountered with warizume.

Although the notation of the *Sōkyoku Taiishō* is rather precise, it sometimes does not include left-hand ornamentations such as *jū* (hiki-iro), and *en* (ato-oshi), that may be found in
scores of Ikuta and Yamada-ryū. Such different interpretations, however, which to a certain
degree are independent of notation, are partly the result of different traditions in the schools or
subschools, as well as different personal interpretations by individual players. In the field of
left-hand ornamentation limited freedom is given to the performer, who, in general, must follow
quite strictly the tradition he has been taught.

In compositions for voice and koto, the traditional score reproduces the voice part only by its
text, not by its melody. This omission of any form of musical notation for the voice part is
probably a result of the fact that the vocal and instrumental parts are so closely related that
representation of the vocal melody may seem superfluous. Also it must be borne in mind that,
until quite recently, scores only functioned as memory aids: the music, voice as well as
koto parts, was exclusively learned by rote. Even today, when printed scores are frequently
used in instruction, the inclusion of musical notation for the voice part is rarely encountered.
When such notation occurs, the same symbols are used as those for the accompanying instrument.

Whatever the system of notation used, tempo indications are not given in traditional koto
music, although certain scores of modern compositions may sometimes include them. The
tempo in which a performer interprets a composition depends entirely on his knowledge of
the tradition.

The above observations on notation, although not covering every detail, are sufficient to
give the reader an adequate insight into the possibilities and limitations of the three most
important koto notations. The average Japanese player reads one notation only, either that
of the Ikuta or the Yamada-ryū. Knowledge of older notations is limited to the more special-
ly-educated among professionals.

Example 15. *Hachidan* dan 8, m. 5-7.

CHAPTER V

PLAYING TECHNIQUES

The player of the koto sits on the floor cross-legged (gagaku, kyōgoku), kneeling (Ikuta and Yamada-ryū), or with one knee raised (Tsukushi-goto).[1] The instrument is in front of him, its right end slightly to his right. During the Nara period the right end of the instrument was kept on the player's knees, as is still done today with the Korean *kayakeum*, an instrument closely related to the koto. The Ikuta player sits at an oblique angle, facing somewhat to the left.

The tsume are worn on thumb, index finger, and middle finger of the right hand, with the plectra on the palmar side. The strings are plucked near the ryūkaku, although experienced players may play farther away also, in order to change tone color. Quite frequently this happens in Tsukushi-goto and shinkyoku. The main playing finger is the thumb, which plucks the string in a movement away from the player. After plucking the string, the tsume comes to rest against the next string. This basic technique apparently has been considered so obvious that it has been taken for granted, for it has never been included in the lists of playing techniques.

The technique of the zokusō had its origin in that of the gakusō, and gradually developed toward more complexity in Tsukushi, Yatsuhashi, Ikuta, and Yamada-ryū. Contact with Western music since the Meiji era eventually forced the koto musicians to adapt their instrumental techniques to the rapidly changing music and to develop those of the left hand especially.

Traditionally the standard classical techniques are classified in seventeen standard techniques for the right hand *(Migite jūshichi-hō)* and eight for the left hand *(Hidarite hachi-hō)*. Keeping in mind the omission of the basic plucking technique with the thumb, the following enumeration gives a fairly complete insight into the technical possibilities of the koto.

Techniques for the Right Hand [2]

The techniques are organized in the following groups: single tones (1 and 2); two strings simultaneously (3, 4, and 5); glissandi (6 through 10); lengthwise "scraping" of one or two strings (11 through 14); and melodic patterns (15 through 18).[3]

1. *Sukuizume*. An upstroke with the thumb. The string is plucked with the back of the tsume in an upward motion. This technique occurs rarely in older forms such as kumiuta and danmono but is frequently met in later music.

2. *Uchizume*. The palmar surface of the middle finger, between the first and second joint, taps a string. This technique occurs typically in the Yamada-ryū and is not met in older types of koto music.

3. *Awasezume*. Two strings, in most cases an octave apart, are plucked by thumb and middle finger. Slight variations occur in the execution of awasezume among the various schools. In Tsukushi-goto, the lower pitch comes well before the higher; in the Ikuta-ryū this time difference is very short, while in the Yamada-ryū the strings are plucked simultaneously. In shōfu, players refer to awasezume as "shan."

4. *Kakite*. Two neighboring strings are plucked by either the index finger or the middle finger in a succession so rapid that the result is almost a single sound. Again, small variations may occur among the schools. In the Ikuta-ryū, the playing finger goes slightly upward after plucking the second string, without coming to rest against the next higher string; the Yamada performer may (not "must") continue the movement of his finger in the same direction until it stops against the next string. Kakite executed by an Ikuta performer will sound light; by a follower of the Yamada-ryū it may sound somewhat heavier. In shōfu, kakite is referred to as "shan."

5. *Oshiawase*. As in kakite, two neighboring strings are played in rapid succession, but this time by the thumb, while the lower-pitched of the two strings is pressed down by the left hand far enough to raise its pitch to that of the higher. The result, therefore, is a unison. Shōfu for oshiawase is "shan" or "ryan," shan being mostly used by Kyōto musicians. It should be noted that shan is used for all three double techniques.

6. *Uraren, ren, or sararin*. This graceful, downward glissando is one of the characteristic koto sounds that first impress Westerners on hearing this instrument. The technique varies not only from school to school, but also from city to city in the same school. The Ikuta ryū in Kyōto begins uraren with a rapid horizontal vibration with the tsume of the index finger upon the string on which the glissando is to start. This takes about half the time allowed for the uraren. The same tsume then moves lightly downward, and the glissando is concluded by plucking the last two or three strings with the thumb somewhat more loudly. The technique in the Ikuta-ryū in Ōsaka is similar, the only difference being that the downward glissando is made using the tsume of both index and middle fingers, thus producing a double glissando. A completely different beginning is made in the Yamada-ryū: the highest string is plucked by the tsume on the index finger in a "hooking" motion, the hand rotates rapidly, and the glissando follows. Uraren mostly begins on string 13, frequently ending on string 1, although different beginnings and endings are not rare. "Sararin" is the shōfu for this technique.

7. *Hikiren or shan-ren*. An upward glissando over all strings. The first two strings and the last two or three are played quite distinctly; the glissando in between is either extremely soft or even omitted altogether. Shōfu is "shan-ren."

8. *Han-hikiren*. Han-hikiren is like hikiren, but begins upon an intermediate rather than the first string. The shōfu is "shan-ren."

9. *Hikisute*. This again is a form of hikiren. This time the movement does not stop upon the highest-pitched string, but a lower one. Shōfu: "shan-ren."

10. *Nagashizume, ryū, or kararin*. This is a downward glissando. The two —sometimes three —highest-pitched strings and the lowest two are plucked distinctly, while the intermediate glissando is played very lightly. When the glissando stops on a string higher than string 1, the technique is called *han-ryū*. Nagashizume is like hikiren, but is played downward rather than upward. Shōfu is "kararin." Nagashizume, like the other glissandi, is found in danmono and kumiuta as well as in later developments of koto music.

11. *Chirashizume, chirashi, or san*. A fast, light, half-circular movement with the tsume of the middle finger lengthwise along a string from right to left. Usually a lower-pitched string is selected. Shōfu: "shu."

12. *Waren*. A fast slide along a string, usually 1, from right to left, with the tsume of the middle finger. The beginning of the movement is fast. Toward the end, the tsume moves upward, often touching string 2 as it rises. Shōfu is "shu."

13. *Surizume*. Two neighboring strings, usually selected from the first six, are scraped by the tsume of the index and middle fingers, from right to left and, after a short pause, back to the right. Shōfu is "shū-shū."

The previous three techniques produce scraping noises rather than tones. All three occur in older as well as in newer music.

14. *Namigaeshi*. A combination of "shan" and "shu." Strings 1 and 2 are plucked in rapid succession, followed by "shu" on two higher-pitched strings by the tsume of index and middle fingers. The conclusion is a repetition of the "shan" with which the pattern began. This technique is occasionally encountered in kumiuta, as well as in later music. Shōfu is "shan-shu-shan."

15. *Warizume*. Two neighboring strings are plucked twice by the index and middle fingers, respectively, after which the main tone of the pattern, which normally is the octave of the lower-pitched of the two, is plucked with the thumb. This very common technique in all forms of koto music is idiomatic for the instrument where the normal position of the hand is such that the interval spanned between the thumb and index and middle fingers is an octave. Shōfu is "sha-sha-ten," "sha-sha-chin," or "sha-sha-tsun."

Example 16.

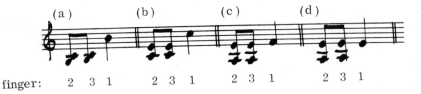

finger: 2 3 1   2 3 1   2 3 1   2 3 1

The above examples of warizume show how the interval at the beginning of this technique may differ from position to position as a result of the tuning of the instrument. Where the final string is lower than string 6, the octave leap (which is no longer within the range of the instrument) is replaced by a sixth or even a fifth, as shown in examples (c) and (d).

16. *Kakezume.* This technique, like the following two, *hankake* and *hayakake,* is a melodic pattern derived from related patterns in gagaku.[4] Kakezume consists of five tones: two neighboring strings are plucked in ascending order by the index finger; the middle finger follows with a similar sequence of two strings, but starting one string lower; the thumb concludes the pattern by plucking a string which sounds an octave higher than the third tone of the pattern. The time values of the first four tones are equal (one time unit; in Western notation, a quarter), the last tone usually is longer. In performance, a player is careful to sound the second and fourth tones somewhat softly by making an upward movement after plucking these strings rather than, as normally would be done, continuing the hand movement until the plucking finger comes to rest against the next higher string. In shōfu, kakezume are recited "ton, ren, ton, ren, ten" although variations are encountered, such as, for example, "ton, ten, ton, ten, ten."

The more important of the five tones of a kakezume pattern are the third tone and, especially, the fifth, two tones, therefore, with an interval of an octave. In the *Sōkyoku Taiishō* this is explicitly shown by printing at the beginning of each such pattern the name of the final string, followed by "kake" in katakana. For example, *to kake* accompanies a kakezume pattern which ends on *to* (11).

It is musically significant that these "kake patterns" represent a certain order of strings, not intervals. The intervals that are heard depend on the location of the kake pattern and the tuning of the instrument. The following three examples, all in the tuning hira-jōshi, show the influence of the location of the pattern on its intervallic structure:

Example 17.

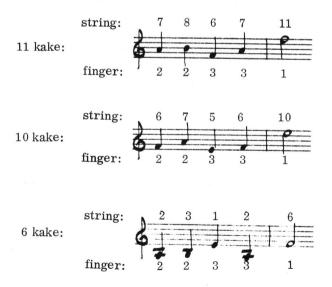

Example 18 shows the different intervallic structures of the same kake pattern performed in two different tunings:

Example 18.

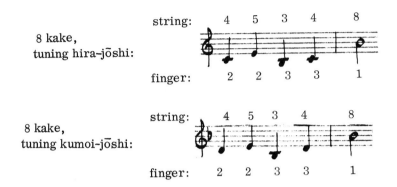

8 kake,
tuning hira-jōshi:

8 kake,
tuning kumoi-jōshi:

17. *Hankake.* This includes three different forms of melodic patterns, all of which are closely related to kakezume. Hankake differs from the kakezume pattern by the omission of one or two of the five tones. Hankake —this time using the term in a more limited sense —omits the second tone; *tanhan,* the fourth *mukōhan* omits the fourth and the fifth. Consequently, mukōhan are not octave patterns. Ordinarily, however, the octave of the third tone of mukōhan will be heard very soon after the pattern itself is concluded.

The example of hankake shown below is the only form in which this specific pattern occurs in hira-jōshi. It is significant, as will be made clear later (see Chapter XI), that *ku-kake* (kake on string 9) only occurs in the hankake form, never as kakezume. Similarly, *to-kake* (kake on string 11) in kumoi-jōshi occurs only as hankake (see Chapter XII). *Ku-kake* (kake on string 9), on the other hand, may be found in kumoi-jōshi in the five-tone form (kakezume) as well as in the four-tone (hankake), although such occurrence is rare.

Tanhan, like mukōhan, although usually found in lower registers, is less limited to specific locations than hankake. This is especially true of tanhan, which is encountered as kake on strings *shichi* (7), *hachi* (8), *ku* (9), *to* (11) and *i* (12) *kake.* Numerically, *hachi* and *i* -kake prove to be the most important, followed by *shichi, ku,* and *to* -kake. The composer Mitsuhashi Kengyō distinguishes himself from his predecessors by his relative preference for i-kake in its tanhan form.

Mukōhan is somewhat more limited in its pitch locations than tanhan and begins only on strings *san* (3), *shi* (4), *roku* (6), or *shichi* (7). More than half of the mukōhan pattern start on string 3, about one-fourth begin with string 6.

Kakezume and the various forms of hankake are of great importance in kumiuta and may be considered characteristic of the form. Typically, a kumiuta phrase begins with a kake pattern,

Example 19. Three forms of hankake in hira-jōshi.

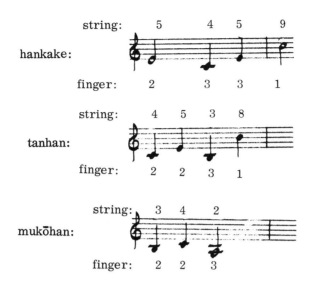

although there are many exceptions, usually toward the end of a piece. But, whereas kakezume may occur at the beginning of any phrase, hankake, tanhan, and mukōhan tend to be limited to specific locations in the course of an uta. Hankake occurs most frequently at the beginning of the second half of an uta (that is, at the beginning of the fifth phrase), less frequently at the beginning of the first phrase, rarely elsewhere. Tanhan and mukōhan both appear mostly toward the end of an uta, especially at the beginning of the seventh and eighth phrases.

18. *Hayakake*. The notation of this "fast kake" is not the same in newer texts as in older, and in actual practice it may be performed in still a third way. The *Sōkyoku Taiishō* notates haya-kake as a regular kakezume that should be performed four times as fast as a regular kakezume (in Western notation; in sixteenths rather than in quarter notes). A modern text, the *Yamada-ryū Koto no Kagami*, gives different note values, and the actual modern practice is still different:

Example 20.

(a) *Sōkyoku Taiishō:*

(b) *Yamada-ryū Koto no Kagami:*

(c) Modern practice:

Basing our judgment on the authority of the *Sōkyoku Taiishō*, which is generally considered quite accurate, it seems probable that in performance practice hayakake has changed since the eighteenth century. One cannot be certain, however, because until recently koto instruction did not employ written material. The difference between the *Yamada-ryū Koto no Kagami* and modern Ikuta-ryū practice is minimal, the additional tone to be heard in actual performance being played very lightly, as if in passing. Unlike kakezume and hankake, hayakake has survived in later developments of sōkyoku, a circumstance that may have been responsible for its gradual modification.

Hayakake are frequently found in kumiuta, although their importance is less than that of other patterns discussed earlier. A hayakake occurs less exclusively at the beginning of a phrase, although it may frequently be encountered there. Early kumiuta used hayakake less frequently than later ones, for example, those by Mitsuhashi Kengyō.

In addition to the hayakake patterns in sixteenth notes and their derivatives, similar patterns in eighth notes occur which, however, are not named. Here also modern performance practice deviates from the notation of the *Sōkyoku Taiishō*:

Example 21

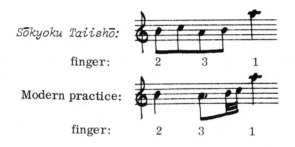

This pattern, which is directly related to hayakake, is to be found especially in later kumiuta.

19. *Yokozume*. Several strings, usually three (sometimes only one string) are scraped with the side of the tsume of the thumb. The tones usually correspond to a descent from scale degrees V to I. This technique, not included in the traditional right-hand techniques, occurs occasionally in kumiuta, but once only in danmono.

The *Sōkyoku Taiishō* (Vol. 6) lists only twelve right-hand techniques as used in kumiuta. Comparing these twelve with the nineteen given above, it appears that those listed here as Nos. 2, 5, 8, 9, 11, 13, and 19 are not mentioned in the older source. The absence of uchizume (No. 2), a later technique, needs no comment. Oshiawase, which does exist in kumiuta, must have been considered a left-hand rather than a right-hand technique. Hanhikiren (No. 8) and surizume (Nos. 11 and 13) are variants of waren. The conclusion to be drawn is that practically all traditional right-hand techniques developed before 1779, when the *Sōkyoku Taiishō* was published.

Techniques for the Left Hand

Seven of the following eight left-hand techniques are executed to the left of the movable bridges and serve the purpose of providing pitches that are different from those provided by the open strings. The function of the first technique does not go beyond the provision of a new, uninflected pitch. In the following six (Nos. 2 through 7) the pitch is changed after the string has been plucked and the function of these techniques is largely ornamental in terms of microtonal pitch deviations. Number 8 differs from the others in its function (change of timbre) as well as in playing position.

1. *Kō (oshide)*. In order to obtain a pitch higher than that provided by an open string, the left hand presses the string down to the left of the movable bridge before the right hand plucks. Depending on the amount of pressure, the pitch can be raised a minor second, a major second, or a minor third.

Ichijū oshi raises a pitch a minor second; *nijū oshi*, a major second; and *sanjū oshi*, a minor third. Sanjū oshi requires so much pressure that it is extremely hard to perform and therefore is rarely used. Bearing in mind the usual tuning of the koto in minor seconds, major seconds, and major thirds, it is logical that kō is often applied on the lower-pitched of two strings a major third apart, thus filling in the gap in the scale.

2. *Oshihanashi*. This technique begins like kō, but the string is released before the next is plucked. The pitch slides down from that of the pressed string to that of the open strings.

3. *En*. A string is pressed down after it has been plucked. The pitch slides up, normally to the next higher tone of the scale. This is normally referred to as *ato-oshi*, "after push."

4. *Kasaneoshi*. After it is plucked, a string is pressed down, released, and pressed down again in rapid succession. [5]

5. *Chitsu* or *tsuki-iro*. After it is plucked, a string is pressed down and released immediately. This technique functions as an expressive pitch accent.

6. *Ju* or *hiki-iro*. A string is taken between thumb and index finger and pushed to the right, then released. The pitch becomes slightly lower. Its function is entirely ornamental.

7. *Yōgin* or *yuri-iro*. This is a vibrato, made with index, middle, and ring fingers, again to the left of the movable bridge. This technique is relatively new and does not occur in kumiuta and danmono.

8. *Keshizume, soede*, or *soe-iro*. A special sound effect, caused by lightly touching a vibrating string with the nail of the index finger (sometimes the thumb) immediately to the right of the movable bridge.

The average koto player does not know many of the "official" terms mentioned above and, while speaking about his music, never uses them. Instead, he refers to these techniques by their shōfu. For example, rather than using the term warizume, he will say "sha-sha-ten," and so on.

As the technique of the zokusō is a further development of that of Tsukushi-goto which, in turn, derived from gakusō techniques, a comparison of the technical arsenals of zokusō and gakusō may provide an insight into the development of instrumental techniques. The gakusō uses the following techniques.

Right-hand techniques:

1. *Sugagaki.*
2. *Shizugaki.*
3. *Hayagaki.*

These three techniques, which occur typically at the beginning of a phrase, are similar in that their basic interval is an octave, which may occur between the last two tones of the pattern (sugagaki and hayagaki), or between the second and the last, interrupted by two "passing" tones (shizugaki). As with the kakezume pattern in zokusō, the last tone of each pattern is the most important.

Example 22. (a) sugagaki, (b) shizugaki, and (c) hayagaki

Shizugaki and hayagaki both are extremely important patterns in the koto part of gagaku compositions, most of which consist almost exclusively of either shizugaki or hayagaki patterns. Sugagaki, in contrast, does not occur in the course of a gagaku composition, but only in the *netori,* the short introductions, and in the *tomede,* the concluding sections. The various kakezume patterns in kumiuta were derived from these three gagaku techniques.

4. *Kozume.* These are single notes that appear between two shizugaki or hayagaki patterns and are played with the thumb. Kenjun developed these single notes into short melodies that connect the kakezume patterns of his kumiuta, and in this, as in other ways, showed how he was influenced by gagaku.[6]

5. *Sawaru.* Sometimes not only kozume but also a second note (played on the fourth beat of the measure) appears between two shizugaki or hayagaki patterns. This additional note is called sawaru. The following example, taken from the koto part of *Etenraku* in hyōjō (measures 37, 38, and 39) in a transcription by Shiba (1955: 11), shows a sequence of shizugaki, kozume, sawaru, and another shizugaki.

Example 23.

shizugaki   kozume   sawaru   shizugaki

6. *Kaeshizume*. An upstroke with the tsume of the thumb. This technique corresponds to sukuizume of the later koto schools.

7. *Ren*. A downward glissando with the tsume of the thumb. The term has survived in solo koto music, although the other terms, uraren and especially sararin, are more popular.

8. *Musubite*. Several consecutive strings are plucked with the back of the tsume of the thumb in ascending order. The following example, taken from *Bairo* (m. 34), shows a sequence of hayagaki and musubite. The transcription is by Shiba (1955: 27). Musubite did not survive in solo koto music.

Example 24

hayagaki   musubite

9. *Tsumute*. Two strings are plucked simultaneously with the tsume of thumb and index finger in an upward motion. This technique corresponds to awasezume in solo sōkyoku.

Comparing these gakusō techniques with classical koto techniques, we notice that a good deal of the latter have been derived, with more or less modification, from the older tradition. Musubite, the ascending glissando with the thumb, did not survive in solo koto. Instead, hikiren and hikisute (which are also upward glissandi) appeared, but played with the middle finger — a technique that never occurred in gakusō techniques. Lengthwise scraping of strings is exclusively found in later sōkyoku.

Left-hand techniques:

Nowadays, the player of the gakusō uses his right hand exclusively. Old texts, however — for example, the *Jinchi Yōroku* (a partbook for the koto dating from the late twelfth century) — show a rather elaborate system of left-hand techniques that were mainly applied following shizugaki and hayagaki patterns. Reconstruction of these lost techniques has been attempted by Dr. Robert Garfias. The explanations given below are based on his work.[7]

1. *Oshiiri*.[8] A string is pushed down after being plucked. This technique, therefore, corresponds to en or ato-oshi in sōkyoku.

2. *Oshihanashi*. A string is pushed down before it is plucked and released afterwards. The technique is the same, therefore, as oshihanashi in later koto music.

3. *Nidooshihanashi*. The execution of this technique is not quite clear. It represents either a double afterpush or a combination of the previous two techniques: a pushing down of the string before plucking, a release after plucking, followed by a second push. The first interpretation corresponds to kasaneoshi in zokusō.

4. *Toriyuru*. This technique is the same as ju or hiki-iro in zokusō.

This brief enumeration makes it clear that the essential left-hand techniques of sōkyoku existed in gagaku.

PART II

DANMONO

CHAPTER VI

DANMONO: THE FIRST DAN

Before the foundation of the Ikuta-ryū in 1695, there existed only two forms of sōkyoku, the vocal-instrumental kumiuta and the purely instrumental danmono. When in the second half of the eighteenth century the first collections of koto music began to appear,[1] no attempts to separate the forms was made. Indeed, although without sufficient reason, danmono sometimes have been classified as kumiuta. The two forms actually have no more in common than the period in which they were composed and the fact that both consist of a number of separate movements (called "dan" in danmono and "uta" in kumiuta), each of which contains a set number of beats. The differences between the forms are decisive. Aside from the fact that the kumiuta is vocal-instrumental and the danmono exclusively instrumental, in the latter the number of dan varies from piece to piece, while in the former the number of uta tends to be fixed (six). A dan contains 104 time units (of one quarter) and an uta 128; musical material and construction also are different and distinctive for each form.[2]

The danmono repertoire is limited today to seven or eight compositions. Their titles show the number of dan of which they consist: *Godan* (five dan), *Rokudan* (six dan), *Shichidan* (seven dan), *Hachidan* (eight dan), *Kudan* (nine dan), *Kumoi Kudan* (nine dan in (hon) kumoi-jōshi). The tuning of *Kumoi Kudan* distinguishes this composition from all other danmono, which use hira-jōshi. Traditionally classified as a danmono, although having a quite different construction, is *Midare,* which sometimes is called *Jūdan* (ten dan) or *Jūnidan* (twelve dan), thus nicely (though unvoluntarily) illustrating the meaning of the word *midare* ("confusion"). To this repertoire may be added the instrumental introduction to the nineteenth-century composition *Akikaze,* which is constructed according to the principles of danmono. Sometimes one finds a title given in longer form, for example, *Rokudan no Shirabe* or *Hachidan no Shirabe.* Shirabe means "investigation" and thus these titles may be translated as, respectively, "Investigation in Six Movements" and "Investigation in Eight Movements." It is not quite clear what the object of these "investigations" may be, but, as will be shown later, they seem to concern not only a process of checking the correctness of the accordatura, but also a systematic exposition of the modal characteristics of the *chōshi* involved.[3]

To Yatsuhashi Kengyō is traditionally attributed the authorship of the best known danmono performed today: *Rokudan, Midare,* and *Hachidan.* However, as was mentioned on page 10, there is little reason to assume that Yatsuhashi Kengyō was the composer of these pieces. Several of his kumiuta are known to be no more than arrangements of earlier compositions of Tsukushi-goto, and these danmono could also have existed before, in some form or other.[4]

Indeed, Kikkawa Eishi (1961: 6) points out that for the most part instrumental Tsukushi-goto compositions of the *Rinzetsu* type very likely were the source for the early danmono, especially for *Midare*, which originally was called *Midare Rinzetsu* and is still so referred to in the Yatsuhashi-ryū (and occasionally even later). The repertoire of the Yatsuhashi-ryū may provide information about the chronology of danmono, which is still unclear. In addition to *Midare Rinzetsu*, this repertoire includes one danmono, *Kudan no Shirabe*, that is related to *Rokudan*, rather than *Kudan*. Indeed, the composition is practically identical to *Rokudan*, the major difference being that dan four, five, and six are repeated, thus making a total of nine dan rather than six. The Yatsuhashi-ryū thus corroborates the antiquity of *Rokudan* and *Midare*. [5]

The old Okinawan repertoire for the koto may also shed light on the danmono chronology. We have seen that this music closely resembles an older type of zokkyoku for koto which is extinct in Japan today, and which must have been exported to Okinawa around 1600. Seven instrumental pieces in this Okinawan koto repertoire are systematically called: *Ichidan* (one dan), *Nidan* (two dan), *Sandan* (three dan), *Shidan* or *Yondan* (four dan), *Godan* (five dan), *Rokudan* (six dan), and *Shichidan* (seven dan). The first five, which have other titles as well and are not danmono at all, formally strongly resemble simple shamisen compositions; *Rokudan Sugagaki* and *Shichidan Sugagaki* (the complete titles of these pieces), on the other hand, are closely related to the Japanese *Rokudan* and *Shichidan*. The complexity of these two compositions sets them apart from the rest of the Okinawan repertoire. Two factors tend to substantiate their antiquity: the tuning used is an anhemitonic pentatonic tuning, used also in Tsukushi-goto and zokkyoku; their form is somewhat less polished and less strict—for example, the numbers of beats per dan correspond only roughly to those of the Japanese versions. The Okinawan repertoire for the koto then, corroborates the hypothesis that *Rokudan* is one of the oldest danmono, and allows *Shichidan* to be grouped with *Rokudan* and *Midare* in the chronology. [6]

With the examination of the repertoires of Tsukushi-goto, Yatsuhashi-ryū, and Okinawan "Yatsuhashi-ryū," we exhaust the immediate resources for determination of the chronology of danmono. Comparison of early printed sources might be expected to open other possibilities. The result, however, is disappointing. The oldest source, the *Shichiku Shoshinshū* (1664), mentions a number of kumiuta by Yatsuhashi Kengyō, but no danmono. Ninety years later another text, the *Busō Gafushū* (1755), mentions all the danmono in the repertoire with the exception of *Kumoi Kudan*, which appears for the first time in 1772, in the *Kinkyoku Shifu*. [7] *Kumoi Kudan*, then, seems to be the last of the danmono, which may be corroborated by its classification as a *shinkyoku* (new piece) in the *Sōkyoku Taiishō* (1779). [8]

Stylistic analysis of the repertoire might be assumed to provide a final means for discovering the chronology of the danmono. However, conscious conformism of the Japanese koto composer, who strives toward stylistic homogeneity in a form rather than diversity, strongly limits the possibilities of such analysis. Only *Godan* [9] and, to a lesser degree, *Hachidan*, are set somewhat apart by their rhythmic complexity and, therefore, may be considered younger.

A tentative chronology of the danmono repertoire, based on the above evidence, and divided into three groups, is as follows:

1. *Midare, Rokudan, Shichidan;*
2. *Kudan, Hachidan, Godan;*
3. *Kumoi Kudan;*
4. *Akikaze no Kyoku.*

A more detailed chronology seems unjustified speculation.[10]

Before proceeding with an analysis of the danmono, the general characteristics of the form may be briefly summarized. Danmono are instrumental compositions for the koto consisting of a varying number of movements ("dan," literally: "steps"). Each dan, with the exception of the first, consists of one hundred and four beats, usually arranged in twenty-six 4/4 measures.[11] The first dan is four to eight beats longer. The tempo is slow at the beginning, but gradually increases from dan to dan until, toward the end of the last dan, the original slow tempo is resumed. The tuning is normally hira-jōshi, the only exception (disregarding the late *Akikaze)* being *Kumoi Kudan.* Since the nineteenth century, danmono have often been performed on two kotos, one, the *honte,* playing the original part in hira-jōshi, the other, the *kaete,* playing an ornamental part in kumoi-jōshi.[12] Many danmono, especially *Rokudan,* were adapted to other instruments, and it is possible to hear these pieces played on shamisen and shakuhachi as well as performed by a sankyoku ensemble.

The danmono constitute a small repertoire of such homogeneity that uninitiated listeners, Japanese as well as Westerners, have much trouble distinguishing one from another. The display of artistic originality was strange to the Japanese composer of the seventeenth and eighteenth centuries; his homage to his great and venerated predecessors was shown by approaching the ideal of the set example as closely as possible, and his individuality was allowed to be expressed in subtle variations upon, rather than in drastic deviations from, the model.[13] This homogeneity of the danmono repertoire almost automatically suggests an analytical method that somewhat departs from the usual procedure for the analysis of a number of compositions. A simultaneous rather than a piece-by-piece analysis promises insights into the formal characteristics of the danmono as a form that could hardly be obtained otherwise. Also, because of this homogeneity, it seems unnecessary to present a detailed analysis of *all* dan in each composition. Therefore, a simultaneous analysis of the first dan of all danmono (with the exception, because of its irregular construction, of *Midare)* will be undertaken initially. When the functioning of this first, and therefore crucial, dan is fully understood, the relation of later dan will be shown, chiefly through one representative composition. The exceptional *Midare* will be discussed separately.

In the following examples, *Kumoi Kudan* has been transposed down a fourth in order to make comparison with the other compositions, in hira-jōshi, easier by giving it the same pitch as first degree of the scale. *Akikaze* is also reproduced with tone e' as fundamental. The few additional beats in the first dan are the result of the presence of a *kandō,* a short introduction consisting of no more than an opening formula with cadential characteristics. In order to permit better comparison with later dan, the kandō will not be included in the numbering of the measures. The pieces will be presented in their presumed chronological order, which, at the same time, automatically organizes them by chōshi in the order hira-jōshi, transposed hon-kumoi-jōshi, and *Akikaze*-chōshi. Finally, in the transcription of *Hachidan* the barlines have been shifted two beats; thus, the piece starts with an "anacrusis" rather than on the first beat as it is usually notated. This alteration allows for a clearer comparison with the other pieces. It also shows the somewhat greater length of the kandō of Hachidan.

In Example 25, the kandō, the opening formulae of the first dan of each danmono, are brought together.

Example 25. Danmono, Dan 1, Kando: (a) *Rokudan, Shichidan, and Kudan;*
(b) *Hachidan;* (c) *Godan;* (d) *Kumoi Kudan;* (e) *Akikaze*

Bearing in mind that the actual register of *Kumoi Kudan* differs from that of the others although the notation suggests it to be the same, we observe:

1. The kandō for all examples are short and include no more than three or four tones. The most common length is four beats (five out of seven examples), and only *Hachidan*, with six, and *Akikaze*, with eight beats, deviate from that norm. *Akikaze*, incidentally, somewhat later in the (first) dan shows an irregularity in its construction, eventually "returning" these four extra beats of its kandō.

2. The register is low for all pieces.

3. All kandō start with tone e' (degree 1 of the mode).

4. All move down to tone b (degree V). This downward movement is either direct *(Ro-kudan, Shichidan,* and *Kudan)*; or interrupted by one *(Hachidan)* or two *(Akikaze)* "shan," or by the inclusion of the passing tone c' *(Godan),* or by the alternation of the first degree with its lower neighbor *(Kumoi Kudan)*.

5. After reaching tone b (degree V), all examples in hira-jōshi continue their downward movement to tone a (degree IV); thus, all three basic degrees of the mode are represented. The fourth degree may occur as a single tone *(Hachidan* and *Godan),* or as part of a "shan" in which degree IV is combined with degree I *(Rokudan, Shichidan,* and *Kudan)*.

6. In *Godan,* the function of tone c' as a passing tone in the basic e'-b(-a) pattern is prac-tically irrelevant when the manner in which the koto player performs it is considered: as if touching it accidentally while proceeding to a more important goal. The group of three tones, e'-c'-b, in the characteristic rhythm of dotted eighth, sixteenth, and quarter, is a good example of the well-known "kororin" pattern. The passing tone in such patterns is always played very lightly and sometimes may be omitted altogether, in which case the "kororin" pattern changes to "ten-ton." Such a change from "kororin" to "ten-ton," or the reverse, does not alter the "musical intention."

7. The exchange tone d' (degree VII) in *Kumoi Kudan* is the only case in which a tone re-quiring left-hand pressure for its production is introduced so early in the composition; normally, such tones do not occur until later in the composition.

8. At this point it becomes clear that one main function of the formula e'-b-a (in scale de-grees I-V-IV) is that of outlining the basic tones of the mode; in other words, it is a melodic cadence.[14]

9. In terms of durational values, the kandō is very simple. Essentially no more than two va-lues are required: half and quarter notes, the longer value being reserved for degree I, the other for degrees V and IV. Inclusion of passing and exchange tones introduces shorter note values (dotted quarters, dotted eighths, eighths, and sixteenths), all of which, however, can clearly be seen to be subordinate to the basic half-quarter-quarter pattern.

10. Although ornamentation will be treated in more detail later, the frequent occurrence of "ju" (hiki-iro) (⤻) on tone e' (degree I), which is of relatively long duration, can be seen.

Following the kandō, the dan may be subdivided into five phrase groups, the limitations of which are determined by descending cadences typical of the danmono repertoire. Such cadences begin on either degree I or V (in the present transcriptions, tones e and b) and invariably des-cend to a degree one fourth lower. Cadences beginning with degree I descend to degree V (from tone e to tone b), those beginning with degree V descend to degree II (from b to f). Because degree II, as we will see later, functions as a descending leading tone, cadences beginning with degree V frequently will be concluded by an additional first degree: V-II-I (b-f-e). Thus, in the dan under discussion, the phrases of phrase group I end with a cadence including degrees I and V (tones e' and b), those of group II end one octave higher, those of group III include degrees V and II (tones b" and f"), etc. It is characteristic that number and length of phrases constituting phrase groups are not identical for all groups. New melodic goals are realized in the first main phrase of each group, and confirmed by the subsequent phrases, the character of which is supporting. It may be noticed that the length of the phrases varies considerably: one and a half measures (phrase group III, phrase 2), two measures (group I, both phrases; group II, both supporting phrases), three measures (main phrases of groups III, IV, and V), and four measures (main phrase of group II, supporting phrase of group IV. This specific division of the dan into five groups, containing ten phrases of very different dimensions, is the result of internal evidence within the modern versions of the repertoire, as well as historic evidence, provided by a prototype –*Sugagaki* –and earlier versions –danmono in the Yatsuhashi-ryū and in Okinawa –(Adriaansz 1970). The following chart may give an insight into the phrase structure and cadential characteristics of the dan:

Phrase group	Phrase	Cadence
I (m. 1-4)	1 (m. 1-2)	I-V (e'-b)
	2 (m. 3-4)	"
II (m. 5-12)	1 (m. 5-8)	I-V (e"-b')
	2 (m. 9-10)	"
	3 (m. 11-12)	"
III (m. 13-17)	1 (m. 13-15)	V-II (b"-f")
	2 (m. 16-17)	"
IV (m. 17-23)	1 (m. 17-20)	I-V (e"-b')
	2 (m. 20-23)	"
V (m. 24-26)	1 (m. 24-26)	I-V (e'-b)

In the following discussions the division of the dan into five phrase groups is observed, with the exception of phrase group II, the greater length of which explains its separate discussion of its first phrase (measures 5-8) and its supporting phrases (measures 8-12).

Phrase group I (measures 1-4)

The following observations may be made:

1. Phrase group I is composed of two phrases of two measures, each of which is concluded by a descending melodic cadence of the same type as that of the kandō (including tones e' and b).

2. The register moves up. The usual goal centers around tone b' (degree V). The highest tones reached in measures 1 and 3 are shown below.

	Measure 1	Measure 3
Rokudan, Godan	b'	c"
Shichidan	f'	e'
Kudan	a'	b'
Hachidan	b'	b'
Kumoi Kudan	a'	a'
Akikaze	b'	f♯'

Tone b' is not the goal of the melodic ascent in *Shichidan* and *Kumoi Kudan*. Nevertheless, in *Kumoi Kudan* tone a' in both measures 1 and 3 is followed by the left-hand technique "en" (ato-oshi) which produces tone b'. *Shichidan* remains the only piece in which, in these first four measures, the melody moves above tone e' (the highest tone of the kandō) only once –to f', a half step above. In three of the seven cases, the highest tone is reached in measure 3, thus providing a gradual increase in melodic tension.

Example 26. Danmono, Dan 1, Phrase group I (mm. 1-4): (a) *Rokudan,*
(b) *Shichidan,* (c) *Kudan,*   (d) *Hachidan,*   (e)   *Godan,*
(f)   *Kumoi Kudan,*   (g) *Akikaze.*

3. The tonal material has increased considerably beyond that found in the kandō and includes for:

Rokudan	:	a, b, c', e', f', a', b', c'';
Shichidan	:	a, b, c', d', e', f';
Kudan, Hachidan	:	a, b, c', d', e', f', a', b';
Godan	:	a, b, c', d', e', f', a', b', c'';
Kumoi Kudan	:	b, d', e', f', g', a';
Akikaze	: E, e, b, c', e', f♯', a' b'.

All tones of the scale that can be produced on open strings have now appeared, in low register, in each of the compositions, except tone c' which is not used in *Kumoi Kudan*. All pieces but *Rokudan* and *Akikaze* use one tone produced by left-hand pressure, d' (degree VII). *Kumoi Kudan*, having already used tone d' in the kandō, now introduces a second such tone, g' (degree III).

4. The function of tones e, a, and b (degrees I, IV, and V) is still that of skeletal tones. Tone c' (degree VI) again functions as a passing tone in "kororin" patterns *(Shichidan, Kudan, Hachidan, Godan,* and *Akikaze:* measures 2 and 4). In measure 3 of *Rokudan,* however, tone c'' temporarily replaces tone b' and is heavily stressed. Tone f' (degree II) functions as upper leading tone for tone e' (degree I), and assumes, therefore, an important melodic function (all examples except *Akikaze* in measures 1 and 3). Tone d' (degree VII) functions as lower leading tone at metrically important locations *(Shichidan, Kudan, Hachidan, Godan,* and *Kumoi Kudan* in measures 1 and/or 3).

5. The highest tones in measures 1 and 3 are reached as follows:

	Measure 1	*Measure 3*
Rokudan	*warizume:* b-b'	immediately: c''
Kudan	ascent: d'-e'-f'-a'	ascent: d'-e'-a'-b'
Hachidan	" : d'-e'-f'-a'-b'	immediately: b'
Godan	" : d'-e'-f'-a'-b'	ascent: a'-(f')-c''
Kumoi Kudan	" : d'-e'-f'-a'	immediately: a'
Akikaze	immediately: b'	

In measure 1 a preference is seen for a fast stepwise ascent that includes the lower leading tone (d'). In measure 3, this procedure occurs only once; an immediate or practically immediate attack of the highest tone appears to be the norm. *Shichidan* and measures 3 of *Akikaze,* in which the melody does not rise above f' and f♯', respectively, deviate from these norms.

6. The important cadence, which was first outlined in the kandō, starts on degree I and descends to V or sometimes to IV. This cadence reappears in measures 2 and 4. In measures 1 and 3 new melodic cadences are introduced that start from tone b' (degree V) or a' (degree IV) to tone e' (degree I). The cadence from degree V often begins with a dotted eighth-sixteenth rhythm. When this cadence starts on the beat, tone f' normally returns to a' before reaching its goal, e' *(Rokudan,* measures 1 and 3). A direct descent occurs when the cadence does not begin on the beat, in which case the opening tone b' is preceded by lower *(Kudan,* measure 3; *Godan,* measure 1) or upper neighbor *(Godan,* measure 3). The effect of the latter two is clearly syncopated.

The cadence from tone a' (degree IV) to e' is less conspicuous and does not use the characteristic dotted rhythm of cadences starting from degrees I or V.

7. Although maintaining a generally quiet character, the rhythmic movement is increased considerably in comparison with the kandō. With the exception of rare occurrences in *Shichidan*, *Kumoi Kudan*, and *Akikaze*, the half note has disappeared and quarter and eighth notes are used, occasionally enlivened by dotted eighth-sixteenth kororin patterns. There is more rhythmic activity in measures 1 and 3 than in measures 2 and 4. Combined with higher pitches in measures 1 and 3, this clearly points to a regular tension-release pattern, in which the tension is represented by measures 1 and 3, the release by 2 and 4.

8. A number of characteristic left-hand ornamentations are summarized below. As the time values of the notes on which these occur, as well as the notes directly following the ornament, are significant, these are included.

Four of the five "ju" (hiki-iro) are found in *Akikaze*. Somewhat anticipating, it may be mentioned that the sequence ju—chitsu on the same tone, as found in *Akikaze*, is not unusual, especially in slow movements.

Ornament	Pitch	Time Value	Following Pitch	Occurrences
En (ato-oshi)	a'	1/2, 1/8	e'	2
	a'	1/4, 1/8, 1/16	f'	3
	a'	1/8	b'	3
	c''	1/8	b'	1
Ju (hiki-iro)	f'	1/2	e'	1
	f♯'	1/2, 1/4	f♯'	2
	b'	1/2	e'	1
	b'	Dotted 1/4	a'	1
Chitsu (tsuki-iro)	f♯'	1/2	e'	1
Oshihanashi	a'	1/4		1

Phrase group II, phrase I (measures 5-8)

The positive, purposeful, "masculine" character of this phrase is in strong contrast to the more elegant, somewhat hesitant and "feminine" character of the preceding four measures. Notwithstanding this obvious contrast, the musical material of these new four measures has been carefully anticipated.

These observations may be made:

1. The group of four measures is subdivided into two groups of two measures, not, as in measures 1-4, by a cadence, but by a break in the melodic movement and an interruption in the regular rhythmic motion.

Example 27. Danmono, Dan 1, Phrase group II, phrase I (mm. 5-8):

(a) *Rokudan,* (b) *Shichidan,* (c) *Kudan,* (d) *Hachidan,* (e) *Godan,*
(f) *Kumoi Kudan,* (g) *Akikaze.*

2. The widening of the range begun in the preceding four measures continues. This time the goal is tone e'' (degree I), which, except in *Akikaze*, is reached in the first half of measure 8. Measures 5 and 6 have their highest point on tone a' (degree IV) in measure 6, and without exception this tone is followed by an *ato-oshi*, by which tone b' (degree V) is produced.

Tone e'' is the highest tone for all examples except *Kumoi Kudan*, which goes to f''. Disregarding the fact that the register is higher, no new tones are introduced except in *Rokudan*, where for the first time tone d'' is found in measure 7. This piece is here, as previously, distinguished by its very careful, balanced, and elegant handling of the tonal material.

3. The melodic material of all pieces except *Akikaze* consists basically of the tones of the in-scale in its ascending form: e-f-a-b-d-e. The initial tone e may be introduced by tone d or even the group a-b-d, in which case tone a is also the concluding tone of the preceding group of four measures *(Kumoi Kudan)*. *Akikaze* "returns" the extra measure of its kandō and so has only three measures here, with the result that its presentation of the scale figure is incomplete, consisting of an ascent employing only the three basic tones, e', a', b', and e''.

The notes of the ascending in-scale are frequently interrupted by insertions of "shan" on strings 1 and 2 (degrees I and IV), between each two scale tones. This device is most consistently shown in *Shichidan*. In other cases, a break is made at the end of measure 6, where the halfway point in the scale (tone a') is given a longer time value, following which the second half tends to be made rhythmically livelier by the use of more tones of shorter time values *(Hachidan)* or by syncopation *(Godan)*. The melodic sequence of measures 5-6 (d'-e'-f'-a'), is foreshadowed by a similar sequence, although in shorter time values and therefore less conspicuous, in measure 1.

4. Measure 8 in most cases concludes by the descending cadence from tone e to b (a) (degrees I to V (IV)), which may be called pattern I. "Pattern" rather than "cadence" is appropriate because, as will be seen later, the figure has not always a concluding function. This kind of melodic pattern plays an important role as a constructive element in danmono. Another such cadential pattern was met in measures 1-4: the descent from tone b (a) to e (degrees V (IV) to I). In addition to descending patterns from one basic tone to another, ascending patterns appear as well, although they are somewhat less conspicuous than the descending ones. The descending patterns often combine their melodic content with characteristic rhythms. Ascending patterns are more purely melodic, showing little preference for set rhythms, and usually have no cadential function. They appear between degrees I and IV (V) and between (IV) V and I.

Making an inventory of the patterns, we arrive at the following:

Example 28,

Pattern I: descent from I to V (IV)

I VI V (IV)

Pattern II: descent from V (IV) to I

(V) IV II I

Pattern III: ascent from (VII) I to IV (V)

VII I II (III) IV (V)

Pattern IV: ascent from (IV) V to I

(IV) V VII I

It will be seen that in their most complete form these patterns span an interval of a fifth and consist of four tones. When the range is reduced to a fourth, either degree IV or V will be omitted. Degree I occurs in all patterns. In pattern III we notice a typical use of degree VII, which is especially conspicuous when the pattern does not proceed beyond degree IV.

Returning to measures 5-8, the melodic content of these measures may be classified as follows: pattern III (measures 5-6), IV (7-8), and I (8).

5. Only *Akikaze* introduces new time values in these four measures: a group of two thirty-seconds in combination with a double-dotted quarter. Syncopation, encountered earlier in the syncopated version of kororin on pattern I *(Hachidan,* measure 4; *Godan,* measure 1), appears again as a device to enliven a strict duple meter using a limited number of time values, mainly quarter, eighth, dotted eighth-sixteenth, and occasional half notes.

6. The ornamentation may be summarized as follows:

Ornament	Pitch	Time Value	Following Pitch	Occurrences
En (ato-oshi)	a'	1/2	b	3
	a'	Dotted 1/4	f'	1
	a'	1/4	shan, b, b'	3
	c''	1/8	b'	2
Ju (hiki-iro)	e'	1/4	shan	1
	f'	1/4	shan, e'	3

7. In terms of melodic tension, these measures differ somewhat from the previous four, in which a regular alternation of tension and release was observed. The absence of a cadence in measure 6 causes the melodic tension to continue past the point where a release might be expected; instead of a T-R-T-R pattern, we find T——T-R with the first T representing a pattern of two measures' length.

Example 29. Danmono, Dan 1, Phrase group II, phrases 2 and 3 (measures 9-12):
(a) *Rokudan,* (b) *Shichidan,* (c) *Kudan,* (d) *Hachidan,* (e) *Godan,*
(f) *Kumoi Kudan,* (g) *Akikaze.*

1. Measures 9-12 are comparable to 1-4 in construction: two groups of two measures, each group concluded by pattern I. The main difference is the higher register in 9-12, *Hachidan* shows a literal repetition of measures 1-4 in the higher octave.

2. In the course of these four measures, the range widens further, in all cases except *Shichidan* reaching the highest string (tone b"). At the same time, the whole compass of the melody, lowest as well as highest tones, has moved up in such a way that the actual melodic range spans no more than approximately an octave. (Shan and octave displacements are disregarded in this connection.)

3. The tonal material is still the same as before, six tones: e, f, a, b, c, and d. In *Shichidan,* however, a seventh tone is introduced: g" (degree III), lower leading tone for degree IV, as part of a variant of pattern III. Here we may anticipate and state that degree III will appear mainly when degree IV assumes a certain independence and importance; as this is not very often the case, the use of degree III is relatively rare.

4. The treatment of the melodic material is similar to that of measures 1-4 and can in most cases be characterized as an alternation of ascending and descending melodic patterns. The highest agreement between the several compositions is reached in measures 10 and 12, where pattern I occurs in all instances except *Kudan* (measure 10).

5. As to time values and rhythm, these measures are similar to the preceding eight. Syncopation is found only in *Hachidan* (m. 11) and *Godan* (mm. 9 and 11).

6. Ornaments used are the following:

Ornament	Pitch	Time Value	Following Pitch	Occurrences
En (ato-oshi)	a"	Dotted 1/4, 1/4	f"	6
	a"	1/8	b"	1
	c"	1/8	b	1
Ju (hiki-iro)	f"	1/4	f"	1
Chitsu (tsuki-iro)	f"	1/4	e"	1
	f"	1/8	e'	1
Yuri	d"	1/2	(d")-e"	1
	d"	Dotted 1/4	e"	1
Oshihanashi	a"	1/4		1

7. The general similarity to measures 1-4 results in a similar tension-release pattern: T-R-T-R.

Phrase group III (measures 13-17)

In the first twelve measures following the kandō, the complete range of the koto has been systematically explored. The register gradually moved higher in a development based upon the basic tones of the mode, I and IV or V. The goal has been the highest string; now that it has been reached, the first part of the dan is completed, and the whole outlook changes. Quadratic phrase structures with their clear definition are abandoned in favor of phrases of less regular length. The following example, measures 13-17, presents the third phrase group in its entirety.

Example 30. Danmono, Dan 1, Phrase group III (measures 13-17): (a) *Rokudan*,
(b) *Shichidan*, (c) *Kudan*, (d) *Hachidan*, (e) *Godan*, (f) *Kumoi
Kudan*, (g) *Akikaze*.

1. The length of this phrase group consists of four and a half measures. The subdivision of this part is irregular: the first phrase, consisting of three measures (13, 14, and 15) represents a shortened version of measures 5-8. The second phrase (measure 16 and the first half of 17) with its echo-like recollection of measure 15, is strongly supporting in character.

2. The range moves in the highest octave. The subdivisions, however, are also characterized by their respective ranges. Disregarding octave displacements (so typical of the koto idiom), the range of the first phrase (measures 13-15) is from d'' to b''; that of the second phrase (measures 16-17), e'' to b''. The downward octave displacement in *Kumoi Kudan* is a necessary deviation: it must be remembered that the notation here is a transposition down a fourth. Tone f'', therefore, represents the highest string in this composition.

3. The tonal material is essentially unchanged. Tone g'' (degree III) here appears for the second time, this time in *Hachidan* (measure 15) as a passing tone and therefore functionally distinct from its use in measure 11 in *Shichidan*.

4. Melodically, nothing new is offered: patterns III, II, and I provide the basic material.

5. Time values are the same as in the foregoing parts. Thirty-seconds, previously encountered only once, in *Akikaze*, now occur also in older compositions, especially in measure 16 *(Shichidan, Kudan,* and *Kumoi Kudan)*. Syncopation is found only in *Godan* (measure 17).

6. The following ornaments are used:

Ornament	Pitch	Time Value	Following Pitch	Occurrences
En (ato-oshi)	a'	1/2	b	1
	a'	1/4	a'	1
	a''	1/2, 1/4, 1/8	b'	5
	a''	1/4	c''	1
	a''	1/2, dotted 1/4	a''	4
	a''	1/2	b''	1
	b''	1/4	a''	1
Ju (hiki-iro)	f♯'	1/2, 1/4	e'	2
Chitsu (tsuki-iro)	f♯'	1/2	e'	1
	a''	1/8	b''	1

Akikaze again presents an example of the sequence ju-chitsu in measures 13-14.

7. The tension-release pattern for measures 13-17 is T-T-R, T-R.

Phrase group IV (measures 17-23)

The function of groups IV and V combined is to lead back to the low register in which the dan began. Group IV starts in the second half of measure 17 with a passage of transitional character that descends and is followed in the second half of measure 20 by an ascent, similar to that of measures 5-8, although shortened; it concludes with a descent, in most instances to tone a', in measures 24-26, the end of the dan.

Example 31. Danmono, Dan 1, Phrase group IV (measures 17–23): (a) *Rokudan*, (b) *Shichidan*, (c) *Kudan*, (d) *Hachidan*, (e) *Godan*, (f) *Kumoi Kudan*, (g) *Akikaze*.

Concerning phrase group IV the following observations can be made.

1. Three measures of transitional character begin in the second half of measure 17 and continue through the first half of measure 20 (phrase 1), where an ascending phrase of three and a half measures' length commences (phrase 2). Like similar phrases encountered before, this second phrase can be subdivided into two parts: the second half of measure 20 through 21, and measures 22-23.

2. The range is still in the higher octave, but in measure 22 a rapid descent begins which continues through the last phrase to the end of the dan.

3. In *Rokudan* (measure 19) a new tone, f♯", is introduced. This "secondary dominant" is a rather common phenomenon in koto music, especially in its later forms. One may admire the composer of *Rokudan* for his exemplary care and feeling for proportion and balance in the introduction of this single new tone, which by its rare use is the more striking. It is placed at one of the critical points in the dan: at two-thirds of the length.

Tone g" (degree III) appears for the third time, as a lower neighbor in *Shichidan* (measure 22).

4. Melodically, these measures may be described as a sequence of patterns II (measures 18-20), III (measures 20-21), II (measure 22), and I (measure 23).

5. No new time values are introduced. The movement is quiet, proceeding for the most part in quarter and eighth notes, occasionally enlivened by a dotted eighth-sixteenth group. Syncopation, as may be expected by now, is limited to *Hachidan* (measures 19 and 22) and *Godan* (measures 19 and 22). Notice that the syncopations tend to occur in the same measures in both pieces and are part of kororin patterns.

6. Ornaments are used as follows:

Ornament	Pitch	Time Value	Following Pitch	Occurrences
En (ato-oshi)	a'	1/4	e'	1
	e"	1/4	c"	1
	a"	1/4, 1/8	e'	3
	a"	Dotted 1/4, 1/8, 1/16	f"	4
	a"	1/8	b"	2
Ju (hiki-iro)	d"	1/2	d"	2
	d"	1/2	e"	1
Chitsu (tsuki-iro)	a"	1/8	b"	2
Yuri	d"	1/2	d"	2
	d"	1/2	e"	1
Waren (shu)				1

7. The tension release pattern for measures 18-23 is T-R, T-T-R.

Example 32.   Danmono, Dan 1, Phrase group V (measures 24-26): (a) *Rokudan,*
(b) *Shichidan,* (c) *Kudan,*   (d) *Hachidan,*   (e) *Godan,* (f) *Kumoi Kudan,*
(g) *Akikaze.*

Phrase group V (measures 24-26)

The last phrase of the first dan consists of an ornamented form of a descending scale from e'' to e', followed by a form of pattern I as a cadence.

1. The length of this last phrase is three measures.

2. The upper focus of the range is tone e'', often accompanied by its upper neighbor, f'' or f♯''. In *Kumoi Kudan* the range is extended to include tone g'', in *Akikaze* it does not go beyond tone c''. The lower limit, for the pieces in hira-jōshi, is tone a or shan on a and e', with *Godan* as an exception, ending the dan on tone c'. This conclusion in *Godan* is certainly irregular; similar deviations are to be found in this piece at the conclusion of later dan. (Precisely how this is "irregular" will be discussed in detail in Chapter VIII.) A liberty of this kind, taken at the end of a movement where convention tends to govern most strongly, provides another reason for classification of *Godan* as a later danmono. *Kumoi Kudan* and *Akikaze* both end on tone b, which may well be because neither is composed in hira-jōshi. It will be seen to be characteristic of danmono that all dan, except the final one, tend to end on a degree other than the first. The most frequent final degrees in earlier dan are degrees IV and V. Other degrees used as a final tone, such as found, for example, in *Godan,* must be considered exceptions.

3. Tone f♯'' occurs, almost as a surprise so late in the dan, in measure 24 in no fewer than three pieces *(Shichidan, Godan* and *Kumoi Kudan).* *Rokudan,* which had introduced this tone earlier in measure 19, does not use it here. Its function here is comparable to its function in *Rokudan:* a "dominant" for tone b', the central tone in measure 25. Prolonged in this function, the f♯ could indicate a modulation to degree V; when so transitory as here, however, it can be termed a "secondary dominant."

4. Melodically, the three measures are a sequence of patterns I, II, and I.

5. Time values are, as before, mainly eighths and quarters with an occasional dotted eighth-sixteenth. Longer values logically occur in the last measure, a traditional means in many types of music to bring a movement to an end.

6. The following ornaments occur:

Ornament	Pitch	Time Value	Following Pitch	Occurrences
En (ato-oshi)	e'	1/2	c'	1
	a'	1/4, 1/8	e'	2
	a'	1/4	f'	1
	a'	1/4	b'	1
	f''	1/8	e''	1
Ju (hiki-iro)	c''	1/4	b'	1
Chitsu (tsuki-iro)	e''	1/8	c''	2

An upstroke on a repeated tone occurs once, in measure 25 of *Kudan*. This technique is very rare in danmono and kumiuta, though it may be observed that it very frequently occurs in later forms of koto music.

7. The tension release pattern is T-T-R.

Conclusions Concerning the First Dan

Up to this point in the analysis, we have been concerned exclusively with phrase to phrase considerations, and have hardly allowed ourselves a panoramic view of the dan as a whole. In the course of these considerations we have observed that the compass of the phrases was selected in a conspicuously systematic manner. This phenomenon allows us to organize the five phrase groups according to their range as follows: Part I (ascent, phrase groups I and II), Part II (climax, phrase group III), and Part III (descent, phrase groups IV and V). The schema on page 84, showing the function of the parts in the totality of the dan structure, is divided into these three parts preceded by the kandō, with their subdivisions and respective ranges. The heading "Pattern" refers to the melodic-cadential patterns discussed earlier; "Tones" refers to those tones on the koto that cannot be obtained from the open strings, that is, to tones requiring left-hand pressure; "T-R" refers to tension-release; and "Form" is an attempt to characterize a phrase as a whole in terms of melodic content. The inclusion of the categories "Phrase" and "Phrase group," finally, may show the relationship between phrase structure and total structure.

The inclusion of "Tones" in a schema that is mainly concerned with constructive elements requires explanation. The reader will observe that in general these tones are introduced at quite definite locations—here, in odd-numbered measures—as long as the phrase structure remains quadratic. Also, they are chiefly to be found in patterns III and IV; when they occur in pattern II or—very rarely—pattern I, they always have a rather "unorganic" function, that of a neighbor tone, for example, and are never an integral part of the pattern itself. This relationship of these tones with the four patterns automatically results in their involvement in the tension-release patterns. A glance at the schema is sufficient to show that tones d and g, that is, degrees VII and III, coincide with moments of tension. It may be concluded, therefore, that degrees III and VII are vehicles of strong melodic tension.

It will be observed that in the subdivision of the dan into kandō and Parts I, II, and III, first consideration has been given to the range. The kandō does not go beyond the range of a fifth, which means that only the lowest five strings are used. The function of the first part proper is to incorporate the entire range of the instrument. Part II, limited to the higher octave, functions as a climax and therefore is short. Part III, finally, leads back to the lower register in which the movement began.

The structure of the phrases also distinguishes the three parts from one another. In Part I, phrases are built very regularly, each consisting of two or four measures, and each subdivisible into sub-phrases of two measures. Because the phrase structure of Part II is much more integrated, it is rather difficult to distinguish the end of one and the beginning of the next phrase; moreover, the length of the phrases is very irregular. All this contributes to the feeling of climax, especially in measures 17-18. The structure of Part III is somewhat less irregular, which contributes to a certain degree to a quietness reminiscent of Part I without, however, reintroducing the strict quadratic structure.

Part I. Ascent

Range	kandō	\(a\)–\(b'\)				\(d'\)–\(e''\)				\(a'\)–\(b''\)			
Measure	\(a\)–\(e'\)	1	2	3	4	5	6	7	8	9	10	11	12
Pattern	I	II* / III	I	II* / III	I	III		IV	I	II* / III	I	II	I
Tones		d'		d'		d'		d''		d''	d''	g''	
T.R.		T	R	T	R	T	T	T	R	T	R	T	R
Form			A				B				A		
Phrase		1		2			1				2		3
Phrase group		I							II				

Part II. Climax

Range	\(d''\)–\(b''\)				
Measure	13	14	15	16	17
Pattern		III	II	II	
Tones	d''		g''		
T.R.	T	T	R	T	R
Form		(B–A)			
Phrase		1		2	
Phrase group				III	

Part III. Descent

Range	\(b''\)–\(a''\)					\(e''\)–\(a\)			
Measure	18	19	20	21	22	23	24	25	26
Pattern	III* / II	I	III	I	II	I	I	II	I
Tones	d''	f♯''	d''	d''	g''		d'' / f♯''	d''	
T.R.	T	R	T	T	T	R	T	T	R
Form	A				B			A	
Phrase		1			2			1	
Phrase group				IV				V	

*The patterns followed by an asterisk occur only in *Rokudan*.

The use made of the four patterns corroborates the tripartition.   While pattern I occurs prominently in Parts I and III, Part II characteristically employs pattern II.   Although range is not and cannot be the only element considered in laying out the structure of the dan, it is probably the most conclusive of the three elements mentioned above.   Phrase structure and the occurrence of the four patterns may be no more than accompanying phenomena, functionally dependent on variation in range.   The gradual expansion of the range seems a logical and meaningful way of progression on this instrument.

The letters given at the bottom of the schema show the following form: A-B-A; (B-A); A-B-A.   The parentheses around the letters representing Part II indicate that this part employs elements of both B and A without clearly separating them.   In this tripartite form the third part appears to be a shortened and varied reprise of the first one.   It should be noted that all the melodic material is presented in Part I; in the latter parts this same material reappears, slightly modified, in different combinations. These circumstances inevitably lead to the   consideration of a theory developed by Takano Kiyoshi, according to whom an individual dan in a danmono should be considered as being a sonata-type form (Takano 1935: 77).   According to Takano, the first part of the dan represents the exposition; the second part, the development; and the last part, the reprise of the sonata form.   Considering the construction of a dan (in terms of letters, which never is sufficient!), there indeed is a certain similarity with the sonata form.   A second obvious consideration shows the fallacy of this theory, however: the material of the danmono represented by the letters A and B can by no means be compared with the themes of a sonata form because it completely lacks the distinctive melodic-rhythmic characteristics that distinguish one sonata theme from another, nor is there the contrast of different keys.   Takano's theory for a time found followers in Japan, but most of them are now convinced that danmono better be explained in its own terms, without recourse to Western forms and terminology.

CHAPTER VII

DANMONO: THE LATER DAN

Analysis of the seven first dan of the repertoire has shown a severe construction that strives for and attains a balance of non-symmetrical units. Comparison of the first dan reveals that all compositions contain closely related melodic material. The absence of strongly contrasting musical elements in the different pieces suggests the composers' aims to have been the invention of subtle melodic shadings of and slight variations on conventional material rather than the introduction of new ideas.

Two interesting questions now present themselves. (1) Is the material of all the dan of a given danmono as basically similar as is the material of the first dan of all seven danmono? (2) Structurally, does the same convention that governs the construction of equivalent units in the first dan of various pieces also govern the construction of successive dan in a single piece? Accepting an affirmative answer to the first of these questions as an hypothesis, successive dan of the piece selected may be subjected to simultaneous phrase-by-phrase comparison, the first phrase group of the first dan being compared with musical units employing the same thematic material in the other dan, then the second phrase group, and so on. Because it may occur that a given melodic unit in the first dan corresponds with a section having a different phrase structure in a later dan (compare, for example, the first four measures of the first dan of *Rokudan* with the corresponding ten measures of its sixth dan in Example 33), it will be necessary to present the structural analysis of the various dan independently from the melodic analysis presented below.

Rokudan has been selected for this further thematic analysis for several reasons. First, because it is qualitatively probably the best of the seven danmono. Second, because it may well be the oldest of the seven, and therefore the model for the later ones. And finally, because in actual musical practice, *Rokudan* is representative not only of danmono in particular, but of Japanese music in general.

The following example shows the first four measures (phrase group I) of the first dan, together with the corresponding measures of the following five dan.

The symmetry of this first statement presented in dan 1 in two plus two measures is repeated in dan 2 and 3. Dan 5 also uses four measures for this first phrase, but lacks the two plus two symmetrical construction, one uninterrupted phrase taking the place of the original two phrases. In view of the gradual increase in tempo from the beginning through the last dan, a procedure characteristic of danmono and especially noticeable in the second half of a composition, this is a constructive change that should not surprise us. The two plus two symmetry is broken earlier also, in the fourth dan, which, like dan 6, requires more than four measures to complete the first statement; dan 4 uses five and a half measures; dan 6, ten.

Taking the first phrase in dan 1 as the basic statement, dan 2 shows only subtle variation. Dan 3 deviates somewhat more than dan 2, yet remains closely similar to dan 1, for the seeming differences turn out to be only superficial. The "sararin" with which the dan opens may sound quite unlike the opening of dan 1, but can nevertheless be described as a variant of the same pattern (II): the descent from degree V to I. As for the tones g' and d' in measures 3 and 4, these do not, indeed, appear in dan 1, but such tones are not standard at the beginning of a composition and therefore should not be expected there.

Example 33. *Rokudan.*

Dan 4 contains the two main elements of the phrase in dan 1: the two descents from tone b' to "shan" on strings 1 and 2 (tones a and e'). However, the descents have been shortened and are preceded by two and a half measures that concentrate mainly on tone e', alternating it with the "shan," a procedure that will be met in certain other danmono also. Although still employing the same material, dan 5 deviates rather strongly: there is an ascent of one and a half measures, and the remaining two and a half measures have a descent that is a variation of the descent found in the first two measures of dan 1. Thus, the melodic movement is ascent-descent, rather than descent-descent. Dan 6 begins with the first four descending notes of dan 1, but postpones the expected sequence by the insertion of a number of "sha-sha-ten," before completing the descent in measure 6. The final "shan" of the descent is repeated three times, then a shortened repetition of the whole statement in the first four measures of dan 1 is given (second half of measure 8 through measure 10).

Up to this point, all six dan have explored only the lower register.

Example 34 shows measures 5 through 8 of the dan 1 (the first phrase of phrase group II) with its transformations in dan 2 through 6.

Example 34. *Rokudan.*

Dan 2 and 3 adhere closely to the model given in dan 1 and consist of two plus two measures. Dan 4 this time recovers the extra one and a half measures used in the completion of the previous phrase and ends, like dan 1, 2, and 3, at the end of measure 8. Through measure 7, dan 5 closely follows the example of dan 1, but replaces "sha-sha-ten" by "shan-ten" (measure 5). In measure 8, however, a typical destruction of symmetry occurs in the repetition of the previous measure, lengthening the phrase to five measures. Such repetition—literal or varied—of a short melodic unit frequently occurs in danmono. Since dan 6 consisted of ten measures for the first phrase, it does not present a version of phrase two. The melodic content of the second phrase is so similar in dan 1 through dan 5 that further discussion of it seems unnecessary.

The register is the same for all dan.

The treatment of the remainder of phrase group II, shown in Example 35, exhibits more variety than the previous one.

Only dan 2 and 4 follow the regular scheme of two plus two measures of dan 1. Dan 3 shortens the four measures of the original to one three-measure phrase and ends in measure 11 rather than 12. Dan 5 and dan 6, on the other hand, are extended through measure 16. In dan 5 this is again accomplished by the standard procedure of varied repetition: measure 10 is repeated in a varied form in measures 11-12 and again in measures 13-14.

Example 35. *Rokudan.*

Dan 2, as before, remains very close melodically to dan 1. Dan 3 through 6 are distinguished by their conspicuously limited use of eighth notes, which again may be explained by their faster tempo. The predominant time value in these later dan is the quarter note, together with the dotted eighth-sixteenth combination which, especially in the typical way in which these rhythms are performed on the koto—lightly passing over the sixteenth—is almost identical to a quarter value.

Dan 5 and 6, notwithstanding their seemingly different melodic appearance, are both characterized by descending patterns similar to those in dan 1. Although measures 18-23 have not been illustrated yet, it should be noted that a short section in dan 6 (from the second half of measure 13 through the first half of measure 15) corresponds to the second half of measure 20 through the first half of measure 22 of dan 4.

Example 36.

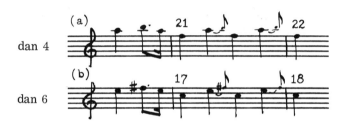

In dan 6 for the first time a real modulation (to the fifth degree) throughout a whole phrase occurs. This modulation sets the phrase sharply apart from all the rest.

Two techniques occur in the measures under discussion here that have not been met before: "waren" in measure 9 of dan 2, and "keshizume" in measure 9 of dan 4. This represents the only occurrence of keshizume in danmono. [1]

With the exception of dan 5, which remains in a lower register, all dan have moved up to the highest register.

Example 37 contains Part II of dan 1 (phrase group III), together with its equivalents in dan 2 through 6.

As before, dan 2 closely follows dan 1, but this time with one rather significant change: the displacement an octave down in measures 14 through 17. Dan 3, one measure behind at the beginning of this phrase, joins the general structural plan in measure 17 by the use of varied repetition of a short melodic unit. Such pattern repetition is often encountered in the climax, not only in *Rokudan* but in other danmono also. Dan 4, 5, and 6, already ahead at the beginning of this section, increase their lead to five, respectively four measures. Dan 4 is distinguished by the occurrence of syncopation in measures 12-13, 16-17, and 19-20.

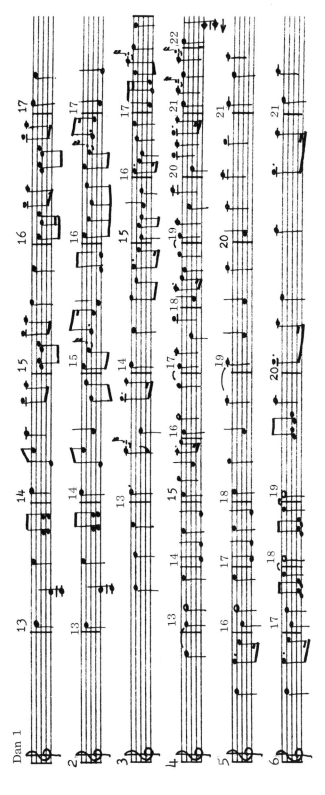

Example 37. *Rokudan.*

Melodically, this part offers some interesting features. Dan 1 through 3 agree in the general plan of an ascent followed by descending patterns. In dan 4, 5, and 6 there is one ascent only, interrupted by a static dwelling on tones e" and a" alternated with their lower octave or "sha-sha-ten." The ascending figures in dan 4 and 5 are distinguished from those in dan 1 through 3 by the use of tone g" rather than f", thus giving stronger emphasis to the following a" (degree IV) rather than to b" (degree V).

As for the register in which this part of the dan moves, there is less agreement here than before, although in general higher registers are favored. Dan 1, 3, 4, and 5 move entirely in the highest octave, while dan 2 and 6 do not go above the middle register.

Complete convergence is reached again in measures 22-23, with all dan descending from tones b" to e" (Example 38). Dan 4 through 6, which contain no more than this cadence, deviate strongly from dan 1 through 3. In the melodic content of measures 20 through 23, the first three dan are distinguished from the last three by the use of an ascending passage followed by descending cadences ending on b' or e"; dan 4, 5 and 6 have only a descent to tone b'. The ascent of dan 3 is unlike those in dan 1 and 2 in that it employs tone g", rather than f". This occurrence of g" as a lower leading tone, like that of the b-flat in measure 21 as an upper leading tone, emphasizes the importance of tone a" (degree IV). The occurrence of this specific ascent in dan 3 anticipates the similar ascents in dan 4 (measures 13-15), dan 5 (measures 16-18), and dan 6 (measures 15-17), which have already been shown.

Example 38. *Rokudan.*

In measure 19 of dan 6 a ritardando sets in which continues until the original slow tempo of dan 1 is reached in measure 23.   This is the usual procedure toward the end of a danmono.   The technique "oshiawase" occurs, twice repeated on tone b", in measures 21 and 22.   This emphatic dwelling on tone b (degree V) serves to announce the final cadence of this last dan, which moves from tone b" (degree V) down to tone e' (degree I).

In these measures all dan are in the highest register.

The concluding three measures (phrase group V) follow as a logical conclusion from the foregoing, and in dan 1, 2, 3, and 5, because of their common goal, show a strong similarity.

All dan except dan 2 and 4 descend from tone e" in measure 24, interrupt the descent in measure 25, emphasizing tone b' before reaching the final cadence in measure 26.   Dan 2 and 4 do not start the descent on tone e" in measure 24, but in measure 25 emphasize tone b', as do the other dan.   All dan have the same range here, from approximately e" down to a (e' for dan 6).

In measure 26 the first five dan share the descending cadence from tone e' (degree I) through tone b (degree V) to shan or tone a (degree IV), while dan 6 concludes the piece on tone e' (degree I), played in unison on strings 1 and 5.   It may be possible to extend these final cadences back to begin the descent with tone b' in measure 25.   The conclusion of the piece on the first degree is not unique to *Rokudan* but typical, as we shall see later, of danmono in general. The descent by means of "sararin" in measure 25 of dan 6 will also be shown to be typical.

Example 39.   *Rokudan.*

There is a certain similarity between dan 4 and dan 6 in measures 24 and 25. Note that dan 4 concludes its cadence uniquely on tone "a" (degree IV) alone, rather than on "shan" also involving tone e (degree I). The contrast between measures 24-26 of dan 4, with their subtly syncopated longer time values, and all that precedes in this dan, is striking. Here is an aesthetic highpoint that is unique and is one of the reasons *Rokudan* may be termed the most interesting and lovely of the danmono. The simplicity, the thinning from complexity, that is the result of the longer time values of the 24th and 25th measures is, as it were, repeated in a different way by the simplicity of the conclusion on a single note. Compare dan 5, and the "shan" in dan 1-3.

The foregoing melodic analysis of *Rokudan* has shown that the structural scheme of dan 1 is followed fairly closely through dan 4. More pronounced deviations, although never the introduction of new material, occurs in the last two dan, mainly as a result of the faster tempo. The adherence to the same musical material, which recurs throughout the entire composition in more or less varied forms, combined with a certain degree of structural similarity, makes justifiable the use of the term "variation form" to describe this danmono. Exception, therefore, should be taken, at least as far as *Rokudan* is concerned, to the description given by William P. Malm: ". . . a basic theme is presented and with each successive dan it is subjected to variation while new material is interpolated between the phrases of the original theme" (Malm 1959: 180-181). When the musical material consists of descending and ascending patterns between the three main tones of the mode, it becomes so flexible (and, therefore, so excellently fit for variation) that the word "theme" seems inappropriate if applied to these patterns, because a theme, by definition, requires a more characteristic profile. Even if one should be willing to consider these basic materials as themes, one would have to distinguish two themes, rather than "a basic theme." The analysis has not revealed "new material interpolated between the phrases of the original theme," unless one can consider the appearance of the e-g-a pattern in measures 20-21, later repeated in measures 13-15 and 16-18, of dan 4 and 5, respectively, as new material. But to do this seems to slice the distinction between new and existing materials too thinly. Nor is it, as will be seen, only *Rokudan* that is in conflict with Professor Malm's description.

The above discussion has revealed that the structure of the dan of *Rokudan* does not always agree with that of the opening dan. Precisely how the phrases of the six dan of *Rokudan* are distributed is shown in the chart on page 95.[2] Each phrase is represented by a bracket, accompanied by a letter-numeral combination that symbolizes the melodic content and the register of the phrase. The letters, A and B, describe the melodic content in the most general sense, indicating merely whether a phrase is characterized mainly by descending material (A) or ascending (B). The Arabic numeral following the letter indicates the register used in the phrase: 1 stands for the lowest register which is used only in the kandō (a to e'); 2 for an approximate octave between tones a and a' or b'; 3 for the middle register (approximately between tones e' and e"); while 4 represents the highest register (between tones a' and b"). The agreement in construction of dan 1 through 3 on the one hand, and 4-6 on the other hand, is immediately apparent.

Similar charts for *Shichidan, Kudan, Hachidan, Godan, Kumoi Kudan, Akikaze,* and *Midare* show in what respects the analysis of *Midare* has given general information about all danmono. *Midare*, though included in the charts, will be discussed later, as it is in matters of construction rather than in musical material that this composition is distinguished from the "regular" danmono. The chart of *Midare* shows that it cannot be considered a normal danmono because of the irregular length of its dan.

ROKUDAN

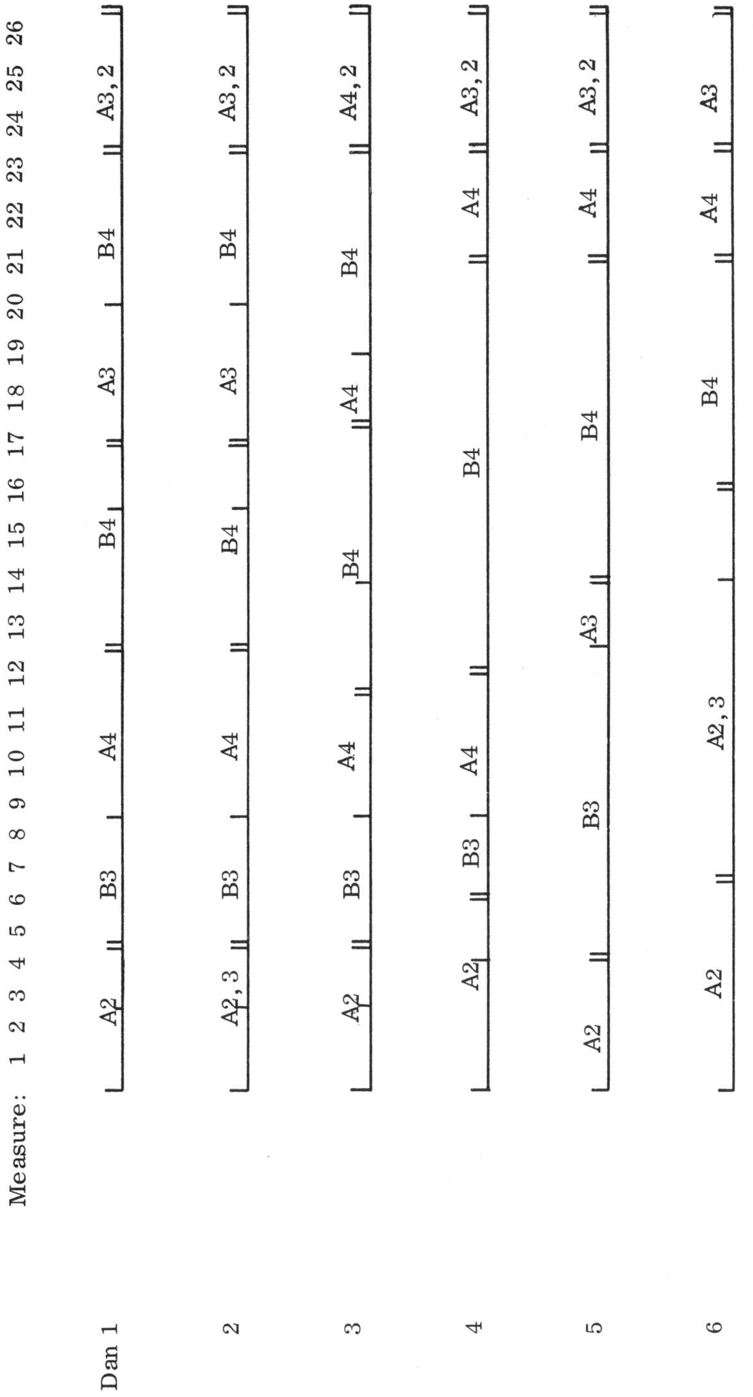

Measure: 1 2 3 4 5 6 7 8 9 10 11 12 13 14 15 16 17 18 19 20 21 22 23 24 25 26

Dan 1   A2   B3   A4   B4   A3   B4   A3, 2

2   A2, 3   B3   A4   B4   A3   B4   A3, 2

3   A2   B3   A4   B4   A4   B4   A4, 2

4   A2   B3   A4   B4   A4   B4   A4   A3, 2

5   A2   B3   A3   B4   A4   A3, 2

6   A2   A2, 3   B4   A4   A3

SHICHIDAN

Measure:	1	2	3	4	5	6	7	8	9	10	11	12	13	14	15	16	17	18	19	20	21	22	23	24	25	26
Dan 1			A1			B3				A4					B4			A4			B4			A3, 2		
2			A2			B3				A4					B4			A4			B4			A3, 2		
3			A2			B3				A2				B3					A2				A4			
4			A4, 3			B4				A4				B4, 3				A3			B1	A4		A2		
5			A1			B3				A4					B4			A4			B4			A3		
6			A1			B3, 4					A4				B4			A4					A2			
			A4, 3			B3				A3					B3			A3			B3			A3		

KUDAN

Measure:	1 2 3	4 5 6 7 8 9	10 11 12 13 14	15 16 17	18 19 20	21 22 23	24 25 26
Dan 1	A2	B3	A4	B4	A4	B4	A3, 2
2	A3, 2	B3	A4	B4	A4	B4	A3, 2
3	A2	B3	A4	B4	A4	B4	A3, 2
4	O1	B3	A4	B3	A3	A4	A3, 2
5	A2	B3	A4	B4	A4	A4	A3, 2
6	A2	B3	A4	B3	A2	B2	A2
7	A3	B3, 4	A4	B4	A4	A4	A3, 2
8	A2	B3	A4	B4	A4	B4	A3, 2
9	A2	B3	A4	B4	A4	B4	A3

HACHIDAN

Measure: 1 2 3 4 5 6 7 8 9 10 11 12 13 14 15 16 17 18 19 20 21 22 23 24 25 26

Dan										
1	A2	B3	A4	B4	A4	B4	A3, 2
2	A2	B3	A4	B4	A4	B4	A3, 2
3	A2	B3	A4	B4	A4	B4	A3, 2
4	A1	B3	A4	B4	A4	B4	A4, 2
5	A2	B3	A4	B4	A4	A4	A3, 2
6	A2	B3	A4	B4	A4	B4	A3, 2
7	A2	B3	A4	A4	B4	B4	A3, 2
8	A2	B3	A4	B4	B3	B4	A4, 3

GODAN

Measure:	1	2	3	4	5	6	7	8	9	10	11	12	13	14	15	16	17	18	19	20	21	22	23	24	25	26
Dan 1			A2			B3				A4				B4				A4				B4			A3, 2	
2			A2			B3				A4				B4				A4				B4		A4	A4	
3			A4			B4, 3				A3				A3				B3				A4			A3, 2	
4			A2			B2, 4				A4				A3					B3			A4			A3, 2	
5			A1			B2, 3				A3				A4, 3				A4				A4			A3	

KUMOI KUDAN

Measure:	1 2 3 4	5 6 7	8 9 10 11	12 13 14 15	16 17 18 19	20 21 22 23	24 25 26
Dan 1	A2	B3	A4	B4	A3	B3	A3, 2
2	A2	B3	A4	B4	A4, 3	B3	A3, 2
3	A2	B3	A4	B4	A4, 3	B2	A3, 2
4	A2	B3	A4	B4	A4, 3	B2	A3, 2
5	A2	B3	A4, 3	B4	A3	B3	A3, 2
6	A2	B3	A4	B4	A4, 3	B3	A4
7	A3	B3	A4	B4	A4, 3	B3	A4
8	A2	B3	A4	B4	A4	B3	A3
9	A2	B2	A4	B4	A3	B3	A3

AKIKAZE

Measure:	1	2	3	4	5	6	7	8	9	10	11	12	13	14	15	16	17	18	19	20	21	22	23	24	25	26
Dan 1		A2					B2			A3				A1		B2		A3	A3		A3				A2	
2		A2				B4					A3			A3				A2			B3			A3, 2		
3		A2					A3			A4				B3				A3			A2				A2	
4		A1					B3			A3				B4			B4				A2			A3		
5		A3					B3					A4	A4, 3			B2		B2					A1			
6		A2				B3			A1		B3					B4			B4	A4		B3			A3	

MIDARE

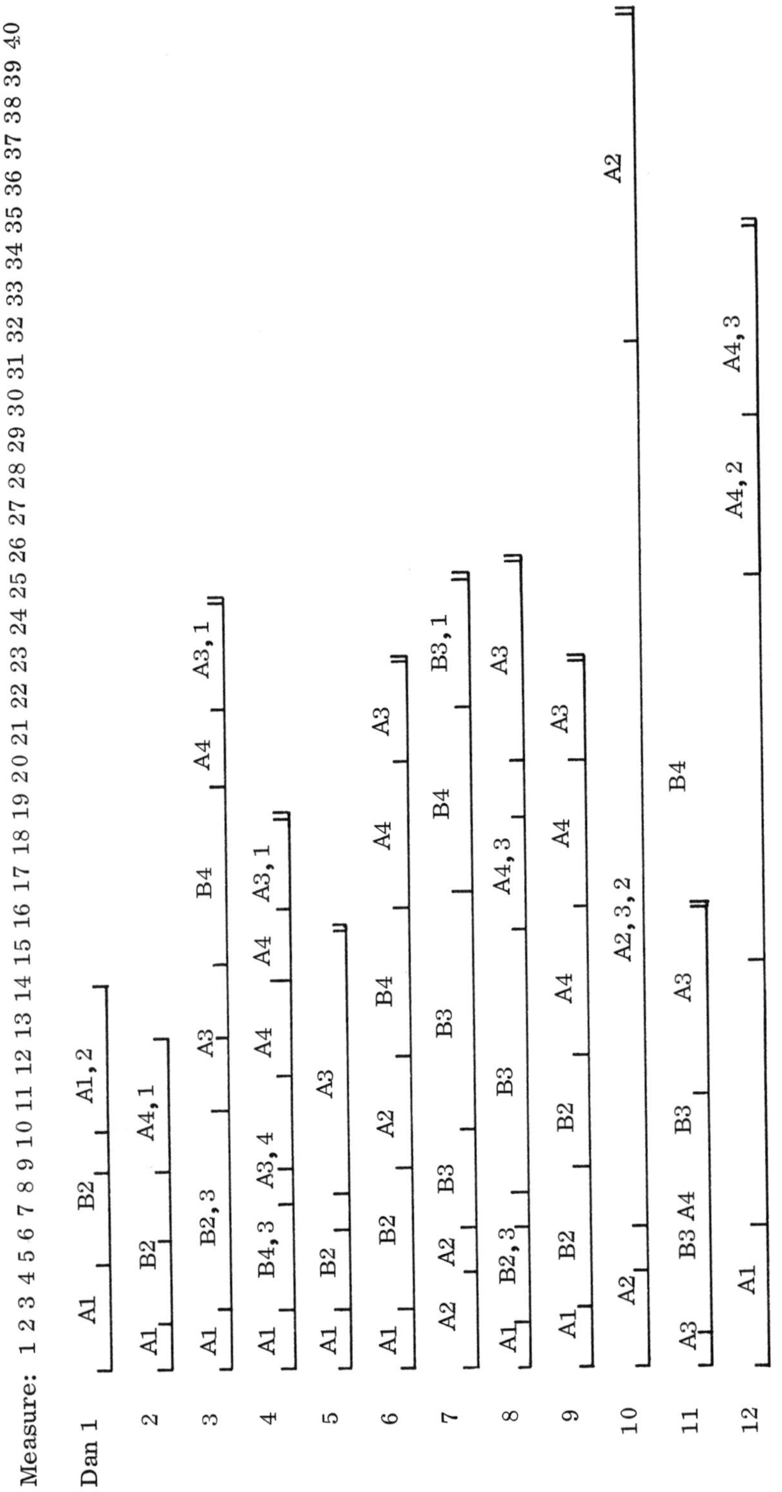

Measure: 1 2 3 4 5 6 7 8 9 10 11 12 13 14 15 16 17 18 19 20 21 22 23 24 25 26 27 28 29 30 31 32 33 34 35 36 37 38 39 40

Dan 1   A1   B2   A1,2

2   A1   B2   A4,1

3   A1   B2,3   A3   B4   A3,1

4   A1   B4,3   A3,4   A4   A4   A3,1

5   A1   B2   A3

6   A1   B2   A2   B4   A4   A3

7   A2   A2   B3   B3   B4   B3,1

8   A1   B2,3   B3   A4,3   A3

9   A1   B2   B2   A4   A4   A3

10   A2   A2,3,2   A2

11   A3   B3 A4   B3   A3   B4   A4,2   A4,3

12   A1

Before interpreting the preceding charts, the following two factors should be pointed out. (1) Because of increasing variation as a danmono proceeds, the character of the original thematic material becomes less and less pronounced. In several cases the letters in the charts represent at best approximations which may not be interpreted too literally. (2) An increasing tendency toward structural integration sometimes makes the precise location of causurae difficult and subject to more or less arbitrary interpretation. The limitations of the various phrases as given in the charts was determined by evidence provided by the composition under discussion, as well as by structural characteristics of the total repertoire in its modern form and in its historic perspective. The most constant and dependable structural element appears to be the phrase group, which therefore will provide the basis for the following considerations of the structure of the total danmono repertoire. In this discussion *Midare*, because of its exceptional form, will be excluded.

The structure of the first dan, consisting of five phrase groups with their various subdivisions, may serve as a point of departure. This particular structure, which may be represented as I 1, 2; II 1, 2, 3; III 1, 2; IV 1, 2; V 1, appears to be by far the most common: it occurs in thirty-four of fifty dan. This basic structure may be shortened either by the omission of one or more of the supporting phrases, by the combination of two short supporting phrases into one of greater length, or by the combination of a supporting phrase with its main phrase. In "regular" danmono the subdivision of the dan into five sections is never departed from (in *Midare*, however, examples may be found), and never is the dan subdivided into more units than those occurring in the first dan. The various structures are listed below in order of their frequency of occurrence.

I 1, 2; II 1, 2, 3; III 1, 2; IV 1, 2; V 1	34 examples	(*Rokudan* 1, 2; *Shichidan* 1, 2, 4, 5, 6, 7; *Kudan* 1 through 9; *Hachidan* 1, 3, 4, 7; *Godan* 1, 3, 4; *Kumoi Kudan* 1 through 9; *Akikaze* 1)
I 1, 2; II 1, 2, 3; III 1 ; IV 1, 2; V 1	7 examples	(*Hachidan* 2, 5, 6, 8; *Godan* 2; *Akikaze* 2, 6)
I 1, 2; II 1, 2 ; III 1, 2; IV 1, 2; V 1	4 examples	(*Rokudan* 3; *Godan* 5; *Akikaze* 3, 5)
I 1 ; II 1, 2 ; III 1 ; IV 1 ; V 1	2 examples	(*Rokudan* 5, 6)
I 1 ; II 1, 2, 3; III 1, 2; IV 1 ; V 1	1 example	(*Akikaze* 4)
I 1, 2; II 1, 2, 3; III 1 ; IV 1 ; V 1	1 example	(*Shichidan* 3)
I 1, 2; II 1, 2 ; III 1 ; IV 1 ; V 1	1 example	(*Rokudan* 4)

Three compositions tenaciously cling to the basic structure: in *Kudan* and *Kumoi Kudan* this plan is never departed from, while in *Shichidan* only one dan occurs in which a supporting phrase is combined with its main phrase. The greatest variety, on the other hand, may be observed in *Rokudan* and *Akikaze*, each of which contains no less than four structural types. The structural variety displayed in *Rokudan* and *Akikaze* has undoubtedly contributed in making these two compositions among the most captivating of the repertoire; the two *Kudan* and *Shichidan*, on the other hand, are quite uninteresting compositions, which is reflected in the academic pedantry with which their composers slavishly followed the once established structural pattern.

The location of the caesurae also appears to be patterned. They are shown in the following five charts, organized according to the number of phrases contained in the dan.

1. Five phrase groups, ten phrases:

Patterns of Caesura Location	Frequency	Location
2, 4; 8, 10, 12; 15, 17; 20, 23;	27	*Rokudan* 1, 2; *Shichidan* 1, 2, 4, 5, 7; *Kudan* 1-8; *Hachidan* 1, 3; *Godan* 1; *Kumoi Kudan* 1-9
2, 4; 8, 10, 12; 15, 16; 19, 23;	1	*Hachidan* 4
2, 4; 8, 10, 12; 15, 17; 19, 23;	1	*Akikaze* 1
2, 4; 8, 10. 12; 16, 17; 20, 23;	1	*Kudan* 9
2, 4; 8, 10, 12; 14, 16; 20, 23;	1	*Hachidan* 7
2, 4; 9, 11, 12; 15, 17; 19, 23;	1	*Godan* 3
2, 4; 9, 10, 13; 16, 17; 20, 23;	1	*Shichidan* 6

2. Five phrase groups, nine phrases:

Patterns of Caesura Location	Frequency	Location
-, 4; 9, 11, 12; 14, 17; 21, 23;	1	*Godan* 4
2, 4; 8, 11, --; 14, 17; 19, 23;	1	*Rokudan* 3
2, 4; 8, 11, --; 15, 17; 19, 23;	1	*Akikaze* 3
2, 4; 9, 12, --; 15, 17; 20, 23;	1	*Godan* 5
2, 4;11, 13, --; 15, 17; 20, 23;	1	*Akikaze* 5
2, 4; 8, 10, 12; 16, --; 20, 23;	3	*Hachidan* 2, 6; *Akikaze* 2
2, 4; 8, 10, 13; 17, --; 20, 23;	1	*Godan* 2
2, 4; 8, 10, 13; 18, --; 19, 22;	1	*Hachidan* 5
2, 4; 8, 10, 14; 18, --; 20, 23;	1	*Akikaze* 6
2, 4; 9, 11, 13; 16, --; 20, 23;	1	*Hachidan* 8

3. Five phrase groups, eight phrases:

Patterns of Caesura Location	Frequency	Location
-, 4; 8, 10, 12; 16, 19; 23, --;	1	*Akikaze* 4
2, 4; 8, 10, 12; 16, --; 23, --;	1	*Shichidan* 3

4. Five phrase groups, seven phrases:

Patterns of Caesura Location	Frequency	Location
4, 6; 8, 12, --; 21, --; 23, --;	1	Rokudan 4

5. Five phrase groups, six phrases:

Patterns of Caesura Location	Frequency	Location
-, 4; 12, 14, --: 21, --; 23, --;	1	Rokudan 5
-, 6; 14, 16; --; 21, --; 23, --;	1	Rokudan 6

Thus organized, the phrase structure of the dan needs no comment. Once again *Rokudan* and *Akikaze* are distinguished by a relatively high degree of variability: in terms of phrase length they represent five and six varieties respectively. This time they are joined by *Godan* and *Hachidan* (five and six varieties), a circumstance which undoubtedly is connected with the greater rhythmic complexity of these two compositions. *Shichidan* and especially *Kudan* and *Kumoi Kudan* again almost constantly employ the standard structure.

The quadratic structure of the phrases which so frequently is found in the first part of a dan reflects a standard ordering of melodic material. Thus, a four-measure phrase normally consists of two sub-phrases of two measures each. Similarly, the non-quadratic phrase structure encountered in the second and third parts of a dan is the result of an organization of non-symmetric units. Studying these irregularly built phrases, it appears that in many cases the symmetry is broken by the repetition, mostly in a varied form, of short melodic fragments, often about one measure in length. Examples of this varied-repetition procedure are typically found in the region of measures 15-19. A few examples from different pieces, all at the same location in the dan, illustrate the principle (see Example 40).

Midare is not cited here because of its different structure, while *Akikaze* provides no examples of repetition at this particular location (and thereby is set apart from the other danmono). The principle appears to be similar for all examples: a short melodic unit is repeated in a varied form, in the process of which the length of the original is increased during the repetition. Notice that all examples essentially give no more than an elaboration on pattern II, the descent from degree V to I. *Rokudan* and *Shichidan* start out with exactly the same material, which in the latter is somewhat more elaborated than in the former. In passing, some attention should be given to a difference in aesthetic quality between these two fragments: where *Shichidan* somewhat mechanically repeats the warizume four times, in *Rokudan* the "sha-sha" is at the beginning of measure 16 alternated with a slight variation, hereby avoiding the monotony that here characterizes *Shichidan*. The last three examples, from *Kudan, Godan,* and *Kumoi Kudan,* show varied repetition occurring more than once, in which case the first repetition may be shorter than its original.

Example 40. (a) *Rokudan,* dan 1; (b) *Shichidan,* dan 2; (c)*Hachidan,* dan 2; (d) *Kudan,* dan 8; (e) *Godan,* dan 1; (f) *Kumoi Kudan,* dan 7.

The systematic use of the various registers of the instrument as observed in the analysis of the first dan is in general followed through the later dan. Strict adherence to this pattern, however, would result in monotony, and several variations occur:

1. The final dan of a danmono always ends in register 3 rather than register 2, as a result of the ending on the first degree that characterizes the conclusion of a danmono.

2. Inner dan sometimes end in register 1 (*Akikaze,* dan 5); register 3 (*Shichidan,* dan 5; *Akikaze,* dan 4); or register 4 (*Godan,* dan 2).

3. Usually a dan opens in register 2, but a beginning in other registers occasionally may be observed: register 1 (*Kudan,* dan 4; *Godan,*   dan 5; *Akikaze,* dan 4); register 3 (*Kudan,* dan 7; *Akikaze,* dan 5); or register 4 (*Shichidan,* dan 4 and 7; *Godan,* dan 3).

4. The middle part occasionally uses registers other than register 4, replacing it by register 3 (*Rokudan,* dan 6; *Shichidan* dan 3; *Kudan,* dan 6; *Hachidan,* dan 8; and *Godan,* dan 4), or register 2 (*Shichidan,* dan 7; *Kudan,* dan 4; and *Akikaze,* dan 5). The occurrence at this location of a lower register in a relatively high number of final dan (three out of seven) may be explained as a preparation for the ascent in the following phrase, which, in turn, prepares the final cadence.

Note that *Kumoi Kudan* is distinguished by its strict following of the standard formal scheme in melodic content as well as in rhythm.

The three-part structure of the typical dan (phrase groups I and II; III; and IV and V) has been found to obtain throughout the entire repertoire. In summary, the main characteristics of the three parts, based on the first dan, in which the formal aspects of danmono are most clearly demonstrated, are as follows:

In the first part proper (that is, after the kandō), the register moves systematically from low to high. Two basic melodic species are introduced in regularly alternating phrases of quadratic structure. Normally, the melody is limited to the degrees of the scale. The character of the first part, which normally is twelve measures long, is that of an exposition.

The second part, about six measures in length, contrasts with the first part by moving to the highest register and by abandoning the quadratic phrase structure for one which is very irregular. The melodic materials, still the same as in the first part, are no longer clearly separated, the rhythm has lost its quiet regularity, and the occurrence of accidentals adds to the general feeling of crisis and climax.

In the third part, finally, the melody gradually returns to the low register in which the dan opened. The phrase structure remains irregular, but the melodic materials are clearly separated, while the rhythm regains some of the quietness of the first part. The character of the third part is that of a denouement.

This short description almost inevitably brings to mind the *jo-ha-kyū* concept.[3] This typically Japanese aesthetic theory has deliberately not been discussed before this point because the contemporary koto musician is not concerned with it; in the past this may have been different, since the theory is mentioned in the sixth volume of the *Sōkyoku Taiishō.* The concept has been applied to the ancient Japanese court dances, *bugaku,* and to Buddhist chanting, *shōmyō.* It found its greater refinement in the theoretical writings of the Nō-playwright, Zeami (1363-1443). The three words refer to a division of a work into three parts: *jo,* an introduction; *ha,* literally "scattering" or "breaking apart," a development toward a climax; and *kyū,* a denouement. In the first dan of a danmono, the initial part indeed shows a jo-character in the gradual introduction of the material and the progressive development of the range of the instrument. The second part, during which a crisis develops through the irregular phrase structure and intermingling of musical materials, is easily equated with ha, while the third part, with its quieter character and partial return to the original order, fulfills the requirements of a kyū.

Regarded as a whole, a danmono consists of a number of separate, independent movements. Aside from the gradually increasing tempo from the first through the last dan, no attempt is made to organize these movements into larger units. *Midare,* however, lacking the structural benefits of the normal danmono because of its irregular dan, shows an organization on a larger scale: several dan are grouped together as distinguishable units. There are three of these groupings and in their sequence they conform to the jo-ha-kyū concept. The organization into these three groups is as follows: dan 1 through 5, dan 6 through 9, and, finally, dan 10, 11, and 12. With the exception of the third, all dan of the first part are marked by brevity. Their musical content is closely related, the tempo is slow and the character quiet. The close similarity of dan 5 to dan 1 elegantly rounds off the first part. All dan of the first part end on "shan" on tones a and e', tone a (degree IV) being the more important structurally.

All dan of the second part except the seventh end on degree I. Their length is approximately the same as those of regular danmono. The tempo of this part is faster and the character much livelier than that of the first part. A striking structural feature is the slightly varied repetition of dan 6 and 7 by dan 9 and 10. Dan 8, closely related to dan 1 and 5, refers back to the first part.

The tenth, eleventh, and twelfth dan, which bring *Midare* to a close, are undoubtedly a later addition: these dan do not occur in the version of *Midare* according to the Yatsuhashi-ryū. Dan 12 is in its musical material related to dan 7 and 10; the repetition of previously stated material helps to achieve unity.[4]

CHAPTER VIII

DANMONO: OTHER CONSIDERATIONS (I)

Melodic Movement

The general melodic movement in danmono may best be described by reference to the registers used. The registers are systematically explored in the course of each dan, in which process guidance is supplied by the three most important degrees of the scale, I, IV, and V.

The melodic material of danmono has been seen to consist in essence of no more than downward and upward progressions from one of the three basic tones of the scale to the next. The most common progressions are the descending patterns: pattern I progresses from degree I down to V, sometimes extended through IV; pattern II, from degree V or IV down to I; pattern III, an ascending pattern, from degree I to IV or V; and pattern IV, also ascending, from degree IV or V to I. The last two patterns may include degrees III and VII. In summary:

```
Pattern  I:  degrees  I     VI   V    (IV)
         II:          (V)   IV   II   I
         III:         I     II   IV   (V), or (VII)   I    III   IV
         IV:          (IV)  V    VI   I  , or (IV)    V    VII   I
```

Descending patterns form the basic material of what in the formal analysis has been symbolized by the letter "A"; ascending patterns, especially pattern III, form the material for "B."

Cadences

The most conspicuous use of the patterns, especially the descending ones, is made in cadences, where they are often met in connection with specific rhythms consisting of dotted eighth-sixteenth and quarter combinations, that in shōfu are referred to as kororin. These very characteristic melodic-rhythmic patterns may best be illustrated in the final cadences of dan.

In considering these final cadences, it should be remembered that all danmono, including *Midare*, close their last dan on the first degree of the scale. The majority of the "inner" dan, however, do not end on the first degree, but close with pattern I, a descent from degree I to V, mostly followed by shan, sometimes by degree IV. This "kororin-shan" or "ten-ton-shan" is so conspicuous in its regular repetition that to the unprepared listener the final conclusion on degree I at the end of the last dan comes as a surprise, almost suggesting an ending on the "dominant" rather than the "tonic."

The final cadences may be divided into three groups: those ending on degree I, those ending on degree V, and finally those ending on degree V followed by shan or degree IV. Considering the cadences on degree I first, we find a clear distinction between those found at the end of final dan and those at the end of inner dan. Example 41 shows the final cadences of the various last dan.

The most common type, the first example, occurs at the end of four of the eight pieces and consists of sararin from the highest string down to tone f'', which is ornamented with a ju (hiki-iro) before resolving to the final tone e', which is played on strings 1 and 5 simultaneously (oshiawase), thus emphasizing the first degree. The final cadence of *Shichidan* is closely related and merely replaces sararin by another glissando, kararin. Basically, both glissandi are variants of the regular cadence from degrees V to I. If this is recognized, the final cadence of *Kumoi Kudan* becomes less deviant than it appears at first sight: there is a short kororin from b' to f', followed by the almost conventional hiki-iro resolving on tone e'. The final tone, however, is a single tone. The conclusion of *Midare* somewhat resembles that of *Kumoi Kudan* but the descent is broken by a return to tone a' before reaching the final e'. *Akikaze*, finally, has a rather different ending, although one that essentially consists of a sequence from degrees V to I. The sequence is interrupted by a surizume, the sole appearance of this technique in danmono. In vocal-instrumental music, however, surizume occurs rather frequently, especially at the end of an instrumental prelude or interlude, and it will be recalled that the danmono part of *Akikaze* functions as an introduction for a vocal composition.

Example 41. Danmono. Final Cadences: (a) *Rokudan, Kudan, Hachidan, and Godan;* (b) *Shichidan;* (c) *Kumoi Kudan;* (d) *Midare;* (e) *Akikaze.*

Cadences on degree I at the conclusion of dan other than the last dan occur in *Midare* at the end of dan 5, 6, 8, 9, 10, and 11; in *Shichidan,* dan 5; *Kudan,* dan 8; *Hachidan,* dan 3 and 6; *Godan,* dan 2 and 3; and *Kumoi Kudan,* dan 5, 6, and 7.   This cadence is not found concluding inner dan in *Rokudan* and *Akikaze.*   Cadences on degree I may be classified into (1) those reached from degree V above; (2) those reached from the higher octave; and (3) those reached from the "dominant" of degree V (raised degree II).   Examples of these three categories are given in Example 42.

Example 42. Danmono. Final Cadences: (a)*Kumoi Kudan,* dan 5; (b)*Hachidan,*
dan 3; (c) *Godan,* dan 3; (d) *Godan,* dan 3; (e) *Midare,* dan 6;
(f) *Midare,* dan 11; (g) *Midare,* dan 10; (h) *Kudan,* dan 8

Kumoi Kudan shows an almost straight descent from tones b' to e' (degree V to I), interrupted by only a lower octave of I. The rhythmic pattern of a double dotted quarter-sixteenth which occurs at the beginning of the cadence is found frequently. *Godan,* dan 2, shows the only case in which a dan ends on tone e''. Final cadences from degrees V to I are very rare, and the three examples given above are the only instances before the final dan. *Godan,* dan 3, represents a unique case. Here the final cadence from tone b' to e' is preceded by no more than a single tone e''. *Midare,* dan 6 and 11, on the other hand, represent a very common group, consisting of a downward scale from e'' to e'. In dan 6 a straight descent is made, in dan 11 the cadence on its way downward turns back from f' to a' (degree IV) before continuing to tone e'. Such interruptions of the descending scale are frequently met. Other examples are found in *Midare,* dan 5, 8, and 9; *Shichidan,* dan 5; and *Kumoi Kudan,* dan 7. *Midare,* dan 10, and *Kudan,* dan 8, show the inclusion of tone f♯'' in the cadence. *Midare,* dan 10, presents a regular descent, interrupted by shan; *Kudan,* dan 8, is the only case in which an ascending cadence occurs at the conclusion of a dan. Notice also the repetition of tone d'' (degree VII) performed in alternating downstrokes and upstrokes, a rare phenomenon in danmono. The ending on a shan on tones a and e', in which the shan represents tone e' rather than tone a, is very uncommon —the two examples given here *(Hachidan,* dan 3, and *Kudan,* dan 8) are the only occurrences.

Final cadences from degrees I to V may be subdivided in a similar way according to whether the final descent is preceded by a descent or an ascent. Representative examples are given below.

Example 43. Danmono. Final Cadences of Inner Dan: (a) *Kumoi Kudan,* dan 2;
(b) *Kumoi Kudan,* dan 4; (c) *Akikaze,* dan 1; (d) *Akikaze,* dan 3;
(e) *Akikaze,* dan 4; (f) *Akikaze,* dan 5.

The phenomenon of dan concluding on tone b (degree V) is limited to *Kumoi Kudan* and *Akikaze* and is therefore not found in compositions in hira-jōshi.   Thus there are few occurrences (12). The conclusion of tone b followed by shan on e and b in *Kumoi Kudan*, dan 2, is unique.   The descent over a complete octave, as exemplified by *Kumoi Kudan*, dan 4, is the most common form of the cadences on degree V, occurring seven times.   The f♯ in *Akikaze* is simply part of the tuning and not the result of the occasional raising of this degree that so often happens in hira-jōshi.   However, note the difference in function between the f♯ in the final cadence of dan 1 and that in dan 3.   In dan 3 it functions as a "dominant" for the fifth degree, in dan 1 it is an inconspicuous part of a descending scale.   The last three examples *(Akikaze,* dan 3, 4, and 5) are unique occurrences.

The last group of cadences, those from degrees V through I to shan or IV, is the most frequently represented.   On the basis of the preceding group of notes, the following subdivisions may be made: (1) start from tone a' (degree IV); (2) start from tone b' (degree V);   start from tone c'' (degree VI).   Representative examples are given in Example 44.

Example 44. Danmono. Final Cadences of Inner Dan: (a) *Kudan*, dan 1; (b) *Rokudan*, dan 3; (c) *Kudan*, dan 6 and 7; (d) *Kudan*, dan 2, and *Godan*, dan 4; (e) *Shichidan*, dan 6; (f) *Midare*, dan 3 and 7; (g) *Shichidan*, dan 3; (h) *Hachidan*, dan 1 and 2.

The first type, the start from degree IV, occurs very rarely *(Kudan,* dan 1, given here, and *Midare,* dan 1). The second type, that beginning with degree V, is the most frequently encountered (19 of 29 examples). The examples from (b) through (e) show subtle differences. These involve the inclusion or exclusion of tone c' between e' and b; the repetition of tone e' before continuing the cadence to tone b; the replacement of the final shan by a single tone a or by waren; or a retracing to tone a' after tone f' has been reached, before continuing the downward movement. *Shichidan,* dan 3, shows the exceptional case of a cadence ending on tone a' rather than a. The third type, the start from degree VI, is a rather undistinctive variant of the second type. It is represented five times in all. The example from *Hachidan,* dan 1 and 2, shows a syncopated kororin (from tone b') that is typical of this piece as well as of *Godan.*

Comparing the three main types of cadences, the most commonly met form descends a complete octave, from either degree I or V. Rarely is the higher tone of the octave preceded by its upper neighbor. A descent from degree IV to lower IV is rare and occurs only twice in the danmono repertoire. Final cadences using less than an octave are found only where the final tone is the first degree, and they move between degrees V and I.

To conclude the survey, some irregularities occurring in *Kudan* and *Godan* must be mentioned. They throw an interesting light on the apparent need composers felt to compose dan of precisely twenty-six measures of 4/4 in length. The following example, transcribed from current Japanese notations, shows three instances of the end of a dan and the beginning of the next.

Example 45. (a) *Kudan,* dan 8-9; (b) *Godan,* dan 1-2; (c) *Godan,* dan 3-4.

The last beats of dan 8 of *Kudan* clearly belong to the following dan. The final tone of the first dan in *Godan* is not reached before the first beat in the second dan, while the last three beats of dan 3 in *Godan* belong organically to dan 4. The notation of these examples is undoubtedly the result of an obligation felt to compose dan of the required length. *Godan,* however, allows another interesting observation: its composer probably desired to make a stronger connection between these dan rather than to present a sequence of independent movements.

Mode

The example of a notational transposition of a piece in kumoi-jōshi, *Kumoi Kudan,* transposed to the same first degree as that of the other compositions in hira-jōshi, allowed the observation that the difference between the two chōshi lies chiefly in register and not in modal quality. Where, for example, a kandō in hira-jōshi moves between strings 5 and 1, a similar movement between strings 7 and 4 will produce a similar musical effect in kumoi-jōshi, the only practical difference being the generally higher sound of the latter chōshi. In general, where compositions in hira-jōshi use a lower register, those in kumoi-jōshi will use a higher one; on the other hand, the highest register in hira-jōshi corresponds to a lower register in kumoi-jōshi: the transposition must be, rather than a fourth up, a fifth down, because of the limits of the range of the instrument. Pieces in kumoi, therefore, tend to move for longer time spans in the middle register of the koto than do pieces in hira-jōshi.

A difference between the two chōshi results from the identical tuning of strings 1 and 2 in both tunings. In hira-jōshi these strings correspond to degrees I and IV; in kumoi-jōshi to V and I. Thus, a similar use of shan on strings 1 and 2 results in musically different functions. This may explain the absence of shan at the end of final cadences in *Kumoi Kudan,* an absence that sets these cadences distinctly apart from those in hira-jōshi. In general, however, the difference between hira-jōshi and kumoi-jōshi hardly goes beyond those of mere transposition.[1] It is legitimate, therefore, to draw conclusions regarding the use of tonal material for both chōshi simultaneously.

The degrees of the in-scale are as follows:

I	II	III	IV	V	VI	VII	(I)
e	f	g	a	b	c	d	(e)

The open strings of the koto are tuned to the following selection from the scale:

I   II   IV   V   VI   (I)

The omission of degrees III and VII strongly suggests a subsidiary importance for these degrees, an assumption that has been corroborated by analysis. Analysis has also shown three of these five tones to be more important than the other two:

I   IV   V   (I)

These three degrees, the first three of a cycle of fifths (and again the reader should remember that these three tones and their octaves are the only tones produced on strings that are tuned in perfect fifths or their inversion, perfect fourths) form the basis of the tonal material of several musical civilizations, including, for example, those of the Far East as well as that of India and that of the West. In Japanese sōkyoku also, degrees I, IV, and V constitute the basic tones of the mode. The function of these tones may be summarized as follows:

Degree I: (1)   First tone in patterns I and III.

       (2)   Final tone or very important supporting tone in patterns II and IV.

       (3)   First and final tone of all danmono.

       (4)   Final tone of several inner dan.

Degree V: (1)   First tone of patterns II and IV.

       (2)   Final tone or important supporting tone in patterns I and III.

       (3)   Infrequently, final tone of inner dan of compositions in hira-jōshi; usual final tone of inner dan of *Kumoi Kudan* and *Akikaze*.

Degree IV: (1)   Frequently, final tone in pattern I and in the subsidiary form of pattern III (VII I III IV).

       (2)   Important supporting tone in pattern II.

       (3)   Frequently, first tone in pattern IV.

       (4)   Final tone (as such often represented by shan) of numerous inner dan.

Degrees I, V, and IV are used as first and final tones in the patterns that have been seen to form the building material of the danmono. These three tones, therefore, must be considered to constitute the most basic tonal material.

Degrees II and VI, the remaining two scale degrees represented on the open strings of the koto, never assume an emphasis comparable to that of degrees I, IV, and V. The melodic importance of these two tones may be judged in their functions within the composition.

Degree II: (1)   As part of pattern II, degree II may function as upper leading tone for degree I and as such receives strong emphasis. This function is especially clear when in a cadence the sequence from II to I is interrupted by a return to degree IV before I is reached. When this interruption does not occur, the leading tone function is hardly perceived and degree II in effect serves as a passing tone.

       (2)   As part of pattern III, degree II usually receives a noticeable amount of stress.

       (3)   Rarely, degree II occurs as a lower neighbor (in terms of koto strings) of degree IV. An example is found in *Godan*, dan 1, measure 11. Example 46 shows the three functions of degree II.

Example 46. (a) *Kudan*, dan 1; (b) *Rokudan*, dan 1, (c) *Godan*, dan 1.

Degree VI: (1) Degree VI appears almost exclusively in descending passages.

(2) It is a passing tone in pattern I.

(3) Degree VI rarely receives stress. When stressed, the degree usually precedes a kororin cadence from degree V.

Occurrences of degree VI as a passing tone and as the relatively stressed upper neighbor of degree V are shown in the following example:

Example 47. (a) Various kandō; (b) *Godan*, dan 4.

Comparing the relative importance of degrees II and VI, it appears noteworthy that the former, in its function as upper leading tone, tends to be emphasized; the latter is mostly unstressed.

The last two degrees of the scale, VII and III, are produced by left-hand pressure. Their frequency is considerably less than that of the other degrees.

Degree VII: (1) Degree VII occurs in ascent only, and somewhat assumes the function of a lower leading tone.

(2) It is often the first tone in pattern III, in which function it is stressed.

(3) As a lower neighbor for degree I, degree VII does not receive stress.

(4) As a light passing tone, degree VII appears in pattern IV between degrees V and I.

The functions of degree VII are illustrated in the following example.

Example 48. (a) *Hachidan*, dan 1; (b) *Kumoi Kudan*, kandō; (c) *Shichidan*, dan 1; (d) *Rokudan*, dan 1.

In general, the occurrence of degree III is rare. When it does occur, its function is similar to that of degree VII.

Degree III: (1) Like degree VII, degree III is used in ascending passages only.

(2) Degree III appears stressed as the first tone of an ascending passage (pattern III).

(3) As a lower neighbor of degree IV, it does not receive stress.

(4) Passing tone in pattern III.

The following example shows the use of degree III.

Example 49. (a) *Shichidan,* dan 1; (b) *Shichidan,* dan 1; (c) *Hachidan,* dan 1.

The order of the relative importance of the degrees of the in-scale, therefore, is: I, V, IV, II, VI, VII, and III.

Besides the seven degrees of the in-scale, three other tones are encountered in danmono: f#', f#", and b♭", in scale degrees II#, and V♭. As in Western Music, the introduction of tones other than those belonging to the scale proper can mean either modulation or a temporary appearance of a secondary dominant or subdominant. The latter is the more usual and will be considered first. The locations of the raised and lowered degrees that indicate secondary dominant or subdominant are given below:

	II#	V♭
Midare	4:16*; 5:11; 8:22; 10:38; 12:12	
Rokudan	1:20; 2:23; 3:19	3:21
Shichidan	1:24; 3:15, 16	4:18
Kudan	6:8; 9:9, 10	7:3
Hachidan	6:12	4:17; 5:11
Godan	1:24; 2:18; 4:20	2:16
Kumoi Kudan	1:24; 3:17, 24; 6:17	5:17
Akikaze		2:7; 4:17; 5:11, 14; 6:19

*Dan 4, Measure 16.

The distribution of these "secondary dominants" is interesting. A large majority is located between measures 17 and 21, that part of the composition which was previously characterized as having a connective character. Another concentration is found on or just before measure 24, the point at which the last descent from tone e" to the lowest tone sets in. Few of these accidentals occur in the first part of the composition, and tone b♭ never occurs in the first dan. A parallel appears to exist between quiet and regular quadratic phrase structure, and restriction to the degrees of the scale, on the one hand, and phrases of irregular length and the appearance of accidentals on the other hand. Complex phrase structure and accidentals clearly work together in producing the effect of a climax.

The explanation of the functioning of these secondary dominants offers no problems: as in equivalent Western situations, a temporary shift in tonal functions occurs.[2] Normally, the first degree functions as tonal center; when this function is temporarily yielded to degrees IV or V, accidentals will occur in order to provide the new center with the appropriate super-structure up to its fifth. The following example shows the necessity for the introduction of accidentals in order to maintain the same tonal relations when the tonal center shifts.

Example 50.

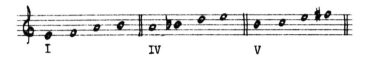

The most common shift made is to degree V; that to degree IV occurs less frequently. Example 51 shows the principle so clearly that it needs no comment. *Kumoi Kudan* and *Akikaze*, although not in hira-jōshi, behave no differently.

Example 51. (a) *Rokudan*, dan 1; (b) *Kudan*, dan 6; (c) *Shichidan*, dan 4;
(d) *Kumoi Kudan*, dan 5; (e) *Akikaze*, dan 2.

Modulation is, in principle, no different from the preceding: the occurrence of accidentals announces a shift in tonal center which in the case of a modulation is continued for at least four measures. The following chart shows the locations and kinds of modulation in danmono.

				new tonal center:	
Midare	:	dan 8, measures	11-18;		V
Rokudan	:	" 6, "	11-18;	"	V
Shichidan	:	no modulation			
Kudan	:	dan 8, measures	20-24;	"	V
Hachidan	:	" 5, "	1-4 ;	"	V
	:	" 5, "	19-22;	"	V
	:	" 8, "	18-25;	"	V
Godan	:	" 3, "	8-12;	"	IV
	:	" 3, "	17-23;	"	IV
	:	" 5, "	13-20;	"	IV
Kumoi Kudan	:	" 5, "	20-23;	"	V
Akikaze	:	no modulation			

The length of sections of modulation is approximately four or eight measures, with an equal distribution of both. If the frequency of modulation increased as danmono continued to be composed, which is very likely, then the relatively higher number of phrases of modulation in *Hachidan* and *Godan* corroborates our assumed later date of composition for these two pieces. The exceptional modulation to degree IV (rather than to degree V) in *Godan* may also point to a relatively late date of composition. A typical example of a modulation to degree V in dan 6 of *Rokudan* has been discussed on page 90. An example of modulation to degree IV is given below.

Example 52. *Godan*, dan 5.

Ornamentation

For all practical purposes ornamentation in koto music can be considered identical to left-hand technique. All left-hand movements are concerned with the production of pitch changes after a string has been plucked. In the only exception, kō (oshide), a string is pushed down before it is plucked in order to produce a pitch that is not available otherwise. To permit an understanding of the functioning of these left-hand ornaments in a composition, those occurring in *Rokudan* will be studied in detail, after which comparison with the ornamentation in other danmono will permit a check on the validity of the conclusions drawn from the analysis of

Table 1

Ornament in *Rokudan*	Ornamented	Pitch Preceding Ornament	Pitch Following Ornament	Time Value	1	2	3	4	5	6	Total
En (ato-oshi)	a'	f'	e'	♪	3	3					6
	a'	f'	f'	♪					1		1
	a'	shan (a–e')	b'	𝅗𝅥				2			2
	a'	e'	b'	𝅗𝅥		1	1			1	3
	a'	e''	b'	♪	1						1
	c''	b'	b'	♪		2	1				3
	c''	e''	b'	𝅗𝅥		2					2
	e''	shan (a–e')	c''	♪						1*	1
	e''	c''	c''	♪						1*	1
	a''	f''	e''	♪	1						1
	a''	e''	f''	♪		1	1	2			4
	a''	f''	f''	♪	1		1				2
	a''	f''	f''	♪	1						1
	a''	f''	b''	♪						1	1
	a''	f''	b''	♪		1	1				2
Total					7	10	5	4	1	4	31
Chitsu (tsuki-iro)	f''	f''	e''	♪	1						1
Total					1						1

*Combined with oshiawase.

Table 1 (continued)

Ornament in *Rokudan*	Pitch Ornamented	Preceding Ornament	Following Ornament	Time Value	Freq. Dan 1	2	3	4	5	6	Total
Ju (hiki-iro)	e'	shan	shan	𝅗𝅥.						2	2
	e'	shan	shan	𝅘𝅥	1	1	1		1		4
	e'	--	b	𝅗𝅥	1						1
	e'	f'	b	𝅗𝅥			1				1
	f'	shan	shan	𝅘𝅥				1	1		2
	f'	shan	e'	𝅘𝅥	1	1	1				3
	f'	a'	e'	𝅗𝅥						1	1
	f''	e''	f''	𝅘𝅥	1						1
Total					4	2	3	1	2	3	15
Keshizume	e''							2			2
Total								2			2
Yuri	b''			𝅗𝅥				2			2
Total								2			2

Rokudan. Table 1 shows all left-hand ornaments found in *Rokudan*.   From left to right are given the name of the specific ornament (and in most cases the name by which this ornament is popularly referred to, in parentheses), the pitch on which the ornament occurs, the pitches preceding and following the one ornamented, the time value of the tone, and finally, the number of times the ornament is used in each dan.

It must be kept in mind that the ornamentation given here represents the practice of one master, Hagiwara Seigin, which not only may but certainly does differ in details from the ornamentation of other performers.   However, as Hagiwara Seigin is a leading musician in the Ikuta-ryū in Kyōto, her teaching can be taken as representative of the Kyōto style, and as Kyōto was and is one of the centers of the Ikuta-ryū, her performance may be considered as representative of that school.   At the same time, it must also be kept in mind that ornamentation is perhaps the only aspect of koto music which, under certain conditions, allows a limited freedom to the performer.   He will consciously —or more frequently unconsciously —follow unformulated rules that control where certain ornaments *may* be used; but no rule states where these *ad libitum* ornaments *must* be used.   Despite the above reservations, there is no doubt that the table is representative of what happens in ornamentation and, therefore, conclusions may be legitimately drawn from it.

Five out of eight possible ornaments (see Chapter V) are used in *Rokudan*.   One of these five, keshizume, which produces a change in timbre, cannot be regarded as a melodic ornament and is, in addition, by no means generally used.   Oshihanashi, kasaneoshi, and yōgin are not used.   Examination of the table reveals that on certain pitches certain ornaments are preferred, or at least that this is true of the two occurring frequently enough to allow generalization, en and ju.   Chitsu, yuri, and keshizume occur too infrequently to allow any conclusions other than the observation that they are found here on tones f" and e" (degrees II and I). En shows a pronounced preference for the fourth degree: of thirty-one times that en is used, it occurs twenty-six times on degree IV (thirteen times on tone a'; eleven times on tone a"; and twice on tone e" which, being used during a modulation to the fifth, functions here as degree IV) against five times on degree VI.   Ju occurs a total of fifteen times, eight of which are on degree I (tone e') and seven on degree II (six times on tone f'; once on tone f").   Conspicuous as unornamented degrees are degrees III, V, and VII.   As degrees III and VII are produced by left-hand pressure, one cannot expect these degrees to be ornamented too often (the only ornaments possible on these degrees are oshihanashi, kasaneoshi, and yuri).   Any attempt to explain the absence of ornaments on degree V at this stage would be premature.   More information should be first acquired from other pieces.

It seems a general tendency to approach tones ornamented by en and ju from below (en, 28 of 31 occurrences; ju, 12 of 15).   Ju may also be applied to the first note of a composition —unprepared, therefore (see the kandō).   More revealing than the approach to an ornamented tone is its continuation.   The following table shows the degrees ornamented by en, the degree following the one ornamented, and the frequency of the occurrence of these combinations in *Rokudan*.

When degree IV is ornamented by en, the movement is downward in seventeen cases (ten times to degree II, seven times to degree I) and upward in nine cases (to degree V). All five times that degree VI is ornamented with en, it is followed by degree V. Thus, in general, the tendency is to move downward, the only important exception being upward motion from degree IV to V.

Table 2

En (ato-oshi)

On Degree	Following Degree	Frequency
IV	I	7
IV	II	10
IV	V	9
VI	V	5

A similar table for ju is given below.

Table 3

Ju (hiki-iro)

On Degree	Following Degree	Frequency
I	shan	6
I	V	2
II	shan	2
II	I	5

Ju also has a tendency to be followed by a lower tone. This may be degree V (after degree I), degree I (after II), or shan, after either degree II or I, consisting of tones a and e' (degrees IV and I). It seems that a degree ornamented by en or ju is usually followed by one of the three basic tones (I, IV, or V), an observation that is supported when it is remembered that degree II if it follows a fourth degree ornamented by en is invariably followed by degree I.

There is a difference between the time values of pitches with which en and ju are used: en is used with pitches of relatively short duration (mainly eighths, rarely quarters and halves); ju occurs on long values (quarters and halves). This difference may be explained at least partly by the fact that in execution ju requires more time than en.

The following two examples show some typical uses of en and ju.

Example 53. The use of en in *Rokudan*: (a) *Rokudan,* dan 2; (b) dan 1; (c) dan 1; (d) dan 1; (e) dan 6.

Example 54. The use of ju in *Rokudan:* (a) kandō; (b) dan 1; (c) dan 1.

Summarizing the findings about ornamentation in *Rokudan*, we find that four degrees are ornamented: I, II, IV, and VI. Degrees III, V, and VII are not ornamented. Five left-hand ornamental techniques are used; in order of frequency, they are: en, ju, yuri, keshizume, and chitsu. En is used primarily with degree IV; ju with degrees I and II. Both en and ju are regularly preceded and followed by lower tones (mainly degrees I, V, and II), the only exception being degree IV ornamented by en, which may be followed by degree V. En occurs primarily with pitches on shorter time values, especially eighths, ju on longer values, mainly quarters and halves. No further conclusions are possible at this point.

Table 4 presents the most important information concerning ornamentation in all danmono. It shows the ornament, the tone on which the ornament occurs, and the frequency of occurrence in each composition. Since time values and preceding and following tones behave in the same way as in the patterns shown in *Rokudan*, these were not included. Two ornaments that do not occur in *Rokudan* are found, oshihanashi and kasaneoshi. En and ju are the most frequently used left-hand ornaments in all the danmono, as they are in *Rokudan*, en occurring a total of 396 times and ju a total of 117 times. Chitsu, appearing only once in *Rokudan*, is next in importance (26 times), closely followed by yuri (21 times). Oshihanashi, kasaneoshi, and keshizume appear in only one composition each (in *Hachidan*, *Midare*, and *Rokudan*, respectively).

The general characteristics of the most important ornaments, en and ju, are what they have already been found to be in *Rokudan*: en appears primarily on tones a' and a'' (degree IV), tone c'' (degree VI), and tone e'' (degree IV, in its five occurrences in passages involving modulation to the fifth; in the remaining instances degree I). Occasionally, it is found on tone f (degree II), and, exceptionally, on tone b (degree V). As in *Rokudan*, ju occurs primarily on tones e and f (degrees I and II). Occasionally it is found also on tones c, a, and b (degrees VI, and V).

Table 4

	Tone	Midare	Rokudan	Shichidan	Kudan	Hachidan	Godan	Kumoi Kudan	Akikaze	Total
					Frequency					
Oshihanashi	a'					1				1
	a''					1				1
Total						2				2
En (ato-oshi)	e'					1 a	2			3
	f'	8				1		3		12
	a'	36	13	16	28	15	11	41	19	179
	b'	1								1
	c''	19	5	7	4	7	5	2	1	50
	e''	4*b	2*	2	4	2 a	5	4	6	27
	f''	3		1		1			2	7
	a''	8	11	23	32	19	22		1	116
	b''					1				1
Total		79	31	49	68	47	43	50	29	396

Table 4 (continued)

	Tone	Frequency								Total
		Midare	Rokudan	Shichidan	Kudan	Hachidan	Godan	Kumoi Kudan	Akikaze	
Kasaneoshi	a''	1								1
Total		1								1
Chitsu (tsuki-iro)	f♯'								2	2
	a'						2			2
	b'	5			1					6
	c''			1	1		3			5
	e''					2				2
	f''		1	1	2	1				5
	a''						4			4
Total		5	1	2	4	3	9		2	26
Ju (hiki-iro)	e'	17	8	2	3	1	2		6	39
	f'	6	6	4	2	6	5	1	6	36
	a'	3			3		2		1	9
	b'	3			1				2	6
	c''	3		5	4		3		1	16
	f''	1	1		4	2	2		1	11
Total		33	15	11	17	9	14	1	17	117
Yuri	d'							1		1
	b'							2		2
	d''	4						1	6	11
	b''		2							2
	c'''					2				2
Total		4	2		2			4	6	18
Keshizume	e''		2							2

*Combined with oshiawase.
[a]Modulation to dominant in all cases.
[b]Modulation to dominant in one case.

En appears to be conventionally used in descending patterns I and II. The first general rule for the application of en may be formulated as follows: in patterns I and II, the second note of the pattern may be ornamented with en. Example 55 shows three instances of en following degree IV, II, and VI. Brackets show the limits of the pattern. Examples (a) and (b) both consist of pattern II, but different tones are ornamented (tone a' and tone f'', respectively). The difference is that in example (a) the passage starts with tone b', but in example (b), with tone a''. Both have in common that the second note of the pattern is ornamented with en.

Example 55. (a)*Midare*, dan 1, measure 8; (b)*Shichidan*, dan 4, measure 10; (c)*Shichidan*, dan 1, measure 8.

Descending patterns are frequently interrupted before the final tone is reached. When this occurs, the interrupting tone may be followed by en.

Example 56. (a)*Rokudan*, dan 1, measure 1; (b)*Shichidan*, dan 2, measures 24-25; (c)*Midare*, dan 4, measures 16-17.

Another conventional use of en occurs in the ascending pattern III. The ornamented degree in this case is always degree IV. All examples in this category give the impression that the fourth degree is "attracted" by the stronger fifth degree.

Example 57. (a)*Kudan*, dan 3, measures 5-7; (b)*Shichidan*, dan 7, measures 18-19.

If the function of en may be described as somewhat dynamic in character, that of ju, the second important ornament, is largely static. Typically, this ornament occurs mainly with pitches of relatively long time values. Ju occurs primarily on basic degrees of the scale (I, IV, and V) and the upper neighbors of degrees I and V (degrees II and VI). In the latter case, degrees II and VI ornamented by ju are most frequently followed by I and V, respectively (occasionally VI is followed by I). Where degrees II and VI ornamented with ju are followed by their lower neighbors, they seem to be attracted by those basic degrees, and the use of ju in this context may be compared with that of en on degree IV, followed by degree V. Typical uses of ju are shown in the following example.

Example 58. (a)*Shichidan*, dan 7, kandō and measures 1–2; (b) *Akikaze*,
dan 1, measures 2–3; (c) *Godan*, dan 3, measures 2–3.

Chitsu or tsuki-iro occurs rather generally on degrees I, II, IV, V, and VI. It is a somewhat ambiguous ornament owing to its resemblance to en. Most typically it is used as a pitch accent. The following example shows the various uses of chitsu. In the first two (a) and (b), chitsu is shown occurring on relatively long note values, where it functions as an expressive pitch accent. The other examples, both from *Godan*, show a use of chitsu that can hardly be distinguished from en. En has been seen to occur at similar locations—where, because of the short value of the ornamented note, it becomes practically identical with chitsu. Modern printed scores of *Godan* do not exist, and the frequent occurrence of chitsu, rather than en, in the handwritten copy that was used for this study may probably be attributed to an idiosyncrasy of the copyist. Chitsu often occurs on the second of a tone repetition, the first of which is ornamented with ju. See the above example (a).

Example 59. (a)*Midare*, dan 8, measures 5–6; (b) *Godan*, dan 5, measures
24–26; (c) *Godan*, dan 3, measures 14–15; (d) *Godan*, dan 3,
measure 21.

Yuri is applied on degrees obtained by left-hand pressure, mainly degree VII. Twice it occurs on degree VI (*Hachidan,* dan 3, measures 16 and 18) when this degree is produced on string 13 by left-hand pressure. When yuri is encountered on degree V, it always occurs on a unison on two neighboring strings that is obtained by oshiawase (see (b) and (c) in the following example). Yuri is an expressive ornament, somewhat related to ju. When yuri occurs on degree VII, it is followed by the next higher degree, I (see (a), (d), and (e) in the following example). Like ju, yuri requires a pitch of rather long time value.

Example 60. (a) *Midare,* dan 7, measures 15–18; (b) *Kumoi Kudan,* dan 2, measures 22–23; (c) *Rokudan,* dan 6, measures 21–22; (d) *Midare,* dan 4, measures 4–5; (e) *Kumoi Kudan,* dan 1, measure 1.

Yuri is favorably used on repeated tones of long value, adding interest and melodic tension. Aside from its occurrence in tone repetitions, yuri is found in ascending passages, preferably on degree VII—which thereby receives additional emphasis.

The occurrence of oshihanashi, kasaneoshi, and keshizume is so rare that no more than a few general remarks can be made. Oshihanashi, which occurs only in *Hachidan* (dan 1, measures 3 and 11), provides two tones on one string by releasing a pressed down string after it has been plucked. Two tones are heard, connected by a slide. The function is no different from that of two separate tones played on different strings and the effect is mainly coloristic. Kasaneoshi is a double en: after being plucked, a string is pressed down, released, and pressed down again. Its function is no different from that of en. An example occurs at the conclusion of *Midare* (dan 12, measure 34) on a pitch of long time value. The purely coloristic effect of kasaneoshi has been mentioned above in the discussion of *Rokudan*.

In conclusion, the use of ornamentation in danmono may be stated to be at least partly determined by modal requirements. This concerns especially the most characteristic left-hand ornaments, en and ju: en because of its occurrence in melodic patterns that are determined by the three basic tones; ju because it occurs either on the most important degrees, I and V, or on their upper neighbors, degrees II and VI, which normally are followed by the lower two basic tones. However, there are instances where ornamentation is determined by purely coloristic or structural needs, and this makes it impossible to regard ornamentation in this genre of koto music from an exclusively modal point of view.

CHAPTER IX

DANMONO: OTHER CONSIDERATIONS (II)

Rhythm

Of the ryhthmic aspects of danmono, mainly time values of notes have been considered to this point. Briefly summarizing the findings of the analysis of the first dan, which are equally valid for the later ones, a danmono can be stated to use primarily quarter and eighth notes. Half notes occur occasionally, chiefly in the kandō, rarely in the course of a composition. Whole notes are truly exceptional. Dotted rhythms are found frequently, mostly as a subdivision of quarter values into dotted eighth-sixteenth or (occasionally) two thirty-seconds; they occur less frequently as a subdivision of a half value: double dotted quarter-sixteenth or two thirty-seconds or dotted quarter-eighth. The dan in the first half of a danmono use more eighth notes, later dan more quarter notes, a logical change in view of the increasing tempo.

Syncopation has been mentioned a few times, mostly in connection with *Hachidan* and *Go-dan*. This leads logically to the question of musical meter. Danmono, as well as practically the whole of the classic koto repertoire, is traditionally notated in duple meter, either 4/4 or 2/4, a difference that roughly can be equated with the notation of the Ikuta and Yamada schools, respectively. Different notations of one and the same composition inevitably present the question as to which of the two is the correct one. A decision is not easily made. Modern Ikuta notation developed logically from older notations, such as that of the *Sōkyoku Taiishō*, which were also in four and which, in their turn, stemmed from still older national traditions, notably that of gagaku, in the repertoire of which there is one piece, *Etenraku*, which can be shown to be the direct ancestor of the koto kumiuta. Tradition, however, though it may serve as an explanation, is not necessarily a justification, and indeed it is not difficult to point out places where the meter suggested by the barlines rather deviates from the actual rhythm. Sometimes it may happen that a notation in 2/4 eliminates certain discrepancies that occur in 4/4, but never all of them. Apart from this occasional advantage of a notation in 2/4, this notation has the disadvantage that it suggests a rhythmic accentuation that is not compatible with the easy, relaxed grace with which danmono tend to move. For this reason the older notation in 4/4 has been used for the transcriptions in this study.

A notation in 4/4 (or, for that matter, in any consistent meter) becomes more easily acceptable when it is taken into account that the barlines provide only a convenient spacing of time into groups of four beats and do not imply that the first, and to a lesser degree also the third, beats are stressed beats. In Japanese music this implication is still more frequently untrue than in Western music. Yet, quite often danmono do organize themselves into regular patterns of four beats, sometimes by a certain regularity in the sequence of more or less stressed and unstressed beats, at other times by sequences of time values that cause certain expectations of regular rhythmic proceedings in the mind of player or listener. Without expectations of this kind it would be impossible to speak of syncopation. Japanese musicians, under the influence of Western music, have occasionally attempted to notate their classic koto music in Western notation in a way more compatible with the expectations suggested by the barlines. The following is an example of *Rokudan* taken from a recent publication (Miyagi 1963: 39).

Example 61. *Rokudan*, dan 1, measures 1-8.

This beginning may seem promising, but soon the inconsistencies between the actual patterns of emphasis and the notation become apparent. Mr. Miyagi has avoided the confusion of almost constantly changing time signatures which would have been the price for consistency. Indeed, after the beginning two measures in 3/4, the notation holds to 2/4 until the very last two measures of the dan, which are in 3/4. The actual patterns of emphasis in the above example are correctly notated as follows:

Example 62. *Rokudan*.

The disadvantages of this more correct notation weigh heavier than its one advantage, consistency, and the best solution seems to maintain the traditional notation in 4/4 throughout, bearing in mind that this notation does not imply the presence of stressed and unstressed beats in the Western sense.

To return to syncopation, syncopations occurring in danmono may be classified according to those in which the stress is moved a time value of a quarter, and others where the change is an eighth. The first category may be subdivided into two-note patterns and more extensive melodic units. Example 63 shows instances of syncopated two-note patterns.

Example 63. (a) *Midare*, dan 8; *Akikaze*, dan 5; (b) *Hachidan*, dan 3;
(c) *Rokudan*, dan 4; (d) *Kudan*, dan 4; (e) *Shichidan*, dan 4.

The above have in common the characteristic that a lower or a higher neighbor is once or more frequently repeated on an unstressed beat before resolving into one of the three basic tones. Notice that the lower neighbor is no more than a major second below the basic tone and therefore in two of the three cases a tone that has to be obtained by left-hand pressure. Notice also the related left-hand ornaments, yuri and ju (in *Midare* and *Shichidan)*, and the en before the lower final tone is reached in *Hachidan* and *Shichidan*. *Hachidan* presents the only instance of stress moved the value of an eighth. Two-tone syncopations are, although not frequent, regularly encountered in all danmono except *Kumoi Kudan*.

The next example shows metric shifts of a quarter note for more than two tones.

Example 64.   (a) *Kudan*, dan 6; (b) *Godan*, dan 5; (c) *Akikaze*, dan 4.

This type of syncopation shows no essential differences from that previously discussed. It is, however, less frequently found and does not occur in *Rokudan*, *Shichidan*, *Midare*, *Hachidan*, and *Kumoi Kudan*; that is, it is absent in general from the older examples of danmono, *Kumoi Kudan* excepted.

Syncopations in which the stress is displaced a time value of an eighth are limited to two pieces, *Hachidan* (dan 1 and 2), and *Godan*. In *Godan* these syncopes occur so frequently that the character of this composition is largely determined by them.   They are completely absent from *Rokudan*, *Shichidan*, and *Akikaze*, and occur only once each in *Midare*, *Kudan*, and *Kumoi Kudan*. Representative examples are given in Example 65.

The first five examples have in common a syncopated kororin pattern that is shifted a time value of an eighth.   Different ways of approaching kororin, that is, from above and below, are shown in examples (a) and (b).   Sequences of two syncopated kororin patterns are given in examples (c) and (d).   In the last the metric balance is restored by a third kororin.   Examples (f) and (g) show "free" syncopated melodies; in example (f) this melody is combined with a syncopated kororin.

Syncopation, in conclusion, is a rather important element in the rhythm of danmono.   In older compositions such as *Rokudan*, *Shichidan*, *Midare*, and *Kudan*, as well as in the late *Kumoi Kudan* and *Akikaze*, its use is very limited and restricted to the not too conspicuous shift of a quarter time value.   A shift of an eighth, which occurs once each in *Midare* and *Kudan*, becomes a common feature in the first two dan of *Hachidan*, and in dan 1 through 4 of *Godan*, which in this respect seems almost a systematic development of *Hachidan*.

Example 65. (a) *Midare*, dan 2; (b) *Kudan*, dan 1; (c) *Hachidan*, dan 1;
(d) *Godan*, dan 1; (e) *Hachidan*, dan 1; (f) *Godan*, dan 1;
(g) *Kumoi Kudan*, dan 2.

Right-hand Techniques in Danmono

A wide variety of right-hand techniques are employed in danmono. They are tabulated in Table 5. In this table, the frequency of occurrence of various techniques is shown for each dan. An exception is made for kakite (shan) which is used so frequently that tabulation is pointless. Its presence in a dan is therefore merely indicated by an asterisk. The techniques are presented in the order in which they were discussed in Chapter V.

Table 5

Composition	Dan	Sukuizume	Awasezume	Kakite	Oshiawase	Uraren (Sararin)	Hikiren	Nagashizume (Kararin)	Hanryu	Waren	Surizume	Warizume	Hankake	Hayakake	Yokozume
Midare	1	1		*								2			
	2			*								1			
	3	2		*		2			1			2			
	4			*								4			
	5			*										1	
	6			*					1	1		10			
	7	1		*						2		2			
	8			*				2		3		4		1	
	9			*					1	1		8		1	
	10	3		*						3					
	11	2		*											
	12		1	*						1					
Total		9	1	*		2		2	3	11		33		3	
Rokudan	1			*								5		1	
	2	1		*							1	2		1	
	3	1		*		1						2		1	
	4			*							1	1			
	5			*								4			
	6		1	*	1	1					1	7			
Total		2	1	*	1	2					3	21		3	
Shichidan	1			*											
	2	1		*								13			
	3			*		1						4			
	4			*							1				
	5			*	1				1		1	4			
	6			*						1	1				
	7		1	*	2					2	3				
Total		1	1	*	3	1			1	3	6	21			
Kudan	1	1		*								4			
	2			*						1	3	3			
	3	1		*								5		1	
	4			*						1	1	10			
	5			*	1						3	7		1	
	6			*								1			
	7			*							1	3			
	8	1		*	1					1		5		1	
	9	1	1	*		1						4			
Total		4	1	*	2	1				3	8	42		3	

Table 5 (continued)

Composition	Dan	Sukuizume	Awasezume	Kakite	Oshiawase	Uraren (Sararin)	Hikiren	Nagashizume (Kararin)	Hanryu	Waren	Surizume	Warizume	Hankake	Hayakake	Yokozume
Hachidan	1			*											
	2			*	1							1			
	3			*				1							
	4			*									1		
	5			*										1	
	6			*	1			1						3	
	7			*	1	1		3		1		4			
	8		1	*											
Total			1	*	3	1		5		1		5	1	4	
Godan	1			*											
	2	1												1	
	3			*											
	4	2													
	5		1	*		1						7			1
Total		3	1	*		1						7		1	1
Kumoi Kudan	1									1					
	2			*	1	1								2	
	3	1		*						1					
	4			*						2					
	5			*											
	6	1		*											
	7	1		*								2		1	
	8				1							14		1	
	9			*	1										
Total		3		*	3	1				4		16		4	
Akikaze	1			*									1		
	2	1		*		1		1						1	
	3	1	1	*			1							3	
	4			*											
	5	2		*							1	2			
	6			*						1					
Total		4	1	*		1	1	1		1	1	2	1	4	

No fewer than thirteen of the total of nineteen right-hand techniques discussed in Chapter V occur in danmono. This, naturally, does not mean that all thirteen techniques are used in one composition: ordinarily, a single composition employs seven to ten different techniques. The selection of these thirteen techniques is to some extent distinctive for danmono; later, it will be shown that in kumiuta a slightly different choice is made. Absent from danmono are the following techniques: uchizume (which never occurs in older types of koto music); two varieties of upward glissando, hanhikiren and hikisute; chirashizume; namigaeshi; and kakezume.

Four of the thirteen techniques are used only once or twice: hikiren and surizume are found in *Akikaze* alone, hankake (in the form "tanhan") in *Hachidan* and *Akikaze,* and yokozume in *Godan* alone. These four, therefore, cannot be considered representative of danmono. Nine right-hand techniques remain that are regularly used, namely:

kakite,	appearing in 8 pieces in 58 dan (of a total of 62 dan)		
warizume,	"	" 8	" " 32 "
sararin,	"	" 8	" " 9 "
waren,	"	" 7	" " 22 "
sukuizume,	"	" 7	" " 20 "
hayakake,	"	" 7	" " 17 "
awasezume,	"	" 7	" " 7 "
kararin,	"	" 5	" " 14 "
oshiawase,	"	" 5	" " 11 "

A number of these techniques typically occur at the end of a danmono; sararin and awasezume have been seen in this location. Oshiawase with its somewhat emphatic character sometimes is also used toward the end of a composition, especially on tone b" (degree V), where it may be used in combination with yuri. In this connection an example occurring in the sixth dan of *Rokudan* has already been discussed. Similar cases occur in *Shichidan,* dan 5, and *Kumoi Kudan,* dan 9. Oshiawase is also found on tones c" and f" (degrees VI and II), upper leading tones for basic degrees V and I, to which they resolve.

Example 66. (a) *Shichidan,* dan 7; (b) *Hachidan,* dan 7.

In the example from *Hachidan,* the final shan takes the place of the expected tone e'.

Waren usually appears as a replacement for shan and is normally followed by either kororin or kararin. The following examples show some typical uses occurring after kororin or at the end of an ascent. Like sararin, kararin appears to be a more dramatic substitute for kororin.

Of these examples, the two from *Midare* show especially the applicability in similar locations of kororin and kararin. Notice, however, how in example (e) tone g' is followed by shan rather than by a single tone a as in example (d), thus preparing the different continuation by kararin instead of the quieter kororin. Kararin often appears at the end of important sections and in this respect is similar to the somewhat more definitive sararin and the more general kororin. The best example of kararin in cadential function has already been given — the final cadence of *Shichidan* (Example 41). Kararin may also be found at the end of an inner dan —see, for example, the conclusion of dan 3 and 6 of *Hachidan,* and dan 8 of *Kudan.*

Example 67. (a) *Shichidan,* dan 6; (b) *Rokudan,* dan 6; (c) *Akikaze,* dan 5; (d) *Midare,* dan 7; (e) *Midare,* dan 6; (f) *Kudan,* dan 2.

The most representative forms of kakezume are not used in danmono. Hankake appears — twice only —in the form of tanhan in *Hachidan* and *Akikaze.* Hayakake, on the other hand, occurs frequently and is the only form of kakezume that survived from kumiuta into later genres, perhaps because it is so self-effacing, as it were, compared with kakezume itself. In the following example (a) and (b) represent tanhan (c), (d), and (e) varieties of hayakake. Typical fingerings employing index finger, middle finger, and thumb have been added.

Example 68. (a) *Hachidan*, dan 8; (b) *Akikaze*, dan 1; (c) *Kumoi Kudan*,
dan 8; (d) *Kudan*, dan 8; (e) *Midare*, dan 5.

Although not representing one of the officially listed techniques, broken octaves must be mentioned as a device frequently used. This is one of the idiomatic techniques of the koto, on which the normal hand position for the right hand spans an octave between thumb and middle or index fingers. Broken octaves are played in ascending order by middle finger and thumb, but occasionally a sequence of broken octaves will be played by index finger-thumb and middle finger-thumb. The following example from *Godan* shows this procedure.

Example 69. *Godan*, dan 1.

Finally, in the later parts of danmono it often occurs that melody tones are alternated with shan or sha-sha (warizume), thus strongly enhancing the general liveliness that characterizes the second half of a piece. Closely related material is found in almost all compositions at the beginning of these later dan, *Kumoi Kudan* and *Akikaze* excepted. Notice in the following three examples that the barlines may occur at different places in similar musical phrases. This should not be equated with different rhythmic interpretation. Each of the three examples consists of basically the same material.

Example 70. (a) *Midare,* dan 12; (b) *Shichidan,* dan 5; (c) *Kudan,* dan 4;
(d) *Hachidan,* dan 7.

Example 71. (a) *Midare,* dan 10; (b) *Rokudan,* dan 4; (c) *Kudan,* dan 9.

Example 72. (a) *Rokudan*, dan 6; *Godan*, dan 5; (c) *Midare*, dan 6; (d) *Shichidan*, dan 3.

PART III

KUMIUTA

CHAPTER X

FUKI, THE FIRST KUMIUTA

It is accepted as a historic fact that the priest Kenjun, who, as was stated in Chapter I, was attached to the Zendōji on the island of Kyūshū, was the composer of the first kumiuta, the Tsukushi-goto composition called *Fuki*. Legend, however, attributes *Fuki* not to Kenjun, but to a group of seven noblemen who during the reign of Emperor Temmon (1532-1555) stayed at the mansion of Ōuchi Yoshitaka in Suō.[1] They had fled their homes in Kyōto because of the battles that raged there, as well as in other parts of Japan, as a result of a struggle for power among several feudal families (Sansom 1943: 401 ff; Reischauer and Fairbank 1958: 570 ff.). In the relative safety of Suō they whiled away their leisure time in a traditional courtly fashion, each composing a poem to be sung to koto accompaniment using the music of *Etenraku*. In this way, according to tradition, the first kumiuta *Fuki*, was born. Because there were seven noblemen, *Fuki* consisted of seven songs, and when, later, one of the noblemen died, subsequent kumiuta contained no more than six songs. This story appeared in the eighteenth century *Sōkyoku Taiishō* and is retold in later works (Fujita 1930: 23; Kikkawa 1961: 5). Kikkawa Eishi gives a version in which Kenjun is said to have been present among the noblemen during their composition of the poems that became the text of *Fuki*. Although the story does not inspire too much confidence it should not be disregarded altogether.

Throughout the Ashikaga period the Ōuchi were among the most powerful families of Japan. They dominated large sections of West Honshū and North Kyūshū: Suō, Nagato, Buzen, Bungo, and Chikuzen. St. Francis Xavier, who in 1551 spent several months in Suō, described the lord of Ōuchi as the most powerful of Japan. The castle town of Yamaguchi, an important harbor thriving on foreign trade, attracted scholars and nobles from war-torn Kyōto. By the early sixteenth century the city had become a center of culture and elegance. The Ōuchi family strongly promoted the arts, especially painting (Sesshu painted his "long scroll" here in 1486) although the other arts were by no means neglected. In the first half of the sixteenth century Yamaguchi, which was known as one of the strongholds of poetry, was visited by a nō group of the Kanze school (Sansom 1958: 234, 239, and 262; 1962: 380 and 401). In this milieu poetic-musical activities such as the one described above may well have taken place in Suō. The possibility of Kenjun's presence at one of those meetings must be discarded, however, because the fief of Yoshitaka, the then head of the Ōuchi family, was attacked in 1551, shortly after which the power of his family was destroyed. In 1551, Kenjun was four years old.

Etenraku in the sixteenth century had long been, as it has remained until today, one of the most popular compositions in the gagaku repertoire. When, around 980 at the Kyōto court, new texts of contemporary interest were set to existing music, *Etenraku* was one of the favorite melodies used. The new genre, imayō[2] (literally "contemporary songs"), subsequently became very popular and it is frequently mentioned in literary classics such as *Makura no Sōshi* (eleventh century), *Genji Monogatari* (eleventh century), and *Heike Monogatari* (thirteenth century).[3] Therefore, if the noblemen in Suō sang at all, they may well have sung imayō to the music of *Etenraku*.

The legend about *Fuki* contains three points of musical importance. First the connection between Tsukushi-goto and the ancient court traditions of sōkyoku is once more affirmed. Second, a rencontre between the court aristocracy and the priesthood of the Zendōji is mentioned, if not a meeting with Kenjun himself (also a priest) in the feudal mansion of Ōuchi Yoshitaka, yet at least contacts with the priests in Kurume have been likely. Third, the story relates that *Etenraku* was the musical source of *Fuki*, a point that is easily proved by comparing the scores, and that is corroborated by the fact that *Etenraku* is used as an alternative title for *Fuki*.

Not only the music but also the text of *Fuki* can be traced back to a time before Kenjun. Old collections of texts sung to the koto, preserved in the Kofukuji in Nara and the Sampōin in Daigo near Kyōto, the *Kofukuji-Ennenbushi* and the *Shinsōgochō*, contain several texts that are very similar to those of later kumiuta such as *Fuki, Umegae, Kokoro Zukushi, Kiritsubo,* and *Usuyuki* (Takano 1926: 746-751; Fujita 1930: 23-24; Kikkawa 1961: 5-6;). When Yatsuhashi Kengyō, two student generations after Kenjun, composed a new version of *Fuki*, he secured the continuation of the old texts into the present.

The direct link between *Etenraku* and *Fuki* must be looked for in the similarities in the koto parts rather than in their melodies. In Example 73, the notations of *Etenraku, Fuki* of Tsukushi-goto, and *Fuki* of zokusō are given (in Arabic rather than Japanese numerals) one over the other. In the case of the first two, the shizugaki patterns have been written out completely, although the traditional gagaku notation does not give more than the basic octave of the pattern. The tunings, different for gagaku and Tsukushi-goto and again different for zokusō, have been disregarded as irrelevant since the agreement is a matter of string numbers rather than pitches.

Etenraku is not represented in its entirety because only the first sixteen measures (without repetition) have been used for *Fuki*. Its construction is very regular, consisting of eight alternations of one measure of shizugaki and one measure of kozume. Notice the repetition of the first two measures in measures 3 and 4. Because the kozume consist of only one tone, the even-numbered measures in which they occur are conspicuously empty compared to the odd-numbered ones. In the orchestral context this distribution of tonal material works very well. In soloistic music, on the other hand, such a regularly occurring scarcity of tones would be disturbingly monotonous and indeed the even-numbered measures appear to be the places where most of the changes were made. A first step in this direction may be observed in the rinzetsu version of the koto part in *Etenraku*. Comparing this version with the standard one, it appears that the odd-numbered measures remain unaltered, changes being limited to even-numbered measures (measure 11 excepted). In the nokorigaku version of *Etenraku*, the repetition of the first four measures has been written out because it involves variation.

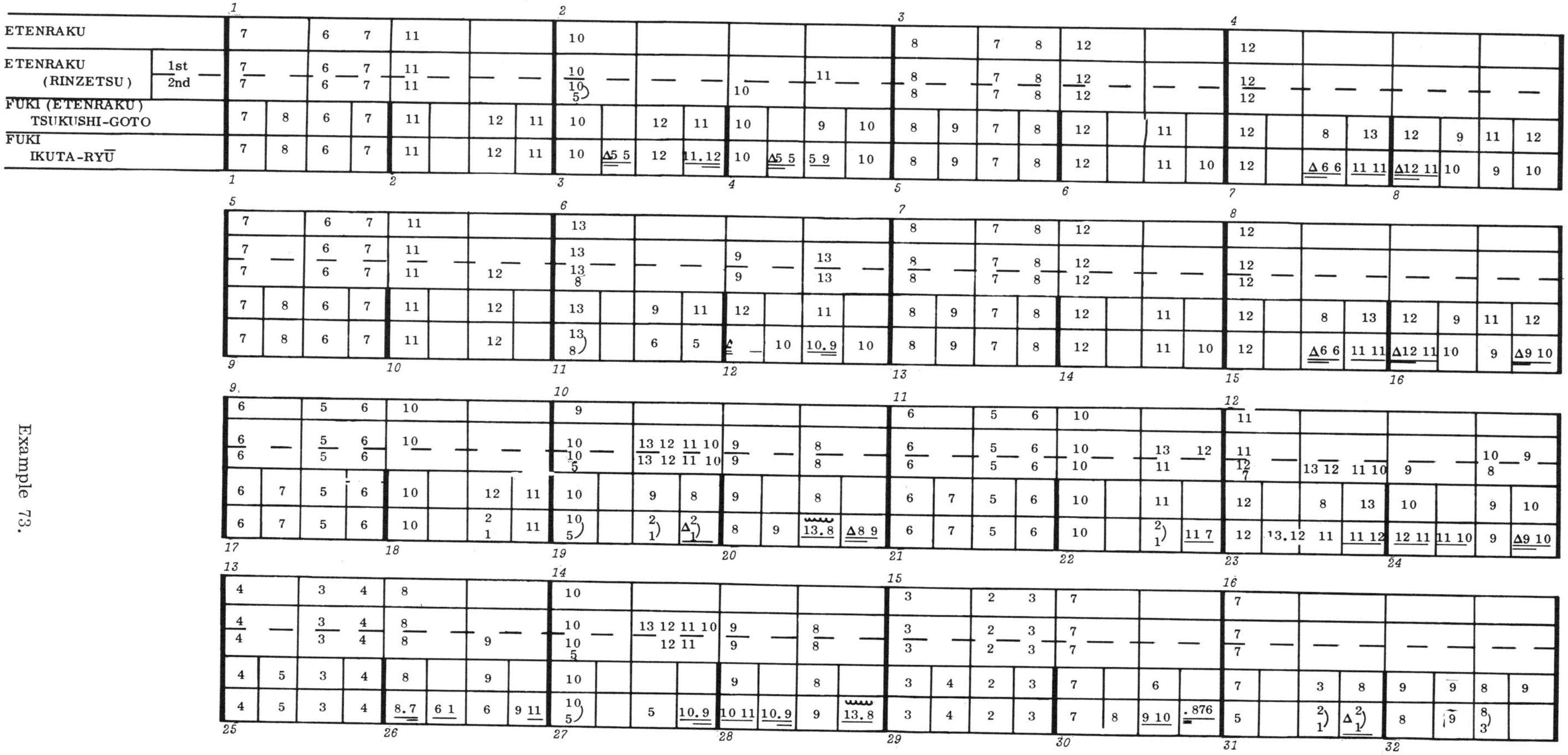

ETENRAKU

ETENRAKU
(RINZETSU)

FUKI (ETENRAKU)
TSUKUSHI-GOTO

FUKI
IKUTA-RYŪ

1st
2nd

Example 73.

More radical changes are found when we compare *Etenraku* with the *Fuki* of Tsukushi-goto. First of all, we notice that the number of measures has been doubled (from sixteen to thirty-two), a logical consequence of the growing number of notes. The gagaku shizugaki pattern has been replaced by a related pattern, kakezume, which resembles a cross of shizugaki and haya-gaki. This relationship between gagaku and sōkyoku patterns will be discussed in more detail later. The agreement between the patterns is more striking than their differences. Both share, as the most essential element, the octave between second and fourth and third and fifth tones, respectively. Moreover, the tones outlined by these octaves are the same for both *Etenraku* and *Fuki*. Not only the octave patterns, but also the kozume of *Etenraku* are, almost without exception, found at the same locations in *Fuki*. In this regard, there are only two differences—between measures 10 and 12 of *Etenraku* and the corresponding measures 20 and 24 in *Fuki*. These differences occur at noteworthy locations in the score of *Etenraku*. Comparing the koto part with the parts of the other instruments of the gagaku ensemble, we note perfect agreement with the exception of the same two kozume. The following example, showing the shō ryūteki, hichiriki, koto, and biwa,[4] illustrates this point.

Example 74. *Etenraku*.

The two deviating kozume, played on strings 9 and 11 respectively, are indicated with arrows. It is noteworthy that the pitches occurring simultaneously on the other instruments are no higher than could be reached on the koto by left-hand pressure. We know that the technique of left-hand pressure existed in gagaku and it would not have been unlikely if it were used at these two places. A certain lack of confidence in the *Etenraku* score at these locations becomes still stronger in view of the rinzetsu version of the koto, which at both measures 10 and 12 disagrees with the standard version, but agrees with the Kenjun *Fuki*. Beyond pointing out that the gagaku score itself shows the koto part in disagreement with the rest of the ensemble at these locations, we cannot yet offer a satisfying explanation for the two deviant kozume in Kenjun's *Fuki*. Intriguing as this discrepancy may be, however, it hardly contradicts the general similarity between the two parts.

Kenjun, using the koto as the only instrument accompanying the voice, was forced to elaborate the instrumental part in order to prevent a monotonous repetition of the same pattern alternated with only a single tone. The most obvious way was to develop the kozume and this he did in a manner similar to, but more consistent than, that already in use in the rinzetsu practice in gagaku. He also made it a common practice to connect, by the addition of a few tones, the final tone of the kakezume pattern with the beginning of the next measure — the place where in gagaku the kozume would normally be encountered. This practice may also be found occasionally in the rinzetsu version, but so rarely that its occurrences must be considered exceptions. In principle, however, all of Kenjun's innovations existed already in gagaku. One might expect a similarity between the rinzetsu version of the koto part of *Etenraku* and *Fuki*, since both are attempts to enliven the material, but this is seldom the case. It is apparent that Kenjun employed the standard, not the rinzetsu, version of the koto part of *Etenraku* as his point of departure in composing *Fuki*.

The changes Kenjun made in deriving *Fuki* from *Etenraku* are characteristic. The chart on page 149 shows the various progressions from tone to tone, first as they appear in *Etenraku*, then as they are expanded by Kenjun in *Fuki*. The columns "Progression *Etenraku*" and "Progression *Fuki*" contain string numbers. In the column "Comment" the main characteristic of the added tones is pointed out. Measure numbers refer to *Etenraku*.

The principle appears simple. Repeated tones on degree IV are enlivened by the insertion of a lower neighbor before the repetition (examples a and b). Where in *Etenraku* degree I or V is preceded by the second lower string, in *Fuki* the gap is filled in, thus creating patterns similar to patterns IV and III in danmono (examples c and d). The descending patterns found in danmono are also used: pattern II (descent from degrees IV to I) occurs in examples (e), (f), and (g); pattern I (descent from I to V) is found in examples (h) and (i). Another upward progression, one not met before, is VI-II-IV (examples j, k, and I). An alternation of degree IV with its upper neighbor, preceded by its lower octave, occurs twice (examples j and k). Notice that the simpler progressions occur in the odd-numbered measures, that is, in the locations corresponding to the progressions from shizugaki and kozume. The even-numbered measures in *Etenraku* contain the progression from kozume to the following shizugaki pattern and correspond with longer and more complex progressions in *Fuki*.

The above shows Kenjun as an arranger rather than a composer. When we compare his *Fuki* with that by Yatsuhashi Kengyō, we find the latter in a very similar role. Yatsuhashi's main innovation consisted of the introduction of a new scale, the in-scale, with which he was familiar because of his past as a shamisen player. Comparing the scores, we find a strong resemblance between the two *Fuki*. All kakezume and all tones corresponding with the original kozume (on the first beat of the even-numbered measures) agree — with the exception of the last measure, which, however, is of no essential importance. Yatsuhashi Kengyō proceeded somewhat farther in the same process that Kenjun had begun by elaborating still more the original kozume. In general outline he follows his model in Tsukushi-goto, but the rhythmic differentiation becomes more subtle, with the use of time values down to sixteenths where Kenjun

	Measure *Etenraku*	Progression *Etenraku*	Progression *Fuki* (Tsukushi-goto)	Progression in Scale Degrees *Fuki*	Comment
(a)	15	7-7	7-6-7	IV-II-IV	Lower neighbor
(b)	3, 7	12-12	12-11-12	IV-II-IV	Lower neighbor
(c)	13	8-10	8-9-10	V-VI-I	Passing tone (Pattern: V-VI-I)
(d)	5	11-13	11-12-13	II-IV-V	Passing tone (Pattern: II-IV-V)
(e)	9	10-10	10-12-11-10	I-IV-II-I	Pattern (IV-II-I)
(f)	1	11-10	11-12-11-10	II-IV-II-I	Pattern (IV-II-I)
(g)	2	10-8	10-12-11-10-9-10-8	I-IV-II-I-VI-I-V	Pattern (IV-II-I) plus lower neighbor
(h)	14	10-3	10-9-8-3	I-VI-V-V	Pattern (I-VI-V)
(i)	10	10-6	10-9-8-9-8-6	I-VI-V-VI-V-II	Pattern (I-VI-V)
(j)	4	12-7	12-8-13-12-9-11-12-7	IV-V-V-IV-VI-II-IV-IV	Upper neighbor VI-II-IV
(k)	8	12-10	12-8-13-12-11-12-10	IV-V-V-IV-VI-II-IV-I	Upper neighbor VI-II-IV
(l)	6	13-8	13-9-11-12-11-8	V-VI-II-IV-II-V	VI-II-IV

did not go farther (at least in this movement) than quarter notes. The occurrence of two sararin contributes to the general impression that Yatsuhashi strove after a finer differentiation of rhythm and more complicated technical means. The technical complexity is important, for it is related to the fact that with zokusō the real professional koto musician emerged. However proficient a Tsukushi-goto performer may have been, he always had another, official profession, that of a priest or a scholar by whom music perhaps was passionately loved, yet to whom it was no more than a gentlemanly *passe-temps,* certainly never a major source of income. Zokusō, on the other hand, came into the hands of professional musicians, often blind, for whom music was a living, not a pastime. Professionalism inevitably leads to technical development. Sōkyoku is no exception.

Various forms of kakezume occur in kumiuta. Almost all of them can be shown to be related to either shizugaki, hayagaki, or sugagaki in gagaku (see Example 75).

Example 75.

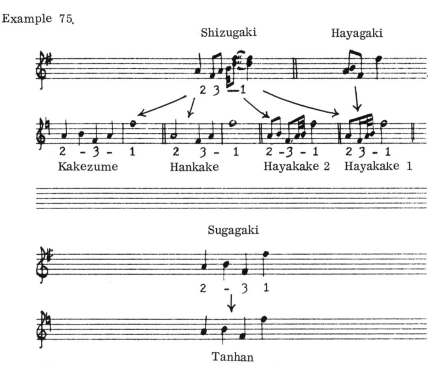

The tuning by Kenjun in *Fuki* seems unrelated not only to any of the three tunings that may be used for *Etenraku* (hyōjō, banshikichō) but also to other gagaku tunings, except for the circumstance that this tuning, like those in gagaku, consists of major seconds and minor thirds. The fact that the tuning of Tsukushi-goto is called ichikotsu-chō does not imply that it is the same as ichikotsu-chō in gagaku: in point of fact, the tuning pattern of ichokotsu-chō in Tsukushi-goto has no exact parallel in gagaku. In practice, all twelve transpositions of the basic tuning pattern of Tsukushi-goto may be called ichikotsu-chō. This practice, however, must be considered to be a corruption of a system that more specifically designates each individual transposition according to the name of the pitch of the second string. Thus, when the name of that pitch is ichikotsu (d), the name of the tuning is ichikotsu-chō; when string 2 is tuned to ōshiki (a), the tuning should be called ōshiki-chō, and so on (Hirano-Kishibe 1955: 24). The origin of Tsukushi-goto's tuning is not clear. In the course of a short discussion of Tsukushi-goto in the *Shichiku Shoshinshū* (Takano 1928: 192-193) the method according to which a koto is to be tuned to ichikotsu-chō is explained as follows: tune string 1 to ichikotsu, string 2 to shimomu, 3 to ōshiki, 4 to banshiki, 5 to ichikotsu, 6 to hyōjō, 7 one octave above 2, 8 one octave above 3, etc. The result is a tuning in which only one pitch, that of the second string, differs from gagaku ichikotsu-chō—see Example 76 (a) and (b). Hayashi (1957: 26) assumes that this tuning, which should represent a transitory stage, was soon (no later than Genroku) modified by replacing the shimomu of strings 2, 7, and 12 by sōjō, as in Example 76 (c). Although this hypothesis deserves serious consideration, the possibility of a mistake in the explanation of the tuning method in the *Shichiku Shoshinshū* may not be excluded. First, because mistakes are by no means absent in this book; second, because no other tuning pattern containing an interval of a sixth between the first two strings is known; third, while the given tuning does not work for the compositions contained in the same work, the modified tuning, which uses sōjō instead of shimomu, does.

Example 76. Ichikotsu-chō in gagaku (a), *Schichiku Shoshinshū* (b), and Tsukushi-goto (c).

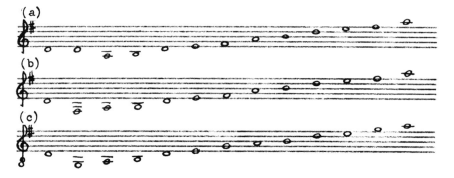

Fuki consists of several uta. In Tsukushi-goto the number varies according to the manuscript, the highest being nine, in which version the second uta is *Umegae*. Later, *Umegae* was to become a separate kumiuta, a fact that explains the close similarity between *Fuki* and *Umegae* in zokusō. Yatsuhashi's *Fuki* consists of seven uta, one more than the usual number. This version of *Fuki* (as performed in the Ikuta-ryū) will be the object of a detailed analysis; since Yatsuhashi Kengyō closely followed his model in Tsukushi-goto, it is not necessary to go into more detail about the older composition.

Before turning to the analysis of the zokusō *Fuki*, however, it is well to summarize the kumiuta heritage from gagaku as exemplified in *Fuki*, bearing in mind that which is true of *Fuki* in this respect is also true generally of all kumiuta:

1. The form of each uta is directly derived from a part of *Etenraku* and consists of thirty-two measures of 4/4 (or 2/2), organized in eight phrases of four measures each. In the case of the first uta of *Fuki*, each of the phrases begins with a kakezume pattern. The severity and symmetry of the form of the first uta leads one to expect that release from these limitations will be sought in later uta, and to a certain degree this happens, although never (except in one atypical piece, *Kambun Otsu no Kyoku*) is the length of thirty-two measures abandoned.

2. The various forms of kakezume apparently were derived directly from related patterns in gagaku.

3. The tempo of the first uta of *Fuki* is about the same as that of *Etenraku*.

4. The tuning of Kenjun's *Fuki* is directly related to hyōjō in gagaku.

Fuki or *Fuki-gumi*, in its arrangement by Yatsuhashi Kengyō, is the best known of all kumiuta, probably because, as the first of the omotegumi, all of which are in hira-jōshi, it is the first to be taught to the students of sōkyoku. Like its model in Tsukushi-goto, Yatsuhashi's *Fuki* is also sometimes called *Etenraku*. The text, consisting of seven poems, was taken from the *Genji Monogatari* and the *Wakan Roei Shū*. The first, introductory uta may be performed as an independent song, in which case it is called *Fuki no Kyoku*.

In the present transcription the songs are numbered 1 through 7, which is modern practice. Older sources, however, consider the first uta as an introduction and start the numbering with the second, thus conforming to the traditional limitation of a kumiuta to six songs.[5] The whole may be preceded by an instrumental introduction, the *maebiki*, of sixteen measures containing musical material closely related to that of the following uta. This maebiki is not included in printed collections before Satō's *Kumiuta Zenshū* (1941). According to Satō, the maebiki is to be performed only on official occasions.

The first uta of *Fuki* contains eight phrases of four measures each and each phrase is opened, and therefore determined by, a kakezume pattern. Consequently, the musical content of this uta may be adequately characterized by the sequence in which these patterns appear. Kakezume patterns are traditionally identified by their final tone (the higher tone of the basic octave) and are so indicated in older notations. Thus, the sequence of kakezume is as follows: 11, 12, 11, 12, 10, 10, 8, 7. Comparing the construction of this first uta with that of the following ones, it becomes apparent that the structure throughout the composition is determined by that of the first uta and, consequently, by the structure of *Etenraku* (see Table 6).

As was expected, the extreme structural severity of the first uta, each phrase beginning with kakezume, is gradually released. In the second uta two "free" phrases occur, while in the seventh uta no more than one kakezume pattern is encountered; typically, it occurs in the last phrase. The reader will recall that the tempo gradually increases from uta to uta, but in the last phrase of the last uta, returns to the initial tempo. Here, as in numerous other kumiuta, this return is accompanied by a return of kakezume. The kakezume in *Fuki* belong to the five-tone type, except one found in the last phrase of uta 5 which belongs to the mukōhan variety. This type is indicated here, as it will be indicated in later cases also, by double underlining. The "total" at the bottom of the chart shows the number of kakezume per uta.

Table 6

Phrase	Uta						
	1	2	3	4	5	6	7
1	11	11	11	11	11	11	
2	12	12	12	12	12	12	
3	11	11	11	11	11		
4	12	12	12	12	7		
5	10				=		
6	10						
7	8	8	8				
8	7	7	7		7		7
					=		=
Total	8	6	6	4	5	2	1

With the strong relationship between the various first, second, third, and so on, phrases established now, a simultaneous analysis of the phrases that will permit direct comparison will be given. Important as the vocal part may be, for the time being it will not be considered. This is justifiable because the voice sings only a version of the melody that occurs in the instrument. The koto part may be considered the more important of the two, being complete in itself, while the voice part is interrupted by many rests. Moreover, the absence of the voice part from older (*Kinkyoku Shifu, Sōkyoku Taiishō*) as well as from most modern notations (*Yamada-ryū, Koto no Kagami*) supports the musical priority of the koto part.

As a logical development of our previous discussion of the historic origin of *Fuki*, the structure of the piece will be our first and main concern. This involves the questions of four measure phrases, the opening of a phrase with a kakezume or the possible replacement of that pattern, the halfway point in the phrase (comparable to the location of the kozume in *Etenraku*,) the ending of the phrase, and the use of specific techniques and patterns.

Fuki, Phrase 1

In Example 77 are shown the first phrases of all seven uta, plus the maebiki. The absence of kakezume at the opening of uta 7 is significant but structurally less important than might be expected. The kakezume pattern is replaced by another octave pattern, warizume, that outlines the same octave between tones f' and f''. With this difference noted, the phrase may be treated like the others. In phrases only four measures in length in which one and a half measures at the beginning are determined by a standard pattern, the important question becomes whether the patterns are continued in standard ways also. Skeletons of the continuation are given in Example 78.

The first tone given in this example for maebiki and each uta represents the last tone of kakezume or warizume involved. Skeletal tones are given in open notes, additional tones in black notes. We notice, first of all, that in all examples there occurs in measure 3 a progression from tone f'' to tone e'', in scale degrees from II to I. A progression from degree II, functioning as an upper leading tone and therefore as a melodic dissonance, to its logical resolution on degree I could be expected. Tone e'' (degree I) remains the melodic axis through the fourth measure except in uta 5 and 6, which proceed to tone b' (degree V).

Example 77. *Fuki*, phrase 1.

Example 78.

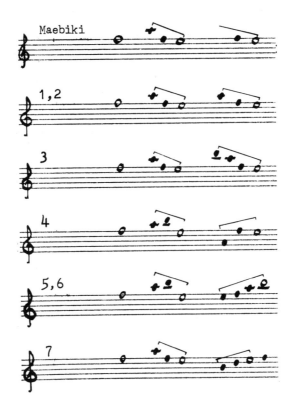

Tone e'' is in most of the cases reached from above, the usual progression being a''-f''-e''. Tone a'' may be replaced by tone a' (uta 4) or shan (maebiki). In addition, tone b'' is included in most of the uta, sometimes by an ato-oshi after tone a'' (Example 77, all uta except the sixth), or by plucking of the thirteenth string (Example 77, uta 4, 5, and 6). In all uta we recognize this descent from degree IV (or V) to degree I to be pattern II as it occurs in danmono. Once, in uta 7, tone e'' is reached from below by the sequence b'-d''-e'' (degrees V-VII-I), reproducing pattern IV of danmono. Tone b'', finally, is reached by the upward progression from tone e'', degrees I-II-IV-V, which is danmono pattern III. (Danmono pattern I appears in first phrases at less essential locations in a connecting function. See the third measures of uta 3, 4, and 7, Example 77). Thus, the kakezume patterns that open the phrases are indeed followed in standard ways, namely, by the same melodic patterns I through IV used in danmono.

Frequently the phrases end in a "codetta," an affirmation of the tone that is reached as the goal of the melodic movement. Where this final tone is tone e'' and is reached from above, it is followed by its lower neighbor before being repeated (maebiki and uta 1, 2, and 3). When this tone is tone b'' and is reached from below, its higher neighbor appears before the tone is repeated (uta 5 and 6). The occurrences of these codettas strongly contribute to the closed character of the phrases. In uta 7, however, the progression beyond tone e'' to tone f'' provides an immediate link to the next phrase.

Compared with the following uta, the rhythm of the maebiki is extremely simple and uniform; it consists of little more than a repeated anapest: quarter, quarter, half. In the uta, most of the rhythmic activity is found in the second half of the phrases, where it adds a new element to the repeated melodic patterns. Notice the characteristic ♪♫♩ rhythm in measures 3 and 4 of the first and second uta. The first two tones of this rhythm, which usually follows a tone of the same denomination in the higher octave, are played with the middle finger. As always, the use of the middle finger widens the range and we can observe this especially in the second half of the phrase of uta 5 and 6. In order to understand the sometimes wide leaps in koto music, we must always consider the characteristic fingerings, and that the use of the middle finger and index finger frequently results in displacements of an octave or more. Passages that initially seem somewhat puzzling can often be clarified by disregarding octave or two-octave leaps. In this light, measures 3 and 4 of the third uta, for example, prove to be little more than a descending scale.

We may summarize as follows:

1. All phrases, whether or not they begin with a kakezume pattern, follow the outline provided originally by *Etenraku*. Only uta 7 does not begin with the kakezume; instead, it employs another octave pattern, warizume, that outlines the same octave.

2. After the conclusion of the opening pattern on tone f'', all phrases develop toward tone e'' in the third measure. This is a logical progression from a melodic dissonance (degree II) to a melodic consonance (degree I).

3. In measure 4, the phrase either continues to center on tone e'' or, less frequently, moves up to tone b'' (degree V) (uta 5 and 6). In all cases, therefore, the phrases move toward a basic degree of the mode, either I or V.

4. The occurrence of codettas strongly affirms the newly reached basic tones. In the first phrases, the codettas require the only use of a tone produced by left-hand pressure, in this case, tone d'' (degree VII). Most phrases form a closed unit. A direct link to the next phrase is found only in uta 7.

5. The sequence of patterns is as follows:

      Maebiki and uta through 4:   II, II
      Uta 5 and 6:   II, III
      Uta 7:   II, IV

6. Rhythmic differentiation is strongest in the second half of the phrases. Anticipating, it may be mentioned that this is typical of the beginning uta, that is, the slower ones. Later uta derive sufficient activity from their faster speed.

Fuki, Phrase 2

The discussion of the remaining phrases requires less detail and on the whole follows the points of the summary given above. Example 79 shows phrase 2.

1. All phrases start with kakezume on string 12 except uta 7, where kakezume is replaced by a warizume that outlines the same octave as the kakezume.

2. As in *Etenraku*, all phrases except maebiki and uta 6 give tone a'' (degree IV) in measure 7. In the two exceptions, tone a'' is replaced by tone e'' (degree I).

3. All uta except 7 reach tone e'' in measure 8. In uta 7 tone f'' is emphasized. It occurs in a characteristic pattern, consisting of two shan, followed by tone f''. Although in many cases this pattern is eventually followed by degree I, its character is so strongly determined by the second degree that it may be referred to as "cadence on degree II."

4. All phrases have a closed ending on tone e'' (degree I), emphasized by a codetta except the second phrase in uta 7, which leads directly to the third phrase.

Example 79. *Fuki*, phrase 2.

5. The distribution of the patterns is as follows:

> Maebiki and uta 1 through 6: II, II
> Uta 7:   II, Cadence on degree II

6. Maximum rhythmic activity is found in the second half of the phrases, except in uta 7.

7. *Ai-no-te* (short instrumental interludes) occur in measures 7 and 8, following the point indicated by an asterisk.

Fuki, Phrase 3

Phrase 3, opening with the same kakezume pattern as phrase 1, allows an interesting comparison:

Example 80. *Fuki*, phrase 3.

1. In all uta except uta 6 and 7, the third phrase begins with kakezume on string 11. In uta 6 that pattern is replaced by a warizume that leads to string 11. In uta 7, measure 9 gives the conclusion of the unfinished previous phrase. In measure 10 of this uta a warizume pattern outlines the same octave as outlined by the kakezume patterns in measure 9 of uta 1-5. As kakezume patterns normally require more than one measure for their completion, this delayed introduction of the basic octave is not structurally alien.

2. All uta develop to tone b'' in measure 11. This is distinctively unlike phrase 1. This different development, of course, has its source in *Etenraku*, but it is a logical one. We have seen that in the third measure of the first three phrases the melodic line ascends to a highpoint which is tone e'' in measure 3, tone a'' in measure 7, and tone b'' in measure 11. The gradual rise of the phrasal peaks corresponds to a rise in tension and, for a moment anticipating by observing that the highpoint of phrase 4 will be tone e'', we can conclude that the climax of the first half of the uta is reached in the third measure of the third phrase.

3. Like phrases 1 and 2, phrase 3 does not always end with the same tone. In five uta this tone is tone e'', in two (uta 4 and 5) it is tone b'', which is the final element in a cadence consisting of a repeated shan followed by tone b. This cadence will be referred to as "cadence on degree V." All phrases form closed units. Only in uta 5 can a tendency toward connection with the following phrase be perceived. The feeling of a definite ending is strengthened by the occurrence of codettas at the end of all phrases except uta 5. Note the use of lower as well as upper neighbor of the final tone in uta 7.

4. The following is the sequence of patterns:

> Maebiki and uta 1, 2, 3, 6, and 7: III, II
> Uta 4 and 5:   III, Cadence on degree V

5. Again, especially in uta 1-6, maximum rhythmic activity is reached in the second half of the phrase.

Fuki, Phrase 4

Phrase 4 shows a general similarity to phrase 2:

Example 81. *Fuki*, phrase 4.

Although all the seven uta still show strong common features, there is less uniformity in phrase 4 than in the preceding phrases.

1.   Kakezume on string 12 opens the phrase in maebiki and uta 1-4. It is replaced in uta 5 by kakezume on string 7, the lower octave of 12; in uta 6 and 7 it is replaced by warizume outlining the same octave.

2.   In measure 15 the opening pattern has developed to tone e'' in maebiki and uta 4 and 5; to tone a'' in uta 1, 2, and 7; to tone b'' in uta 3; and to tone c'' in uta 6.

3.   In measure 16 maebiki and uta 1 come to a complete close upon tone e''. The remaining uta, except uta 6, end with a cadence on degree II, which implies that the phrase leads over directly into phrase 5. In uta 6 the phrase ends on degree II also, with the same implications. Maebiki and uta 1 both end the phrase with a codetta.

4.   The sequence of patterns is as follows:

> Maebiki and uta 1 and 6: II, II
>
> Uta 2, 4, and 7:   II, Cadence on degree II
>
> Uta 3:   III, Cadence on degree II
>
> Uta 5:   IV, Cadence on degree II

5.   In the first three uta the maximum rhythmic activity is again met in the second half of the phrase. Uta 4 and 7 show the more unified rhythmic movement that is often characteristic of uta in faster tempo.

6.   Ai-no-te occur in measure 15 fillowing the point indicated by an asterisk.

7.   The maebiki ends at this point.

Fuki, Phrase 5

The similarity among the uta lessens considerably in measures 17-20.

Example 82. *Fuki*, phrase 5.

1. In strong contrast to the preceding four phrases, phrase 5 opens with kakezume only in uta 1. The substitution of warizume for kakezume, encountered several times in the previous phrases, is conspicuously absent. In uta 2 and 3, however, an awasezume produces the tones e' and e'', the same basic octave outlined by the kakezume in uta 1. A single tone e'' occurs at the same location in uta 6, while in uta 7 a tone e' occurs three times in alternation with shan an octave lower. Therefore, tone e'' is still central in the opening of the phrase in five

of the seven uta. As the preceding phrase in uta 2 through 7 remained unresolved on tone f", tone e" now provides the resolution. In uta 4 and 5, however, the expected resoluton on tone e" does not occur until measure 19 and is reached by way of tones b' (uta 4) and b" (uta 5). Uta 4 moves to tone b' by means of a hayakake pattern, the only occurrence of this pattern in *Fuki*.

2. In the third measure of the phrase, the location of the kozume, all uta agree on tone e". Note that in uta 6 and 7 this tone is reached on the second and third beat, respectively.

3. In uta 1 and 7 measure 20 centers on tone b', in uta 2-5 the center is tone e', and uta 6 concludes the measure on tone f'. Uta 2, 4, and 6 maintain a flux which, however, is provided in different ways: in uta 2 and 4, after tone e' is reached in measure 20, it is left immediately to allow a smooth connection with the next phrase; in uta 6 pattern II remains unfinished on tone f'. A codetta occurs only in uta 1.

4. The following sequence of patterns is found:

> Uta 1:   II, Cadence on degree V
> Uta 2-6:   II, II
> Uta 7:   II, I

5. Maximum rhythmic activity is encountered in the second half of the phrase in uta 1-3, in the first half in uta 4 and 5. In uta 5 this rhythmic activity coincides with the postponed resolution. We may be justified now in concluding that, in general, the maximum rhythmic activity in a phrase occurs just before a resolution. Usually this occurrence will be in the third and fourth measures of a four-measure phrase. Where, however, the resolution is postponed to the succeeding phrase, the increase in rhythmic activity may also be postponed.

Fuki, Phrase 6

The tendency toward freer construction, already clear in phrase 5, is continued in phrase 6 (Example 83).

1. Phrase 6, like phrase 5, opens with kakezume only in uta 1. Tone e", the final tone of the kakezume, is clearly present in uta 2, 5, and 7 (where it is reached by means of a warizume). The same tone is given a certain prominence in uta 3 where in measures 21 and 22 it is the goal of the melodic movement. In uta 4, the position of tone e" requires it to be regarded as the most important tone at the opening of the phrase. In uta 6, however, where tone e' would be expected as resolution of the foregoing tone f', it is conspicuously absent.

2. In most of the previous phrases, the halfway point of the phrase could be easily identified by the occurrence of a longer note value, usually a half note. This was less true of phrase 5; it is not true at all of phrase 6 which, therefore, has a quality of integrality. However, it is possible to determine where the caesura occurs. It falls on tone f" in uta 1 (measure 23, beat 3), uta 2 (measure 23, beat 2), uta 6 (measure 22, beat 4), and uta 7 (measure 22, beat 3). Uta 3 ends the first half of the phrase more conventionally on tone e" (measure 22, beat 4), while uta 4 and 5 employ tone b' (measure 22, beat 4).

Example 83. *Fuki*, phrase 6.

3.   Uta 1, 2, 6, and 7 conclude the phrase on tone e''; in uta 3 tone e'' is followed by tone b'; in uta 4 and 5 tone e' is followed by tone b'. The phrase is convincingly concluded at the end of measure 24 in all cases and in this respect is distinguished from phrase 5. The sequence of a phrase with an open ending followed by a close phrase suggests a two-phrase unit.

4.   The sequence of patterns is somewhat more complicated than that of the preceding phrase, which could be schematized by two patterns. Now, in some instances, three or more patterns are found. Not all are equally important and in the following scheme the less important patterns are closed in parentheses:

Uta 1:	(III), II		II		
Uta 2 and 7:	III,		II		
Uta 3:	(III), II,	(III),	II,	(I)	
Uta 4 and 5:	I,		II,	(III)	
Uta 6:	II,		II		

5. In uta 1 and 2 maximum rhythmic activity is found in the second half of the phrase; in uta 3-7 the rhythmic movement remains approximately constant throughout.

Fuki, Phrase 7

The concluding two phrases in the uta return to a simpler structure. Example 84 shows phrase 7.

1. Kakezume are found at the beginning of phrase 7 in uta 1-3. Uta 4 substitutes kakezume by a broken octave on the same tone (b') in measure 25; in uta 5 tone b' is reached at the beginning of measure 26; in uta 6 a warizume outlines the same octave as the kakezume in uta 1; uta 7 emphasizes tone b' only slightly as the movement proceeds to tone e' at the beginning of measure 26.

2. The midpoint of the phrase is on tone e" in uta 1, 2, 3, and 6, where it occurs on the first beat of measure 27. In uta 4 and 5 tone e" appears on beat 4 of measure 26. Uta 7 deviates by sounding tone b' instead of tone e".

3. The phrase ends on tone b' in all uta except 4 and 7. Measure 28 of uta 4 ends on tone f' and therefore the resolution on tone e' may be expected in the following measure. In uta 7 (the concluding uta) the phrase ends on tone e'.

4. The pattern sequence is as follows:

Uta 1:	II,	I
Uta 2:	II, (III),	II, (I)
Uta 3:	IV, (II),	I
Uta 4:	II,	I, (II)
Uta 5:	IV,	III
Uta 6:	IV,	I
Uta 7:	I, (IV),	II

5. In general, the rhythmic activity is equally divided between both halves of the phrase.

Example 84. *Fuki*, phrase 7,

Fuki, Phrase 8

Phrase 8, the concluding phrase, even more than phrase 7 returns to the regularity of the beginning (see Example 85).

1. Phrase 8 of uta 1, 2, 3, and 7 begins with kakezume on string 7 (tone a'). Uta 5 shows the only example in *Fuki* of a mukōhan-kakezume. Uta 4 develops from warizume on tone e' up to tone a' in measure 30. Measure 29 of uta 6, finally, begins with a broken octave on tones a and a'. Thus, all examples in some way or other emphasize tone a' at the beginning of the phrase.

2. All examples except uta 4 develop to tone e' in measure 31. Uta 4 arrives at tone a'.

3. The end of all uta except 7 is reached by means of a cadence on degree V. This cadence appears in its most typical form in uta 1, 4, 5, and 6; the versions in uta 2 and 3 provide a connection to the next uta, which follows without interruption. Uta 7, the final uta, ends on tone e' played simultaneously on strings 1 and 5. It is preceded by two sararin that begin on tones b'' and e'', respectively, the second one ending on tone a'. This final cadence, one frequently met at the conclusion of a kumiuta, outlines all three basic tones of the mode. It will henceforth be referred to as cadence on degree I. Thus, only two of the seven uta vary the final cadence to lead into the next uta, all others ending conclusively.

Example 85: *Fuki,* phrase 8.

4. The pattern sequence. In measures 29-30 the patterns frequently follow each other in rapid succession. Where it is impossible to determine which is the more important, they are given below in the order in which they occur, connected by a hyphen:

> Uta 1, 2, 5, and 6: IV-II, Cadence on degree V
> Uta 3:   II, Cadence on degree V
> Uta 4:   III, Cadence on degree V
> Uta 7:   II, Cadence on degree I

5. The rhythmic activity tends to diminish in the final cadence, except in those cases where the cadences lead over to the following uta.

In matters of tonal material, rhythm, left- and right-hand techniques, and ornamentation there is considerable agreement between the kumiuta *Fuki* and danmono. As these elements were treated in detail in the discussion of danmono, an intensive treatment of their function in kumiuta would be repetitive and we shall limit ourselves to a brief enumeration.

The basic tonal material of *Fuki* is provided by the open strings, that is, degrees I, II, IV, V, and VI. Degree VII regularly occurs with the function of lower leading tone and as such appears in two ways: first, as a lower neighbor in the sequence I-VII-I at the end of phrases (the so-called codettas); second, as part of an ascending pattern V-VII-I (pattern IV). Degree III, on the other hand, is found only once (uta 2, measure 27 in the ascent I-III-IV, that is, pattern III). Other tones are not used in *Fuki* and consequently secondary dominants and modulations are absent. This, incidentally, may be considered one of the elements that identifies *Fuki* as an early kumiuta. In later kumiuta secondary dominants as well as modulations are by no means rare phenomena.

The rhythm of the koto part of *Fuki* is simple, simpler even than that of danmono, but while considering this it should not be forgotten that kumiuta is a vocal-instrumental form to which the vocal part contributes a considerable amount of rhythmic complexity. Note values in *Fuki* are limited to half notes and quarter notes with a limited number of subdivisions.

Half notes and subdivisions:

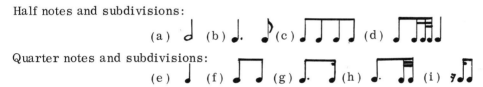

Quarter notes and subdivisions:

Pattern (d) occurs only in hayakake. Patterns (h) and (i) always occur in a descent from degree I to degree V. See, for example, uta 5, measures 14 and 18.

Syncopation is found frequently and consists almost exclusively of the combination eighth-quarter-eighth or a subdivision, either at the beginning or the end of the measure, a displacement of an eighth value that is frequently met in danmono also. Examples of types of syncopation and their locations are given below:

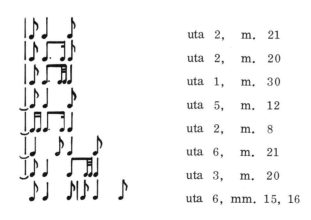

uta 2,   m. 21

uta 2,   m. 20

uta 1,   m. 30

uta 5,   m. 12

uta 2,   m. 8

uta 6,   m. 21

uta 3,   m. 20

uta 6,   mm. 15, 16

With only a few exceptions *Fuki* shares its right-hand techniques with danmono. Kakezume, which strongly stamps the musical character of *Fuki* (and of kumiuta in general), is practically nonexistent in danmono. Hikiren is not used in danmono, but is encountered once in *Fuki's* third uta. Yokozume, which in *Fuki* always occurs on tone d" (degree VII), hardly plays a role in danmono. All other right-hand techniques in *Fuki* are met in danmono as well. Table 7 contains all right-hand techniques encountered in *Fuki*, together with information on their specific uses.

Table 7

Technique	Tone(s)	Uta	Frequency	Typical Location
Awasezume	e'–e'	7	1	End of piece
	e'–e"	1, 2, 3, 5	13	6x in phrase 5
	f'–f"	2, 4, 5, 7	4	Measure 16 (Cadence II)
	b'–b"	2, 4, 5, 7	9	Measures 11, 32 (Cadence V)
Kakite		All		
Oshiawase	b"–b"	M, 3	2	
Sararin	b"–b'	1, 2, 4, 6	6	End phrases in second and third parts
	b"–e"	5	1	
Hikiren		3	1	
Kararin		M, 3	2	
Waren		7	2	
Surizume		2, 4, 5	3	Phrase 5
Warizume		4, 5, 6, 7	34	General
Kakezume		All	32	Beginning of phrases
Yokozume		1, 2, 4	3	End of phrases

A frequently encountered combination is tone d" played yokozume, followed by sararin. See, for example, uta 1, measure 20. Both times that waren is met (uta 7, measures 18 and 22), it is followed by kororin from tone b", a procedure that will be seen to be typical. Surizume is preceded by tone e (degree I) the three times that it occurs.

The concentration of special techniques such as awasezume, sararin, waren, and surizume in Part II, especially phrase 5, is related to the crisis character of this part. Warizume does not appear before the second half of uta 4, after which it plays an increasingly important role. To a certain extent this technique acts as a unifying device in the later uta, a use that coincides with a diminished use of kakezume. To take over the function of kakezume is, as we have seen, part of the function of warizume.

Ornamentation is largely a modal, not a genre, characteristic. Thus, the left-hand techniques in *Fuki* are not distinguished in any way from those used in danmono. The same ornaments occur in the same contexts:

Ornament	Tone(s)
Oshihanashi	a', c"
En (ato-oshi)	a', c", e", a"
Chitsu (tsuki-iro)	e"
Ju (hiki-iro)	f"

The most frequent ornaments are en on tone a (degree IV) and ju on tone f (degree II).

Summary

In summarizing the foregoing analysis, the first important conclusion is that each uta of *Fuki* consists basically of three parts:

Part I contains the first four phrases, the second pair of which may be considered to be a varied repetition of the preceding pair, from which it is separated by a short ai-no-te. The regular four-measure structure is characteristic and the large majority (twenty-six of a total of thirty-two) start with a standardized opening, kakezume, of which no more than two varieties occur. Where kakezume is absent, its place is taken by another octave pattern, warizume, that outlines the same octave as the other kakezume. In phrases 1, 2, and 3 there is only one example of a phrase leading over into the succeeding phrase. Standardized openings and closed endings produce the impression that each phrase forms a unit in itself. This is especially true for phrases ending on tone e (degree I), which is more often met concluding phrase 2 than phrase 1 or 3. The latter two phrases show a tendency to end on tone b (degree V). As in Western music, degree I gives a stronger feeling of stability than degree V. Phrase 4, like phrase 2, ends with an ai-no-te, which in this case, however, shows a strong tendency not to close the phrase in measure 16, but to lead over to phrase 5. In five of the six cases this transition is made by means of a cadence on degree II. The quiet, regular character of Part I justifies its categorization as a "jo."

Part II contains phrases 5 and 6. Contrasting with the first four phrases, the regularity now makes way for a somewhat more integrated structure that is the result partly of the almost complete elimination of the opening kakezume (or their substitute warizume) patterns, partly of the related tendency to provide a flowing connection between phrases 5 and 6. Within the phrases themselves more integration is provided by a less conspicuous restpoint that coincides with the location of the kozume in *Etenraku*. Phrase 5 has a tendency to end on degree V, while phrase 6 in all uta reaches degree I in the last measure (24), although for the sake of connection a further development toward degree V may occur. In comparison with Part I, this second part has the character of a crisis and may therefore be categorized as a "ha."

Part III contains phrases 7 and 8. A certain return to the regularity and relaxation of the first part may be observed. Of the total of sixteen phrases, seven open with a regular kakezume, one with mukōhan kake, one with the substitute for kakezume, warizume, and one with another such substitute, a broken octave. The phrases regain a generally closed character. Only one direct connection from phrase 7 to phrase 8 is made. Phrase 8 closes with some version of the cadence on degree V except in the final uta, where a cadence on degree I is found. The return to the initial regularity of construction, the quiet and relaxed mood, and the low register give this last part the character of a denouement, a "kyū."

Comparison with Danmono

Certain parallels with the structure of danmono may be drawn. Both genres consist of a certain number of separate movements, each movement containing a severely prescribed number of measures, and, in addition, both follow the jo-ha-kyū concept within each movement. In kumiuta as in danmono, the jo consists of regularly constructed phrases of strict quadratic structure. The ha in both genres brings a loosening of the preceding severity, the phrases become less self-contained, and the loss of their independence results in an increased complexity and integration of the ha part as a whole. In the kyū, finally, a certain return to the regularity of the first part may be observed although the original severity is not attained.[6]

Kumiuta as exemplified in *Fuki* shares with danmono certain melodic patterns that connect the basic tones of the mode. However, kumiuta has its own, distinctive set of patterns in the varieties of kakezume that in danmono are practically nonexistent. The final cadences of the inner movements (dan and uta, respectively) are different, each genre showing a distinctive cadence, in danmono "ten-ton-shan," in kumiuta "sha-sha-ten-tsun-shan":

Example 86. Final Cadence of Inner Uta.

Note that while the inner dan in danmono end on shan consisting of tones a and e', giving the aural effect of tone a (degree IV), the inner uta in kumiuta end on tone b (degree V). Both danmono and kumiuta, however, conclude last movements with a sararin from the highest string and end with a unison on tone e (degree I). Although only *Fuki* has been analyzed at this point we may anticipate by observing that the most usual formula in kumiuta is as follows.

Example 87. Final Cadence of Last Uta.

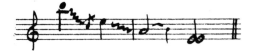

The performance of these sararin is somewhat unusual. The first sararin begins with the normal tremolo on tone b'', the descent to tone c'' is made with the side of the tsume of the middle finger, and the following sararin from e'' to a' is executed like the first.

Fuki has, in addition, another cadence that is somewhat related to the cadence on degree V and that we have referred to as cadence on degree II.

Example 88. Cadence on Degree II.

This cadence is encountered at the end of phrases, especially phrase 4, and always fulfills a connective function, leading over into the following phrase, at the beginning of which, usually, degree II resolves to degree I.

The systematic expansion and contraction of the range, which is a formal principle in danmono, is not found in the same form in *Fuki*. Here, the frequent use of kakezume, outlining a lower octave before reaching the final tone, forces the melody to move in higher registers. The average range of the various phrases of the combined seven uta, disregarding the frequent octave displacements, is given below:

Location	Average Range
Part I, phrases 1-4	(a') d''-b''
Part II, " 5	(e') a'-b''
" 6	e'-b''
Part III, " 7	e'-e'' (b'')
" 8	e'-e''

Without attempting at this stage to draw any general conclusions about preferences for certain ranges at certain locations in kumiuta, we observe that in *Fuki* the successive parts gradually move into lower registers. (Note that the various ranges perfectly match the sequence of kakezume, shown on page 153.) The pattern, therefore, rather than ascent followed by descent as in danmono, is descent from the beginning. Whether this heritage from *Etenraku* is a general characteristic of all kumiuta remains to be seen.

CHAPTER XI

KUMIUTA IN HIRA-JŌSHI

The Direct Influence of Fuki

Analysis of Yatsuhashi's *Fuki* has provided an insight into a genre of musical composition with very distinctive features. We have now to determine which, if any, of the characteristics of *Fuki* reflect the kumiuta genre and which represent only that specific composition. At the outset certain limitations must be accepted as representing standard usage of the term "kumiuta." A koto kumiuta is a vocal-instrumental form consisting of several movements of thirty-two measures of 4/4 that are notable for the frequent occurrence of kakezume patterns at the opening of the phrases. Normally, the phrases are four measures in length. Where these characteristics are absent, a composition may not be called a kumiuta.

A kakezume pattern that opens a phrase occupies about forty per cent of its total length and so much influences further development that the content of the phrase is practically determined by the pattern. Yet, on the other hand, and precisely because of the regularity of its occurrence, when kakezume is absent from the beginning of a phrase, that absence is equally conspicuous. A simple listing of the kakezume patterns in the kumiuta, therefore, will give an insight into the melodic content of these compositions. In order to facilitate comparison with *Fuki*, only kumiuta in the same tuning, hira-jōshi, will be discussed here; kumiuta in kumoi-jōshi, nakazora, and so on, will be reserved for separate treatment in Chapter XII. *Ōtsu no Kyoku*, however, has been included because its tuning, shimo-chidori, is closely related to hira-jōshi. *Kambun Ōtsu no Kyoku*, on the contrary, although it uses the tuning kin-uwa-jōshi, which is also very similar to hira-jōshi, is excluded because the irregular length of its uta is uncharacteristic of kumiuta. At this point the attempt is to establish a standard, not to deal with deviants.

The tabulations in Table 8 contain not only kakezume patterns proper, but also the related patterns hankake, tanhan, kaihan, mukōhan, and hayakake, when these patterns initiate phrases. If the number is followed by a dash, the pattern is han-kakezume. When the string number is underlined once, tanhan-kake is referred to, while a double underlining indicates mukōhan. If the number is followed by a semicolon, the pattern is kaihan; if it is followed by a single parenthesis, the pattern is hayakake. Some kakezume appear later than normal (usually one measure), and where this happens, the string number is given in parentheses. An asterisk indicates an unclassified variant of kakezume which will be discussed later.

176

Table 8

Phrase	Fuki							Umegae						Kokoro Zukushi					
	1	2	3	4	5	6	7	1	2	3	4	5	6	1	2	3	4	5	6
1	11	11	11	11	11	11	7	11	11	11	11	11	11	10	6	11	10	10	13
2	12	12	12	12	12	12		12	12	10	10	10		6	10			13	
3	11	11	11	11	11			11	11	6	8			9-	8	9-		10	
4	12	12	12	12	7			12	12	13	12					13			12*
5	10								10		8	10		13	10				
6	10		8					10				7		8			8		
7	8	8	7		7			8					8		8				10
8	7	7	7					7	7	7	7		7	7		8	7		7
	8	6	6	4	5	2	1	7	5	5	6	4	3	6	5	4	3	3	4

Table 8 (continued)

Tenka Taihei

Phrase	1	2	3	4	5	6
1	11	10	11	10	11	11
2	12	12	10	8	13	12
3	11	8	8			
4		12				12
5		6	10	13		
6	10	13	8	10		
7	8	8			7	
8				8		7
	5	7	5	5	3	4

Usuyuki

Phrase	1	2	3	4	5	6
1	10	11	11	10	11	10
2	(10)	10	12	11	12	8*
3	8	7	11	11		
4	8		11			
5	6					10
6	13	10	10	10	10	
7			7	8	8	
8			7	6*		
	6	4	7	5	4	3

Yuki no Ashita

Phrase	1	2	3	4	5	6
1	13	10	11	11	11	11
2		8	10	10		
3	8					
4		10	13	12	10	10
5	7	6	8	10	10	
6	10					
7		8	8			
8		8	7	7		
	4	6	6	5	3	2

TABLE 8 (continued)

Phrase	Kumo no Ue 1	2	3	4	5	6	Usugoromo 1	2	3	4	5	6	Kiritsubo 1	2	3	4	5	6
1	11	6	8	8	11	—	8	10	11	13	11	—	8	11	11	10	—	—
2	12	10	12	6	10		10	10		12	12		10	10		10	12	
3	11	13	7		6		13				7		8	8	6	13		
4	12		13					8		13	13	12)	12	13	12			
5	10	6					6		10				10					
6		8̲			13		8				11̲		13					
7	8					8				8	8			8	8		8	8
8	6	6				7	7̲	7̲	7̲	8̲		7		7*			7	7
	7	5	4	3	4	2	6	4	3	5	6	2	6	6	4	3	3	2

Table 8 (continued)

Phrase	Suma						Shiki no Kyoku *					Ōgi no Kyoku					
	1	2	3	4	5	6	1	2	3	4	5	1	2	3	4	5	6
1	11	13	10	10	11		8	11	11	11	8	10	8	10.	8	11	13
2		13	12	12	12		13	12	12	12		8	10	12	10	7	8
3	10	8	11	11		11*	9-	11	6)	6)			6	8	8	8	9-
4	13						10	13					13	13	13		
5	10	9-	13				11	(10)	10	10			7				
6	11	10				11	8	10				12	11	10	9-	8	
7	8	8	8	8	8	8	6					8		8			8)
8	8	7	7	7		7	7	7			8		6)	7			
	5	6	6	4	4	4	7	5	5	4	4	4	7	7	5	4	4

*Contains only five uta.

Table 8 (continued)

Akashi

Phrase	1	2	3	4	5	6
1	10	13	8	13	10	
2	7	10	12		12	
3		11		11		
4						
5	9:	9-				
6		10				
7	8	8				8
8	6	7	8|	7*		
	5	7	3	3	2	1

Sue no Matsu

Phrase	1	2	3	4	5	6
1	9-			10:	11	11)
2	13		10			
3	13		6	8		
4	10			13		
5				11	9-	
6		10			11*	
7	8					
8			8)			
	4	2	3	4	3	1

Utsusemi

Phrase	1	2	3	4	5	6
1	11	11	11	12	11	
2		12	13	10	10	7
3	10	8				
4	7		13	13	8	12)
5		10	10	8		
6		11				
7	8	9-	8			
8	7	7|				7
	5	7	5	4	3	3

Table 8 (continued)

Hagoromo

Phrase	1	2	3	4	5	6
1	11	13	11	10	11	
2	12	10	8	10	12	
3	10	8	8			
4	8	7		13		
5		8	10			
6		10				
7	6	8		8		8
8	7			7		
	6	7	3	4	2	2

Wakaba

1	2	3	4	5	6
10			10	11	12*
8			12	13	12)
6			11		11)
13			7	10	12)
10					
			8		
8			10		
6			6	3	4

Miya no Uguisu

1	2	3	4	5	6	7
8						
12						
13						
9–						
4						

Table 8 (continued)

Phrase	Shiki no Fuji 1	2	3	4	5	6	Jichō 1	2	3	4	5	6	Setsugekka 1	2	3	4	5	6
1	9–	10	13				8	10	13		11		13	8	11	9–		
2								7	10		10		7					
3		10		8					9–				10	11				
4	10									9:			12	12				
5	6	8					12											
6	10:		11							10)							7*	
7	8						8			7				8				
8										7		6						7
	5	3	2	1			3	2	3	3	2	1	4	4	1	1	1	1

Table 8 (continued)

Mutamagawa

Phrase	1	2	3	4	5	6
1	7	13	10		8	12
2	10		12			12*
3	8	11				
4	8					
5	8					
6	7	13		13		
7	7		8)			
8	5	3	3	1	1	2

Tamakazura

Phrase	1	2	3	4	5	6
1				8		
2				12	10	
3				8	10	
4						
5						
6			7	10	10	
7				8		
8			1	5	2	

Ukifume

Phrase	1	2	3	4	5	6
1	11	8		9–		
2	8		(10)			
3		(13)				
4						
5						
6	7	7	7			
7						
8	3	3	2	1		

Table 8 (continued)

Phrase	Shiki no Koi*						Shiki no Tomo+				Tomo Chidori					
	1	2	3	4	5	6	1	2	3	4	1	2	3	4	5	6
1	12	9–	10				8	13	11	11	11	13	11	13	11	
2	10						10	13	10				12			
3	8						6	8		11)	8	8	8			
4								10		12)		7	10	13	13	12
5							9–			8	13	11				
6			12					8	12		8			10		
7			13				8				9–	8	10			
8								7			7	8	7	7		7
	3	1	3				5	4	4	5	5	6	6	4	2	2

* Contains five uta.

+ Contains only four uta.

Table 8 (continued)

Hana no En

Phrase	1	2	3	4	5	6
1	11	11	11	13	11	
2	12	8	7	12	12	
3	11				11	
4	12	13		12	7	
5		9– 10			7	
6			11			
7	11	13		8		
8	7=	7	7|		7=	7
	6	6	5	3	5	1

Haru no Miya

Phrase	1	2	3	4	5	6
1	11	11				
2	8	10				
3						
4		10				
5	9–	9–				
6	10	13				
7						
8		8				
	4	6				

Hashihime

Phrase	1	2	3	4	5	6
1	10	13	10	11	10	13
2		8				
3	8	10		8		
4	13		13			
5	10		10	11		10*
6	11	12	11	8		
7	6		13			9)
8	10	10				
	7	5	5	4	1	3

Table 8 (continued)

Phrase	Wakana 1	Wakana 2	Wakana 3	Tachibana* 1	Tachibana* 2	Tachibana* 3	Tanabata* 1	Tanabata* 2	Tanabata* 3	Sakakiba* 1	Sakakiba* 2	Sakakiba* 3	Chio no Tomo 1	Chio no Tomo 2	Chio no Tomo 3	Chio no Tomo 4	Chio no Tomo 5	Chio no Tomo 6
1	8	10	11	11	13	11	11	11	11	8	11	13	11	8	6	10	11	
2					10		12*	12	12				12	10				
3	9–						10	13		8					11*	10	11*	13
4	11	8		11	11								12		7	13		
5				8						11		11	10	8		10		
6												12)		7	11	10		
7	8						8	13		13	13		11		8		8	11)
8	7		7			7	10	7*	7	7		7	7					8
	5	2	2	3	3	2	5	5	3	5	2	4	6	4	5	4	4	3

* Contains only three uta.

Table 8 (continued)

Hatsune

Phrase	1	2	3	4	5	6
1	11	11	6			
2	7				7*	
3	12	11	8	10		
4		13	7			
5	10	10				
6	(13)					
7	9–	7				
8		8				
	6	5	4	1	1	

Tobiume

Phrase	1	2	3	4	5	6
1	11	11	8	11	13	12
2	12	10		12	12	12)
3	11	13	11	11	11	
4			10			
5		7	9–			12
6		10				
7		11	11	10		
8	7		6			7
	4	6	6	4	3	4

Ōtsu no Kyoku*
(shimo-chidori)

Phrase	1	2	3	4	5
1	10	8			
2	8				
3			8*	13	
4	10		10:		
5	8		(10)		
6	13				
7	8)				
8					
	6	1	3	1	

* Contains five uta.   Only uta 1–4 are in shimo-chidori; uta 5 is in han-nakazora 2.

The inclusion of *Fuki* at the head of the charts enables us to perceive immediately that the construction of this composition is shared to some extent by other kumiuta, and thus traces of *Etenraku* are found throughout the entire repertoire, although their distribution is far from even (for example, kumiuta by Mitsuhashi Kengyō show practically no such traces). Uta having at least four phrases that open with the same kakezume patterns as the equivalent phrases in *Fuki* are given in Table 9.

Table 9

Title	Uta	Shared Kakezume in Part			Total Shared Kakezume
		I	II	III	
Umegae	1	4	1	2	7
Usuyuki	3	4	1	2	7
Kumo no Ue	1	4	1	1	6
Tenka Taihei	1	3	1	1	5
Shiki no Kyoku	3	3	1	1	5
Chio no Tomo	1	3	1	1	5
Umegae	2	4	1		5
Hana no En	1	4		1	5
Usuyuki	5	2	1	1	4
Yuki no Ashita	4	2	1	1	4
Shiki no Kyoku	2	1	2	1	4
Utsusemi	2	2	1	1	4
Chio no Tomo	5	2	1	1	4
Hatsune	2	2	1	1	4
Tenka Taihei	6	3		1	4
Suma	5	3		1	4
Hana no En	5	3		1	4
Tobiume	1	3		1	4
Ōgi no Kyoku	3	1	1	2	4
Akashi	2	1	1	2	4
Suma	3	1	1	2	4

As concordances may be the result of mere chance, a minimum percentage of agreement per uta must be arbitrarily designated as the lower limit for structural similarity. The percentage selected is fifty per cent (four phrases); uta having less than fifty per cent concordance are in principle regarded as not of the *Fuki* type, although sometimes a lower percentage of concordance may be accepted when the agreements occur at certain locations in the uta. Thus, cases where only three kakezume agree with the pattern of *Fuki* will be acceptable when either (1) two of the agreements occur at the beginning of the first two phrases of the uta and the third occurs in either Part II or III, or (2) when one occurs in Part I, one in Part II, and the third in Part III. This adds the following uta to the list:

Table 10

Title	Uta	Shared Kakezume in Part			Total Shared Kakezume
		I	II	III	
Usugoromo	5	2		1	3
Hagoromo	1	2		1	3
Tanabata	1	2		1	3
Tanabata	3	2		1	3
Shiki no Kyoku	4	2	1		3
Hatsune	1	2	1		3
Tenka Taihei	3	1	1	1	3
Usugoromo	3	1	1	1	3
Suma	1	1	1	1	3
Utsusemi	3	1	1	1	3

Although even an agreement of two phrases can at times be suggestive, the minimum used here is three. Even if the minimum were two agreements, only one more composition would be added to the list, *Tomo Chidori*, in which the first two phrases of uta 3 begin with the conventional kakezume on strings 11 and 12.

Eighteen of the total of thirty-one uta that show similarity with the structure of *Fuki*, which we shall henceforth speak of as a structural type, are from compositions by Yatsuhashi Kengyō. These eighteen uta represent nine of the total of eleven kumiuta in hira-jōshi by Yatsuhashi (the tenth is *Fuki* itself), and all are in their construction more or less influenced by *Etenraku*. Even *Kiritsubo*, the one kumiuta that thus far has been excluded as not having the minimum number of agreements, shows some traces of the *Fuki* type, especially in uta 3. Thus, a more or less close adherence to the structural pattern of *Fuki* may be considered one of the characteristics of the compositional style of this composer.

No more than an occasional borrowing from the *Fuki* scheme is found in kumiuta by Yatsuhashi's student Kitajima; in the compositions of Mitsuhashi, representing the second generation after Yatsuhashi, the *Fuki* type disappears entirely. The type reappears in Ishizuka's *Hana no En*, a composition that seems deliberately to select *Fuki* as a model and even repeats its fifth uta, text as well as music. The *Fuki* type is also apparent in the anonymous *Tanabata* and especially in *Chio no Tomo*. Yamada Kengyō, a powerful composer who does not suffer from a lack of invention, is archaizing rather than borrowing in the first half of his *Hatsune;* he uses there conventional techniques that he leaves far behind in the second half. Among the secret pieces, *Tobiume*, by Shin Yatsuhashi Kengyō, follows the traditional composition scheme, especially in uta 1 and 3.

Although in a limited sense the *Fuki* type is not used for the form of kumiuta as a whole, yet in a wider sense its influence may be detected generally. That is, the first and second parts of an uta will usually move in higher registers, while the last part almost without exception will descend to the lowest octave, practically forced there by the traditional cadence ending on tone b'.

The *Fuki* scheme is used especially by earlier composers of kumiuta. It falls into disuse in the first half of the eighteenth century, to reappear occasionally in the second half of that century among composers who seem limited to conventionalisms.

Although *Fuki* may share important structural features with later kumiuta, it is unique in the way that its first uta permeates the whole composition, making the later uta appear variations of the first. Certain other kumiuta (especially *Umegae,* which is historically related to *Fuki,* and parts of *Tenka Taihei* and *Usuyuki)* show some mutual relationship among the various uta, but in no other composition are the later uta developed so systematically from the first.

Stylistic Evolution in Phrase Openings

More insight into the styles of the individual composers may be gained by reorganizing the information in the above charts by composer. Only the three most important kumiuta composers, Yatsuhashi Kengyō, Kitajima Kengyō, and Mitsuhashi Kengyō, can be considered, for only these three provide a sufficient number of kumiuta to make the analysis significant. In the following tables the first column shows the phrase numbers, the last column shows the number of phrases that do not open with kakezume, and the remaining columns show the number of phrases that open with kakezume and the strings on which these kakezume occur.

The highest number of occurrences, whether of kakezume or of no kakezume, is indicated for each phrase by underlining; the highest number of a given kakezume in a phrase is shown by a circle. By connecting the circled numbers, profiles are obtained that are different for each composer and that summarize a stylistic idiosyncrasy, namely, the composer's preference among the various kakezume openings. The profile of Yatsuhashi represents exactly the *Fuki* scheme (11-12-11-12-10-10-8-7), while that of Kitajima shows how already the first generation after Yatsuhashi has moved away from the *Fuki* type. Mitsuhashi, the third generation, develops still farther away from *Fuki*.

The most significant changes in preference appear in the first part of the uta. Yet when we study the frequencies of the kakezume of the first four phrases, it appears that the original sequence of 11-12-11-12, although it does not constitute the profiles, is still relatively strongly represented (in number of occurrences) in Kitajima's as well as in Mitsuhashi's kumiuta. On the other hand, the chart for Yatsuhashi reveals that the later preferences of Kitajima and Mitsuhashi were clearly foreshadowed in his compositions. The development from Yatsuhashi through Kitajima to Mitsuhashi therefore is less one of radical innovations than one of gradual changes in emphasis. Even a composer as individualistic as Mitsuhashi seems to express his own character only by making limited choices within definitely determined boundaries.

The development of preferences in the second and third parts of the uta shows less pronounced changes than in the first part. The only change of consequence occurs in the fifth phrase, where the opening kakezume is played one or two strings lower than is usual in kumiuta by Yatsuhashi Kengyō. The profiles also show clearly the tripartition of the uta: phrases 1 through 4 are in the middle to high register, phrases 5 and 6 in the middle register, phrases 7 and 8 conclude in the low register.

Yatsuhashi Kengyō

Phrase Number	Kakezume on String								No. Kakezume
	6	7	8	9	10	11	12	13	
1	2		8		15	(36)		5	6
2	2	1	4		17		(25)	4	19
3	6	2	12	4	2	(15)		3	28
4		2	2		3			(16) 13	36
5	5	2	3	1	(15)	1		3	42
6		1	5	1	(13)	4	1	4	43
7	1	1	(30)		1				39
8	4	(31)	6						31

Kitajima Kengyō

Phrase Number	Kakezume on String								No. Kakezume
	6	7	8	9	10	11	12	13	
1			1	1	3	(6)	1	2	4
2		2			(4)		3	2	7
3	1		(2)		1	(2)		1	11
4		1	1		1		1	(3)	11
5			1	(3)	2	1			11
6					(2)	(2)			14
7			(6)	1					11
8	1	(5)	2						10

Mitsuhashi Kengyō

Phrase Number	Kakezume on String								No. Kakezume
	6	7	8	9	10	11	12	13	
1		1	(6)	4	4	3	2	4	14
2		1	1		(5)		4		27
3			(3)	1	(3)	2		2	28
4			1		1		(3)		34
5	1	1	(2)	(2)					32
6		2			(3)	1	1	1	30
7		(4)	(4)		1			2	26
8	1	(2)	1						33

Another development, that of the change in the relative proportions of "free" phrases (those that do not begin with kakezume) and kakezume phrases, is shown in the same charts but comparison cannot be made in terms of the figures given because of the different number of uta by each composer. Conversion to percentages is given below, arranged by composer:

Percentage of Free Phrases

Phrase	Yatsuhashi	Kitajima	Mitsuhashi
1	8	22	37
2	27	39	71
3	39	61	72
4	50	61	87
5	58	61	92
6	60	78	79
7	54	61	70
8	43	56	89

Taking the Yatsuhashi column as our standard for comparison, in Kitajima's kumiuta the increase in free phrases is considerable, and the very high percentages in Mitsuhashi's work significantly describe an aspect of kumiuta composition in its later stages. A remarkable feature repeated by each of the three composers is the gradual increase in the number of free phrases through the first and second parts of the uta, followed by a decrease in Part III. Reappearance of kakezume phrases toward the end of the uta seems confirmed as a device used to create the required mood for the kyū section. Turning back to *Fuki* for a moment, we recall the same developmental pattern in the course of its seven uta, and in this respect *Fuki* may be considered a foreboding in microform of the historical development of the whole genre. The first uta of *Fuki*, the first kumiuta, with all eight of its phrases opening with kakezume patterns, becomes almost symbolic of an archetype or ideal that was exceptionally afterward realized yet remained formally potent.

Similarly, the last uta of *Fuki*, which is characterized by frequently occurring warizume and by liveliness, set another precedent that was often followed. Closely related to *Fuki's* last uta in the predominance of warizume as well as structurally are *Kumo no Ue* (uta 6), *Usugoromo* (uta 6), *Shiki no Kyoku* (uta 5), *Ukifune* (uta 6), *Tomo Chidori* (uta 6), and *Hana no En* (uta 6). Less consistent relationships are to be found in other kumiuta, for the application of warizume toward the end of the composition is a frequently used device. Note that among the above mentioned compositions are represented not only Yatsuhashi but also Mitsuhashi, Hisamura and Ishizuka.

Ai-no-te

Short instrumental interludes, ai-no-te, occur regularly in *Fuki* at the end of the second and fourth phrases of each uta. When this pattern is compared with later kumiuta in hira-jōshi, it appears that *Fuki's* example was never strictly followed, yet, on the other hand, the end of the second and fourth phrases is the most common location for the insertion of ai-no-te— so common, indeed, that no kumiuta exists in which no example can be found. Yatsuhashi and Kitajima never use ai-no-te at other locations. Mitsuhashi introduces ai-no-te at the end of the sixth phrase, occasionally at the end of the third. Again these locations are logical ones for instrumental interludes, for Part II of the uta ends with the sixth phrase and the end of the third phrase is the point at which the strict formality of Part I tends to break down (observe the lower number of kakezume at the beginning of the fourth phrase). Examples of ai-no-te at the end of phrase 6 may be found in practically all of Mitsuhashi's kumiuta. Interludes at the end of phrase 3 are rather rare (examples may be found in *Tamakazura*, uta 4, and *Ukifune*, uta 1 and 5).

Mitsuhashi's precedent in the use of ai-no-te at locations other than at the end of the second and fourth phrases was followed by composers who came after him. Ai-no-te at the end of phrase 6 are used by Hisamura Kengyō, by the anonymous composers of *Hashime*, *Tachi-bana, Tanabata, Sakakiba*, and *Chio no Tomo*, by Mitsuzaki Kengyō, and, among the composers of hikyoku (secret pieces), by Tsugiyama Kengyō in *Ōtsu no Kyoku*. Ai-no-te at the end of phrase 3 are as rare in kumiuta by later composers as in those by Mitsuhashi Kengyō himself and the only examples are by Hisamura Kengyō in *Shiki no Tomo* (uta 4) and the anonymous composer of *Hashihime* (uta 3). Usually ai-no-te are no longer than one and one-half measures. An exception is found in *Ōtsu no Kyoku*, where the whole eighth phrase of the uta functions as ai-no-te. This may be explained by the circumstance that a new tuning is introduced in the uta immediately following. Moreover, a long instrumental interlude of twenty-eight measures occurs in this composition between uta 2 and 3. Extended interludes of this kind are nonexistent in ordinary kumiuta although not unusual among the hikyoku.

Inasmuch as the ai-no-te occur at the end of phrases, most of them have a cadential character. Cadences on degrees II and V, or variations thereof, are used in this function throughout the compositions of Yatsuhashi Kengyō; the cadence on degree II is occasionally used by Kitajima, Hisamura, and the anonymous composer of *Tanabata*. Examples of frequently met ai-no-te are given below.

Example 89.

Of the above ai-no-te, (a), (b), (c), and (d) are closely related, as are (e) and (f), and (g) and (h). Example (a) is represented in many kumiuta by Yatsuhashi and is also found in *Sue no Matsu* by Kitajima. Example (b) is used by Yatsuhashi in numerous compositions, by Kitajima in *Sue no Matsu,* and by Shin Yatsuhashi in *Tobiume*. Example (c) occurs in several works by Yatsuhashi and in *Tomo Chidori* by Hisamura. Example (d) is met in Yatsuhashi's compositions only. Example (e), the ascending cadence to the first degree of the scale, occurs in its pure form only in *Sue no Matsu* by Kitajima; the related form (f) is used by Yatsuhashi in *Umegae, Kumo no Ue,* and *Kiritsubo,* and also by Kitajima in *Sue no Matsu.* The ascending cadence to degree V is found in its lower position (g) in *Kokoro Zukushi, Tenka Taihei, Usuyuki,* and *Kumo no Ue* by Yatsuhashi, in *Tomo Chidori* by Hisamura, and in *Haru no Miya* by Ishizuka. In its higher position (h) it is used by Yatsuhashi in *Tenka Taihei* and *Usuyuki.* Therefore, most of these standard ai-no-te are used by Yatsuhashi. Occasionally they are used by his student Kitajima and by Hisamura and Ishizuka, while Mitsuhashi does not follow the convention at all closely.

Attention should be drawn to the occurrence in other compositions of a type of ai-no-te that is frequently found in Yatsuhashi's *Fuki*. The following examples taken from *Fuki* (a) and *Umegae* (b) by Yatsuhashi, from *Hagoromo* (c) by Kitajima or Makino, from the anonymous *Hashihime* (d) and *Wakana* (e), and from *Tobiume* (f) by Shin Yatsuhashi will need no further comment.

Example 90.

Cadences

By the mere fact that their location is conspicuous, final cadences of inner, as well as of final, uta stamp their imprint on the character of a kumiuta in a way comparable to the effect of the opening kakezume patterns. The analysis of *Fuki* showed that a distinction must be made between cadences at the end of inner uta, which tend to resolve on degree V of the scale, and those occurring at the conclusion of last uta, which resolve on degree I. This distinction is found throughout the entire kumiuta repertoire, with very few exceptions: only ten times does an inner uta conclude on degree I, only once on degree IV. Degree I for final cadences of inner uta is used by Yatsuhashi in *Tenka Taihei* (uta 2) and *Shiki no Kyoku* (uta 8), six times by Mitsuhashi in *Shiki no Fuji* (uta 3), *Setsugekka* (uta 2 and 5), *Tamakazura* (uta 3), *Mutamagawa* (uta 5), and *Shiki no Koi* (uta 3), and once by Yamada in *Hatsune* (uta 4). Twice, however (in *Shiki no Fuji* and *Tamakazura*), this deviation loses its importance because the cadence serves not only to conclude the phrase but also to provide a connection to the following uta by way of degree V. In a third case *(Shiki no Koi)*, the cadence introduces a modulation from hira-jōshi to han-nakazora. *Wakaba* (by Kitajima or Makino) concludes its first uta on degree IV, introducing a modulation to han-kumoi, and its fifth uta on degree I.

In regard to content, cadences on degree V can be classified into five main types. An overwhelming majority (95 of 148 cadences) belongs to what in the analysis of *Fuki* has been called cadence on degree V. This we shall now refer to as type V(a). Next in importance (19 of 148) is a cadence that first rises from degree V by way of VII to degree I and returns by way of degree VI to V [type V(b)]. Third in importance (16 of 148) is a cadence consisting of a simple ascent from degree I to degree V (pattern III), which will be called type V(c). The last two types, V(d) and V(e), approach degree V from above, usually by descending from degree I to degree IV before reaching degree V (14 of 148), less usually by an uninterrupted descent from degree I to degree V (4 of 148). Representative examples of all five types are given below.

Example 91. Cadences on Degree V: (a) General; (b) *Usugoromo*, uta 5; (c) *Akashi*, uta 2; (d) *Usuyuki*, uta 3; (e) *Mutamagawa*, uta 2.

The distribution of the above five types, plus that of the cadences ending on degree I and IV, is shown in the following chart arranged by composer.

| Composer | Cadence on Degree | | | | | | | |
| | V | | | | | I | IV | Total |
	a	b	c	d	e			
Yatsuhashi	45	4	1	8		2		60
Kitajima	6	6	2	1				15
Kitajima or Makino	7					1	1	9
Mitsuhashi	2	6	10	2	3	6		29
Hisamura	7	1						8
Ishizuka	6							6
Anonymi	15	1		1	1			18
Yamada	3		1			1		5
Shin Yatsuhashi	4			1				5
Tsugiyama		1	2	1				4
Total	95	19	16	14	4	10	1	159

The chart confirms previous findings. Kitajima discreetly varies a pattern established by his teacher Yatsuhashi. But where a strong majority of final cadences of inner uta in Yatsuhashi's compositions employ type V(a), Kitajima divides his attention equally between types V(a) and V(b). Mitsuhashi, as usual, departs farthest from the precedent, favoring type V(c) and only rarely using V(a). Shin Yatsuhashi, as well as later generations of composers, Hisamura, Ishizuka, and Anonymi, who repeatedly have been shown to think in relatively conservative terms, again strongly favors cadence V(a). Yamada shows deliberate archaism in his three uses of this type.

Before moving on to the final cadences of the last uta, attention should be drawn to the fact that twice, in *Utsusemi* (uta 3) by Kitajima, and *Hatsune* (uta 5) by Yamada, the final tone of the cadence is at the same time the first note of the following uta.

Final cadences of the last movement of a kumiuta in most cases (27 of 34) end, like *Fuki*, on degree I. A limited number (7 of 34) end on degree V *(Kokoro Zukushi, Kumo no Ue, Shiki no Kyoku,* and *Ōgi no Kyoku* by Yatsuhashi; *Akashi* by Kitajima; *Wakaba* by Kitajima or Makino; and *Hatsune* by Yamada). Most final cadences, those on degree I as well as those on degree V, use some form of glissando, normally sararin. Twice hikiren is used (in *Suma* and *Utsusemi)*. The most popular type is the cadence encountered in *Fuki,* which concludes eleven kumiuta [see the following example, (a)]. A second type (7 occurrences) gives a fast descent from degree I to degree IV, followed by degree I [Example 92, (b)]. Typically all cadences emphasize their final tone by playing it on two strings either in unison (strings 1 and 5), or in octaves. Normally the final tone is reached at the end of a descent, and once only *(Muta-magawa),* after an ascent from degree IV by way of degrees V and VII. A few of the more representative final cadences are shown in Example 92.

The frequencies with which the different composers end their kumiuta with cadences on I and V are given on the following page.

Composer	Cadence on	
	I	V
Yatsuhashi	8	4
Kitajima	1	1
Kitajima or Makino	1	1
Mitsuhashi	7	
Hisamura	2	
Ishizuka	1	
Anonymi	6	
Yamada		1
Shin Yatsuhashi	1	—
Total	27	7

Example 92. (a) General; (b) *Jichō*, *Setsugekka*, and *Tamakazura*; (c) *Suma* and *Utsusemi*; (d) *Mutamagawa*; (e) *Akashi*.

Mitsuhashi consistently ends his kumiuta in hira-jōshi on degree I. His predecessors use conclusions on degree V as well as I. After Mitsuhashi only Yamada concludes a kumiuta in hira-jōshi on the fifth degree.

Tonal Material and Modulation

The extreme economy of *Fuki* in tonal material is not followed by later composers and Yatsuhashi himself enlarges his arsenal of tonal possibilities in his subsequent compositions. *Fuki* employs only the most basic material: the tones provided by the open strings of the koto (degrees I, II, IV, V, and VI), with the regular addition of degree VII and the rare addition of degree III by means of left-hand pressure. In respect to these two additional tones nothing changes in later kumiuta: degree VII continues to be frequently encountered, while degree III never becomes more than an occasional phenomenon, to be met perhaps once or twice in a composition, or not at all, as in *Shiki no Tomo* and *Tomo Chidori,* both kumiuta by Hisa-mura. As both degrees III and VII function as lower leading tones, the rare occurrence of degree III compared to that of degree VII shows the relatively limited importance of degree IV compared to degree I. Degrees III and VII will usually be found in ascending contexts, and in the whole kumiuta repertoire there occur no more than two exceptions to this rule. Typical uses of these degrees, followed by the two exceptions (c and e), are given below.

Example 93. (a) *Kokoro Zukushi,* uta 2; (b) *Umegae,* uta 3; (c) *Sue no Matsu,* uta 6; (d) *Fuki,* uta 2; (e) *Ōgi no Kyoku,* uta 5.

In addition to the tones of the scale, some raised or flattened tones may occur, the most frequently met of which is tone f-sharp (degree II) which functions as dominant for degree V, the second important degree of the mode. The use of this tone may be transient, in which case it functions as a secondary dominant; or its use may be prolonged, for example, to the duration of a complete phrase. When the latter occurs, we will consider it to indicate a modulation in which degree V temporarily assumes the function of degree I. The use of the sharpened second degree is very common and is absent only from *Fuki* and *Hana no En,* the composition that Ishizuka closely modeled after *Fuki.* Two examples, selected at random, illustrate typical use of the sharpened second degree in the function of secondary dominant.

Example 94. (a) *Akashi,* uta 1; (b) *Suma,* uta 2.

Both examples have been extended to include recurrence of the natural second degree, which shows clearly the transient nature of this secondary dominant. The recurrence of the natural usually is postponed for some time [Example 94 (a)], but sometimes it follows closely after the sharpened tone in a way that traditional Western compositional rules would not allow [Example 94 (b)].

Although the use of a secondary dominant for the fifth degree is common, modulation to the fifth is less frequent. With the progress of time the frequency of modulating passages increases, as is shown in the following enumeration of the compositions containing modulations to the fifth compared with the total oeuvre in hira-jōshi of each composer:

Yatsuhashi	:	1 (*Shiki no Kyoku,* uta 4)	out of 12 kumiuta
Kitajima	:	1 (*Sue no Matsu,* uta 2)	" " 3 "
Kitajima or	:		
Makino	:	1 (*Wakaba,* uta 4)	" " 2 "
Mitsuhashi	:	7*	" " 8 "
Hisamura	:	0	" " 2 "
Ishizuka	:	1 (*Haru no Miya,* uta 2)	" " 2 "
Anonymi	:	5*	" " 6 "
Yamada	:	1 (*Hatsune,* uta 1)	" " 1 "
Shin-Yatsuhashi	:	1 (*Tobiume,* uta 1, 2, 3, and 5)	" " 1 "
Tsugiyama	:	1 (*Ōtsu no Kyoku,* uta 1, 2, and 4)	" " 1 "

*Inasmuch as almost all of the kumiuta in hira-jōshi by Mitsuhashi and Anonymi contain modulations, it seems pointless to list the titles.

The frequency of modulating passages increases from Yatsuhashi to Kitajima and again from the latter to Mitsuhashi. In the compositions of Hisamura a return to the older norm can be observed. In later composers, conventional as they may be in other respects, modulation is a common feature. Usually a kumiuta contains no more than one modulation, but some of the hikyoku have more: *Ōtsu no Kyoku,* for example, contains three modulations, and *Tobiume* no fewer than four. These two compositions in addition contain the longest modulating sections. Normally a modulation lasts one phrase, that is, four measures. *Tobiume* has a modulation that lasts six measures in uta 1, and the same composition and *Ōtsu no Kyoku* each contain a modulation lasting eight measures (in uta 5 and 1, respectively). The last is exceptional and is met elsewhere only in *Chio no Tomo* (uta 6).

Another accidental, b-flat (degree V), is occasionally encountered, but its occurrence is considerably less frequent than that of the raised second degree. Tone b-flat, functioning as upper leading tone for degree IV, is typically used in a descending context and only one exception to this rule is met (*Sue no Matsu,* uta 5). Two examples illustrate the normal and the exceptional use of the flattened fifth degree.

Example 95. (a) *Sue no Matsu,* uta 3; (b) *Sue no Matsu,* uta 5.

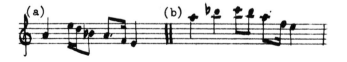

Like the sharpened second degree, the flattened fifth degree may signal a modulation, this time with degree IV as the new fundamental. This modulation, however, is rare and is found only seven times in the entire kumiuta repertoire. The following chart shows the locations of the flattened fifth degrees, the column to the right containing those occurrences that indicate a modulation.

Not unexpectedly, we find a development similar to that of the sharpened second degree. Use of tone b-flat by Yatsuhashi is exceptional: it increases in Kitajima's compositions, but modulation does not occur before Mitsuhashi. Hisamura again does not modulate in his kumiuta, while late composers follow the example of Mitsuhashi. Most modulations, like those to degree V, are four measures long. An exceptionally long one (eight measures) is found in *Shiki no Koi*.

Tone e-flat is met only once, in the long ai-no-te between the second and third uta of *Ōtsu no Kyoku*. This location in a purely instrumental part makes it atypical.

Composer	Accidental Use of b-flat	b-flat in Modulation to Degree IV
Yatsuhashi	*Kokoro Zukushi*, uta 1 *Usugoromo*, uta 2	
Kitajima	*Sue no Matsu*, uta 3 and 5	
Kitajima or Makino	None	
Mitsuhashi	*Miya no Uguisu*, uta 1 *Jichō*, uta 1 *Mutamagawa*, uta 2 and 6	*Setsugekka*, uta 3 *Tamakazura*, uta 3 and 4 *Shiki no Koi*, uta 1 and 2
Hisamura	None	
Ishizuka		*Hana no En*, uta 4
Anonymi	*Hashihime*, uta 1 and 5 *Chio no Tomo*, uta 1 and 2	*Hashihime*, uta 3
Yamada	None	
Shin Yatsuhashi		*Tobiume*, uta 2
Tsugiyama	*Ōtsu no Kyoku*, uta 3	*Ōtsu no Kyoku*, uta 2

In most instances these accidentals are used in such a way that the general character of the mode is hardly touched. A few exceptions should be noted. The first occurs at the opening of *Kokoro Zukushi*, where a raised second degree is introduced before the modality has had sufficient time to settle (Example 96). As might be expected in such an early kumiuta, the balance is soon and adequately restored, but the appearance of the raised second degree immediately after the natural second is very striking. Mitsuhashi occasionally goes so far in his use of raised tones that the aural effect is almost a complete change to a new chōshi. Where,

Example 96. *Kokoro Zukushi*, uta 1.

for example, he raises the second degree in combination with the use of degree III (both effected on the same string with different amounts of pressure), the effect is entirely that of nakazora rather than hira-jōshi. Mitsuhashi, as has been observed, actually changes the tuning in some of his compositions. Examples of transient effect of a new chōshi, without change of tuning, may be found in *Setsugekka* (uta 4) and *Shiki no Koi* (uta 2). The following example from *Setsugekka* is a passage from a composition in hira-jōshi which from a purely tonal point of view belongs to nakazora.

Example 97. *Setsugekka*, uta 4.

Right-hand Techniques

Fuki contains a very limited number of kakezume patterns, all of which can be shown to be derived directly from *Etenraku* through the *Fuki* of Tsukushi-goto. The only kakezume patterns occurring in *Fuki* are those on strings 7, 8, 10, 11, and 12, and all are of the regular kakezume type. Mukōhan is used once on string 7. Tanhan, kaihan, and hayakake are not represented at all. Turning back to the charts at the beginning of this chapter, we see that this small technical arsenal is soon enlarged to its extreme limits. Kakezume come to be used at any location on the koto where the range below the final tone of the pattern allows it, that is, from kakezume on string 7 through string 13. In addition, kakezume on string 6 occurs, although because of the irregular tuning sequence of strings on the lower side, no octave is possible. A regular octave on kakezume on string 6 can be played only in the related tunings shimo-chidori and kin-uwa-jōshi; and actually occurs only in the latter *(Kambun Ōtsu no Kyoku)*. The performance of kakezume on string 6 in kin-uwa-jōshi requires left-hand pressure on the lowest string, an extremely unusual phenomenon in general and in kakezume in particular. The following example shows the kakezume on string 6 as it is normally met in hira-jōshi (a), and the uncommon form that occurs in kin-uwa-jōshi (b).

Example 98. Kakezume on string 6: (a) in hira-jōshi; (b) in kin-uwa-jōshi.

Kakezume on string 6, like kakezume on string 13, is for the first time encountered in *Umegae;* afterward both occur regularly in all compositions. Kakezume on string 9 makes its first appearance in *Kokoro Zukushi.* This pattern occurs only as a hankake, with the second tone omitted, never in its complete five-tone form.

Mukōhan and tanhan kake usually occur in the third part of an uta, where the register is low, and therefore most of these patterns are on string 7 or 8. Less frequent are mukōhan and tanhan on strings 10, 11, and 12. (Note that string 9—which is reserved for hankake— is excluded from this enumeration.) Mukōhan and tanhan are used in the same locations, and the choice between the two patterns seems a matter of personal preference of the composer. Mukōhan is preferred by Yatsuhashi, Hisamura, Anonymi, Yamada, and Tsugiyama; tanhan by Kitajima, Kitajima-or-Makino, Mitsuhashi, and Ishizuka. Again we find composers disposed in the groups that are now familiar. It should be observed that Mitsuhashi, although most of his tanhan kake occur on string 7, has a stronger preference for patterns on higher strings (especially tanhan on string 12) than his fellow composers.

Kaihan kake is very rarely used and is found only in *Akashi* (uta 5), and *Sue no Matsu* (uta 4) by Kitajima, *Shiki no Fuji* (uta 1) and *Jichō* (uta 4) by Mitsuhashi and *Ōtsu no Kyoku* (uta 3) by Tsugiyama. The various types of hayakake, on the other hand, are used often and, unlike the other types, which are met only at the beginning of a phrase, may occur at various positions. In Example 75, which showed the relationship between standard koto-patterns in gagaku and those in kumiuta, three types of hayakake were illustrated. Of these three, hayakake 1 is the most common in kumiuta. It is found on all strings from string 5 through 13, and in addition on raised 6, double-raised 9, raised 11, and raised 13. The less common hayakake 2 occurs only on strings 5, 6, 8, 10, 12, and 13, never on raised tones. One of the very rare examples of hayakake 3 in hirayōshi is encountered in *Shiki no Kyoku* (uta 5, measure 15).

Like kakezume on string 6, hayakake on raised strings 9, 12, and 13 do not contain octaves as basic intervals. The aural effect of all three examples is somewhat "wrong" because of the absence of the basic octave. However, it is physically impossible to press down two strings an octave apart in the time available.

Example 99. Hayakake on (a) string 9, (b) string 12, and (c) string 13.

Finally, a number of variations of kakezume occur that cannot be classified under the preceding categories. Four of these are given in the following example.

Example 100. (a) *Hatsune,* uta 5; (b) *Akashi,* uta 4, and *Tamakazura,* uta 2 ;
(c) *Sue no Matsu,* uta 5, and *Chio no Tomo,* uta 5; (d) *Mutamagawa,* uta 6.

Example (a) is a unique form of kakezume in double note values. Example (b) is related to tanhan. Examples (c) and (d) are forms of hayakake.

All right-hand techniques, other than kakezume, that are used in kumiuta in hira-jōshi are collected in the following table (11) and arranged by composer. Concerning most of these techniques, no more than a statement of use or non-use is necessary, and in these cases the presence of a technique is shown by an x. In a few cases, however, more information is desirable. For awasezume, oshiawase, chirashizume, and yokozume, therefore, the tone(s) on which the techniques occur are given; in the cases of hikisute and hanryu, the tones shown are the concluding tones.

Table 11

	Yatsuhashi	Kitajima	Kitajima or Makino	Mitsuhashi	Hisamura	Ishizuka	Anonymi	Yamada	Shin Yatsuhashi	Shin Tsugiyama
Sukuizume	x	x	x	x		x	x		x	x
Awasezume										
a–a'	x							x	x	x
b–b'	x	x	x	x	x	x	x	x	x	x
c'–c''	x									
e'–e'	x	x	x	x	x	x	x		x	
e'–e''	x	x	x	x	x	x	x	x	x	x
f'–f''	x	x								
a'–a''				x	x	x				
b'–b''	x	x	x	x		x	x	x		
Kakite	x	x	x	x	x	x	x	x	x	x
Oshiwase										
b'				x						
c''		x							x	x
f''		x					x	x	x	x
b''	x	x	x	x	x	x	x	x	x	x
Sararin	x	x	x	x	x	x	x	x	x	x
Hikiren	x	x	x	x	x	x	x	x	x	x
Hikisute										
e''		x		x						
f''										
f#''								x		x

Table 11 (continued)

	Yatsuhashi	Kitajima	Kitajima or Makino	Mitsuhashi	Hisamura	Ishizuka	Anonymi	Yamada	Shin Yatsuhashi	Shin Tsugiyama
Kararin	x	x		x	x		x	x		
Hanryu										
b		x								
f'	x		x	x			x			
a'	x									
b'		x		x						
c''									x	
d''							x			
e''	x	x								
Chirashizume										
e										x
b								x		
e'	x			x	x					
Waren	x	x	x	x	x	x	x	x	x	
Surizume	x	x	x	x	x		x	x	x	
Namigaeshi										
low	x	x	x							
high				x					x	
Warizume	x	x	x	x	x	x	x	x	x	x
Yokozume										
d''	x	x	x	x	x	x	x			x
e''-a'	x	x								

Certain of these right-hand techniques are universal in kumiuta in hira-jōshi: awasezume, kakite, oshiawase, sararin, hikiren, and warizume. Others occur in most kumiuta: waren, surizume, yokozume, and kararin and its related form hanryu. Only hikisute and namigaeshi, therefore, reflect the styles of the different composers. Hikisute is rarely used, being encountered only in *Mutamagawa* and *Tamakazura* by Mitsuhashi, *Hatsune* by Yamada, and *Ōtsu no Kyoku* by Tsugiyama. Two unusual forms of this technique are shown below.

Example 101. (a) *Mutamagawa,* uta 4; (b) *Ōtsu no Kyoku,* uta 3.

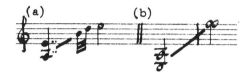

In (a) the hikisute begins with shan on strings 1 and 2, which is followed by an upward glissando, and ends on the last three strings plucked very distinctly. In (b) the hikisute also starts on shan on the first two strings [which in this case, because of the slightly different tuning (shimochidori), produces tones different from those heard in hira-jōshi] and the glissando ends on oshiawase on strings 10 and 11.

Namigaeshi exists in two forms, both of which consist of a sequence of shan-shu-shan. Shu may occur in a lower or a higher register.

Example 102.

In (a) we see the more common of the two, the form frequently used by Yatsuhashi, Kitajima, and Kitajima-or-Makino. The form using the higher register does not occur often but may be found in *Mutamagawa* by Mitsuhashi and *Tobiume* by Shin Yatsuhashi. An incomplete namigaeshi, consisting only of shan-shu, occurs in *Tomo Chidori* by Hisamura.

The more generally used right-hand techniques, awasezume, kakite, oshiawase, and so on, have certain characteristics that should be noted briefly. Awasezume is used mainly with tones e and b, that is, degrees I and V. Awasezume on both degrees occur within the uta as well as in its final cadences. An octave on degree II occurs sporadically in compositions by Yatsuhashi and Kitajima, and may be found in cadences on degree II *(Suma,* uta 6, and *Akashi,* uta 6). A remarkable coloristic effect is obtained when the koto plays a short sequence of octaves. This practice is rare and is used only by Yatsuhashi, Hisamura, the anonymous composer of *Chio no Tomo*, Yamada, and Tsugiyama. Awasezume on tones f, a, and c occur almost exclusively in octave sequences. The examples below illustrate the use of octave sequences in kumiuta.

Example 103. (a) *Kokoro Zukushi*, uta 3; (b) *Hatsune*, uta 6; (c) *Usuyuki*, uta 2; (d) *Ōtsu no Kyoku*, uta 2.

Examples (a) and (b) show how two composers, Yatsuhashi and Yamada, living a century and a half apart, use practically identical material at similar locations (both in measures 5 through 7). Tsugiyama combines two related coloristic effects, oshiawase and awasezume (example d).

Probably it is because of their rather strident effect that sequences of oshiawase are rarely used. A repetition of the same oshiawase occasionally occurs. A double repetition is met in *Wakana* (uta 3) [see Example 104 (a)]. A sequence of two different oshiawase is found in *Hatsune* (uta 3) and in *Akashi* (uta 5) [Example 104 (b)]. Sometimes in a repeated oshiawase the pressed string may be released before the strings are plucked again; after the strings are plucked the lower string will be again pressed down until the pitch of the higher string is reached. Example 104 (c) illustrates this procedure. A yuri may be performed on the repeated oshiawase, as illustrated in example (d). Finally, an oshiawase may be released after the strings are plucked, allowing the lower of the two strings to return to its original pitch [Example 104 (d)]. All of these manipulations with oshiawase are rather infrequently encountered.

Example 104.   (a) *Wakana*,   uta 3;   (b) *Hatsune*, uta 3;   (c) *Tenka Taihei*, uta 5;
(d) *Jichō*, uta 3;   (e) *Suma*, uta 5.

Kakite (shan) is a very common right-hand technique.   A sequence of kakite, however, is extremely rare and is used twice only in the kumiuta repertoire, both times by Yatsuhashi. These two occurrences are shown below.

Example 105.   (a) *Suma*, uta 2;   (b) *Shiki no Kyoku*, uta 2.

Of the various forms of glissando, the use of sararin is general in kumiuta as it is in danmono, and hikiren, which is rare in danmono, is also very common.   Sararin may descend to almost any tone from f″-sharp down, but preference is shown for tones f″, b′, and e′ played on string 1. Hikiren by definition includes the complete range of the instrument.   Hikisute, a technique related to hikiren, is limited to only a few examples.   Kararin and its relative, hanryū, are less popular than sararin and hikiren and are not, for example, used by Ishizuka at all.   All these forms of glissando are quite colorful, especially when several of the same or different kinds are combined, as happens rather frequently.   The practice of combining glissandi is followed by practically every composer.   Example 106 shows combinations of hikiren-kararin-hikiren (a), hikiren-sararin-hikiren (b), and a sequence of three sararin (c).

Example 106. (a) *Umegae*, uta 1; (b) *Yuki no Ashita*, uta 1; (c) *Jichō*, uta 1.

Chirashizume, surizume, and namigaeshi are not to be found in danmono and may be considered kumiuta techniques. Waren, which is related to the three, exists in danmono also. Chirashizume characteristically occurs on tones e and b (degrees I and V). It is infrequently used. Often it is repeated once or more, as, for example, in *Kokoro Zukushi*, uta 1.

Example 107. *Kokoro Zukushi*, uta 1.

Yokozume appears in three different characteristic situations, one of which has been discussed in connection with the most typical final cadence of a kumiuta. Another form, used almost generally throughout the entire repertoire, consists of a single tone d'', played in yokozume technique, followed by a sararin to tone b'. We have seen this form already in *Fuki*. A less common form—used only by Yatsuhashi and Kitajima—consists of a descending figure of four tones from d'' to a' in sixteenths.

Example 108. *Kumo no Ue*, uta 5.

This figure occurs at the end of the second phrase. It may be stated that yokozume in general shows a tendency to occur at or toward the end of phrases.

Left-hand Techniques and Rhythm

Left-hand techniques, it has been noted, are determined by modal requirements, rather than by the genre in which they occur. Oshihanashi, en, chitsu, and ju are found in later kumiuta, as they are in *Fuki*. They present nothing that has not previously been discussed in the analysis of danmono.

Nor do we find that later kumiuta differ rhythmically from *Fuki* . Basically, the koto part of all kumiuta is very simple, containing the time values, rhythmic units, and syncopations that were discussed in Chapter X. If this rhythmic stock seems too simple to be of interest compared with the greater rhythmic complexity of danmono, it should be remembered that we are considering only the koto part, to which the voice part adds considerable rhythmic interest. The almost constant rhythmic shifting in the vocal part necessitates a relatively simple rhythm in the instrumental part.

Summary

We have examined the later kumiuta in hira-jōshi by taking the first kumiuta, *Fuki,* as a point of reference. This approach has allowed productive analysis which may be summarized as follows. The specific structure of *Fuki,* which is determined by the sequence of the kake-zume at the opening of the phrases and is derived from the structure of the first part of *Eten-raku,* can be traced, either directly or in a more general form, throughout the entire kumiuta repertoire. Direct influence, revealed by phrase openings similar to those at the same locations in *Fuki,* permeates the whole oeuvre of Yatsuhashi, to a certain degree influences the work of Kitajima, and disappears with Mitsuhashi. With the last composer the development of kumiuta, in fact, reached its end, although for a while new kumiuta were composed. The more general influence consisted of the use of the middle to high register for the first two parts, the low register for the last part, of an uta. Another direct influence of *Fuki,* the shaping of the last uta after the model of the concluding movement of that composition, may be traced through a number of compositions by Yatsuhashi, Mitsuhashi, Hisamura, and Ishizuka. The very strong coherence among the uta of *Fuki* is a unique feature of this specific composition.

Ai-no-te, which in *Fuki* occur exclusively at the end of second and fourth phrases, continue to be used at these locations. Beginning with Mitsuhashi, ai-no-te occasionally are found at the end of the sixth phrase, rarely at the end of the third. Thus, in general these interludes contribute to the outlining of the tripartite form, which follows the jo-ha-kyū concept. Most of the ai-no-te consist of a cadence-like passage and are no longer than a measure and a half.

The development of kumiuta through the three most important generations of composers shows an increasing proportion of free phrases and a decreasing proportion of kakezume phrases, diminishing of the direct influence of the *Fuki* structure, and increasing importance of ai-no-te. All these factors reflect the same trend: a loosening of the very tight construction exemplified by *Fuki*. The number of modulations also increases, until with Mitsuhashi they are by no means unusual. These modulations are of a limited duration, usually four measures, exceptionally eight.   Remaining longer in new tonal areas would require a change in the tuning of the koto, a step that is taken several times by Mitsuhashi.   As in Western music, the modulations are made to tonal centers that are closely related to the original one, to degree V ordinarily, less frequently to degree IV.

Composers after Mitsuhashi rarely added anything new to the form.   One can understand why, not long after Mitsuhashi, Yasumura pronounced his famous decree prohibiting the composition of new kumiuta.

CHAPTER XII

KUMIUTA IN OTHER CHŌSHI

The Modal Identity of the Tunings

Most kumiuta are composed in hira-jōshi and the use of the other tunings —the kumoi, naka-zora, and akebono groups, and *Akikaze*-chōshi —is limited to a small part of the repertoire. Our brief meeting with hon-kumoi-jōshi in the analysis of danmono shows that this tuning be-haves as a transposition of hira-jōshi to the fourth degree and reveals no changes that could be termed modal. Thus, the relationship between hira-jōshi and kumoi-jōshi may be likened to the relationship between two major (or two minor) keys a fourth apart in Western music. The *Sōkyoku Taiishō* (Vol. 6) confirms this, stating that the starting string (degree I) in kumoi-jōshi is string 2, in hira-jōshi string 5. The sequence of intervals in the two tunings on the koto is the same, namely: minor second, major third, major second, minor second, and major third (corresponding to degrees I, II, IV, V, and VI of the *in-*scale). The nakazora and akebono groups of tunings, which have their first degrees on strings 3 and 6, respectively, show exactly the same sequence of intervals. The fact that the different tunings have the same intervallic structure makes possible the use of the same mode in compositions in different tunings. Theoretically, more than one mode may be realized in a single tuning, but in practice this is not done. The scale used in all compositions in tunings having the same sequence of intervals is the same, the in-scale, and the functions of the scale degrees are unchanged. There exist only two tunings (han-nakazora 2 and *Akikaze* -chōshi) in which the sequence of intervals differs. Han-nakazora 2, however, will be shown to behave modally as han-naka-zora 1, that is, to use the in-scale also. This leaves *Akikaze* as the only kumiuta in a dif-ferent mode. It will be considered separately.

Hira-jōshi remained the most popular tuning through the entire period during which kumiuta were composed. The historic development of the form, therefore, is reflected in kumiuta composed in this tuning. Ornamentation (left-hand technique) has been shown to be a direct result of modality. As the mode does not change in any tuning except Akikaze-chōshi, orna-mentation is naturally applied in the same way except, possibly, in *Akikaze;* that is, in all compositions, the same types of ornaments appear on the same degrees. Techniques for the right hand are not functions of mode, and consequently we find that in this respect even *Aki-kaze* shows no essential differences from the rest of the repertoire. In the following discussion of kumiuta in tunings other than hira-jōshi, we shall limit ourselves, therefore, to illustrating the basic modal identity of the kumoi, nakazora, and akebono groups with hira-jōshi; to pointing out certain adaptations that result from "irregularities" in the tuning of the first two or three strings; and to drawing attention to hitherto unencountered phenomena when they occur. A large proportion of the secret kumiuta was composed in tunings other than hira-jōshi and thus some particulars of this special group will be discussed in this chapter.

The first kumiuta in hon-kumoi-jōshi, *Kumoi no Kyoku*, by Yatsuhashi Kengyō, begins its first two phrases like several kumiuta in hira-jōshi, with kakezume on strings 11 and 12. Example 109 shows the first phrase of *Kumoi no Kyoku* with a related phrase taken from a composition in hira-jōshi on (mainly) the same scale degrees and another phrase, also in hira-jōshi, that begins with a kakezume on the same string (11).

Example 109. (a) *Kumoi no Kyoku*, uta 1; (b) *Kokoro Zukushi*, uta 1; (c) *Umegae*, uta 5.

Examining example (a) and example (b) we find that the first three measures are identical in scale degrees: both phrases open with han-kake on degree VI, and the melody moves down and up between degrees I and IV, but in the fourth measure the phrases are no longer identical. Anticipating, we may note that the regular occurrence in hira-jōshi of han-kake on degree VI (string 9) is shared by kumoi-jōshi, where the string involved is string 11.

At first glance, example (c) appears even more similar to example (a) than does example (b). In Japanese notation the similarity would be even more striking, because the string numbers involved are, with the exception of the second tone, identical: 7, (8), 6, 7; 11, 12, 11; 10, 9, 10, 11; 12, 11, 10, 9, 10. The small differences between the phrases are significant because they are the direct result of the differences between the two tunings. First, whereas *Kumoi no Kyoku* opens with a han-kake, *Umegae* opens with a complete kakezume because the last tone in the pattern in *Umegae* is f" which is not degree VI, the only degree in hira-jōshi on which han-kake occurs. Second, the last beat in the third measure in *Kumoi no Kyoku* shows tone g", degree VII, which is a commonly used degree in all tunings in the in-scale. If this tone were in the *Umegae* phrase, it would be degree III, the least used of all degrees. What we find, in fact, is tone f", degree II.

As a second illustration of the basic modal identity between kumoi-jōshi and hira-jōshi, (a) and (b) in Example 110 show a practically complete transposition, including a cadence on degree V: (a) is simply a fourth lower than (b) with the most important deviation in the shan, which in (a) consists of degrees I and V and in (b) of degrees IV and I, both shan sounding identical.

Example 110. (a) *Kumoi no Kyoku,* uta 1; (b) *Usuyuki,* uta 2.

Since compositions in kumoi-jōshi are modally no different from compositions in hira-jōshi, both tunings allow the use of similar musical material, the only difference being the register.

One example may suffice to illustrate the modal identity with hira-jōshi of nakazora, akebono, and their related tunings. The four phrases, taken from kumiuta in han-kumoi-jōshi, hira-jōshi, nakazora, and akebono, share the same basic progression (degrees V–IV–IV) in their second, third, and fourth measures. The phrase in han-kumoi-jōshi (a) shows no modal differences from the others.

Example 111. (a) *Kan no Kyoku,* uta 2; (b) *Haru no Miya,* uta 1; (c) *Haru no Miya,* uta 4; (d) *Haru no Miya,* uta 5.[1]

Indeed the han-tunings (han-kumoi-jōshi and han-nakazora) are used in such a way that their aural effect is completely that of kumoi-jōshi and nakazora, respectively. Han-tunings occur only in the course of a composition, and are never used for a complete piece. They exist merely as a convenience for the performer. Although a player may show a respectable skill in changing the tuning of his instrument while playing, such changes require a certain amount of time, which makes it worthwhile to reduce them to the minimum. A complete retuning from hira-jōshi to nakazora, for example, requires the position of four bridges to be altered (those under strings 6, 7, 11, and 12); retuning from hira-jōshi to han-nakazora can be accomplished by moving only two bridges (6 and 7). One of these han-tunings, han-nakazora 2, has been mentioned as having a different intervallic structure than the usual. Normally a koto tuning represents degrees I, II, IV, V, and VI of the in-scale; in han-nakazora 2 the degrees are I, II, IV, V, and VII. The difference is the presence of degree VII in the tuning instead of degree VI. The observation deflates the consideration that han-nakazora 2 may represent a different mode, for previous analysis has made it clear that in the tunings with the usual interval relationship the string that is most frequently pressed down is the one that raises degree VI to degree VII. Han-nakazora 2 does not represent a different mode, but rather is a tuning that provides degree VII as an open string. Degree VI is easily provided by string pressure. When we study the rare examples of compositions that employ han-nakazora 2 (*Miya no Uguisu*, uta 2, and *Ōtsu no Kyoku* uta 5), we see that the portions in this tuning behave like those in nakazora. Degree VI appears in both *Ōtsu no Kyoku* and *Miya no Uguisu*, although Mitsuhashi Kengyō uses the degree only rarely, which sometimes results in a somewhat unusual descent from degree I to degree V by way of degree VII rather than VI. The following passage from *Miya no Uguisu* contains an example of this unusual appearance of degree VII in descending motion. A comparable phrase, also from *Miya no Uguisu*, illustrates the more common use of degree VI in this context.

Example 112. *Miya no Uguisu.*

Another difference between han-nakazora 2 and nakazora is in kakezume on string 11. It is used only once in *Ōtsu no Kyoku*. The following example shows kakezume on string 11 in nakazora, followed by its variation in han-nakazora 2.

Example 113.

Notwithstanding the above small deviations, the basic character of the mode remains un-altered. Han-nakazora 2 may be at most considered to represent a variation of nakazora, definitely not a separate mode.

Structure

The general structural outline that we described in our examination of kumiuta in hira-jōshi — four-measure phrases, frequently opening with a kakezume pattern, thirty-two measure uta — is preserved in the kumoi, nakazora, and akebono groups. Only two structural irregularities must be noted, both of them found among the secret pieces, namely, in *Yaegaki,* uta 2, and *Kō Genji,* uta 4. Both uta conclude with a 2/4 measure which in *Yaegaki* results in two beats more, and in *Kō Genji* in two beats less, than the norm.

Example 114. (a) *Yaegaki,* uta 2; (b) *Kō Genji,* uta 4.

In terms of the phrase structure,[2] it may be observed that in general the influence of the *Fuki* structural model has diminished strongly in these tunings, to the point that in most kumiuta it has disappeared completely. This should not, however, be attributed to the fact that the tunings are new, but rather to the historical development of the genre. Most kumiuta in tunings other than hira-jōshi were composed relatively late in the history of the genre. The only important concordances with the phrase organization of *Fuki* are found in compositions in kumoi-jōshi, which, significantly, after hira-jōshi, is the oldest tuning used in kumiuta. The beginning of the first kumiuta to be composed in kumoi-jōshi, *Kumoi no Kyoku,* strongly reminds us of *Fuki* because its first two phrases open with kakezume on strings 11 and 12, respectively. The sixth phrase also reflects traditional structure by beginning with kakezume on string 10, while if phrase 7 does not begin with the usual kakezume on string 8, at least it opens with another low form, kakezume on string 7. Finally, the kakezume on string 7 at the opening of the fourth phrase is an octave replacement of kakezume on string 12 (exactly as in *Fuki*, uta 5). Thus the agreement between the first uta of *Kumoi no Kyoku* and *Fuki* is undeniable. This is the only instance in which similarity with *Fuki* can be shown so directly, however, and, as might be expected, this is a composition by Yatsuhashi Kengyō.

The proportions of kakezume phrases and free phrases in the kumiuta in the kumoi, nakazora, and akebono groups of tunings are generally similar to those in the compositions in hira-jōshi. The number of free phrases increases in the course of a composition as in the course of the history of the form. An exceptional instance of all phrases opening with kakezume is found in the nakazora group in the first uta of *Yaegaki*, by Shin Yatsuhashi Kengyō. This is the only time that this is found after *Fuki*. In the akebono group, exceptionally high numbers of kakezume phrases (high, that is, in view of the location in the last uta of the composition) are found in *Haru no Miya*, uta 6, and *Kō Genji*, uta 5, kumiuta by Ishizuka Kengyō and Tsugiyama Kengyō, respectively. Such a high number is unusual in Tsugiyama's work. A reasonable explanation is that only this last uta is composed in the akebono tuning (those preceding are in nakazora) and the new chōshi may be best established by the use of kakezume phrases. The same explanation may apply to *Haru no Miya* as well, for it is a composition that changes tuning twice.

Ai-no-te

Ai-no-te in kumiuta in these less common tunings tend to be more frequent and longer than those in kumiuta in hira-jōshi. In part this is simply an expression of the later date at which compositions in kumoi, nakazora, and akebono groups were composed; it is, in addition, a consequence of the fact that several of the compositions are hikyoku (secret pieces). *Kan no Kyoku*, a hikyoku in kumoi-jōshi, contains ai-no-te of three measures (uta 2, 3, and 4, all in the eighth phrase) and four measures (uta 2, phrase 4; uta 5, phrase 8). This composition may be preceded by no less than two instrumental preludes, *Kin no Shirabe* and *Gin no Shirabe*, containing thirty-two and sixty-two measures, respectively.[3] Among the non-secret kumiuta only *Hien no Kyoku*, by Yasumura Kengyō, is preceded by an extensive instrumental introduction. It is uncertain whether this zensō was composed by Yasumura himself, for it did not appear in print at the same time as the publication of the kumiuta in volume four of the *Sōkyoku Taiishō* in 1779 but, rather, not until the seventh volume was brought out in 1903.

Two other hikyoku, *Koryū Shiki Genji* and *Tōryū Shiki Genji*, are distinguished by the occurrence of instrumental preludes and interludes. *Koryū Shiki Genji* opens with an introduction of four measures which, in another tuning, is repeated at the beginning of *Kagami no Kyoku* (*Koryū Shiki Genji* is in shimo-chidori, *Kagami no Kyoku* in ura-chidori). The prelude is in both cases called a *jo*.

Example 115. Jo of *Koryū Shiki Genji* and *Kagami no Kyoku*.

Tōryū Shiki Genji, a composition in karigane-chōshi, opens with an extensive koto introduction of unusual construction that is characterized by many reprises. The form is A:, B:, A:, B:, C:, introduced and followed by a 2/4 measure. Interludes of thirty-two measures are found in *Koryū Shiki Genji* between uta 2 and 3 and between uta 4 and 5, and in *Tōryū Shiki Genji* between uta 4 and 5. Instrumental preludes and interludes therefore appear characteristically in hikyoku, although not in all of them. The non-secret *Hien no Kyoku*, however, stands as an exception.

In the Yamada-ryū all kumiuta are traditionally prefaced by a short instrumental introduction of six beats, called *shirabe*. These shirabe are ascribed to Yamada Kengyō or to his student Yamaki Kengyō. Closely related shirabe, however, precede the kumiuta of the Yatsuhashi-ryū. Transcriptions of all shirabe are given on page 452.

Cadences

As in kumiuta in hira-jōshi, the large majority of inner uta of compositions in the kumoi, nakazora, and akebono groups of tunings, conclude on degree V, a smaller number on degree I, while in exceptional cases an inner uta may end on degrees II or VI. The most common cadence is an adaptation of the cadence on degree V found in hira-jōshi.

Example 116. Cadence on Degree V in (a) hira-jōshi, (b) hon-kumoi-jōshi,
(c) shimo-chidori, (d) shimo-chidori, (e) ura-chidori, and
(f) karigane.

Cadences (d), (e), and (f) in the above example deserve brief comment, for they do not blend tonally as do (a), (b), and (c). The point is simply that the shan that opens the cadences are always played on the first two strings, regardless of the pitches that result. In the case of the minor seconds the effect is jarring and it is only slightly less so in (d).

In a few kumiuta (*Tamakazura*, uta 1 and 2, *Kan no Kyoku*, uta 2) the stronger connections between movements are provided by withholding the resolution of the final cadence until the beginning of the following uta. Conclusions on degrees VI and II lead one to expect degrees V and I, respectively, to follow. They do not, in these cases, and the sense of suspense at the end of these unresolved cadences functions to bridge into the next uta.

Conclusions of final uta are usually made on degree I, occasionally on degree V, exceptionally on degree IV. Cadences on degrees I and V occur as they do in hira-jōshi. In occurrences of a conclusion on degree IV (*Kasumi no Kyoku* and *Shiki no Koi*), the impression given is of a deliberate modulation after a quite convincing cadence on degree I, in the voice as well as in the koto.

Example 117. (a) *Kasumi no Kyoku;* (b) *Shiki no Koi.*

Secondary Dominants and Modulation

The use of secondary dominants and modulations in the compositions in the kumoi, nakazora, and akebono groups of tunings is similar to that in those in hira-jōshi. The frequency of their occurrence in the kumoi group is somewhat higher than in hira-jōshi. Once again this may be explained as a direct result of later dates of composition. Modulations occur in every kumiuta composed entirely in kumoi-jōshi or a related tuning. They are absent from *Wakaba* and *Shiki no Fuji*, each of which contains only two uta in kumoi-jōshi. Most modulations are made to the fifth degree, some to the fourth, as in hira-jōshi, and the length of modulating sections is, again as usual, four measures, although occasionally longer modulations, up to 9 measures, are found (*Kumoi no Kyoku*, uta 6, *Omoigawa*, uta 6, *Kan no Kyoku*, uta 2, and

Kasumi no Kyoku, uta(3). It is noteworthy that in all pieces in the kumoi group that end on degree V, a modulation to the fifth degree occurs either in the very last phrase (*Omoigawa* and *Kan no Kyoku*), or rather shortly before the last phrase *(Kumoi no Kyoku)*. Also, one conclusion on degree IV is preceded by a phrase that modulates to the fourth degree *(Kasumi no Kyoku)*.

Secondary dominants occur somewhat less frequently in nakazora than in hira-jōshi and modulations are truly exceptional. When modulations do occur, they are to the fifth only. They are found in *Shiki no Koi,* uta 5, and *Kō Genji* uta 2 and 4. In kumiuta in the akebono group, modulation is equally rare, occurring only in *Tōryū Shiki Genji,* uta 2 and 4.

Right-hand Techniques

The occurrence of kakezume patterns in their complete form is in the kumoi, nakazora, and akebono groups of tunings exactly as it is in hira-jōshi. The kake occurs consistently on the sixth degree of the scale. The other patterns, tanhan, mukōhan, and kaihan, occur relatively less frequently than in hira-jōshi. Hayakake occurs, as in hira-jōshi, not only at the opening of phrases but also within the phrase.

Normally, a kumiuta opens with a kakezume pattern. This is not the case in *Hien no Kyoku,* which begins very unconventionally. The first four notes, although not played with index and middle fingers, sound as if they were starting a kakezume pattern. The octave on the first beat of the second measure, however, is not the expected tone (Example 118). Kakezume are never ornamented. The unique variation in *Hien no Kyoku* ornaments three of the four tones in the first measure, thereby achieving an effect unlike that of a conventional kakezume.

Example 118. *Hien no Kyoku,* uta 1.

A few right-hand techniques occur that have not been met before. In *Hien no Kyoku* (uta 5), the fifth string is tapped with the left hand. This technique should not be confused with the technique called uchizume, common in the Yamada-ryū, in which the string is tapped with the right hand. In Example 120, diamond-shaped notes indicate the strings that are tapped with the left hand.

Example 119. *Hien no Kyoku,* uta 5.

An indefinite pitch is produced in *Ōtsu no Kumi* (uta 5) by plucking string 13 with the index finger of the left hand in an upward motion to the left of the bridge. An unusual form of hikiren, played with the inner side of the tsume of the middle finger, occurs in *Tōryū Shiki Genji* (uta 4):

Example 120. (a) *Ōtsu no Kumi*, uta 5; (b) *Tōryū Shiki Genji*, uta 4.

Akikaze no Kyoku

Mitsuzaki Kengyō, the composer of *Akikaze*, consciously followed the traditional kumiuta form, six uta of thirty-two measures each, and also maintained the traditional use of kakezume patterns. The composition does not consist merely of a kumiuta, however, but also of a dan-mono, which serves as an instrumental introduction. The tuning is distinguished from the usual kumiuta tunings by containing one, rather than two, half-steps. It shows the following intervallic structure. For comparison, the structure of other tunings is also given:

Akikaze-chōshi: M2, m3, M2, m2, M3
Other tunings: m2, M3, M2, m2, M3

The singularity of Akikaze-chōshi involves only one tone.

As we have observed, *Akikaze* follows the traditional procedures. Structurally, each uta consists of three parts that express the jo-ha-kyū concept. This tripartition is frequently made more explicit by the location of ai-no-te at the end of the second, fourth, and sixth phrases, in other words, halfway through at the end of the first part, and between the second and third parts. The length of the ai-no-te is not unusual, about one measure and a half, except at the end of phrase 6 in uta 4, where it lasts for three and a half measures.

Because of the different chōshi, most of the final cadences of the inner uta differ somewhat from those met in other kumiuta. Uta 1, 2, and 3 all conclude on the fifth degree, and uta 5 on the second. This last example of an unresolved cadence is similar to those we have met before. The expected first degree does not occur; instead, the second degree smoothly leads over into the beginning of the sixth uta, which starts on the same degree. The final cadence of the composition ends on degree V.

It is typical of Akikaze-chōshi that two of the three uta closing on degree V emphasize the second degree at the beginning of the cadence. Degree II in this tuning is a perfect fifth higher than degree V, rather than a diminished fifth as in all other tunings. The final cadence of the first uta is introduced (as a homage to the past?) by a sararin.

Example 121. Final Cadences: *Akikaze,* uta 2, 3, and 1.

Like most kumiuta, no matter in what tuning, *Akikaze* uses only two accidentals, namely, the raised sixth degree and the lowered second. Other chōshi raise the second degree and lower the fifth. In *Akikaze* the second does not need to be raised in order to serve as secondary dominant for the fifth degree because in its unaltered form in this tuning the second degree already is a perfect fifth above the fifth degree: the secondary dominant is inherent in the tuning. Lowering the fifth degree in order to provide an upper leading tone for the fourth degree could be done in *Akikaze,* but does not happen, probably because use of the fourth degree as a temporary tonal center would involve a lowering of the second degree as well.

The lowered second degree in *Akikaze* may be seen, analogously to the lowered fifth in other chōshi, as a temporary upper leading tone. A parallel explanation of the raised sixth as analogous to the raised second in other tunings turns out to be less easy, because to assign this tone the function of temporary dominant of the fifth degree becomes, in the given context, rather far-fetched. The three occurrences of the raised sixth degree are found in the first, fourth, and sixth uta. Note that the tuning changes between examples (a) and (b): degree I in example (a) is tone e, while in examples (b) and (c) it is tone b (Example 122).

In the first of the three examples, tone c''-sharp might indeed be interpreted as a secondary dominant for the fifth degree, which appears in the last measure. The same explanation for (b) raises some problems. Although the fifth degree does appear in the third measure (tone c-sharp), its role as compared with that of the altered tone is relatively so unimportant that this explanation seems forced. As for (c), the fifth degree does not occur at all. Another explanation for the raised sixth seems required and may be developed from a consideration of an ambiguity within the tuning itself. Turning back for a moment to other tunings, we may observe that each consists of two identical parts. In hira-jōshi, for example, these parts are tones e-f-a and b-c-e. In Akikaze-chōshi the two parts of the structure, which consist of the tones e-f sharp-a and b-c-e, are unequal. The introduction of the raised sixth degree

Example 122. *Akikaze*, uta 1 (a), 4 (b), and 6 (c).

may probably best be interpreted as an attempt to restore balance between the two parts. This interpretation can explain the above example and also all occurrences of the flattened second degree, which results in a temporary transformation of Akikaze-chōshi into hira-jōshi as shown in Example 123.

Example 123. Akikaze, uta 1 (a) and 5 (b).

The occurrences of alterations in *Akikaze* are very limited, and all are shown in Examples 122 and 123. Modulations do not occur in this composition, Mitsuzaki showing himself in this respect more conservative than his immediate predecessors.

The kakezume chart (see Appendix C) for this composition shows a remarkably restrained use of this pattern. The absence of kakezume on lower strings (6 and 7) is to be explained by the unusual tuning of the lower strings which cannot provide the octave the pattern requires. Yet apart from the physical limitation in the lower register, Mitsuzaki does not use all possible kakezume. This may be a result of the relatively short time spent in each of the two tunings. Hankake occurs only on string 9. Tanhan, mukōhan, and kaihan-kake are absent. A sparse use is made of hayakake.

As for the remaining right-hand techniques, and those for the left hand, *Akikaze* follows the usual paths. In the latter half of the composition, warizume plays its customary role. Where it uses string 6 as its final tone, it receives a very special and almost poignant color as a consequence of the "empty" octave on sha-sha. The generally melancholy mood of *Akikaze* is largely determined by this octave between the first two strings, which may explain why Mitsuzaki devised this specific tuning.

With *Akikaze no Kyoku* we reach the end of the kumiuta tradition. Looking back over the findings in this chapter concerned with compositions in other tunings than hira-jōshi, we may conclude that the use of those chōshi did not present musical problems to the composers because no modal change occurred, except in *Akikaze*. The basic changes were only in register.

The use of tunings other than hira-jōshi seems partly responsible for the classification of certain kumiuta as hikyoku and therefore it is in this chapter that we have encountered other characteristics of the secret pieces, such as extensive instrumental introductions and ai-no-te. It should be emphasized that these are characteristics not of the tunings, but of the secret repertoire. *Akikaze* is distinguished from other kumiuta by its use of a complete danmono as introduction, and by its unique tuning, which was shown to have an asymmetric internal organization as compared with that of all other tunings. This tuning determined the choice of kakezume patterns made in *Akikaze*, while its asymmetry determined the alterations and their functions.

CHAPTER XIII

THE VOCAL PART IN KUMIUTA

In the sixth volume of his large work, *Sōkyoku Taiishō,* Yamada Shōkoku states that in kumiuta the voice is king, the strings (the koto) servant. This judgment by an authority deserves attention because it seems to contradict the evaluation that has been followed thus far in this study, namely, that the instrumental part represents the musical base of the composition, upon which the voice merely adds a version of the same melody which may be more complex rhythmically, but is never completely independent. Several strong reasons caused us to consider the koto, rather than the voice, to be the carrier of the composition. First, the koto part has uninterrupted continuity, while the vocal part, because of the numerous pauses, is more a collection of fragments. Second, in regard to rhythm, it is musically more sensible to view the vocal part in relation to the instrumental part, not the reverse: the koto is played on the beat most of the time, with only occasional deviations in the form of simple syncopations; the voice, on the contrary, often proceeds off the beat, following the koto, joining it again at the end of a phrase. A third argument may perhaps be found in the classification of this music as *sōkyoku*—that is, koto music, not vocal music. This last point alone may not be very convincing, yet when we consider that the term sōkyoku existed at a time when purely instrumental music for the koto was practically nonexistent, it cannot be entirely disregarded.

Yet, neither can Yamada Shōkoku's statement be ignored altogether. First, there is the fact that the text is a significant quantity in the total work. Second, the singer and the koto player are one and the same person who, regardless of what may be the musical base of the composition, voice or koto, must devote his major expressiveness to his singing and regard his koto playing as an accompaniment, the mood of which he must adapt to that created by his singing, which, in its turn, is influenced by the requirements of the text. From this point of view Yamada Shōkoku is clearly right, even though from a musico-analytic point of view there can be no doubt about the primacy of the koto part.

We know that the form kumiuta received its name from the fact that its composers selected their texts not from one but from various old literary sources, carefully combining a number of unrelated poems into cycles of—usually—six songs. This at least was the practice in the beginning. Later certain kumiuta were composed that used unified texts rather than composites. Although these works were, in the literal sense of the word, no longer kumiuta, yet musical factors rather than textual criteria actually defined the form and since these were consistently followed, the old term could legitimately continue to be used. Examples of kumiuta with unified texts are *Ukifune, Miya no Uguisu,* and *Akikaze no Kyoku.* A noteworthy group of kumiuta has the four seasons as its subject matter. The type can be traced back at least as far as Tsukushi-goto and can be followed through compositions by Yatsuhashi Kengyō *(Shiki no Kyoku)*, Mitsuhashi Kengyō *(Shiki no Fuji* and *Shiki no Koi)*, and Hisamura Kengyō *(Shiki no Tomo)*. These kumiuta are distinguished from the "standard" ones because they contain a smaller number of uta, basically four, one for each season. The cycle may or may not be preceded by an introductory uta. Another group of kumiuta, *Wakana, Tachibana, Tanabata,* and *Sakakiba,* also treats the sequence of seasons. Each of these four compositions (the authorship of which sometimes is ascribed to Yaezaki Kengyō), consists of three uta. The complete cycle of the four kumiuta, *Shiki no Kumi,* contains twelve uta, corresponding to the twelve months of the year.

In the Japanese language stress accent is absent and the importance of quantity is slight. Poetry in this language, therefore, does not employ poetic feet. Since practically every syllable consists of a consonant followed by a vowel, the number of combinations is very limited and as a result rhyme is so easy that it poses no challenge. The main structural device used by the Japanese poet is lines of a fixed number of syllables: normally a line consists of five or seven syllables. The most important Japanese poetic forms develop this principle. The *tanka,* for example, consists of five lines of five, seven, five, seven, and seven syllables, respectively; the *haiku* of three lines of five, seven, and five syllables, respectively.[1] Kumiuta texts tend to employ lines of five or seven syllables in length, but not consistently, and lines of four, six, and eight syllables are occasionally found. The number of lines usually agrees with the number of musical phrases, that is, there are eight.

The *Sōkyoku Taiishō* contains instructions concerning vocal performance which, since they were written at a time when kumiuta was still a relatively flourishing form, give a good insight into the ideal of performance practice in the second half of the eighteenth century. Modern practice, it should be noted, closely follows the same procedures. The kumiuta voice, according to Yamada Shōkoku, should be neither too heavy nor too thin, and the singer should strive after the right vocal quality, that is, not sensual, without vibrato, and with extreme care for correct intonation. The delivery should be devoid of roughness, and the connection between the syllables as well as the execution of the *fushi-mawashi* should be smooth (fushi-mawashi is a collective term for various kinds of subtle vocal ornamentations, such as light glottal stops, single spoken syllables just before a leap, and light accents in sustained tones). The singer should understand the meaning of the text as well as the structure of the music, the jo-ha-kyū sequence in general and the crucial locations in the musical structure in particular. Balance is the ideal, emotions should be controlled, and no undue melancholy displayed. When singing in low register intensity should be maintained; when singing in high register, the singer should be careful not to be carried away.

Yamada Shōkoku even goes so far as to warn against bad "stage manners." The performer must preserve a dignified attitude, should not close his eyes, nor beat time.[2] Such deportment may still be observed today, and the modern performer maintains a mask-like composure and is careful not to display emotion.

These instructions all work together toward one goal: the realization of a musical ideal of aristocratic reserve, of balance, and the avoidance of anything that might contain the slightest hint of vulgarity. Yet with Yatsuhashi's kumiuta a new kind of koto music appears which was disdainfully labelled zokusō, "vulgar koto music," by the guardians of the older traditions. It has been shown in the preceding chapters that technically kumiuta developed from older forms without any important break in the continuation. Now it appears that aesthetically also kumiuta followed the tradition.

Kumiuta may be described as melogenic, that is, the composition is oriented toward the music rather than the text. In general, direct influence of text on music is limited in musical genres with strictly predetermined forms. Kumiuta with its severely prescribed form does not allow for influence of the text on the musical structure. The formality of kumiuta goes beyond structure alone and permeates all patterns of behavior in and around the music. This formal attitude hardly provides a fertile ground for picturesque elements, such as musical illustration of the text, and, in fact, this is reduced to the minimum. Where it does occur, however, it is objectified (and thereby formalized again) by its strictly conventional use. For example, wind and cold may be illustrated on the koto by glissandi and lengthwise scraping of the strings. A section of the fourth uta of *Shiki no Kyoku* may serve as an example of illustration of the text (Example 124). The text "kaze fukeba suzushi(kute)" ("it is cool when the wind blows") is illustrated at two places: during the syllable "fu" of fukeba ("if it blows") the koto player performs a glissando over all strings;[3] the word "suzushi" (cool) is introduced by lengthwise scraping of the strings.

Beyond these occasional word illustrations, the relation between text and music can be described only in the most general terms: a general agreement of the structures of each (normally, a line of poetry corresponds with a phrase in the music) and a melismatic treatment of the words in the melody, in which process the syllables are about equally divided over the musical phrase.

Example 124. *Shiki no Kyoku*, uta 4.

Rhythmic interplay between voice and instrument is one of the most striking features of Japanese vocal-instrumental music in general. In an early study on Japanese music by Abraham and Von Hornbostel the relationship is nicely described in their mention of a "Gesangstück mit Koto-Begleitung, in welchem Gesang und Instrument forthwährend in Synkopen einander entgegenarbeiten" (Abraham and Von Hornbostel 1903: 333). When sixty years later William P. Malm describes the same phenomenon, he informs us that "this is not called a syncopation but rather a form of 'neutrality' *(fusoko-furi)*" (Malm 1963: 50)—fusoko-furi being the term the Japanese use to indicate that the vocal line is sung without strong rhythmic accents. The description by **Dr.** Malm seems partly to contradict the older one, but in view of the fact that Japanese music in general rarely uses strong rhythmic accents, it is better to consider his statement a refinement, rather than a contradiction, in which his choice of the word "neutrality" to describe the rhythmically free effect of the vocal performance may be appreciated.

Practically any phrase of any kumiuta may be selected to demonstrate the principle of vocal-instrumental collaboration and the choice of the first two phrases of the first uta of *Fuki* as representative is based only upon the function of this composition as a model for later ones.

Example 125.

The first two lines,

> Fuki to iū mo
> Kusa no na

contain six and four syllables, respectively. We notice that the shorter line coincides with a shorter musical phrase in the vocal part, a measure and a half being left to the koto for an ai-no-te. In general, there may be a connection between the number of syllables in a verse line and the length of the phrase in the vocal part, but this may by no means be elevated to a general law, for kumiuta, as this short example shows, are quite melismatic—a fact that allows the composer practically complete freedom. In most cases the syllables are so placed that they do not coincide with new notes in the koto. This practice, by avoiding a conflict in attention, promotes easy comprehension of the text.

The rhythmic interplay between voice and koto appears rather complex, and frequent shifts, mostly to an eighth after the beat, may be observed in the vocal part. See, for example, most of measure 2, the end of measure 6, and several separate tones in measures 3, 4, and 5 which fall between the beats. This rhythmic shift, however, is far from consistent, and Dr. Malm's suggestion that it might be more correct to bar a vocal line to start on the second half of the instrument's first beat (Malm 1963: 50-51) certainly could not be very practically applied in this specific example, no more than in kumiuta in general. In fact, the return of the vocal part to the beat is as important as its occasional departures from the beat. Rhythmic shifts in the voice line are used to create tension, which is released by returns to rhythmically tension-less locations on the beat in an alternation that may be compared with the tension-release pattern in traditional Western harmony provided by the use of dissonance and consonance. In the present example, rhythmic release is reached at the beginning of measures 3, 4, and 7, and in all cases is preceded by tension-creating shifts of an eighth. Maximum release is obtained where a melodic consonant in the voice part, preferably the first degree, coincides with the same degree in the koto on the first beat of the measure, especially on longer note values. See the beginning of measures 3 and 4, and compare these with the beginning of measure 7 where in the voice part release is reached rhythmically on the first beat, but melodically not until the third beat. Moreover, the koto plays degree IV rather than I on the first beat, adding to the amount of tension, which it then prolongs until the end of the ai-no-te. Notice how the koto after the sixteenth rest in measure 7 seems to disregard completely the tone just heard in the voice by quietly finishing its pattern II (the descent from degree IV via degree II to degree I). Compare this "harmonic dissonance" with very similar figures in measures 3 and 4, where voice and koto blend almost perfectly. This kind of figure, consisting of a low sixteenth and eighth after a rest of a sixteenth, usually appears at the end of a cadence in the voice line, thus securing continuation of the rhythmic motion.

Melodically the vocal part appears to be a variation of the koto part. Or, better, perhaps, voice and koto both are variations of an abstract melody that as such is absent from the composition. This abstract melody for the first phrase would consist of tone f" (the final tone of the kakezume) and the resolution of that melodic dissonant into tone e" in measure 3, at which point the goal of the melodic movement is reached, to be affirmed by a codetta in the remainder of measure 3 and in measure 4. Similarly, the second phrase essentially consists of no more than a descending cadence from tone a" to tone e" that is heard twice in the koto, once in the voice. In both phrases the voice line rises somewhat higher than the koto, in the first to tone b", in the second to tone c'". Essentially measures 6 and 7 are similar to measures 2 and 3: after reaching the main starting tone as sounded by the koto, that is, tone f" in measure 2 and tone a" in measure 4, a descending cadence to tone e" is performed, the skeletal tones of which in the voice are tone b"-f"-e" (degrees V-II-I). The second phrase differs from the first only in that it is more ornamented. Note that in both phrases the final tone of the cadence is followed by the "codetta" that typically occurs frequently in the koto part also. The second part of the first vocal phrase is no more than a kind of melodic echo of the first half, consisting only of tone e" and its upper and lower neighbors. The importance of degree II (tone f), already noted in earlier analysis, is clear in the vocal part also.

In both phrases the voice does not enter until the kakezume pattern in the koto is well on its way. This we will find to be a general practice that strongly contributes to the sectional character of kumiuta.

Kakezume on strings 11 and 12, the patterns with which the first two phrases of *Fuki* open, are frequently encountered and thus provide material for comparison that may lead to more general conclusions about the relationship between voice and koto. In several instances, these phrases in the koto part not only share the same opening kakezume, but are identical throughout. Two such phrases from Yatsuhashi's kumiuta will now be examined. The koto part of the first of these two examples is (f) of the following example; above it, (a) to (e) are five vocal melodies that are sung to that koto accompaniment. Each of these appears at the beginning of an uta.

Example 126.   (a) *Kokoro Zukushi,* uta 3; (b) *Tenka Taihei,* uta 5; (c) *Umegae,* uta 6; (d) *Usugoromo,* uta 5; (e) *Shiki no Kyoku* uta 2; (f) koto accompaniment.

In this example a koto phrase occurs in five different kumiuta in the same form, and in each occurrence as accompaniment to a vocal line that differs from, although it is related to, each of the other vocal lines. Uniformity in the koto phrases, therefore, is not necessarily paralleled by uniformity in the corresponding vocal phrases. We have previously commented upon the recurring nature of the musical material in the koto part, and have shown that this material reduces to a very few patterns that form the building blocks, and we have also amply shown the structural similarity of a number of kumiuta. Recurring material in structurally-like contexts obviously risks becoming monotonous. The simplicity of the rhythm in the koto part increases that risk, but is countered by the rhythmic complexity of the vocal-instrumental relationship. So, similarly, the possible monotony of recurring melodic material in the koto part is countered by the use of a variety of corresponding vocal lines. The changes shown in Example 126 (a)-(e) are, therefore, although slight, highly important. Such subtle shading, rather than strong contrast, is basic in much Japanese art, not only in music but also in literature, drama, and the graphic arts. In the area of music this basic dissimilarity to the dominant Western approach creates a barrier to understanding by Westerners. The interdependency between a homogeneous repertoire and subtle mutations in individual compositions is an aspect of the aesthetic of the danmono and kumiuta traditions that by this point can be appreciated as vital, and that will be reviewed in Chapter XIV.

Returning to Example 126, we see that the voice line in all five cases is limited in accord with the simplicity of the koto phrase (probably the most straightforward of all phrases that begin with kakezume) to the bare essentials. In each instance the outline is determined by the koto and basically consists of two progressions from tone f" to tone e". The voice follows the koto closely and uses only three tones, d", e", and f", that is, degree I and its upper and lower neighbors, except (c) which includes both higher and lower tones (degree V) as well. Rhythmic shifts are most explicit in the first two measures; in the third measure, rhythmic and melodic tension are released to resume again in a milder form in the fourth measure. The rhythmic interplay between the two parts, voice and koto, creating tension in the second measure by being one-eighth out of phase, releasing that tension in the third measure, where the voice carefully sounds a tone on the second beat while the koto remains inactive, and interlocking, finally, in the last measure, can be advantageously illustrated by reducing the two parts to their rhythms only. Such a reduction is given below. Here the five vocal lines are represented by a single line that is approximately their common denominator [and that happens to be (d) in Example 126].

Example 127.

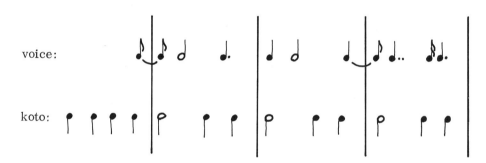

The final double-dotted quarter-sixteenth may also be performed as dotted quarter-eighth, but this makes no essential difference. Note that the voice starts on the last eighth of the first measure, following the general rule that a kakezume must begin alone. The entrance of the voice is indeed as late as possible and thus the kakezume functions as a miniscule introduction. In three of the five pieces the first note in the voice is tone f", agreeing with the basic octave of the kakezume pattern. In the two other cases the singer begins on tone d", the lower neighbor of the fundamental e", before attacking tone f', the upper neighbor.

The second phrase we wish to examine is the first phrase in *Tenka Taihei* (uta 1), *Umegae* (uta 1), *Fuki* (uta 1 and 2), and *Umegae* (uta 2). The koto part, as in the preceding example, begins with kakezume on string 11, and though its first half is identical to that of the previous example, the second half is considerably more complex. This relative complexity is fore-shadowed in the vocal lines which melodically as well as rhythmically are markedly more complicated than the very simple lines in Example 126. The difference between the two ex-amples is immediately clear when the rhythmic abstract of the latter is compared with that of the previous one.

Example 128. (a) *Tenka Taihei*, uta 1; (b) *Umegae*, uta 1; (c) *Fuki*, uta 1;
(d) *Fuki*, uta 2; (e) *Umegae*, uta 2; (f) koto accompaniment.

Example 129.

The principle of the rhythmic interrelationship is the same in both phrases, but the realization here is more complicated than in Example 127, and of a considerable refinement. Note, for example, the delicate rhythmic interlocking in the fourth measure.

Like the vocal lines in the preceding example, (a), (b), and (c) either begin immediately on tone f", or reach that tone by way of tone d". *Fuki,* (c), however, begins on the last quarter instead of the last eighth of the measure. In all three cases, the voice rises slightly above the koto and includes tone b" (degree V). The second half of the phrase in (a), (b), and (c) shows no tones other than tone e" and its immediate neighbors. Melodically the phrase ebbs away, but its vitality is maintained by the finely differentiated rhythm.

As for (d) and (e), they are practically identical, and are distinguished from (a), (b), and (c) by their wider range and their omission of tone f" at the beginning of the second measure. Rather than taking over tone f from the basic octave of the kakezume pattern in the koto, they use the first tone of the pattern, tone a. Although they begin high, almost inevitably they ascend still further to tone c'", hereby including both upper and lower neighbor of tone b" (degree V) (compare this with the previous example, where degree I similarly appears with upper and lower neighbors), before beginning a descent at the end of which the koto is joined again at the beginning of the third measure. The widening of the range in the first half of the phrase makes logical the extension of the range in the second half to include tone b". Example 128 (e) begins at an earlier point in the first measure than the others, which may be explained by the greater number of syllables of its text (seven rather than six). Example 128 (d) has a variant at the beginning of the third measure which is not essential, but rather a form of vocal ornamentation that may or may not be applied by the singer.

Examples 126 and 128 have shown that the development of the vocal melody is largely determined by its opening. For example, when the first note is tone f" (degree II), the melody can continue immediately with tone e" (degree I), or leap up to tone b" (degree V) before descending to tone e". When the first tone is d", tone f" is sung before tone e" follows. Finally, when the first tone is a", the melody rises until it includes tones c'" and b", before descending to the goal of the melodic movement, tone e". When the melody rises to at least tone b", tone e" is approached by what seems to be a typical vocal cadence: (a"-) b"-f"-e" [(IV-) V-II-I]). Recognizing the importance of the beginning of the phrases, it appears justifiable to compare similar equivalent portions of different phrases, for example, the first two measures and a half (after which usually a caesura occurs), which enlarges our analytical material considerably. Working with complete phrases, we were limited to early compositions of Yatsuhashi Kengyō; using now the first half of the phrases, we shall be able to include not only other works by Yatsuhashi, but also those by other composers (Kitajima, Kitajima-or-Makino, Mitsuhashi, Hisamura, Ishizuka, Anonymi, and Shin Yatsuhashi). We shall find that the basic vocal patterns have been met already in previous examples, although naturally minor variations occur in abundance. These patterns can be summarized as follows:

1. The voice starts on tone f" (degree II). The goal of the melodic movement, in agreement with the koto part, is tone e" (degree I).

    a. Tone e" is reached directly. See, for example, *Suma,* uta 5, phrase 3; *Utsusemi,* uta 5, phrase 1; *Tobiume,* uta 4, phrase 3 and uta 5, phrase 3.

b. The melody first descends to tone d" (degree VII), then returns to tone f", after
    which it continues to tone e" (*Umegae*, uta 6, phrase 1; *Kokoro Zukushi*, uta 3,
    phrase 1; *Tenka Taihei*, uta 5, phrase 1; and *Shiki no Kyoku*, uta 3, phrase 1).

c. The initial tone f" is not tied over to the next measure but sung twice. After alter-
    nating with its lower neighbor, tone e", the melody develops in a way similar to
    type b. See, for example, *Fuki*, uta 3, phrase 1, and *Ukifune*, uta 1, phrase 1.

d. The final tone e" is reached by means of a vocal cadence (a"-)b"-f"-e". Usually
    the highest tone occurs in the second half of the measure (*Tenka Taihei*, uta 1,
    phrase 1; *Tachibana*, uta 3, phrase 1); once it is found at the beginning as well
    as later in the measure (*Fuki*, uta 1, phrase 1). The following example illustrates
    each of these types, and also shows their common basis in the koto accompaniment.

Example 130. (a) *Utsusemi*, uta 5, *Tobiume*, uta 5; (b) *Kokoro Zukushi*, uta 3;
              (c) *Ukifune*, uta 1; (d) *Tachibana*, uta 3; (e) *Fuki*, uta 1;
              (f) koto accompaniment.

2. The voice begins on tone d" (degree VII).

    a. The melody proceeds by way of tone f" directly to tone e", which may or may not be followed by a codetta (*Umegae*, uta 5, phrase 1; *Yuki no Ashita*, uta 5, phrase 1; *Usugoromo*, uta 3, phrase 1 and uta 5, phrase 1; *Kiritsubo*, uta 3, phrase 1; *Shiki no Tomo*, uta 4, phrase 1; and *Tobiume*, uta 4, phrase 1). Closely related is *Shiki no Kyoku*, uta 2, phrase 1, which descends to tone d" in short note values before repeating tone f" and continuing to e".

    b. The melody proceeds by way of tone f" to tone e", followed by the cadence b"-f"-e" (*Umegae*, uta 1, phrase 1).

        Example 131.   (a) *Yuki no Ashita*, uta 5, *Usugoromo*, uta 5, *Shiki no Tomo*, uta 4, *Tobiume*, uta 4; (b) *Shiki no Kyoku*, uta 2; (c) *Umegae*, uta 1; (d) koto accompaniment.

3. The voice starts on tone a" (degree IV). All examples of this type show the same procedure: a continuation to tone c", followed by tone b" with its lower neighbor, tone a", and concluding with the vocal cadence b"-f"-e". A codetta may or may not follow the final tone. Examples occur in *Fuki*, uta 2, phrase 1; *Umegae*, uta 2, phrase 1; *Kumo no Ue*, uta 1, phrase 1; *Utsusemi*, uta 1, phrase 1; and *Tomo Chidori*, uta 1, phrase 1.

        Example 132. *Tomo Chidori*, uta 1.

In Examples 130, 131, and 132, the same material recurs regardless of the beginning tones. For example, the sequence b"-f"-e" is found in all three examples. The same is true of the simplest combination, f"-e", which may or **may** not be preceded by tone d". Example 131 (c) consists of the combination of both of these patterns. A melodic sequence may be realized in different rhythms. For example, *Fuki*, uta 1, phrase 1 (Example 130e), which occupies only two measures and a half, basically contains the same patterns as the complete second phrase in the fifth uta of *Suma* (Example 133). The fact that *Fuki* begins with kakezume on string 11 and *Suma* with kakezume on string 12 influences only the very beginning of the voice line.

Example 133. *Suma*, uta 5.

Just as the koto part can be explained in terms of melodic patterns that consist basically of upward and downward movements from one basic tone to another, so also the voice part can be understood as a selection and combination of preexisting melodic patterns that are related to, but different from, those for the koto. This phenomenon is not characteristic of kumiuta alone, but has been shown in other genres of Japanese vocal music as well (Harich-Schneider 1958-1960: 332 ff.; Malm 1963: 166 ff.).

Prototypical vocal melodic patterns are not considered in Japanese musical theory, nor are they recognized as such by the performing musicians. The only way to discover these patterns is through musical analysis. In melodies so finely differentiated as those of kumiuta it is often difficult to decide whether a melodic fragment is merely an ornamented version of a known pattern, or a different, new pattern. The following list, therefore, contains only the more obvious vocal melodic patterns. They are organized in four groups according to their final tones, which may be tone e, a, b, or f. (See Example 134.)

Several patterns in the third group are transpositions of patterns in the first group. Compare I (b), (c), and (d) with III (b), (c), and (d). Similarly, some patterns belonging to group IV are identical to patterns in group I except for the last tones. Indeed, patterns belonging to group IV give a feeling of incompleteness. Since all these patterns typically occur on tones e, b, and f, these duplications seem inevitable. Patterns I (a) and III (a), each consisting of only two tones, may seem too short to be considered real melodic patterns. However, in Example 130, pattern I (a) has been met in no less than four examples in such independent positions that its inclusion as a melodic pattern seems legitimate. Similarly, examples of pattern III (a) occur in independent roles in, among others, *Miya no Uguisu*, uta 1, phrase 1.

Example 134.

Some of these patterns, for example, I (a), I (b), III (a), and III (b), may be used at the beginning of a phrase in the voice part, but more frequently simple opening formulae consisting of two tones are found. The most common such formulae consist of an ascending second to tones e, f, a, or b. Somewhat less frequently these same tones are reached from an upper neighbor or by an upward leap of a third or a fourth. The following example shows in its upper staff the frequently encountered opening formulae, and in the lower staff, several that are less common.

Example 135.   Opening Formulae in the Vocal Part.

Thus far, analysis of the interrelationship between voice and koto has attempted to establish principles rather than examine in detail how certain specific koto patterns accompany other specific patterns in the voice part.   The word "accompany" here may be somewhat misleading, for our evaluation makes the koto part the controlling element in this two-part interplay.   What is meant is simply that when these specific patterns occur in the koto, other specific patterns tend to occur simultaneously in the voice.

One of the koto patterns most often used, not only in kumiuta but also in danmono, consists of a descending figure of three or four tones in a variety of rhythmic realizations, for example, a combination of half and quarters, or quarter notes only, or the dotted eighth-sixteenth-quarter sequence that constitutes the kororin pattern.   When any of these descending figures is used in the instrumental part, very often a related, but slightly deviating figure will occur in the voice. The relationship between voice and koto is simplest when the koto performs the descent in quarter values.

Example 136.   (a) *Fuki*, uta 1, *Umegae*, uta 2; (b) *Yuki no Ashita*, uta 2;
(c) *Yuki no Ashita*, uta 2; (d) *Kokoro Zukushi*, uta 1.

Examples (a) and (d) show the simplest combination of unornamented versions of vocal and instrumental patterns. In the voice tone b'' (degree V) is emphasized, while the same tone in the koto occurs only weakly and rather vaguely as an ato-oshi. The vocal parts of (b) and (c) show a slightly ornamented version of the same figure. The principles of this kind of ornamentation will be discussed in detail later.

When, in the pattern above, the first note in the koto is extended to the value of a half note, the initial note of the vocal pattern is replaced by a small group of four notes in order to adapt the pattern to the changed length.

Example 137. *Umegae*, uta 1.

Descending figures of the kororin type occur very frequently in the koto part. The voice usually shows the same pattern that is illustrated in Example 137. Example 138 illustrates the combination of kororin patterns in the koto with the voice. All the voice parts agree in outlining the same sequence, tones a-b-f-e (degrees IV-V-II-I). Voice-koto combinations of this type are very common.

Example 138. (a) *Umegae*, uta 3; (b) *Umegae*, uta 6; (c) *Tomo Chidori*, uta 1; (d) *Hashihime*, uta 1; (e) *Kokoro Zukushi*, uta 6.

Somewhat less frequent is a related form in which the vocal pattern is used in a very characteristic rhythm.

Example 139. (a) *Yuki no Ashita*, uta 3; (b) *Fuki*, uta 1; (c) *Suma*, uta 2, and *Ogi no Kyoku*, uta 1; (d) *Kumoi no Kyoku*, uta 2; (e) *Sue no Matsu*, uta 3.

Kororin figures beginning on the second half of the beat form the most prominent type of syncopation in the koto part of kumiuta. When these occur, the voice normally sings in a straight eighth movement and does not participate in the syncopation. Thus, when the koto part shows a certain rhythmic complexity, the voice balances with rhythmic simplicity. The following two examples combine two syncopated kororin patterns that follow one another closely, and therefore are rather exceptional. Single syncopated kororin occur very frequently and may be found in practically all kumiuta.

Example 140. (a) *Usuyuki*, uta 5; (b) *Kumo no Ue*, uta 5.

Kororin patterns occur in the vocal part as well. Here, sometimes the seventh degree is used in descending motion, a phenomenon unthinkable in the koto part, where the seventh degree appears only in ascents, the sixth both in ascent and descent. Where these patterns occur together in voice and koto, both versions, one with the seventh degree and the other with the sixth, may be found.

Example 141. (a) *Fuki*, uta 5; (b) *Sue no Matsu*, uta 1.

In the above example the conflicting seventh and sixth degrees are marked with an x. Noêl Péri drew attention to this remarkable phenomenon and explained that "si la voix le donne haussé [that is, the use of the seventh degree], c'est simplement pour produire une de ces dissonances passagères si fréquentes et si recherchées dans ce genre de musique" (1934: 42). M. Péri was undoubtedly right in his observation about the frequency of passing dissonance in kumiuta, but otherwise his explanation is not acceptable. The appearance of the seventh degree in descending passages in the voice part must be seen as the result of the general tendency of the voice to lag behind quite consciously. In the example from *Fuki* when tone d" appears in the voice, it "imitates" the preceding tone d" in the koto, not (yet) tone c", which occurs one sixteenth before. In the example from *Sue no Matsu*, the tone d" is held over from the preceding tone d" in the voice. Dissonances in kumiuta are a result, not a cause, and when M. Péri regards passing dissonances as "recherchées," he assumes a stronger concern for subtleties of vertical construction than actually is the case in seventeenth-century Japanese composition.

In passages that first ascend and afterwards descend, the sixth and seventh degrees are occasionally found in the vocal part in ascent and descent, respectively, simultaneously with the same degrees in the reverse order in the koto. This may be explained as a retarded response by the voice. (See Example 142).

Codettas in quarter notes in the koto normally are imitated in the voice part where, however, the lower second appears as a sixteenth. The phenomenon is so common that examples may be found in almost any kumiuta. The note in the koto preceding the final tone is typically followed immediately by the corresponding tone in the vocal part, which in turn is followed by a concluding tone with the value of a dotted quarter. (See Example 143).

Example 142. (a) *Umegae*, uta 4; (b) *Yaegaki*, uta 4.

Example 143. (a) *Hagoromo*, uta 1; (b) *Utsusemi*, uta 4; (c) *Sue no Matsu*, uta 1; (d) *Tamakazura*, uta 3.

Final Cadences

Last phrases in the vocal part are as standardized as those in the koto. Here, also, *Fuki* shows itself to be the true prototype upon which all later kumiuta are based. The final vocal phrases of all seven uta of *Fuki* are reproduced in the following example.

Example 144. Final Phrases in Vocal Part: *Fuki*.

Uta 1, 2, 5, and 6 reach the final tone e' (degree I) at the beginning of measure 31. This is also true of uta 3, but here tone e' is followed by an ascent to tone b' (degree V). In uta 4 a descent similar to those in the other uta is interrupted on tone f' (degree II), after which the melody ascends to tone b', as in the preceding uta 3. The most common conclusion for the voice at the end of an inner uta, in later kumiuta as well as in *Fuki*, is on the first degree in measure 31, after which the koto completes the uta with a cadence on degree V. In two uta, the voice follows the koto in its final cadence. In the last uta of *Fuki* (7) the vocal line develops toward tone e', the first degree, which is reached at the end of measure 30 but is followed by tones d', e', and f', giving the vocal conclusion of the piece a remarkably labile ending and leaving the restoration of stability to the short postlude by the koto. In general, therefore, the vocal part ends on the first degree in most uta, with a short ascent to degree II or degree V sometimes following the final tone of the cadence.

Not only the final tone, but also the way in which the final tone is approached is typified in *Fuki* for the entire repertoire. These typical cadential formulae are indicated in Example 144 by brackets. No more than three types occur:

1. IV-V-II-I   (uta 1, 2, 3, 4, and 7)
2. IV-V-II   (uta 4)
3. V-IV-II-I   (uta 5 and 6)

With the help of these three cadential formulae, which may be followed by ascents to degrees V or II, the vocal conclusions in all kumiuta can be classified. Of the three, the first occurs in an overwhelming majority of cases and the other two, therefore, may be considered more or less exceptions.

Similarity of vocal conclusions, and even of complete final phrases, often goes far beyond the very general outlines of the above three formulae. This is especially true of the final phrases of concluding uta. The most typical cadential phrase in the vocal part in the last uta is shown in Example 145.

Example 145.

This cadential phrase, which except for its beginning is identical to the last phrase of *Fuki*, occurs at the conclusion of *Umegae, Tenka Taihei, Kumo no Ue, Kiritsubo, Suma, Utsusemi, Hagoromo, Tomo Chidori, Hana no En,* and *Tobiume,* and thus is used by the composers Yatsuhashi, Kitajima, Hisamura, Ishizuka, and Shin Yatsuhashi. Closely related are the last phrases of *Kumoi no Kyoku* and *Chio no Tomo.* Identical, but with the three last notes omitted, are the final phrases of *Wakana, Tachibana, Tanabata,* and *Sakakiba,* and, slightly varied, *Jichō.*

The only examples of a IV-V-II cadence, followed by an ascent to degree V, to conclude a last uta, occur in *Kokoro Zukushi*, *Tamakazura*, and *Hien no Kyoku*. The V-IV-II-I cadence is found at the end of *Hatsune*, where it is followed by an ascent to degree V.

Example 146. (a) *Kokoro Zukushi*; (b) *Tamakazura*; (c) *Hien no Kyoku*;
(d) *Hatsune*.

Vocal Ornamentation

As in Western music, ornamental techniques in Japanese vocal music can be classified into two main types: first, ornamentation in the wider sense, comparable to the practice of diminution in Western music during the Renaissance and the Baroque, and, second, *fushi mawashi*, which are roughly equivalent to agréments, "small ornaments." The parallel with Western music can be drawn farther: the "diminutions" in Japanese music were originally improvised (compare Harich-Schneider 1958-1960: 191-192) but later, as in kumiuta, were prescribed by the composer, while the agréments, although partly prescribed, always represented a limited field for the personal initiative of the performer. This situation in Japan around 1700 is very close to that in contemporaneous Europe.

The extent of vocal ornamentation can be shown in the following example, in which the vocal part of the first twelve measures of *Fuki* is given complete on the upper staff, and without ornamentation on the lower staff. The latter denuded version of the melody is an artificial construction, as such neither known to nor used by the Japanese musician.

Example 147.   The vocal part of the first twelve measures of *Fuki*, complete
and without ornamentation.

Agréments are found in the small groups of notes in short time values in measures 6 and 7,
while good examples of the practice of diminution appear in measures 6 and 11. This short
example shows that analysis of ornamentation must take into consideration whether the object
of the ornamentation is a single note (for example, tone b'' in measure 2, tone e'' in measures
3, 4, and 7), or a progression of two notes (a' to b' in measures 9-10, f' to e' in measure
11), or a still larger group (the complete sixth measure). These considerations form the
basis of our classification of vocal ornamentation, which is based upon material from the complete kumiuta repertoire.

A. *Ornamentation of single tones.*

This type of ornamentation is applied to first, fourth, and fifth degrees of the scale,
the three basic degrees of the mode. The principle is simple: once or twice the tone
is alternated with its lower neighbor or, rarely, with both upper and lower neighbors.
The value of the ornamented tone is at least a dotted quarter, usually a half note.
The rhythm may vary. In the following example, (a) through (f) represent ornamentation of various basic tones with lower second only, while examples (g) through (i)
show the main tone (tone e'', degree I) with upper and lower neighbors.

Example 148. (a) *Umegae*, uta 3; (b) *Fuki*, uta 1; (c) *Kokoro Zukushi*, uta 1;
(d) *Kiritsubo*, uta 3; (e) *Yuki no Ashita*, uta 2; (f) *Miya no Uguisu*, uta 1; (g) *Fuki*, uta 4; (h) *Fuki*, uta 1; (i) *Fuki*, uta 1 and 2.

Ornamentation of single tones is a common phenomenon and examples may be found in any kumiuta. The selection given here is arbitrary and, although representative, by no means complete.

B. *Ornamentation of a sequence of two tones.*

1. Ascending seconds.

Three basic types may be distinguished:

a. An oscillating movement, in which the ascending second is repeated.

Example 149. (a) *Fuki*, uta 1, 2; (b) *Usuyuki*, uta 4; (c) *Akashi*, uta 4.

b. An infrafix is inserted after the first tone. This added lower tone may be a second or a third below the opening tone, depending on the location of the original second and also that of the preceding tone.

Example 150. (a) *Fuki*, uta 7; (b) *Kokoro Zukushi*, uta 3; (c) *Ōgi no Kyoku*,
uta 2; (d) *Fuki*, uta 3; (e) *Kiritsubo*, uta 2; (f) *Kokoro Zukushi*,
uta 2.

A lower second as an infrafix automatically occurs when the first tone of the ascent is
the fifth degree (tone b' in this example) and is normal when the first tone of the
ascending second is the first degree (tone e), except when this is followed by a
raised second degree (f-sharp). When the first tone of the ascending second is
degree IV of the scale (tone a), it will be followed by a lower second, if this tone
already preceded the ascending second [see (a); the preceding tone is given in
parentheses]; when this is not the case [example (e)], the first tone of the ascending second will be followed by a lower major third.

c.   A suprafix after the rising second has been performed, followed by a repetition of the
second or only its last tone. The suprafix may be a minor second, a major second,
a perfect fourth, or an augmented fourth above the higher of the two tones constituting
the original ascending second.

Example 151. (a) *Shiki no Tomo*, uta 1; (b) *Fuki*, uta 1; (c) *Ukifune*, uta 3;
(d) *Kumo no Ue*, uta 2; (e) *Sue no Matsu*, uta 1; (f) *Fuki*, uta 2.

2. Descending seconds.

Four types may be distinguished:

a. An oscillating movement, in which the second is repeated.

Example 152. (a) *Kokoro Zukushi,* uta 5; (b) *Suma,* uta 2; (c) *Shiki no Koi,* uta 1.

b. A suprafix is added after the first tone of the descending sound. This additional tone will be a major second above the first tone of the original interval.

Example 153. (a) *Fuki,* uta 4; (b) *Hagoromo,* uta 2.

c. Original interval plus infrafix. The additional tone will always be a major second below the lower of the two tones constituting the descending second.

Example 154. (a) *Fuki,* uta 6; (b) *Shiki no Fuji,* uta 4; (c) *Fuki,* uta 1 and 2; (d) *Akashi,* uta 5; (e) *Hagoromo,* uta 4; (f) *Umegae,* uta 3.

d. Descending second plus two suprafixes. These additional tones will be a major third and an augmented fourth above the first of the two tones of the descending second. This form of ornamentation occurs only on a progression from degree II to degree I, or from degree VI to degree V, but is very frequently met.

Example 155. (a) *Utsusemi,* uta 5; (b) *Kumo no Ue,* uta 4; (c) *Ōgi no Kyoku,* uta 4.

3. Ascending thirds.

   a. An oscillating movement [Example 156 (a) and (b)].

   b. Major ascending third plus infrafix [Example 156 (c) and (d)].

Example 156.   (a) *Tenka Taihei,* uta 2; (b) *Fuki,* uta 7; (c) *Sue no Matsu,* uta 1; (d) *Kumo no Ue,* uta 3.

4. Descending thirds.

   Two types of ornamented descending thirds occur:

   a. Oscillating movement [Example 157 (a) through (d)].

   b. Descending third plus suprafix [Example 157 (e) and (f)].

Example 157. (a) *Tenka Taihei*, uta 1; (b) *Kokoro Zukushi*, uta 5; (c) *Usuyuki*, uta 1; (d) *Jichō*, uta 6; (e) *Kumo no Ue*, uta 1; (f) *Ōgi no Kyoku*, uta 1.

5. Ascending fourths.

Ascending perfect fourths occur in only one ornamented form, an oscillating move-ment. Their location is between the fifth and first degrees.

Example 158.. (a) *Tenka Taihei*, uta 1; (b) *Usugoromo*, uta 1; (c) *Suma*, uta 1.

6. Descending fourths.

a. Oscillating movement [Example 159 (a) and (b)].

b. Descending fourth plus infrafix. The additional tone will be a major second be-low the higher of the two tones forming the fourth [Example 159 (c), (d), and (e)].

c. Descending fourth plus infrafix. The infrafix will be a major second below the lower tone of the fourth [Example 159 (f)].

Example 159. (a) *Sue no Matsu*, uta 2; (b) *Fuki*, uta 1; (c) *Usuyuki*, uta 6;
(d) *Fuki*, uta 1 and 2; (e) *Sue no Matsu*, uta 3; (f) *Fuki*, uta 3.

7. Descending fifths.

Only one form occurs: an oscillating movement between degrees V and I.

Example 160. *Fuki*, uta 5.

C. *Ornamentation of a group of three or more tones.*

1. Ascent over a range of a fourth or a fifth. Ornamentation over the range of a
fourth occurs only in a sequence of degrees I-III-IV (rarely) or II-IV-V (frequently); over the range of a fifth only in the sequence I-II-V. An infrafix will
be added.

Example 161. (a) *Suma,* uta 1; (b) *Akashi* uta 4; (c) *Setsugekka,* uta 1.

2. Descent over the range of a fourth or a fifth. The degree on which the descent ends is either I or V.

    a. An oscillating movement of the first two tones [Example 162 (a), (b), and (c)].

    b. An oscillating movement of the first three tones [Example 162 (d)].

Example 162. (a) *Shiki no Fuji,* uta 3; (b) *Suma,* uta 1; (c) *Suma,* uta 3; *Shiki no Kyoku,* uta 4 and 5; (d) *Fuki,* uta 4.

3. The (IV-) V-II-I cadence.

This very popular cadence occurs in an almost endless variety of versions, a few of which are given below.

Example 162. (a) *Suma,* uta 1 and 2; (b) *Kumo no Ūe,* uta 1; (c) *Fuki,* uta 2; (d) *Fuki,* uta 1; (e) *Fuki,* uta 2; (f) *Fuki,* uta 7; (g) *Ukifune,* uta 3; (h) *Kokoro Zukushi,* uta 1.

In the above summation of ornamental techniques no distinction is made between ornamentation by diminution and the use of small ornaments and, indeed, in many cases it is hard to draw a line between the two. Both types tend to follow similar laws. The duration of the figure, combined with the values of the notes involved, determine whether the figure is a small ornament or a form of diminution.

In general, longer note values are broken up in a motion that consists mainly of eighths and sixteenth notes, although occasionally values up to a dotted quarter may be encountered. On the other hand, thirty-seconds are by no means rare. The generally regular movement is often interrupted by two rhythmic figures, ♪♬ and ♪.♬♩ . In the first, the two sixteenth notes form a descending second; the first three notes of the second rhythm almost always consist of a rising and falling second, followed by a higher second.

The last two vocal techniques to be considered, glottal stop and spoken syllables, belong strictly to the fushi mawashi, the small ornaments. The glottal stop is performed very discreetly in strictly fixed configurations, namely, before one of the three basic tones when this is preceded by its lower neighbor, or when a basic tone is preceded by both upper and lower neighbor, in which case the glottal stop is performed just before the upper neighbor. Sometimes the final basic tone may be omitted. See Example 164 (g).

Example 164.   (a) *Fuki*, uta 1; *Kiritsubo*, uta 1; (b) *Ōgi no Kyoku*, uta 4;
(c) *Suma*, uta 5; *Utsusemi*, uta 1 and 2; *Miya no Uguisu*, uta 1;
(d) *Kumo no Ue*, uta 2 and 3; (e) *Jichō*, uta 2; (f) *Hien no Kyoku*,
uta 3; (g) *Chio no Tomo*, uta 1; (h) *Ōgi no Kyoku*, uta 5.

Spoken syllables are isolated phenomena, which never occur in groups. They invariably appear on the second half of a beat, in a value of an eighth and are followed by medium high to high tones with preference for the latter.

Example 165. (a) *Usuyuki*, uta 2; (b) *Akashi*, uta 6; (c) *Haru no Miya*, uta 4; (d) *Kiritsubo*, uta 4; *Omoigawa*, uta 4; (e) *Fuki*, uta 5; *Yuki no Ashita*, uta 4; and *Hagoromo*, uta 5.

Before summarizing, we must mention two instances in which the normal relationship between voice and koto hardly obtains. They are to be found in two of the earlier compositions by Yatsuhashi Kengyō (*Fuki*, uta 1, 2, 3, 4, and 5, and *Tenka Taihei*, uta 1). Since the fifth uta of *Fuki* was taken over by Ishizuka Kengyō, the same phrase occurs also in *Hana no En*, uta 5. In these unusual phrases the connection between voice and koto is minimal. They only occur after kakezume on string 11 in the koto part. The voice moves upward, finding its point of support on the strong tones of the mode, e, f, a, and b.

Example 166. *Fuki*, uta 5, phrase 3.

ta- ta- zu- mu wa

Summary

In the relationship between the voice and the koto the most important factor is that both follow the same general outline. It would be wrong to state that one is a variation of the other, since in most of the cases neither of the two can be said to present the melody in its original, simple form. Instead, each gives an individual version in its own idiom, of a basic melody which as such is not presented. In the construction of their respective melodies, koto and voice have each their own set of melodic patterns. Most of these patterns are quite flexible and can be realized in different rhythms. As the koto frequently opens its phrases with kakezume patterns, so the voice has a number of opening formulae, many of which consist of no more than two tones, frequently an ascending second to first, second, fourth, or fifth degree. Codettas, mostly occurring on either first or fifth degree of the mode and including lower, upper, or both lower and upper neighbors, occur frequently in koto as well as voice.

Like the koto, the voice also employs a number of characteristic closing formulae, the most frequently encountered cadence being (IV-) V-II-I. Often the final cadence of an uta is extended until it includes the whole final phrase. All forms of final cadences in the voice part for the whole repertoire are represented in *Fuki*.

The rhythm of the vocal part cannot be regarded as independent and can be understood only in its relation to the koto. Often the voice lags about one eighth note's distance behind the koto and joins the instrument at crucial points in the melody, that is, at the end of cadences. This alternation of "off the beat" and "on the beat" in the voice part causes an alternation of tension and release that in function is similar to alternations of dissonance and consonance in traditional Western harmony. The rhythmic balance between the two parts is carefully observed: when the rhythm of the koto is complicated, that of the voice will tend toward simplicity, and vice versa. The delicately interlocking parts result in a combined rhythm of considerable complexity and refinement.

The musical form of kumiuta is rigidly predetermined and excludes any influence of the text on the musical structure, hereby reducing the possibilities of musical illustration of the text to a minimum. Text and music agree in their general structure, that is, eight phrases in the music correspond with eight lines in the text. Without exception, the vocal melody is melismatic.

As for the present scores of kumiuta, it should be remembered that they show a certain pedantic precision which does not quite reflect the spirit of the performance. In a good kumiuta performance the melody soars freely, elegantly, and without effort over the koto accompaniment and the listener hardly ever suspects the rhythmic intricacies that are revealed only in notation.

CHAPTER XIV

CONCLUSION

Kumiuta and danmono stand at the beginning of one of the most important musical developments of the Tokugawa period (1600-1868), the literature of sōkyoku. During the seventeenth century they were the only forms of classic koto music to be composed. Following the establishment of the Ikuta-ryū in 1695, the kumiuta form gradually yielded its place to newer developments until, in the second half of the eighteenth century, the composition of kumiuta was formally prohibited by Yasumura Kengyō. Notwithstanding that prohibition, a few more kumiuta were composed, but the form had apparently lost vital contact with the times, and these later compositions rarely added much of value. Danmono, although not subjected to formal prohibition, declined simultaneously with kumiuta. Today, although both forms —the Old Testament of koto music —are highly valued *in abstracto*, kumiuta are performed only rarely by a small number of specialists, while, in addition to *Midare*, only one or two danmono, *Rokudan* and *Hachidan*, remain part of the standard repertoire of the modern koto player.

In the form in which they are known today, kumiuta go back to Yatsuhashi Kengyō (1614-1685), the composer of thirteen kumiuta and the founder of a modern school of koto music, zokusō, which has continued into the present. The origins of kumiuta go farther back in history, however, for Yatsuhashi Kengyō based his compositions on those of an older school, Tsukushi-goto (today practically extinct), which in turn is rooted in still older forms that may go back as far as the Heian period. *Fuki*, by legend the first kumiuta of the Tsukushi school, was derived from a gagaku composition, *Etenraku*, and served as base for an arrangement by Yatsuhashi Kengyō, the kumiuta *Fuki* as it is known today. The origins of danmono, on the other hand, are to be found among popular forms of koto music, which probably were incorporated into the repertoire of Tsukushi-goto before being adapted to zokusō. Today, fifty-three kumiuta and seven danmono are known.

We have observed that both danmono and kumiuta are tightly constructed compositions. The two forms share a number of significant characteristics: both consist of a number of independent movements (called uta in kumiuta and dan in danmono), that are performed in a gradually increasing tempo with return to the original tempo in the last measures of the composition, as also occurs in gagaku. Uta and dan both contain a strictly prescribed number of measures that are organized into three parts corresponding to the jo-ha-kyū aesthetic concept, a concept frequently applied in Japanese music. There are also basic differences between the two forms apart from the fact that kumiuta are vocal-instrumental and danmono strictly instrumental. The numbers of measures in uta and dan are different. Kumiuta show a very regular structure of four-measure phrases that in danmono occurs only in the jo-section of a dan, the ha and kyū sections having more integrated phrase structure. Finally, the number of uta within a kumiuta tends to be six, while the number of dan in a danmono varies between five and nine.

One of the most striking features revealed by analysis is the strong homogeneity of both repertoires. This is especially true of danmono. Every first dan opens with a short opening formula, the kandō, in which the three basic tones of the mode are outlined in the lowest register of the instrument and the range is no more than a fifth. In Part I of all first dan (the jo section), the melody moves gradually and systematically up, finding its points of melodic support on the basic tones, until by the end of the part the highest string of the koto has been reached. The phrase structure is sectional and regular (quadratic). Part II, the climax (the ha), moves entirely in the highest octave, and the phrase structure, in contrast to that of Part I, is irregular and integrated. Part III (the kyū), finally, leads back to the low register, and here the phrase pattern, again sectional, is less irregular than in Part II without, however, returning to the quadratic structure of Part I. The first dan of every danmono follows this basic structure so closely that all corresponding subdivisions have exactly the same length with the points of melodic support occurring on the same tone at the same locations. Moreover, the melodic material of all first dan is basically the same: it consists of elaborations upon no more than four prototypical melodic patterns that move upward or downward between basic tones of the mode. Parts I and III of all first dan agree in using the same basic patterns, while Part II characteristically uses a different pattern. Later dan are more or less closely related to the first dan, and a careful use of the term variation form is justified for danmono.

The kumiuta repertoire also exhibits homogeneity, but to an extent that is shown more as continuity in historical development than as similarity of detail among all individual compositions. The first kumiuta of the zokusō repertoire, Yatsuhashi's *Fuki*, derives not only its structure and its use of specific melodic patterns (kakezume) which are characteristic for kumiuta, but also its basic melodic content directly from the *Fuki* of Tsukushi-goto, which in turn derives these from *Etenraku*. The first uta of Yatsuhashi's *Fuki* is severely constructed, opening each of its eight phrases with a kakezume pattern. In the following uta this initial regularity is gradually released, and kakezume patterns are sometimes replaced by other octave patterns, notably warizume. Kumiuta composed later show an increasing tendency to diminish the number of kakezume patterns. The specific form of *Fuki* was an example for many subsequent kumiuta and its structure is characteristic of Yatsuhashi Kengyō. Gradually this direct influence diminished. Traces are still present in kumiuta by Yatsuhashi's student Kitajima Kengyō; they disappear in those by Mitsuhashi Kengyō, who was a student of Kitajima. The indirect influence of *Fuki*, showing in the use of higher registers for the first two parts of an uta and a lower register for the third part, is traceable through the entire kumiuta repertoire. An uta normally consists of eight phrases of four measures, phrases 1 through 4 forming the first part (the jo), phrases 5 and 6 the second part (the ha), and phrases 7 and 8 the third part (the kyū). Sectional, quadratic structure is continued through the composition and through the history of the form also, although tendencies toward stronger integration between the two phrases of the ha section are usually apparent (compare with danmono). Short instrumental interludes, ai-no-te, and rests in the vocal part at the end of numerous phrases contribute to the sectional character of kumiuta. The melodic material consists, in addition to the characteristic kakezume patterns, of the same four basic melodic patterns used in danmono. Voice and koto are closely related. Both may be considered versions of the same abstract melody, which as such is not present in the compositions and which in its vocal and instrumental realization is adapted to the specific idioms of voice and koto. Like the koto, the voice has its set of melodic patterns which are related to, although somewhat different from, those of the instrument. One of the most significant elements in the voice-koto combination is refined rhythmic interplay. Often voice and instrument are out of phase, the voice usually the value of one eighth behind. At other places, notably cadences, they join. Alternations of out-of-phase and in-phase passages result in tension-release patterns that may be compared with similar patterns in Western music caused by alternation of dissonance and consonance in traditional harmony. The combination of voice and koto strives toward a careful balance, greater activity in the koto being balanced by lesser activity in the vocal part, and vice versa. Similar phrases, or segments of phrases, in the koto parts, which permeate the entire repertoire, are accompanied by slightly different vocal phrases in different compositions. The vocal part, thus, by subtly varying from piece to piece, contributes to the identity of each composition. The influence of text upon music is limited to a few conventionally-used word illustrations in the koto part.

Notwithstanding a high degree of conformity among kumiuta and danmono composers, there are indications of a general development of musical style in a certain slackening away from the formal severity of the early kumiuta and the increasing number of accidentals, which function as secondary dominants or appear as part of modulating sections. In the course of time, syncopations in danmono increased in number as the form evolved. These factors permit construction of a chronology for danmono, the composers of which in most cases are unknown.

We therefore find ourselves confronted with two contemporary musical repertoires each of which shows a homogeneity that by Western standards is highly unusual. Clearly aesthetic concepts, different from those in the West, are active in these forms of Japanese music. Rather than the distinct contrasts typical of much Western music, here subtle shadings of basically similar material are preferred. The listener educated only in Western music requires a careful musical reorientation to attune his ears and his mind to the perception of finely differentiated rhythms and shadings in melody and dynamics.

The persistence with which the composers of kumiuta and danmono closely followed their respective musical models, *Fuki* and *Rokudan*, imprinting their individual stamps upon the established forms in the most discreet and restrained way, reflects an aesthetic point of view that is considerably older than kumiuta and danmono and that was not restricted to music. We must look for those who speak with words for explication of the thought of a period, though we find in the music expressions aesthetically related to that thought. In his guide to the composition of poetry, Fujiwara no Teika (1162-1241) stresses the importance of studying and following the style of the old masters, although he also emphasizes the need for originality:

In the expression of the emotions originality merits first consideration. The words, however, should be old ones.... The style should imitate the great poems of the masters of former times. One must discard every last phrase of the sentiments and expressions written by men of recent times.... One should impregnate one's mind with a constant study of the form and expression of ancient poetry (Tsunoda, DeBary, and Keene 1964: 179-180).

Fujiwara no Teika's pronouncements not only reflected the classic tradition of the immediately preceding Heian period, but also defined the canons for Japanese versification for later times. These canons, transferred to music, can explain the aesthetic underlying the composition of danmono and kumiuta. Although such exceptionally homogeneous repertoires, as well as the tenacity with which once-established forms are continued through long periods of time, the possibility of an explanation (at least partly) by a limited creative imagination should be considered also. This additional explanation might be supported by the following factors. (1) The production of even the most outstanding composers is very limited (the most productive kumiuta composer, Yatsuhashi Kengyō, composed no more than thirteen kumiuta, while composers such as Ishizuka Kengyō and Yasumura Kengyō are known for no more than one composition). (2) The fact that professional practice of sōkyoku was practically exclusively limited to blind men severely limited the use of available talent. (3) The fact that these blind musicians were organized into a professional guild, which not only regulated musical society, but also expected its members to adhere to certain compositional rules, made it possible also for musicians of limited creativity to fulfill the average requirements of composition. In point of fact, the percentage of mechanically produced compositions is rather high throughout the entire Edo period, that is, the time during which the Shoku-ʷashiki was in power. A parallel might be observed within the guild of the Meistersinger of Western Europe, where strictly defined compositional rules led to a similar stifling of individual creative imagination.

A younger contemporary of Yatsuhashi Kengyō, the poet Bashō (1644-1694), revolting against conformity, insisted that poetry should "change with every year and be fresh with every month.... I do not seek to follow in the footsteps of the men of old; I seek the things they sought" (Keene 1955: 38). Thus, Yatsuhashi Kengyō and his followers, although initiating a renaissance in koto music, paradoxically gave allegiance to the earlier aesthetic concepts. In this sense, therefore, they did not reflect the time in which they lived. Significantly, kumiuta flourished mainly in the Kansai district, especially in Kyōto, the enclave of the conservative aristocracy who were the carriers and preservers of ancient traditions. No less significantly, the Ikuta-ryū was founded in 1695 to fulfill a need for newer and livelier music. Finally, it is also significant that Hasetomi's attempts to establish the Ikuta-ryū in Edo, the most modern city of Tokugawa Japan, failed because the people of Edo rejected kumiuta as old-fashioned and too sedate. From the beginning, kumiuta and danmono were oriented toward the past, rather than the present.

Although aesthetic theory may reveal factors underlying musical composition, rarely can it explain intrinsic musical value. Our observation that kumiuta and danmono reflect principles that at the time of their composition were accepted by one part of Japanese society, and rejected by another, does not alter the objective fact that both forms represent highpoints in the history of Japanese music.

PART IV

AN ANTHOLOGY OF KUMIUTA AND DANMONO

INTRODUCTION

In the following anthology of kumiuta and danmono an attempt has been made to represent the widest possible variety of musical and technical characteristics of both forms. Thus, the collection represents all groups of instrumental tunings and all generations of kumiuta composers. Several kumiuta contain elements that are more characteristic of the composition per se than of the form as a whole. For example, at the end of *Kumoi no Kyoku* another version of uta 5 with an *ad libitum* second koto part has been added; an instrumental prelude and interlude occur in *Hien no Kyoku* and *Otsu no Kyoku*, respectively; the kumiuta *Akikaze* is preceded by a purely instrumental danmono. The danmono part of *Akikaze* is frequently performed together with *Rokudan*, which in this transcription has been added in the upper staff. Because of the different tunings of the two compositions, certain adaptations in *Rokudan* may be (but not always are) made. In the version of Hagiwara Seigin, which was used here, the alterations in *Rokudan* are placed within parentheses. These alterations are not used when *Rokudan* is performed as a solo composition.

All transcriptions, kumiuta as well as danmono, follow the tradition of the Ikuta-ryū in Kyōto, as represented by its foremost koto musician, Hagiwara Seigin. Local traditions in other musical centers of Japan may differ, but only in minor detail. These differences appear strongest in the vocal part of kumiuta. Those interested in stylistic differences are recommended to consult Sato's *Kumiuta Zenshū* as a source of comparison. The *Kumiuta Zenshū* is the only printed collection of kumiuta that gives notation of the vocal melody as well as the koto part.

In general, koto music lends itself easily to transcription into Western notation. Some instrumental and vocal techniques required the introduction of a few additional symbols, most of which were borrowed from Japanese notation. The following list contains these symbols and the names of the techniques that are represented by them. *

---

*For a complete description of these techniques, see Chapter V.

: sararin (ren uraren)

: nagashizume (kararin)

: hikiren

: waren, chirashizume; diamond-shaped notes indicate the sounded tones

: surizume

ス   : sukuizume

ケ   : keshizume

ヨ   : yokozume

: en (ato-oshi); the small note indicates the time value of the new tone

ヒ   : ju (hiki-iro)

ツ   : chitsu (tsuki-iro)

: glottal stop

: a spoken syllable

The translations of the poems, although adequate, have no literary pretensions; they are included merely to give the reader an insight into their content.

FUKI

1. Fuki to yūmo
   Kusa no na
   Myōga to yū mo
   Kusa no na
   Fūki jizai
   Toku arite
   Myōga arase
   Tamae ya

Fuki is a kind of grass,
Myōga is also a kind of grass.
May I receive the gift of wealth and fame,
May I receive divine favor.[1]

2. Haru no hana no
   Kinkyoku
   Kafūraku ni
   Ryūkaen
   Ryūkaen no
   Uguisu wa
   Onaji kyoku o
   Saezuru

The koto pieces Kafūraku and Ryūkaen
Are spring flower music.
The nightingales of Ryūkaen
Sing these same songs.[2]

3. Tsuki no mae no
   Shirabe wa
   Yosamu o tsuguru
   Akikaze
   Kumoi no
   Karigane wa
   Kotoji ni otsuru
   Koegoe

Koto music played in the moonlight
Is in tune with the autumn wind
Which tells us of cool nights.
The sound of wild geese in the sky
Descends upon the bridges of the koto.[3]

4. Chōseiden no
   Uchi ni wa
   Shunjū
   Tomeri
   Furōmon no
   Mae ni wa
   Tsuki no kage
   Ososhi

Spring and autumn
Are brought to a standstill
In the Chōseiden.
The shade of the moon
Passes slowly
Across the front of the Furōmon.[4]

5. Kokiden no
   Hosodono ni
   Tatazumu wa
   Taredare
   Oborozukiyo no
   Naishi no kami
   Hikarugenji no
   Taishō

Who are they
Standing in the corridor of the Kokiden?
They are Oborozuki-no-naishi-no kami
And Hikari Genji no Taishō.[5]

6. Tazo ya kono   Who is that
    Yachū ni   Who knocks at my door so late at night?
    Saitaru kado o   No matter how loud he knocks,
    Tataku wa   I will not open,
    Tataku tomo   Because we did not agree upon this in the evening.
    Yomo akeji
    Yoi no yakusoku
    Nakereba

7. Shichiseki no   Is it impossible
    Heifū mo   To vault a seven feet high screen
    Odoraba nado ka   If one jumps as high as one can?
    Koezaran?   Why is it that the sleeve of a beautiful silk dress
    Raryō no   Is not torn off
    Tamoto mo   When one pulls at it so desperately?[6]
    Hikaba nado ka
    Kirezaran?

---

[1]A play on the words Fuki ("butterbur"), Fūki ("wealth and fame"), and Myōga ("Zingiber myoga," as well as "divine favor").

[2]*Kafuraku* and *Ryūkaen* are gagaku compositions. Ryūkaen, in addition, is the name of a garden with beautiful flowers and willow trees.

[3]"Descends upon the bridges of the koto" = "Harmonizes with the sounds of the koto."

[4]Chōseiden ("The Palace of Long Life") is the name of a Chinese palace of the T'ang dynasty; Furōmon ("The Gate of Eternal Youth") is the name of one of the gates of this palace.

[5]This poem is based upon the book *Hana no En* of the *Genji Monogatari*. Oborozuki-no-naishi-no-kami and Hikari Genji are characters in this book. Kokiden is the name of a palace in the *Genji Monogatari*.

[6] The poem is based upon an anecdote of Shih Huang-ti of the Ch'in period.

FUKI

Yatsuhashi Kengyō
(hira-jōshi)

o. bo. ro. zu. ki. yo no na. i. shi no ka. mi hi. ka. ru. ge.n. ji no ta. i. sho

KUMOI NO KYOKU

1. Hitome shinobu no
   Naka nareba
   Omoi wa mune ni
   Michinoku no
   Chiga no shihogama
   Na nomi nite
   Hedateshi mi o zo
   Kogaruru

   Since ours is a secret love
   Passion overflows my heart.
   The salt kilns of the Near-Shore, in Michinoku,
   Despite their name are far away,
   And I burn with longing.[1]

2. Wasururu ya
   Wasuraruru
   Waga mi no ue wa
   Omowarede
   Adana tatsu
   Uki hito no
   Sue no yo ikaga
   Arubeki

   Has he forgotten me?
   I do not think of myself,
   But I fear for the future
   Of that heartless man:
   Other people may think badly of him.[2]

3. Tamasaka ni
   Au tote mo
   Nao nuremasaru
   Tamoto kana
   Asu no wakare mo
   Kanete yori
   Omou namida no
   Sakidachite

   Although we meet only once in a long while
   My sleeves become all the more wet.
   My tears flow now
   While I am thinking of tomorrow's farewell.

4. Ame no uchi no
   Tsurezure
   Mukashi o omou
   Orikara
   Aware o soete
   Kusa no to o
   Tataku ya matsu no
   Sayokaze

   To pass the long hours of a rainy night
   I have been thinking of olden times.
   Further deepening my melancholy mood
   The night breeze in the pine trees
   Knocks at the door of my hermitage.

5. Mi wa ukifune no
   Kajio-o tae
   Yorube mo sara ni
   Araiso no
   Iwa utsu nami no
   Oto ni tsurete
   Chiji ni kudakuru
   Kokoro kana

   Helpless as a drifting boat with broken helm
   My fortune has no place to go.
   As the roaring waves dash and break
   On the rocks of the dreary sea shore,
   So does my heart break in a thousand pieces.

6. Kumoi ni hibiku
   Narukami mo
   Otsureba otsuru
   Yo no narai
   Saritote wa
   Waga koi no
   Nadoka wa kanawa
   Zarubeki

It is the way of this world
That the thunder which rolls in the sky
Sometimes strikes the earth.
Why then will my love not be fulfilled some day?
It also must be.

---

[1] This poem contains several double entendres. The words "shinobu" and "michinoku" in "hitome o shinobu" (lit. "to avoid other's eyes," that is, a secret relationship) and "omoi wa mune ni Michinoku" ("my mind is full of affection") also refer to the place Shinobu in the district of Michinoku (Northern Japan). The word "chiga" in "Chiga no shiogama" ("a salt kiln of Chiga") refers simultaneously to the town of Chiga in Michinoku, famous for its salt industry, and the word "chikai" ("near by"); the salt kiln, moreover, is associated with the verb "to burn."

[2] Adapted from a poem in the *Shūi-shū*.

KUMOI NO KYOKU

Yatsuhashi Kengyō
(hon kumoi-jōshi)

hi _ to _ me   shi_ no_   bu   no

na_ ka   na_ re_   ba

o_ mo_   i   wa   mu_   ne   ni

mi chi_   no_ ku   no

chi. ga no shi. ho. ga. ma

na. no. mi mi. te

ke. da. te. te mi o zo

ko. ga. ru. ru

a. da. na ta. tsu

u. ki ki. to no

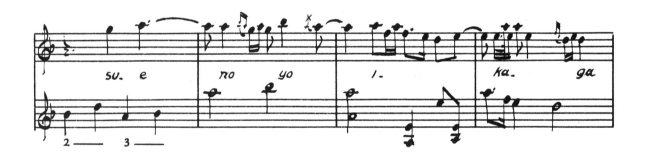

su. e no yo i. ka. ga

a. ru. be. ki

ta. ma. sa. ka   ni

o.   to.   te   no

na. o   nu. re.   ma.   sa.   ru

ta. mo.   to   ka. na

a. su ro wa. ka. re mo

ka ne. te yo. ri

o. mo. u na. mi. da no

sa. ki. da. chi te

a. me no   u. chi no

tsu. re. zu.   re

mu. ka. shi o   o. mo. u

o. ri. ka.   ra

a.   wa.   re.   o   so.   e.   te

ku.   sa   ro   to   o

ta.   ta.   ku   ya   ma.   tsu   no

sa.   yo.   ka.   ze

mi wa   u. ki.   fu.   ne   no

ka. si   o   ta.e.   te

yo. ru.   be   mo   sa.   ra   ni

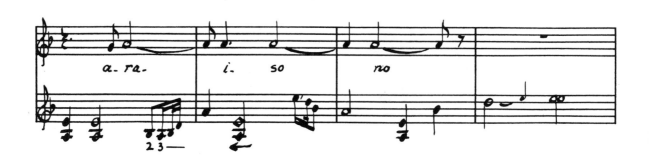

a. ra.   i.   so   no

i_ wa   u_ tsu   na.   mi_ no

o_ to   ni   tsu   re_   te

chi_   ji   ni   ku_da_   ku_   ru

ko_ ko_   ro ka_   na

ku. mo.   i   ni   hi   bi.   ku

na. ru.   ka. mi   mo

o. tsu.   re.   ba   o.   tsu.   ru

yo   no   na.ra.   i

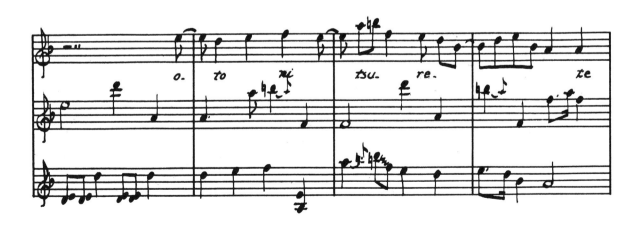

SUE NO MATSU

1. Sue no matsuyama
    Nami kosu tomo
    Kawaranu iro wa
    Matsugae ni
    Kimi ga chitose no
    Kagirinaki
    Migiwa no ike ni
    Kame asobu

    Even if waves should flow
    Over Sue no Matsu mountain,
    As the sprigs of a pine tree
    Remain green for a thousand years,
    You will not change.
    A tortoise plays on the brink of a pond.[1]

2. Mi ni shimiwataru
    Aki no koro
    Tsuki mo kumanaki
    Neya no to ni
    Kaerusa tsuguru
    Kudakake no
    Madaki ni naku zo
    Urameshiki

    Autumn: the time when deep feeling fills one's heart
    Outside our bedchamber
    The moon is shedding her silvery rays.
    Suddenly a rooster crows at the door,
    Telling me it is time to go.
    Alas! The rooster crows before the drawn.

3. Nakanaka ni
    Ima wa tada
    Omoi taenamu
    To bakari o
    Hitozute narade
    Yū yoshi mo
    Arade kogaruru
    Mi zo tsuraki

    As I cannot see you,
    And only through a messenger
    Can tell of the pain of my inner burning,
    I now end my life because of my yearning for you.[2]

4. Shinobu yama
    Shinobu yama
    Aware shinobu no
    Michi no gana
    Hito no kokoro no
    Oku made mo
    Mide ya yaminamu
    Waga omoi

    Ah! I wish there were a way
    To meet you in secret.
    Then I would penetrate deep into your heart
    So that my anxiety might be eased.[3]

5. Sayo chidori
    Yomosugara
    Naku wa ware o
    Tō yaramu
    Suma nu sumai no
    Monouki ni
    Namida o sōru
    Koegoe

    Is it to visit and console me
    That the plovers sing all night?
    Living in this house at Suma
    I feel so melancholy
    That their voices bring me to tears.

6. Chigiriki na
   Katami ni sode o
   Shibori tsutsu
   Sue no matsuyama
   Nami kosaji towa
   Ikani īkemu
   Ada ni narishi
   Urami kaya

"Both shedding tears we pledged
That the waves would never flow
Over Sue no Matsu mountain."
Under what circumstances
Was the poem composed?
Had they then, from bitter feelings,
Withdrawn their pledge?[4]

---

[1]According to an old saying lovers will not change their vows unless the waves of the ocean will flow over Sue no Matsu mountain: a lovers' pledge. The poem is borrowed from the *Kokinshū*.

[2]This poem is a slightly changed version of a famous poem in the *Goshuishū*.

[3]Based upon a poem in the *Ise Monogatari*.

[4]The quotation was borrowed from the *Goshuishū*.

SUE NO MATSU

Kitajima Kengyō
(hira-jōshi)

ki. mi ga chi to. se no

ka. gi. ri. na. ki

mi. gi. wa no i. ke ni

ka.me a.so. bu

2.

Mi mi shi. mi- wa- ta. ru

a. ki no ko. ro tsu

ki no ku ma. na. ki

ne. ya no to ni

ka- e- ru- sa tsu- gu- ru

ku- da- ka- ke no

ma- da- ki ni na- ku zo

u- ra- me- shi- ki

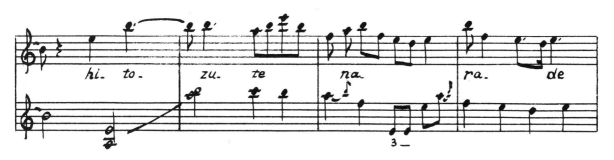

hi. to.   zu. te   na.   ra.   de

i. ū   yo. shi   no

a. ra   de ko.   ga   ru. ru

mi zo tsu.   ra.   ki

hi- to   no   ko_ ko_ ro no

o-   ku ma_ de   mo

mi_ de   ya   ya- mi_   na_ n

wa-ga   o-   mo_   i

su. ma nu suma. i no

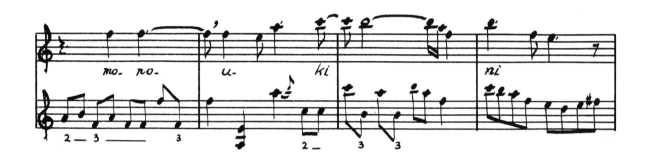

mo. ro. u. ki ni

na. mi. da o sò. ru

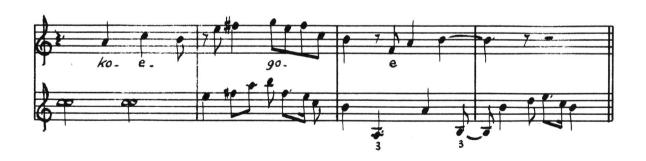

ko. e. go. e

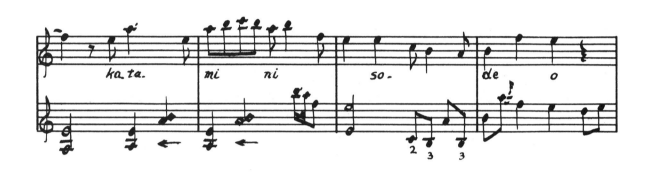

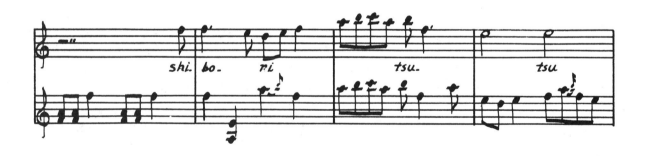

TAMAKAZURA

1. Ikanaru suji to
   Yūgao no
   Tsuyu no yukari no
   Tamakazura
   Mukashi o kakete
   Koi wataru
   Enishi mo ikade
   Asakaranu

I ask from whom she is descended.
She is Tamakazura, a relative of Yūgao.
I love her with all my memory of the past,
Our bond is not shallow.[1]

2. Hatsune yukashiki
   Uguisu no
   Sudachishi matsu no
   Ne o toeba
   Tani no furusu mo
   Mezurashiku
   Haru no hikage zo
   Nodokeki

A nightingale with first sweet song
Calls on the root of the pine tree
From where it first took wing.
The old home in the valley is so dear.
The sunshine of spring is full of peace.[2]

3. Sakura yamabuki
   Toridori ni
   Hana no magaki ni
   Tobichigō
   Kochō no mai wa
   Hakanaku mo
   Akazu kureyuku
   Keshiki kana

Butterflies are fluttering about fences
Where cherries and yellow roses blossom.
Their dances have not ended yet.
Alas! The spring day is growing dark.[3]

4. Koe wa sede
   Mi o nomi kogasu
   Hotaru koso
   Usuki hitoe no
   Nasake nite
   Soreka to bakari
   Wasurarenu
   Omokage zo yukashiki

Like a firefly burning itself silently
You have given me your sympathy
As thin as the lightest silk
Your dear, faintly seen image
Is forever printed in my mind.[4]

5. Saki midaretaru
   Mase no uchi ni
   Toko natsukashiki
   Nadeshiko no
   Moto no kakine ya
   Hito shirezu
   Kokoro ni kakete
   Shinoberi

Among the flowers blooming profusely
Beside the bamboo hedge
Is the ever-sweet fringed pink.
Secretly she remembers and thinks
Of the fence at home.[5]

6. Kagaribi ni
   Tachisō
   Koi no kemuri no
   Yo to tomo ni
   Taenu honō to
   Narinuru wa
   Yukue mo shiranu
   Omoi kana

Every night the smoke of love
Ascending with the fire
Becomes unextinguished flame.
Alas! I am not sure of
Where the smoke is going. [6]

[1-6] All poems are taken from the *Genji Monogatari*: from the books *Tamakazura, Hatsune, Kochō, Hotaru, Tokonatsu,* and *Kagaribi,* respectively.

TAMAKAZURA

Mitsuhashi Kengyō
(hon kumoi-jōshi, hira-jōshi)

i- ka- na ru su- ji to

i-u- ga. o no tsu

yu no yu ka ri no

TA. ma. ka zu ra n

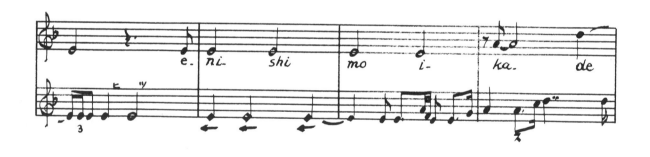

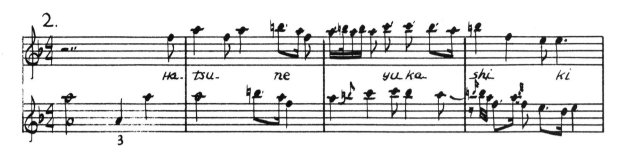

Ha.tsu. ne yu ka. shi. ki

u. gu. i- su no

su. da. chi. shi ma. tsu no

ne o to. e. ba

ta-ni no fu-ru-su no me-

zu- ra-shi-ku

ha-ru no hi-ka- ge zo

no- do-ke- ki

3.

sa- ku- ra   ya- ma- bu- ki

to-   ri-   do- ri   ni

ha- na   no   ma- ga- ki   ni

STRING 8: ½ UP ; 9 : ⅟₁ DOWN

to- bi- chi-   go

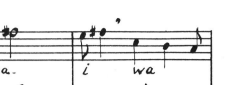

(o) ko- cho no ma- i wa

ha- ka- na- ku mo

2 —— 3 ——

a- ka- zu ku- re- yu- ku

3

ke- shi- ki ka na

3

4.

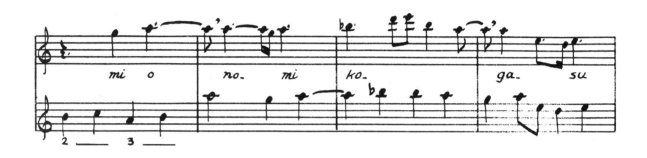

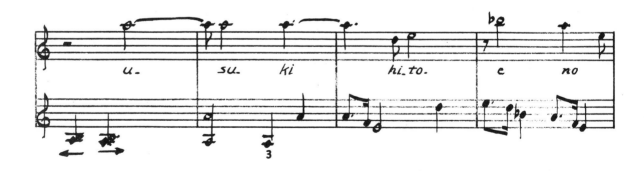

na_ sa_ ke   ni   te

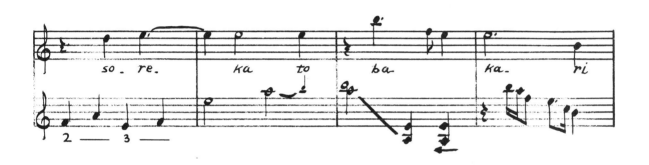

so_ re_   ka   to   ba   ka_   ri

wa_ su_   ra_ re_   ru   o_ mo_   ka_

ge   zo   yu_   ka_   shi   ki

5.

sa- ki mi- da- re- ta-

ru ma- se no u- chi ni

to- ko na- tsu- ka- shi- ki

na- de- shi- ko no no

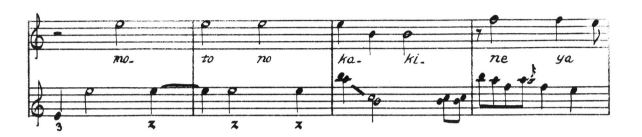

6.

ka. ga. ri. bi ni

ta. chi. so. u

ko. i no ke. mu. ri no yo

do. to. mo ni

ta. e. nu ho. no. o to

na- ri- nu- ru wa

yu. ku- e mo shi. ra. nu

o. mo. i ka. na

SHIKI NO KOI

1. Mono no aware wa
    Kore yori zo
    Shirazaramashi ya
    Shirazarame
    Toki ni tsuke tsutsu
    Utsuru kokoro
    Izureka omoi no
    Tane naramu

    Tender sentiments arise from this our love.
    Don't you know it? How could you not?
    Our hearts respond to the change of seasons:
    A cause of yearning.[1]

2. Ito yori kakeshi
    Midori koso
    Nemidaregami no
    Omokage
    Nagame seshi ma ni
    Iro mo ka mo
    Utsuroi yasuki
    Hitogokoro

    Long, green, drooping branches of a willow
        tree
    Remind me of a face with untied hair after
        sleep.
    So the beauty of a woman quickly fades
    And a man's heart is changed.[2]

3. Usuki nasake no
    Oriwaete
    Ito hakanaku mo
    Naki kurashi
    Tsutsumu ni amaru
    Mune no hi no
    Yosugara mi o ya
    Kogasuramu

    Throughout the day
    She may weep hopelessly
    Over his heartlessness.
    And all through the night
    She may burn herself
    With the fire of her heart,
    Too bright to be hidden.

4. Toshi goto ni
    Ō tote mo
    Neru yo sukunaki
    Chigiri kana
    Nageke tote ya wa
    Teri soru
    Kage ni zo chiji no
    Kanashiki

They[3] may meet once a year:
Their marriage is but a few nights.
The moonlight, which shines as if saying
"Grieve for your unhappy fate,"
Gives them many thoughts
And feeling of sadness.[4]

5. Ozasa ga ue ni
    Tabashiru wa
    Wakare no sode no
    Shiratama
    Omoi furuya no
    Noki ni tsumoru
    Urami mo tokete
    Shinobine

White jewels falling on the sleeves
When we say goodbye
Are like the chain of dewdrops
Running over bamboo leaves.
When meeting again our growing emotion
    and grief thaws
As the snow melts on the eaves of an old
    house
And we weep silently.

---

[1] Poem by Fujiwara Shunzei

[2] The first line is taken from the Kokinshu.

[3] "They" refers to Tanabara: Vega and Altair.

[4] The first two lines are taken from the Kokinshu.

SHIKI NO KOI

Mitsuhashi Kengyō
(hira-jōshi, han-nakazora, nakazora)

1.

2.

na- ga_   me   se_ shi_ ma   ni   i-

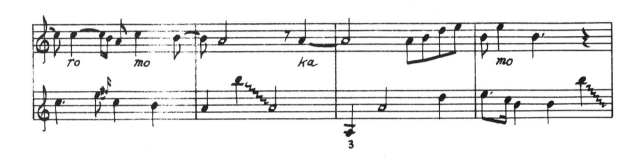

ro   mo   ka   mo

u_ tsu_   ro_ i   ya_ su_ ki

hi_ to_   go_ ko_   ro

3.

u. su. ki na. sa. ke no

o. ri. wa. e. te

i. to wa. ka. na. ku mo

na. ki ku. ra. shi

tsu. tsu. mu   ni   a.   ma. ru

mu-ne   no   hi   no

yo. su.   ga. ra   mi   o   ya

ko-ga.   su.   ra.   n

STRING 6: ½ UP

4.

TO- shi. go. to ni

STRING 7 : ½ DOWN

o to- te mo

2 3

ne- ru yo su ku- na- ki chi

gi ri ka- na na

5.

o. za. sa   ga u. e ni

STRING 11 : ½ UP   STRING 12: ½

ta. ba.   shi. ru wa   wa

DOWN

ka. re   no   so. de   no

shi. ra.   ta.   ma

HIEN NO KYOKU[1]

1. Hisakata no
   Kumo no sode
   Furishi mukashi
   Shinobashi
   Hana ni nokoru
   Tsuyu yori mo
   Kienu mi zo
   Hakanaki

I cherish the old days
When she waved her cloud-like sleeves.
Less enduring than the dewdrops on the flowers
Is my person, not yet passed away.

2. Yo o terasu
   Shiratama no
   Kazu no hikari
   Narazuba
   Amatsu otome no
   Kazashi shite
   Tsuki ni asobu
   Naruramu

Her face seemed to have the brilliance
Of many white jewels,
Illuminating the night.
Or, was like that of a heavenly maiden
With an ornamental hairpin,
Playing in the moon.

3. Kurenai no
   Hana no ue
   Tsuyu no iro mo
   Tsune naranu
   Yume wa nokoru
   Yokogumo no
   Furu sode no
   Namida kana

She had the rare beauty of dewdrops
On a crimson flower.
Awakening from my dream
I see only a bank of clouds in the sky.
Tears fall on my sleeves.

4. Natsukashi ya
   Inishie o
   Shinobu ni niō
   Wagasode
   Nurete hosu
   Kosu no to ni
   Aware nareshi
   Tsubakurame

How precious this memory!
While thinking of the days past,
My sleeves, fragrant with the scent of a fern,
Have become wet.
How lovely! Outside the bamboo screen
Where I hang the wet sleeves to dry
A tame swallow comes to play.

5. Tagui naki
   Hana no iro ni
   Kokoro utsusu
   Kono kimi
   Utsutsu naki
   Omoi koso
   Itodo nao mo
   Fukamigusa

The lord turned his heart
To the unsurpassed beauty of a flower.
He is possessed,
His passions grow even deeper.

6. Chiri yasuki
   Narai to wa
   Yose ni nomi
   Kikishi mi mo
   Utsurō wa
   Waga toga
   Uramu maji ya
   Harukaze

They said it was nature's way
That flowers would soon be gone.
I took it that they talked of others,
But I too fade, and the fault is mine.
I do not blame the breeze of spring.

---

[1]*Hien no Kyoku* is based on *Ch'ing-ping t'iao*, three poems by Li Po. Hien is the name of a beauty, who was loved by Ch'eng-ti during the Han dynasty.

HIEN NO KYOKU

Yasumura Kengyō
(kumoi-jōshi)

STRING 13 : ½ DOWN

(kumoi-jōshi)

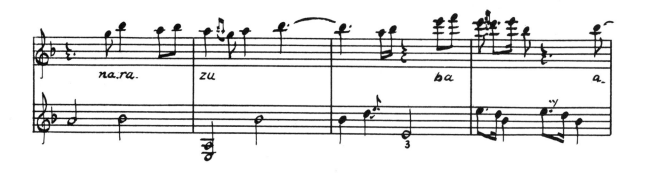

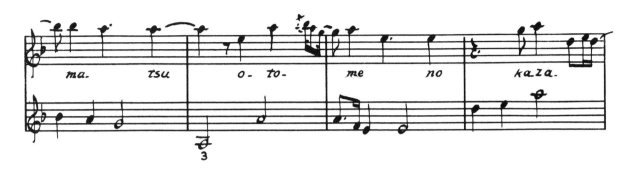

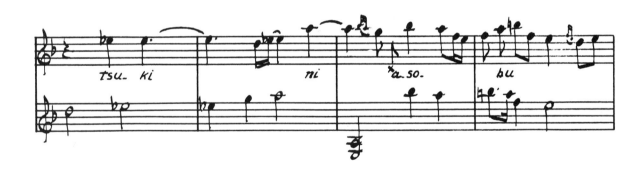

3. ♩ = c. 63

nu. re te   ko. su

ko. su   no   to   ni

a. wa.   re   na. re   shi

tsu. ba   ku. ra   me

1) TAP WITH THIRD FINGER OF LEFT HAND IMMEDIATELY LEFT OF THE BRIDGE.

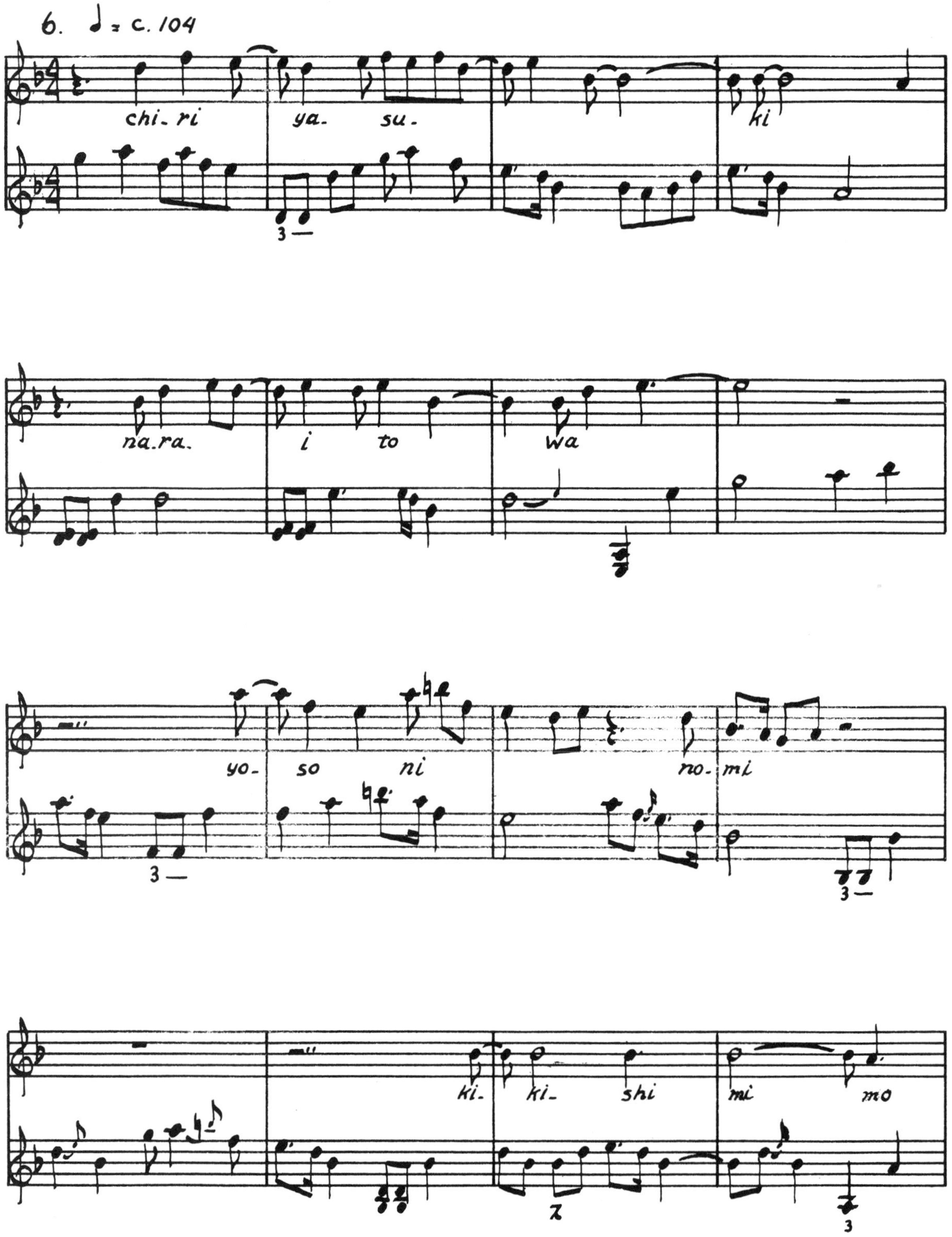
6. ♩= c. 104
chi- ri
ya- su-
ki
na- ra-
i
to
wa
yo-
so
ni
no-
mi
ki-
ki-
shi
mi
mo

HARU NO MIYA

1. Haru no yo no ma no
   Kaze ni fuki
   Hiraku rosei no
   Momo no hana
   Nakaba narazaru
   Miya no mae
   Tsuki no katsura no
   Kage takashi

   At night, spurred by the spring breeze,
   The peach blossoms have bloomed near an
     open well.
   In front of the Biō Palace[1]
   A judas tree casts its tall silhouette
   In the moonlight.

2. Kumoi no sora ni
   Kimi mezuru
   Sugata yasashiki
   Maihime no
   Yo ya samuki tote
   Megumi sō
   Hana no nishiki no
   Tamoto kana

   The Emperor loved a dancing girl with grace-
     ful figure,
   Upon whom he bestowed a beautiful brocade
     dress,
   Thinking of chilly nights.[2]

3. Shizukeki miya no
   Mado no uchi
   Ayanaku hana no
   Kaori kite
   Urami wa nagaki
   Haru no yo ni
   Maki mo eyaranu
   Tamasudare

   Near the windows of the lonely, quiet palace
   Flowers give of fragrance in vain.
   Cherishing the anguish of the heart
   All the spring night,
   She does not dare roll up the bead portieres.

4. Naname ni koto o
   Idaki tsutsu
   Tsuki ni mukaeba
   Oboro naru
   Kage sae yagate
   Kogakurete
   Hitori tsurenaki
   Yowa no toko

   Facing the moon
   She takes her koto.
   The hazy shape of the palace[3]
   Is hidden by trees.
   Helplessly she remains
   In the middle of the night.[4]

5. Ike no fuyō mo
   Oyobi naki
   Hito no tamoto ni
   Fuki wataru
   Kaze no kaori wa
   Nakanaka ni
   Hana yori mo nao
   Kōbashiki

   The wind is more fragrant than flowers,
   For it breathes on the sleeves of her,
   Whose beauty surpasses that of a lotus flower
   In the pond.

6. Kimi ga nasake no
   Wasurarede
   Sutenu ōgi no
   Aki mo fuke
   Katamaku tsuki no
   Yomosugara
   Miyuki no matsu zo
   Hakanaki

I dare not throw the fan away
For I cannot forget his feelings toward me
Now that the autumn has grown old.
How sad to look for the Emperor's visit
All night long, as the moon wanes.

---

[1]*Biō-kyū* (Chinese: *Wei yang kung*): the name of a Chinese palace.

[2]The first two poems are based on *Ch'un kung ch'ü* by Wang Chang-ling.

[3]*Shōyō-kyū* (Chinese: *Chao yang kung*): the name of the Empress's palace.

[4]Poems 3 and 4 are based on *Hsi kung ch'iu yüan* by Wang Ch'ang-ling.

HARU NO MIYA

Ishizuka Kengyō
(hira-jōshi, nakazora, akebono)

Ha- ru no yo no ma no

ka. ze ni fu. ki

hi. ra. ku ro. se. i no

mo.mo no ha. na

na_ ka_ ba   na_ ra_ za_   ru

mi_ ya   no   ma   e

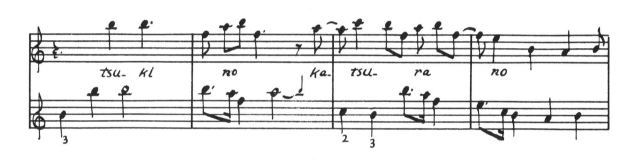

tsu_ ki   no   ka_ tsu_ ra   no

ka_ge   ta_   ka_   shi

2.

ku— mo— i no so— ra ni

ki—mi me— zu— ru

su— ga— ta ya— sa— shi— ki

ma— i— bi— me no

yo_ya sa_ mu_ ki to_ te

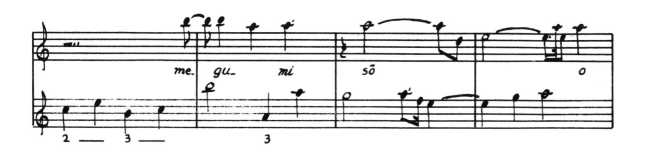

me_ gu_ mi sō o

ha_na no ni_ shi_ ki no

ta_ mo_ to ka_ na

STRING 6 : ½ UP

3.

shi_ zu_ ke_ ki mi_ ya no

2 —— 3 STRING 7 : ½ DOWN

ma do no u_ chi

3

STRING 11 : ½ UP, 12 : ½ DOWN

a_ ya_ na_ ku ha_ na no

2 —— 3 ——

ka_ o_ ri ki_ te

na_ na_ me ni ko_ to o

i_ da_ ki tsu_ tsu

tsu_ ki ni mu ka_ e_ ba

o_ bo_ ro na_ ru

STRINGS 3 AND 4: ½ UP

ke no   fu-   yo mo   o-

yo-   bi   na-   ki

hi-   to   no   ta mo-   to ni

STRINGS 5 AND 10: ½ DOWN

fu-   ki   wa-   ta-   ru

kaze   no   ka—   o—   ri   wa

na—ka—   na—   ka   ni

ha—na   yo—ri   mo   na—   o

kō—   ba—shi—   ki

6.

ki. mi ga na. sa. ke no

wa. su. ra. re. de

su. te. nu ō. gi no

a. ki mo fu. ke

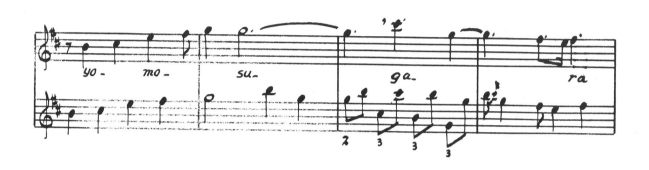

ŌTSU NO KYOKU

1. Haru no omae no
   Ikemizu ni
   Karameku fune no
   Yosōi wa
   Urara ni miete
   Kogu sode no
   Sao no shizuku ni
   Hana kaoru

In the spring garden
A gorgeously decorated boat in the pond.
Water drips from the oars,
Reminding us of fragrant falling blossom.

2. Tsuki no katsura no
   Oikaze ni
   Shirabe awasuru
   Tsumagoto no
   Kikisute kataki
   Orikara ya
   Moyōshigao no
   Hototogisu

I am unable to tear myself
From the charming strains of the koto
Which mingle with the breeze
From the judas tree of the moon,
And now a cuckoo has begun to sing
As if to tempt me to linger a while longer.

3. Asayū tsuyu no
   Hikari mo
   Yo no tsune naranu
   Iroiro
   Tamoto kagayaku
   Senzai no
   Chiji ni midaruru
   Akikaze

Morning and evening
The new sparkles in such unusual colors
That the sleeves glisten with it.
The autumn wind blows
And disperses the dewdrops.

4. Aretaru yado no
   Kakiio ni
   Furi tsumu yuki no
   Tachibana o
   Haraedo moto no
   Sue no matsu
   Nao tatsu nami no
   Omokage

Though sweeping the snow
From fences of a decaying house,
It soon piles up as before.
The sight of falling snow
Is like rising waves.

5. Chiyo yorozuyo no
    Yo mo saki
    Kimi no megumi wa
    Tsukubayama
    Hayama shigeyama
    Kage takaku
    Nigiō tami no
    Ie ie

Through all ages, until the end of time
The benevolence of the Emperor will never end.
Each household prospers because of the abund-
    ance
With which it receives the Emperor's generosity,
Which is inexhaustible as Tsukuba Mountain,
Covered with luxuriant trees and high grasses.

ŌTSU NO KYOKU

Tsugiyama Kengyō
(shimo-chidori, han-nakazora)

2.

tsu- ki no ka- tsu ra no

o- i- ka- ze ni

shi- ra- be a- wa- su- ru

tsu- ma- go- to no ki-

3.

sa_   i_   u   tsu_   yu   no

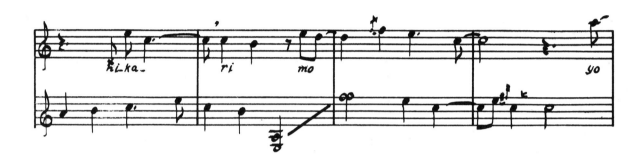

hi_ka_   ri   mo   yo

no   tsu_   ne   na_   ra   nu

i_ro_   i_   ro   ta_ mo_

4.

a-re- ta- ru ya- do no

ka- ki- i- o ni

fu- ri tsu- mu yu- ki no ta-

chi- ba- na o ha- ra- e-

do   mo_ to   no   su_   e

no   ma_ tsu   na o   ta_ tsu   na

mi   no   o_ mo_ ka_   ge

STRINGS 6 AND 11: ½ UP

5.

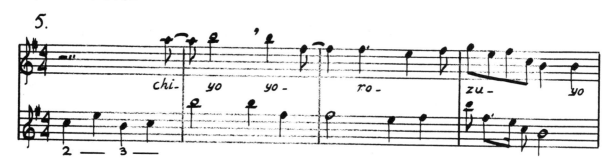

chi— yo   yo— ro—   zu—   yo

no   yo—mō   sa—   ki

ki—mi   no   me   gu—   mi wa

TSU— ku— ba—   ya—   ō.   ma

HATSUNE NO KYOKU[1]

1. Ume ga ka mo
   Misu no nioi ni
   Fuki magai
   Haru no otodo ni
   Haru tateru
   Omae no sama
   Yū kotonoha mo
   Oyobaji

   The fragrance of plum blossoms
   Mixes with the scent of incense
   Within the bamboo screen.
   Spring has come to the Spring Palace
   And the Lady within
   Is indescribably beautiful.

2. Ōmi no ya
   Ōmi no ya
   Nadakaki yama mo
   Yoso naranu
   Haru no kagami ni
   Mukai ite
   Kawaranu kage o
   Utsusan

   In Ōmi is the famous Mirror Mountain[2]
   And this too has meaning for me.
   Facing toward the mirror in spring[3]
   May it reflect an image which never changes.

3. Kyō wa ne-no-hi
   Narikeri
   Chitose no haru o
   Iō tote
   Sonō no komatsu
   Hiki asobu
   Hito no kokoro zo
   Nodokeki

   Today is the day of the Rat.
   To celebrate the everlasting spring
   People amuse themselves
   By pulling up young pine-trees in the garden.
   Their minds are carefree and peaceful.

4. Mezurashi ya
   Kage takaki
   Hana o negura no
   Uguisu
   Sudachishi matsu no
   Ne ni tatete
   Tani no furusu o
   Koto tō wa

   It is surprising that the nightingale
   Who nests amidst the loftly blossom
   Should fly singing to the pine-tree where it
      was born,
   To revisit its old nest in the valley.

5. Hana no ka sasō
   Yūkaze
   Nodoyaka ni
   Fukitaru ni
   Ume mo yōyō
   Himotokite
   Kono tono asobu zo
   Omoshiroki

   The evening breeze,
   Stirring the fragrance of flowers,
   Breathes pleasantly.
   Awakened by the breeze,
   Plum blossoms begin to bloom.
   It is tasteful and enjoyable to play *Kono Tono*.[4]

6. Otoko tōka no
   Akegata
   Mizuumaya nimo
   Araji na
   Wata o kazuki
   Watashite
   Banzeiraku o
   Utaeri

At dawn, after the night of Otoko-Tōka,
Instead of the usual mizuumaya[5]
The musicians were presented with cotton
As they sang *Banzeiraku*.

---

[1]*Hatsune* is based on the book *Hatsune* of the *Genji Monogatari*.

[2]Ōtomo no Kuronushi composed a poem in association with longevity upon Kagamiyama, "Mirror Mountain."

[3]"Kagami-mochi:" are round, mirror-shaped rice cakes.

[4]*Kono Tono:*   a saibara.

[5]Mizuumaya: a light, informal meal to treat Tōka musicians.

HATSUNE NO KYOKU

Yamada Kengyō
(hira-jōshi)

ha   ru   ta. te.   r.u

o.   ma.   e   no   sa.   ma

i.   ū   ko.   to.   no.   ha   mo

o.   yo.   ba.   ji

3. ♩= c.80

kyō   wa   ne_   no_   hi

na_   ri   ke_   ri

chi_ to_   se   no   ha_   ru   o

i_ wa   u   to_   te

su da chi shi ma tsu no

ne ni ta te

te ta ni no FU TU su o

ko to tō wa

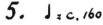

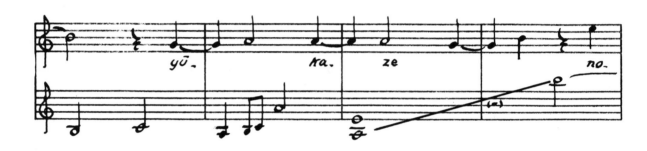

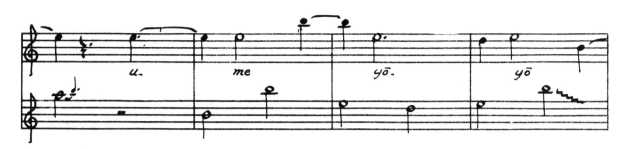

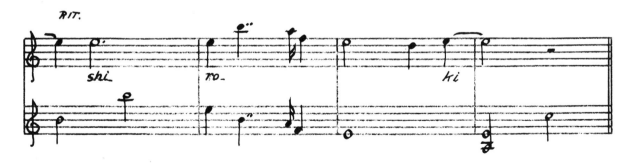

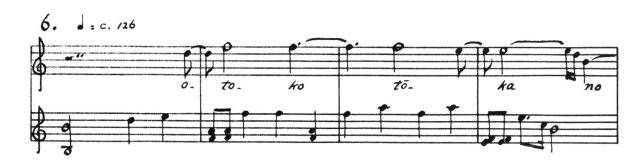

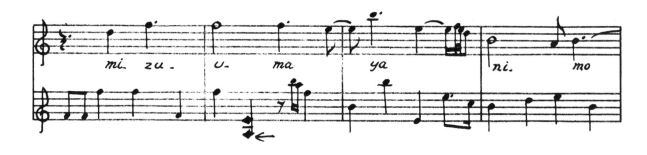

AKIKAZE

1. Motomuredo
   Egataki wa
   Iro ni nan
   Arikeru
   Saritote wa
   Yōka no me koso
   Taenaru
   Monozo kashi

   Though you may seek it,
   Difficult to find is a beautiful face.
   How rare then indeed is the beauty
   Of the daughter of the House of Yō.

2. Kumo no binzura
   Hana no kao
   Geni kaidō no
   Nemuri toya
   Ōkimi no
   Hanare mo yarade
   Nagame akashinu

   Her flower-petaled hair,
   Her flower-like face,
   Are truly like the slumbering kaidō blossom.
   The Emperor always gazes upon her
   Without ever leaving her.

3. Midori no hana no
   Yukitsu modoritsu
   Ikanisemu
   Kyō koko no e ni
   Hikikaete
   Tabine no sora no
   Akikaze

   Alone in the place
   He walks aimlessly
   Longing in vain
   For the lost young flower.

4. Geishō ui no
   Sengaku wa
   Bakai no yūbe ni
   Hizume no
   Chiri o fuku
   Kaze no oto nomi
   Nokoru
   Kanashisa

   After the night of Bakai
   Their lives had seemed touched with enchant-
      ment,
   Filled with heavenly music.
   Nothing is left but sadness,
   The sound of wind blowing through the dust,
   Raised by horses' hoofs,
   And sorrow.

5. Nishi no miya
   Minami no sono wa
   Akikusa no
   Tsuyu shigeku
   Otsuru
   Konoha wa kisahashi
   Tsumoredo tareka
   Harawamu

   In the Southern garden of the Western palace
   The dew weighs heavily
   On the neglected autumn grass.
   Though leaves fall and pile up on the steps,
   Who is there to sweep them away?

6. Enō no
   Kawara wa
   Shimo no hana
   Niō rashiki
   Hisui no fusuma
   Hitori kite
   Nadoka
   Yume o musubamu

The frost flowers are thick
Upon the tile of the mandarin-duck roof.
How can he dream,
Huddled alone under his green quilt?

(ROKUDAN) AKIKAZE

Mitsuzaki Kengyō
(hira-jōshi, akikaze-chōshi)

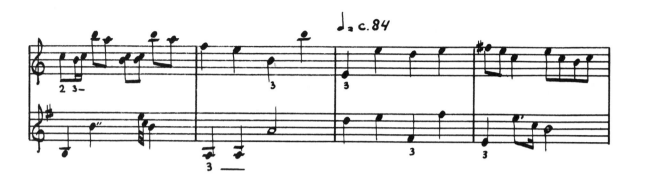

2. ♩ = c. 108

4. ♩ = c. 168

5. ♩ = c. 176

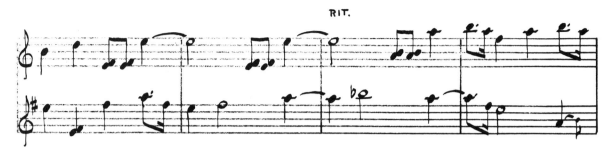

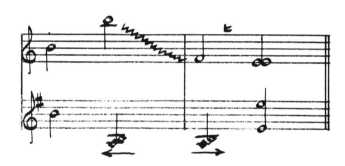

sa. ri. to. te wa yo.

ka no me. ko. so

ta. e. na. ru mo.

no. zo ka. shi

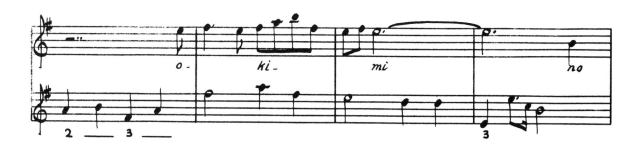

5. ♩ = c. 120

Ni- shi no mi- ya

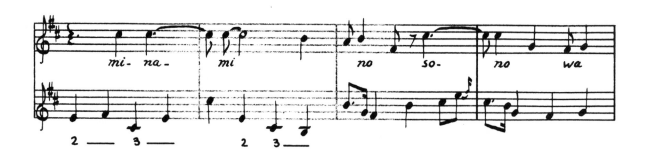

mi- na- mi no so- no wa

a- ki- ku- sa no

tsu- yu shi- ge-

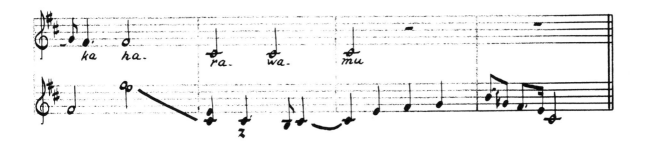

GODAN   (hira-jōshi)

KUMOI KUDAN

(hon kumoi-jōshi)

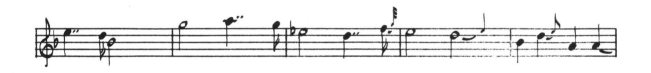

MIDARE

(hira-jōshi)

A TEMPO ♩ = c. 176

9 (VII) ♩ = c. 184

11 (IX) ♩= c. 208

♩= c. 224

12

YAMADA–RYŪ SHIRABE

Tradition in the Yamada-ryū relates that these shirabe were added by either Yamada Kengyō or his student Yamaki Kengyō.   Perhaps they were taken over from the shinkyoku *Shiki Genji,* in which many such patterns occur.   For a possible explanation of the origin of the shirabe, however, the occurrence of similar patterns in the Yatsuhashi-ryū should also be considered (Adriaansz 1972: 73, 75).

Hira jōshi

Hon-kumoi jōshi

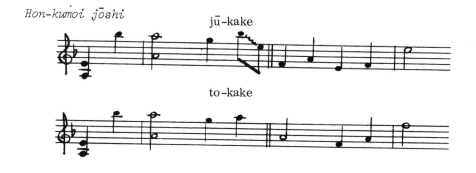

Han-kumoi jōshi

APPENDIXES

APPENDIX A

THE DANMONO REPERTOIRE

Composer	Composition	Number of Dan	Chōshi	Classification
Anonymi	*Rokudan*	6	Hira-jōshi	Omote-gumi
	Hachidan	8	"	Ura-gumi
	Midare	12	"	Ura-gumi
	Kudan	9	"	Naka-yurushi
	Shichidan	7	"	Naka-yurushi
Mitsuhashi	*Kumoi Kudan*	9	Hon kumoi-jōshi	Naka-yurushi
Ikuta (?)	*Godan*	5	Hira-jōshi	Oku-yurushi

454

THE KUMIUTA REPERTOIRE

Composer	Composition (alternate names in parentheses)	Number of Uta	Chōshi	Classification
Yatsuhashi (1614-1685)	*Fuki* (Etenraku)	7	Hira-jōshi	Omote-gumi
	Umegae (Chidori no Kyoku)	6	"	"
	Kokoro Zukushi (Oguruma no Kyoku, Miyakodori)	6	"	"
	Tenka Taihei (Sumiyoshi no Kyoku, Hinazura no Kyoku, Taiheiraku, Taihei Tenka Taihei)	6	"	"
	Usuyuki (Asagao no Kyoku, Shinonome no Kyoku)	6	"	"
	Yuki no Ashita (Aoi no Kyoku, Nahi no Kyoku)	6	"	"
	Kumo no Ue (Musashino no Kyoku)	6	"	Ura-gumi
	Usugoromo (Tegai no Kyoku, Kashiwagi no Kyoku)	6	"	"
	Kiritsubo (Kuina no Kyoku, Aoyagi no Kyoku)	6	"	"
	Suma	6	"	Naka-yurushi
	Kumoi Rōsai	3	Hon kumoi-jōshi	"
	Shiki no Kyoku	5	Hira-jōshi	Oku-yurushi
	Ōgi no Kyoku	6	"	"
	Kumoi no Kyoku	6	Hon kumoi-jōshi	"
Kitajima (d. 1690)	*Akashi*	6	Hira-jōshi	Naka-yurushi
	Sue no Matsu	6	"	"
	Utsusemi	6	"	"
Kitajima of Makino	*Hagoromo*	6	"	Oku shinkyoku
	Wakaba.	6	Hira-jōshi, Han-kumoi-jōshi	"

Composer	Composition (alternate names in parentheses)	Number of Uta	Chōshi	Classification
Kitajima or Ikuta (1655-1715)	*Omoigawa*	6	Hon kumoi-jōshi	Oku shinkyoku
Kurahashi (d. 1690)	*Shin Kumoi Rōsai*	3	Hon kumoi-jōshi	Naka-yurushi
Mitsuhashi (d. 1760)	*Miya no Uguisu*	7	Hira-jōshi, Han-nakazora	Oku ato shinkyoku
	Shiki no Fuji	5	Hira-jōshi, Han-kumoi-jōshi	"
	Jichō	6	Hira-jōshi	"
	Setsugekka	6	"	"
	Mutamagawa (Tamagawa)	6	"	"
	Tamakazura	6	Han-kumoi-jōshi, Hira-jōshi	"
	Ukifune	6	"	"
	Shiki no Koi	5	Hira-jōshi, Han-nakazora, Nakazora	"
Yasumura (d. 1779)	*Hien no Kyoku (Seiheichō)*	6	Hon kumoi-jōshi (Zensō: Kumoi-jōshi)	Oku ato shinkyoku
Hisamura	*Shiki no Tomo*	4	Hira-jōshi	Ura shinkyoku
	Tomo Chidori (Tomo no Kyoku)	6	"	"
Ishizuka	*Hana no En*	6	Hira-jōshi	Ura shinkyoku
	Haru no Miya (Mitsu no Shirabe)	6	Hira-jōshi Nakazora, Akebono	Oku ato shinkyoku
Anonymi	*Hashihime*	6	Hira-jōshi	Naka-yurushi
	Wakana	3	"	Omote-gumi
	Tachibana	3	"	"
	Tanabata	3	"	"
	Sakakiba	3	"	"
	Chio no Tomo	6	"	Ura-gumi
Yamada (1757-1817)	*Hatsune no Kyoku*	6	Hira-jōshi	
Mitsuzaki (d. 1853)	*Akikaze*	6	Akikaze-chōshi	None
Ikuta	*Kagami no Kyoku (Tekagami no Kyoku)*	6	Ura-chidori	Hikyoku

Composer	Composition (alternate names in parentheses)	Number of Uta	Chōshi	Classification
Shin Yatsuhashi	*Yaegaki*	6	Ura-chidori	Hikyoku
	Tobiume	6	Hira-jōshi	"
Tsugiyama	*Ōtsu no Kyoku*	6	Shimo-chidori, Han-nakazora	Hikyoku
	Kan no Kyoku	5	Hon kumoi-jōshi	"
	Kasumi no Kyoku	6	Shimo-chidori	"
	Kō Genji	5	Ura-chidori, Karigane	Goku hikyoku
Anonymi	*Toryū Shiki Genji (Otome no Kyoku)*	5	Karigane	Hikyoku
	Ōtsu no Kumi	6	Karigane	Goku hikyoku
	Koryū Shiki Genji	5	Shimo-chidori	"
	Kambun Ōtsu no Kyoku	5	Kin-iwa-jōshi	"

APPENDIX C

KAKEZUME CHARTS OF KUMIUTA IN TUNINGS

OTHER THAN HIRA –JŌSHI

(a) Kumiuta in the Kumoi Group:

Kumoi no Kyoku

Phrase	1	2	3	4	5	6
1	11-	10		7	10	
2	12	7	7		7	
3	8	7		9-		
4	7	10	10	8		
5		9-	11-			
6	<u>10</u>		7	10		
7	7	12	9-			
8		9				6)
	6	7	5	4	2	1

Wakaba

Phrase	1	2	3	4	5	6
1			10			
2		10	10			
3			12			
4		12				
5		12				
6		10	10			
7						
8						10)
	3	4				

♩ Omoigawa

Phrase	1	2	3	4	5	6
1	10	8	10	12	10	
2	12	10	7	10		
3	8	7	11-	9-	12	
4		12			10	10
5		11-	8		12	
6	12	10	12	10	10	
7	10					
8						
	5	6	5	4	5	1

Phrase	Shiki no Fuji 1	2	3	4	5	6	Tamakazura 1	2	3	4	5	6	Hien no Kyoku 1	2	3	4	5	6
1				12			12		11–				*	8	10	8	10	
2								10					7	10	7)	10)	12	
3													10					
4																		
5							11–						11–		8	11–		
6		10																
7								10					9–					
8			1	1			2	2	1				4	2	3	3	2	

Phrase	Kan no Kyoku					Kasumi no Kyoku						Koryū Shiki Genji				
	1	2	3	4	5	1	2	3	4	5	6	1	2	3	4	5
1	7	11-	9	10		8	7	11-	6-	10	12	8	8	10	13	10
2						7	10		9-	7		7		10	10	12
3			12		7:	10		9-	$9_=$		6*	9-	8	9-	9-	10
4					7	9)						10		9-	9	6
5	(8)	10	10	10		12	6-		8	10			$\underline{7}$			
6						11)						9-			7	7
7				7	9		10	6-	11					6-		9
8	2	2	3	3	2	6	4	3	5	3	1	5	3	4	5	6

(b) Kumiuta in the Nakazora Group:

Miya no Uguisu

Phrase	1	2	3	4	5	6	7
1		9	8	13	8̲		
2							
3							
4							
5		10:	10–	11	8		
6			9̲	8			
7		13	8				
8		3	4		2		

Shiki no Koi

Phrase	1	2	3	4	5
1					
2				10:	
3					
4				9)	
8				2	

Haru no Miya

Phrase	1	2	3	4	5	6
1			8	13		
2				11		
3			8			
4				9)		
5			9			
6			8	8		
8			11)			
			5	4		

Kagami no Kyoku

Phrase	1	2	3	4	5	6
1	11	9	11	11	9	
2			13			
3			7)	8		
4	11	11			11	
5	13					
6	11	11			9	
7			9		6	
8			10			11
	4	3	5	2	4	1

Yaegaki

Phrase	1	2	3	4	5	6
1	11	9	11	11		
2	8	11				
3	6		6			
4	9		11			
5	11			9		
6	8	12)	11			
7	6					
8	8					
	8	3	4	2		

Ōtsu no Kyoku

Phrase	1	2	3	4	5
1					13
4					8
6					11
7					13
					4

(c) Kumiuta in the Akebono Group:

Phrase	Kō Genji					Haru no Miya						Kō Genji				
	1	2	3	4	5	1	2	3	4	5	6	1	2	3	4	5
1		9	10	11)							**12**					6)
2											11					10–
3	9		6	6:						10–	10–					6
4			11													12)
5	8			10						11	11					
6				8		9				9						
7							11				11					6)
8	2	1	3	4		1	1			3	5					5

(d) Akikaze-chōshi:

Torȳu Shiki Genji

Phrase	1	2	3	4	5
1	9	10-	7	8-	11
2		6		8-	
3	8-			9)	
4				11	
5	11				
6	9				
7					
8					
	4	2	1	3	1

Ōtsu no Kumi

Phrase	1	2	3	4	5	6
1		10-	11	9	12	
2	7		10)		9*	
3			8)	10)		
4				8))		
5	8-	8				
6		9		10-		6
7						
8						
	2	3	4	3	2	1

Akikaze no Kyoku

Phrase	1	2	3	4	5	6
1	12	9	9		12	
2			8)	12	10	11
3	7)					
4	10	12	12	13	9-	13*
5						
6	9	9	12	9-	10	
7						
8						
	4	3	3	3	4	2

APPENDIX D

CLASSIFICATION OF THE REPERTOIRE

The Japanese have classified the sōkyoku in various ways, each of which has its merits as well as its limitations. A classification useful to most koto players is one based upon division of the repertoire by school. The Tsukushi, Yatsuhashi, Ikuta, Tsugiyama, and Yamada schools, for example, have each its own repertoire; the performer is normally limited in his choice of pieces to the music available in his school. Considering the koto repertoire as a whole, however, this classification is not too useful because many pieces are played in more than one school. Kumiuta belong to the basic repertoire of Ikuta as well as Yamada-ryū. Originally the compositions of Yamada Kengyō were the exclusive property of the Yamada ryū, but nowadays some of his compositions are played in the Ikuta-ryū also. At the same time, many tegotomono originally the property of the Ikuta-ryū have been taken over by the Yamada-ryū.

Another classification, according to technical difficulty, we have met before. Kumiuta were originally grouped into four classes: *omote-gumi*, *uragami*, *naka-yurushi*, and *oku-yurushi*. Although a similar grouping is not applied to other parts of the koto repertoire, pieces tend to be taught in a rather strict order. This classification has its didactic purposes.

Kumiuta have been the object of a third classification (Sato Showa: *Kumiuta Zenshū)*, one based upon age. This classification distinguishes the following categories:

kokyoku	(old works)	the compositions of Yatsuhashi Kengyō
koshinkyoku	(old-new works)	compositions by Kitajima Kengyō and his students Ikuta Kengyō, Kurahashi Kengyō and Makino Kengyō
chū-koshinkyoku	(middle-old-new)	compositions by Mitsuhashi Kengyō
shinkyoku	(new works)	compositions by Hisamura Kengyō, Ishizuka Kengyō and Anonymi

Still another classification reflects stylistic characteristics. One speaks of classical and modern sōkyoku, the latter being music since the Meiji period that shows Western influence. Classical sōkyoku is divided in *jun-sōkyoku* ("pure" sōkyoku), sōkyoku in jiuta style, and sōkyoku of the Yamada-ryū. Jun-sōkyoku contains kumiuta, danmono, shin-kumiuta (*Akikaze*, Kokingumi), and shinkyoku *(Chidori no Kyoku, Mikuni no Homare, etc.)*. Sōkyoku in jiuta style, mainly performed by koto and shamisen, distinguishes *utamono*, which stresses the vocal part, and *tegotomono*, in which extensive instrumental soli occur *Shō-Chiku-Bai*, *Yaegoromo, etc.)*. Yamada-ryū sōkyoku originally contained only utamono (*Kogō*, *Nasuno*, *etc.)*, but later, although rarely, some tegotomono were composed also *(Miyako no Haru)*. The inclusion of the Yamada-ryū as a separate group in this otherwise practical classification may be objected to because its forms, utamono and tegotomono, are categories that transcend limitations of a single school, and apply to compositions that are, in addition, included anyhow. Modern sōkyoku distinguishes chamber music and works for orchestras consisting of Japanese or a mixture of Japanese and Western instruments.

466

NOTES

NOTES

Chapter I

[1]There are numerous works that treat of Japanese-Chinese contacts. See, among others, Sansom (1958 and 1962), Reischauer and Fairbank (1962), Tsunoda, De Bary, and Keene (1964).

[2]For the composition of the Gagaku-ryō, see Eckardt (1957: 1725) and Garfias (1965: Chapter 1).

[3]For English treatment of gakusō and gagaku in general, see Harich-Schneider (1939: 49-74), Malm (1959: 77-104), Garfias (1965: Chapter 2). In Japanese, the article "Gakusō" in Volume II of the encyclopedia *Ongaku Jiten* (1955-57) is valuable. For musical transcriptions of gagaku in Western notation, see Harich-Schneider (1939), Shiba (1955-56), and Garfias (1965: Volume 2). It should be noted that all Japanese music histories deal with gagaku. Among several of those listed in the bibliography, studies by Tanabe Hisao are particularly useful.

[4]For a discussion of the music in the *Genji Monogatari*, see Yamada 1934.

[5]This story is briefly discussed by Tanabe (1962: 168). The legend is commonplace among koto musicians in Japan.

[6]Tanabe (1962: 171) somewhat oversimplifies by considering the entire Okinawan koto tradition as being derived from zokkyoku. Two of the seven instrumental pieces *(Rokudan Sugagaki* and *Shichidan Sugagaki)* because of their structural complexity resist classification as zokkyoku, the structure of which, like most popular music, is simple. The two pieces are practically identical to *Rokudan* and *Shichidan* in seventeenth-century Japanese sōkyoku.

[7]For detailed discussion of these connections, see Adriaansz 1967 and, more specifically, Adriaansz 1970.

[8]Literally "combined songs." Kumiuta are song cycles. The texts of the individual songs *(uta)* were taken from different sources and, therefore, were not always related to one another.

[9]The term Tsukushi-ryū seems not to have been used before the Bunka-Bunsei periods (1804 to 1830). Earlier, one simply spoke of Tsukushi-goto when referring to the repertoire that Kenjun organized and his followers performed and augmented. The appearance of the term Tsukushi-ryū suggests that up to the first quarter of the nineteenth century, the emergence of newer schools (such as the *Ikuta* and *Yamada-ryū* embodying new styles and compositions made it desirable to distinguish their common precursor as a school also. Although the new term may have been an expression of the nineteenth-century gusto for classification, it is true that the group of musicians this term referred to functioned as, even if they did not consider themselves to be, a school.

[10]This tuning pattern may be transposed to each of the twelve tones of the octave. The name of each specific tuning is derived from the name of the pitch of the second string, which was traditionally considered to be the "tonic." Thus the tuning given above would be called *Ōshiki-chō*.

[11]Kumoi-jōshi is contained in Example 2 on page 8.

[12]The relationship between instruments and tunings of gagaku and Tsukushi-goto will be discussed in more detail in Chapter IV.

[13]For other classifications, which differ slightly from the one given here, see Hirano and Kishibe (1955: 7).

[14]The dengai-hikyoku may be grouped together with the hikyoku.

[15]According to some of the older sources it was not Genjo, but Kenjun, who went to Kyōto. Genjo was chosen here, following Tanabe (1956: 51).

[16]The reason for Hosui's failure is usually said to be his inadequate technique. However, it is hard to believe that Genjo as head of the school would have sent an unskilled player to a place so demanding as the Court in Kyōto. More than anyone else, Genjo must have been capable to judge Hosui's capacities.

[17]Kōtō and Kengyō are professional titles for male blind musicians. The higher rank is Kengyō, which is somewhat comparable to *maestro* in Western music.

[18]An older name for this tuning is *Toko no Shirabe*. Today, however, this term is rarely used.

[19]Although the term zokusō normally indicates the instrument used for koto music since the time of Yatsuhashi Kengyō, it may refer to the music as well. It is possible, for example, to hear Yatsuhashi characterized as "the founder of zokusō."

[20]History, style, and structure of *shamisen kumiuta* are treated in Adriaansz 1971.

[21]*Kumoi Rōsai* is closely related to the shamisen kumiuta *Rōsai*. This is the only example of a direct relationship between koto and shamisen kumiuta. For discussion of the various *Rōsai*, see Adriaansz 1969.

[22]A study of the repertoire of the Yatsuhashi-ryū, which, in addition to compositions by Yatsuhashi Kengyō, contains one kumiuta by Kitajima Kengyō *(Akashi)*, has revealed that in modern practice Yatsuhashi's kumiuta are no longer performed in their original form, but in arrangements by Kitajima Kengyō. In view of this evidence similar reworking of part of the danmono repertoire by Kitajima Kengyō becomes very probable. (Adriaansz 1971.)

[23]See also Kikkawa (1961: 6 and 1965: 149-151).

[24]Traditionally these three kumiuta are the object of an exceptional reverence by the koto musician. It is especially in these three compositions that the deviation between modern practice and the older tradition, as represented by the Yatsuhashi-ryū, is greatest: in point of fact, the san-kyoku have been entirely recomposed, rather than having been the object of minor revisions. The modern versions follow the normal kumiuta form, while those of the Yatsuhashi-ryū deviate very pronouncedly from the established norm. In view of the fact that Kitajima's revisions invariably involve structural normalization, in addition to some general polishing, it may be suspected that the modern versions of *Yatsuhashi no san-kyoku* are not compositions by Yatsuhashi Kengyō at all, but rather creations by Kitajima Kengyō (Adriaansz 1971).

[25]The rank of bettō seems to have been very rare.

[26]Recently Sanada Shin has begun to instruct a small number of students (among whom one professional musician) into the repertoire and performance practice of the Yatsuhashi-ryū. Consequently the chances of survival of this school are rather favorable, in contrast to those of Tsukushi-goto.

[27]Examples of early nagauta and hauta are given in a collection of 1703, *Matsu no Ha*. This collection also contains some pieces in narrative style *(katarimono)*. Later, around the Kampo period (1741-1744), other examples of katarimono appeared *(saku-mono, shi-gedayu-mono,* and *yōkyoku-mono)*. These narrative forms are so rare, however, that they must be considered exceptions to the rule that jiuta are lyrical only.

[28]*Jo-ha-kyū* corresponds to introduction, development, and denouement. See pp. 107-108 for a more detailed description.

[29]The term akebono is not generally used. In Kyōto, for example, only few players know this term. For the majority, this rather rare tuning is namelsss.

[30]Although the most striking developments were made in the field of tegoto-mono, simpler forms in which the composer concentrated on the vocal part, accompanied by shamisen and/or koto *(uta-mono)*, continued to be composed.

[31]For an example of a similar cooperation in the composition of nagauta, see Malm (1963: 97).

[32]"Sankyoku," *Ongaku Jiten*, Vol. 4, p. 187.

[33]"Miyagi Michio" in *Ongaku Jiten*, Vol. 10, pp. 156-157.

Chapter II

[1]The *Tōyō Kanji* is a collection of 1850 ideograms, the use of which is recommended in an attempt to normalize and simplify written Japanese.

[2]The same legend, with certain adaptations to suit a different number of strings, explains the origin of the dàn tranh in Vietnam (Tran Van Khe 1967: 85-86).

[3]Extensive fragments of a *Tōsō*, a koto of the T'ang period, preserved in the Shōsōin in Nara, show an exterior similar to that of later instruments, but an essential difference in construction. The body is formed of a thin topboard, separate sideboards, and a bottom. Hayashi Kenzō, who has given a detailed description of this instrument (1964), traces the history of the scooped-out long zithers in China back to the Warring States (403-221 B.C.), that of the koto of sectional construction to a much later date, around the sixth century A.D. (pp. 271-272). He speculates that a shortage of large trees may have been the reason for this unusual construction. The koto at the Shōsōin is the oldest relic of this type. In Japan, even in the Nara period, the type had been replaced by the koto of scooped-out construction.

[4]The *Sōkyoku Taiishō* explains the names of the highest three strings as onomatopoea.

[5]Although Japan has adopted the metric system in weights and measures, old terminology has not died out, especially in connection with traditional subjects. One momme equals 3.75 grams or 0.1325 oz.

[6]This koto belonged to the late Tsuda Kengyō, and before him to Yaezaki Kengyō. Its dimensions are given as an example of variation from the standards.

Chapter III

[1]The use of the terms "dominant," "subdominant," etc. may seem to be too ethnocentric to be allowable. It will become clear, however, that degrees V and IV in this Japanese scale fulfill modal functions that are sufficiently similar to those of the dominant and subdominant in Western music (although not in the harmonic sense) to allow a careful use of both terms also in this genre of Japanese music.

[2]If it is true that Yatsuhashi is the composer of *Koryū Shiki Genji*, as Satō assumes in his *Kumiuta Zenshū*, then he used a third tuning, *ura-chidori*, which, however, is no more than a variant of hon-kumoi-jōshi. Satō probably based his assumption on a story mentioned in Volume 6 of the *Sōkyoku Taiishō*, relating that Yatsuhashi was the first and only musician to play this secret piece.

[3]The names of the tunings given in Example 8 are those used in the Ikuta-ryū. When occasionally the Yamada-ryū uses different names, these are added in parentheses.

[4]In practice, the tuning will be adapted to the range of the singer. In purely instrumental compositions the first string is usually tuned to pitch d' (ichikotsu).

[5]The only occurrence of kumoi-jōshi in the instrumental prelude (Jō) of *Hien no Kyoku* has been disregarded in this chart. It is not certain whether this introduction was composed by Yasumura Kengyō himself or was added at a later date by someone else. The fact that *Hien no Kyoku* is printed in Volume 4 of the *Sōkyoku Taiishō,* its Jō in Volume 7 (which was published more than a century later), may point in this direction. *Akikaze no Kyoku,* as a shin-kumiuta, that is, a piece composed much later than the others, has also been excluded.

[6] A similar characteristic of modulation practice is also known elsewhere, for example in Java and Thailand. See Hood (1954: 230) and Morton (1964: 224).

[7] Tuning of the gakusō in general follows a similar pattern but begins with string 2 rather than string 1, which is not tuned until all others have been finished.

[8] This has been noted in other genres as well. See Malm (1959: 59, 60).

Chapter IV

[1]The terms *shōfu* and *kuchi-jamisen* are not generally known. Outstanding musicians may make a daily use of the system without having ever heard these terms, which describe the system as a whole.

[2]For an explanation of special symbols in the notation, see pp. 265-266.

[3]Attempts to interpret these notations, the accuracy of which in respect to the rhythm leaves something to be desired, have been made by Hayashi Kenzō (1957). Interpretations of two compositions for koto solo are contained in Adriaansz 1970 and Adriaansz 1972.

[4]In the Yamada-ryū, *ichi,* *ni,* and *san* are represented by different kanji: 壱, 弐, and 参 .

[5]The Yamada notation is used by the Ikuta-ryū occasionally, although this is rather rare.

[6]In recent scores, mainly of shinkyoku, Ikuta notation sometimes incorporates the metric precision of the Yamada notation by taking over the single, double, triple, or quadruple time-value lines, which are printed vertically on the right side of the columns.

[7]The *Sōkyoku Taiishō* shows a remarkable variation in its notation by using the above-mentioned sequence of circles for danmono and a slightly different sequence (large, small, large double, small) for kumiuta.

Chapter V

[1]Female performers, who in recent times have been admitted to the Tsukushi-ryū, changed this unfeminine position into a kneeling one.

[2]Similar listings, although differently organized, can be found in *Sōkyoku Taiishō*, Vol. VI, and *Ongaku Jiten*, VI, 38-39 (article "Sō" by Fujita Toshikazu and Kikkawa Eishi).

[3]That eighteen, rather than seventeen, right-hand techniques are listed here is due to the inclusion of a later-developed technique, *uchizume*.

[4]For a detailed discussion of the origin of these patterns in sōkyoku, see Chapter X.

[5]A related left-hand technique not listed in the official eight left-hand techniques is *yuri*: a pressed-down string is quickly released and pressed down again.

[6]In later times, kozume was occasionally used in parts of compositions which evoked the ancient court atmosphere by the use of gakusō techniques. For an example, see the section *Gaku* in *Kogō no Kyoku* by Yamada Kengyō.

[7]Oral communication with Dr. Garfias.

[8]Since the tradition was interrupted for several centuries, it is not sure that the pronunciation of the kanji which represent these techniques is the same as those that were used before.

Chapter VI

[1]*Kinkyoku Shifu* (1772) and *Sōkyoku Taiishō* (1779).

[2]A term that can include both danmono and kumiuta is *kumikyoku*, to be translated as "combined pieces" or "combination of pieces." See Takano 1935: 73.

[3]As these examples of extended titles indicate, danmono are also known as *shirabemono*. *Midare*, which resists satisfying classification as a danmono, easily fits the somewhat wider category of shirabemono. The term shirabemono does not imply the formal limitations of danmono.

[4]Prototypes of danmono and *Midare* may be found in certain compositions of Tsukushi-goto and in the *Shichiku-shoshinshū (Sugagaki* and *Rinzetsu* respectively). For a discussion of the evolution of these instrumental koto compositions, see Adriaansz 1968, 1970, and 1971, "Midare".

[5]For a discussion of the Yatsuhashi-ryū, see Adriaansz 1971 ("The Yatsuhashi-ryū").

[6]The relationship between the Okinawan and the Japanese koto repertories is discussed in more detail in Adriaansz 1970.

[7]*Kumoi Kudan* often is ascribed to Mitsuhashi Kengyō.

[8]Takano (1935) bases his entire chronology on these eighteenth-century sources, at the same time taking account of their classification as omote, ura, naka, and oku. This combination of late sources and technical rather than historical classification seems to condemn his efforts as futile from the very beginning.

[9]Attributed to Ikuta Kengyō.

[10] For a more detailed discussion, see Adriaansz 1967.

[11]In the Yamada-ryū a dan is organized in fifty-two 2/4 measures.

[12] *Kumoi Kudan* may be heard used as kaete to *Kudan*. It may be questioned whether *Kumoi Kudan* was composed as an independent composition or as a kaete to the older piece. In favor of the former possibility are the following facts: *kaeteshiki* composition is a product of the nineteenth century, while *Kumoi Kudan* had been published already in 1772; kaete are in kumoi-jōshi, *Kumoi Kudan* is in hon-kumoi; finally, the style of *Kumoi Kudan* does not show the ornamental character of a regular kaete.

[13]It has been suggested that the homogeneity of the danmono repertoire may also be explained, at least partly, by a common origin of all danmono in certain zokkyoku. Thus, the two compositions for koto solo reproduced in the *Shichiku Shoshinshū*, *Sugagaki*, and *Rinzetsu* may have given rise to the "regular" danmono and *Midare* respectively. The gradual development from simple and artless one-movement compositions to the complex and sophisticated multimovement forms of strictly standardized structure and content has been the object of two elaborate studies, devoted to the development of danmono and *Midare* respectively (Adriaansz 1970 and 1972, "Midare").

[14]It may be relevant to remind the reader that these three basic tones of the mode are the same three that were obtained by tuning in perfect intervals (fifths and fourths).

Chapter VII

[1]However, keshizume at this location is by no means generally applied.

[2]Because the phrases frequently show an increasing tendency toward integration as the danmono proceeds, the structure of later dan is considerably less obvious than that of the opening dan with its clear caesurae. The ubiquitous "kororin" pattern, which may function as a cadential formula at the end as well as an ornamental figure within a phrase, contributes to the structural ambiguity. In addition, the original character of the phrases—which is either cadential (descending), or proceeding (ascending)—is often abandoned, instead of which both characteristics may become combined within one phrase. Once again historic prototypes and predecessors have contributed to the solution of structural problems (Adriaansz 1970).

[3]See "Jo-ha-kyū," *Ongaku Jiten*, Vol. 5 (1957), p. 159; Malm (1963: 27-28).

[4]In *Midare* the jo-ha-kyū concept can be applied to smaller groupings as well. Thus, the jo (dan 1 through 5) may be subdivided into three groups of dan (1 and 2, 3 and 4, and 5, respectively) which again represent a jo-ha-kyū sequence. A similar grouping may be applied to the ha section (dan 6, dan 7 and 8, and dan 9), but not to the kyū. For a detailed discussion see Adriaansz 1972.

Chapter VIII

[1]Since the Yamada-ryū usually prefers higher registers than the Ikuta-ryū, it often occurs that compositions that are taken over from the older school and that originally were in hira-jōshi will be transposed to kumoi-jōshi, in which case the different musical function of strings 1 and 2 is calmly disregarded. This transfer from chōshi to chōshi would not be possible if any essential differences between the two existed.

[2]The use of such terminology as "tonal function" should not be inferred to suggest harmonic functions as found in Western music.

Chapter X

[1]Nowadays, Yamaguchi prefecture. This prefecture, however, includes only the southwestern area of Honshu, whereas Suō included the northernmost part of Kyūshū as well.

[2]See article "Imayō" in *Ongaku Jiten*, Vol. 1, pp. 123-124; Tanabe (1962), 216-220; Malm (1959), p. 90.

[3]A modern survivor of the Etenraku-imayō is *Kuroda-bushi* (sometimes called *Chikuzen-imayō*). *Kuroda-bushi* derived its name from the Kuroda clan, which lived near Hakata, which today is part of the city of Fukuoka in northwest Kyūshū.

[4]Adapted from Shiba (1955-56), p. 12. In the case of *Etenraku*, Shiba based the transcription of the koto part on an unusual tuning, which employs tone d instead of c♯ for strings 6 and 11. In Example 74, the c♯ was restored, thus bringing the score to agree with the actual performance practice (measures 9, 11, and 12). Compare transcriptions in several of Tanabe's books (a.o. 1959: 62-66).

[5]A similar practice is observed in kumiuta which have the four seasons as a theme and therefore contain four uta. It may happen that there are five songs, in which case the first is considered introductory and is not included in the numbering.

[6] Although the jo-ha-kyū concept is generally known and applied to various genres of Japanese music, its absence in connection with danmono and kumiuta is conspicuous. Repeated inquiry among musicologists and musicians never led to any definite statement on this matter. The only time I found the concept in reference to kumiuta was in the *Sōkyoku Taiishō* (Vol.6), in a context where the singer was recommended to understand the structure of the piece, and also the jo-ha-kyū sequence.

Chapter XII

[1] *Haru no Miya*, also called *Mitsu no Shirabe*, is a good source for the study of the behavior of different tunings because it uses three chōshi, hira-jōshi, nakazora, and akebono, in a systematic sequence. Its composer, Ishizuka Kengyō, handles his musical material in the same way throughout the composition, regardless of the tuning.

[2]For kakezume charts of kumiuta in the kumoi, nakazora, and akebono groups, and also *Akikaze*, see Appendix C.·

[3]These two preludes that introduce a secret piece seem to be treated with special care. I never succeeded in locating a written notation and my own score was made from dictation by Miss Kikuzuki in Kyōto.

Chapter XIII

[1]An attractive introduction   Japanese poetry may be found in Keene (1955). See also Brower and Miner (1961).

[2]One cannot help being reminded of a similar concern about stage manners of the eighteenth-century European performer. François Couperin (1668-1733) gives similar advice to the harpsichord player in his *L'Art de Toucher le Clavecin*.

[3]The word "yūkaze" (eveningwind") is illustrated in a similar manner in the fifth uta (m.7-8) of *Hatsune*.

BIBLIOGRAPHY

BIBLIOGRAPHY

Abraham, O., and E.M. von Hornbostel. "Studien über das Tonsystem der Japaner," *Sammelbände der Internationalen Musikgesellschaft,* IV (1903), 302-360.

Adriaansz, Willem. "Research into the Chronology of Danmono," *Ethnomusicology,* XI, No.1 (1967), 25-53.

----- "On the Evolution of the Classic Instrumental Repertoire for the Koto," *Proceedings of the Centennial Workshop on Ethnomusicology, held at the University of British Columbia, Vancouver,* 68-78. Victoria: Govt. of the Province of British Columbia, 1968.

----- "Rōsai," *Ethnomusicology,* XIII, No.1 (1969), 101-123.

----- "A Japanese Procrustean Bed: A Study of the Development of Danmono," *Journal of the American Musicological Society,* XXIII, No.1 (1970), 26-60.

----- "The Yatsuhashi-ryū: A Seventeenth Century School of Koto Music," *Acta Musicologica,* vol. XLIII, fasc. I-II (1971), 55-93.

----- "Midare: A Study of Its Historic Development," in *Kikkawa Eishi Sensei Kanreki Kinen Rombunshū* (Festschrift for Professor Kikkawa Eishi), Tokyo, 1972.

----- Introduction to *Shamisen Kumiuta,* in press.

Aston, W.G. (translator). *Nihongi.* London: George Allen and Unwin, Ltd., 1956.

Brower, Robert H., and Earl Miner. *Japanese Court Poetry.* Stanford: Stanford University Press, 1961, xvi+527 pp.

Davidson, Archibald T., and Willi Apel. *Historical Anthology of Music,* Vol. I. Cambridge, Massachussets: Harvard University Press, 1959.

Eckardt, Andreas. *Koreanische Musik.* Tokyo: Deutsche Gesellschaft für Natur- und Völkerkunde Ostasiens, 1930. 63 pp.

Eckardt, Hans. "Japanese Musik," *Die Musik in Geschichte und Gegenwart,* VI (1957), 1720-1754.

----- "Koto," *Die Musik in Geschichte und Gegenwart,* VII (1958), 1646-1650.

Ellis, Alexander J. "On the Musical Scales of Various Nations," *Journal of the Society of Arts* (March 1885), 485-527.

Fujita Tonan. *Meikyoku Kaidai.* Itami: Kamigata Kyōdo Geijitsu Hozonkai, Shōwa 31 (1956). 306 pp.

----- *Sōkyoku Jiuta Meikyoku Kashu.* Ōsaka: Hōgakusha, Shōwa 23 (1948). 174 pp.

----- *Sōkyoku to Jiuta no Ajiwaikata.* Ōsaka: Maekawa, Shōwa 5 (1930). 250 pp.

Fujita Toshikazu, and Kikkawa Eishi. "Sō," *Ongaku Jiten*. Tokyo: Heibonsha, 1955-1957, Vol. 6, pp. 37-39.

Garfias, Robert. *Music of a Thousand Autumns: The Tōgaku Style of Japanese Court Music*. Los Angeles: University of California Press, in press.

Gensui. *Kinkyoku Shifu*. Edo: Umemura Saburobei, 1772. 5 vols.

Gulik, R.H. van. "Brief Note on the Cheng, the Chinese Small Cither," *Tōyō Ongaku Kenkyū*, 9 (March 1951), 19-25.

---- *The Lore of the Chinese Lute*. Tokyo: Sophia University, 1940. 224 pp.

Harich-Schneider, Eta. "The Present Condition of Japanese Court Music," *Musical Quarterly*, 39 (January 1953), 49-74.

----- *Rōei, the Medieval Court Songs of Japan*, Monumenta Nipponica Monographs, No. 21, Tokyo: Sophia University Press, 1965. 132 pp.

Hayashi Kenzō. "Edoshoki Zokuyō no Fukugen no Kokoromi-tokuni Shichiku Shoshinshū no Kouta ni Tsuite —," *Nara Gakugei Daigaku Kiyō*, 7, No. 1 (1957), 21-44.

----- *Shōsōin Gakki no Kenkyū*. Tokyo: Kazama, 1964. 370 pp.

Higashiyama Shinji. "Jiuta," *Ongaku Jiten*, IV, 215-217.

Hirano Kenji. "Kinsei Shoki ni Okeru Nihon no Genki Gakkyoku," *Transactions of the Kansai University Institute of Oriental and Occidental Studies*, No. 48, 1961.

----- "Kayō Bungaku to Shite no Sōkyoku." *Kokugo to Kokubungaku*, XXXII, No. 4 (1958), 86-95.

Hirano Kenji and Kishibe Shigeo. *Tsukushi-goto Kenkyū Shiryō*. Shōwa 30 (1955). 25 pp.

Hood, Mantle. *The Nuclear Theme as a Determinant of Patet in Javanese Music*. Groningen, Djakarta: J.B. Wolters, 1954. 323 pp.

Iba Takashi. *Nihon Ongaku Gairon*. Tokyo: Koseikaku Shoten, 1928. 999 pp.

Isawa S. (ed.). *Collection of Japanese Koto Music*. Tokyo: Department of Education, 1888.

"Jo-ha-kyu," *Ongaku Jiten*. V (1957), p. 159.

Keene, Donald. *Japanese Literature*. New York: Grove Press, 1955. 114 pp.

Kikkawa Eishi. *Sōkyoku to Jiuta no Rekishi*. (Introduction to four LP's) Victor SLR 510-513 (1961). 29 pp.

----- *Nihon Ongaku no Rekishi*. Ōsaka: Sōgensha, 1965. 469+40 pp.

Kishibe Shigeo. "Zokusō," *Ongaku Jiten*, II, 276-279.

----- "Classical Japanese Koto Music," *KBS Bulletin*, 21 (Nov.-Dec. 1956), 3-4.

Knott, C. G. "Remarks on Japanese Musical Scales," *Transactions of the Asiatic Society of Japan*, XIX (1891), 373-392.

Komiya Toyotoka (editor). *Japanese Music and Drama in the Meiji Era*. Translated by E. Seidensticker and D. Keene. Tokyo: Ubunsha, 1956. 535 pp.

Kraus, Alexandre. *La Musique au Japon*. Florence: Imprimerie de l'arte della Stampa, 1878. 83 pp.

Lee Hye-ku. *Korean Classical Instruments*. Seoul: The Korea Information Service, Inc., n.d. 42 pp.

Malm, William P. *Japanese Music and Musical Instruments*. Rutland, Vermont, and Tokyo, Japan: Charles E. Tuttle Company, 1959. 299 pp.

-----*Nagauta, the Heart of Kabuki Music*. Rutland, Vermont, and Tokyo, Japan: Charles E. Tuttle Company, 1963. 344 pp.

Miyagi Mamoru. *Koto (Gosen-fu) Kyōsokuhon*. 4th ed. Tokyo: Hōgakusha, 1963. 41 pp.

Morton, David. *The Traditional Music of Thailand*. Los Angeles: University of California Press, in press.

Müller, Dr. L. "Einige Notizen über die Japanische Music," *Mitteilungen der Deutschen Gesellschaft für Natur- und Völkerkunde Ostasiens*, Band I, Heft VI, pp. 13-31; Heft VIII, pp. 41-49; Heft IX, pp. 19-35, 1874-76.

Murasaki Shikibu. *The Tale of Genji*. Translated by Arthur Waley. New York: The Modern Library, 1960. 1135 pp.

Murata Shōsen. *Yamada Ryū Koto no Kagami*. 12 vols. Tokyo: Hakushindō, 1962.

Nakauchi Chōjo and Nishio Tamura. *Koto-uta oyobi Jiuta Zenshū*. Tokyo: Ogawa Kiku-matsu, Shōwa 2 (1924). 463 pp.

Nihonji. See Aston, W. G.

Obata Juichi and Eizi Sugita. "Acoustical Investigations on Some Japanese Musical Instruments. Part IV. The Koto, a Thirteen-stringed Instrument," *Proceedings of the Physico-Mathematical Society of Japan*, 32nd Series, XIII, No. 5 (May 1931), 133-150.

Ongaku Jiten (Music Encyclopedia). Tokyo: Heibonsha, 1955-1957. 12 vols.

Péri, Noël. *Essai sur les Gammes Japonaises*. Paris: Geuthner, 1934. 70 pp.

Piggot, Sir Francis T. *The Music and Musical Instruments of Japan.*   2nd ed. London: B. T. Batsford, 1909. 196 pp.

Reinhard, Kurt. *Chinesische Musik*. Eisenach and Kassel: Erich Roth Verlag, 1956. 246 pp.

Reischauer, Edwin O. *Japan Past and Present*. 3rd ed. New York: Alfred A. Knopf, 1964. 323 pp.

-----and John K. Fairbank.*East Asia, the Great Tradition*. Modern Asia Edition.   Boston: Houghton Mifflin Company; Tōkyō: Charles E. Tuttle Company, 1962. 739 pp.

Ryūkyū Sōkyoku Kun-kun-shi. 3 vols. Naha: Kōyōkai, 1965.

Sansom, Geo. B. *A History of Japan*. Vol. I: to 1334; Vol. II: 1334-1615; Vol. III: 1615-1867. Stanford: Stanford University Press, 1958, 1961, and 1963.

Sansom, G. B. *Japan, a Short Cultural History.*   New York: Appleton-Century-Crofts, Inc., 1962. 558 pp.

Satō Showa. *Kumiuta Zenshū.* 7 vols. Tokyo: Takahashi Ichisaku, Shōwa 16 (1941).

Shiba Sukehiro. *Gagaku*. 2 vols. Tokyo: Ryugin-sha, 1955-56.

Takano Kiyoshi. "Theorie der Japanischen Musik (I). Untersuchungen über die Form der Koto Musik 'Danmono,'" *Tōhoku Psychologica Folia*. Sendai, 1935, pp. 69-169.

Takano Tatsuyuki. "Shichiku Shoshinshu," *Nihon Kayō Shusei*. Vol. 6. Tokyo: Shunjūsha, Shōwa 3 (1928).

----- *Nihon Kayōshi*. Tōkyō: Shunjūsha, 1926. 1090 pp.

Tanabe Hisao. *Gesammelte Werke der Weltmusik.*   Vols. 25 and 34. Tokyo: Shunjūsha, 1931.

----- *Japanese Music*. Kokusai Bunka Shinkokai, 1959. 74 pp.

----- *Nihon Ongaku Kowa*. Tokyo: Iwanami Shoten, 1919. 764 pp.

----- *Nihon no Ongaku*. Tokyo: Bunka Kenkyūsha, 1947, Revised Edition, Shōwa 29 (1954). 337 pp.

----- *Nihon no Ongaku*. Tokyo: Zen-on Gakufu Shuppansha Co. Ltd., 1961. 214 pp.

----- *Nihon Ongaku Gairon*. 3rd ed. Tokyo: Ongaku no Tomosha, Shōwa 36 (1961). 181 pp.

-----*Nihon Ongaku Shi*. Tokyo: Tōkyō Denki Daigaku Shuppanbu, Shōwa 38 (1963). 275 pp.

----- "Sōkyoku," *Ongaku Jiten*. Tokyo: Heibonsha, 1955-57, Vol. 6, pp. 49-56.

Tanaka Giichi. *Gendai Sōkyoku Chōshi Jiten*.   Ōsaka: Maekawa Shuppansha, Shōwa 35 (1960). 173 pp.

----- *Gendai Sankyoku Tembō*. Ōsaka: Maekawa Shuppansha, Shōwa 38 (1963). 481 pp.

Tran Van Khe. *La Musique Vietnamienne Traditionnelle*. Paris: Presses Universitaires de France, 1962. 384 pp.

----- *Viet-nam*. Paris: Buchet/Chastel, 1967. 224 pp.

Tsunoda Ryusaku, William Theodore De Bary, and Donald Keene. *Sources of Japanese Tradition*. New York and London: Columbia University Press, 1958 and 1964. 2 vols.

Yamada Ryū Koto no Kagami.   See Murata Shōsen.

Waterhouse, David. "An Early Fluctuation of the Four-Stringed Kokyū," *Oriental Art*, Vol. XVI, No. 2 (1970): 1-7.

Yamada Shōkoku. *Sōkyoku Taiishō*.   Edo: Fugetsu Sozaemon. Vols. 1-6: 1779, Vol. 7: 1903.

Yamada Takao. *Genji Monogatari no Ongaku*.   Tokyo: Hōbunkan, 1934. 450 pp.

Zedwitz, Freiherr von. "Japanese Musikstücke," *Mitteilungen der Deutschen Gesellschaft fur Natur- und Volkerkunde Ostasiens*,   IV, No. 32: 107; IV, No. 33: 129-145 (1885).

INDEX

Abraham, O., and
    E.M. von Hornbostel, 228
a-chaing, 23
Adriaansz, Willem, 468, 469, 470, 472,
    473, 474, 475
aesthetics, 227, 231, 258, 260, 261
ai-no-te, 14, 15, 161, 164, 173, 193-
    195, 201, 211-212, 218, 219,
    223, 229, 259
Aizu, 25
Akashi, 10, 12, 181, 189, 196, 197,
    198, 199, 203, 204, 207, 208,
    248, 250, 254, 256, 455, 469
Akikaze no Kyoku, 16, 17, 63, 65-85, 94,
    101-106, 110-113, 116, 119-121,
    127-128, 130, 135, 136, 139-143,
    222-225, 226, 264, 399-424, 456,
    465, 466, 472, 476
Aki no Kyoku, 17
Aki no Shirabe 21
Aki no Yama, 7, 11
Amenonori-goto, 22
Aoi no Kyoku, 19
Araki Chikuō, 18
assō, 23
Aston, W.G., 3
ato-biki, 15
ato-uta, 15
awasezume. See koto: playing techniques,
    zokusō, right hand
Azuma-Jishi, 15
bachi, 41
Bairo, 59
Bansei-Jishi, 16
Bashō, 261
Bettō, 11, 470
biwa (no koto), 4, 18, 22
Bizen, 5
Brown, Robert H.,
    and Earl Miner, 476
bugaku, 107
Busō Gafushu, 64
cadence, 109-115, 160, 162, 169,
    196-198, 219, 220, 222, 244-246
Cha no Yū Ondo (Chaondo), 16
cheng, 3, 22, 23

Chidori no Kyoku, 17, 466
Chikuzen-imayō. See *Kuroda-bushi*
ch'in, 6, 22
China:
    cultural contacts with, 3, 4, 5, 22,
    23
    modal system, 31
Chio no Tomo, 31, 187, 189, 190, 194,
    201, 204, 208, 245, 255, 456
Chio no Uguisu, 16
chirashi, 15
chirashizume. See koto: playing tech-
    niques, zokusō, right hand
Chōkonka:
    Chinese poem, 16
    composition by Yamada Kengyō, 19
chōshi. See tuning
chronology (danmono), 63-65
chū-koshinkyoku, 466
classification:
    in Tsukushi-goto, 6, 7, 469
    in Ikuta-ryū, 13, 39, 466, 474
    in Yamada-ryū, 19, 466
Concerto for koto and orchestra
    (Miyagi), 21
Couperin, François, 476
Daigo, 11
dangaeshi, 16
danmono:
    prototypes, 5
    in Japan, 5, 10, 16, 19
    in Okinawa, 5
dansō, 23
dàn tranh, 22, 471
Dazaifu, 5
dengai-hikyoku. See classification;
    Tsukushi-goto
diminution, 246-247
Echigo, 25
Echigo-Jishi, 15
Eckhardt, Hans, 22, 468, 473
Edo, 7, 18, 261
Edo-nagauta, 13
Ellis, Alexander J., 40
en. See koto: playing techniques, zokusō,
    left hand

Etenraku:
    in gagaku, 58, 133, 147-152,
        155, 156, 159, 160, 162, 173,
        175, 189, 190, 202, 211, 258,
        259, 475
    in Tsukushi-goto, 9
    See also *Fuki*
Etenraku-imayō, 475
extra-musical connotations, 29
Fujiike-ryū, 14
Fujita Tonan, 9
Fujiwara no Sadatoshi, 4
Fujiwara no Teika, 260, 261
Fukakusa Kengyō, 15
Fuke sect, 18
Fukeshu, 20
Fuki:
    by Kenjun, 6, 7, 11, 147-155,
        202, 258, 259
    by Yatsuhashi Kengyō, 11, 44,
        148, 149, 151, 154-177,
        189-191, 193, 195-199, 202,
        210, 211, 217, 218, 229,
        230, 232, 233, 234, 235,
        236, 237, 239, 241, 243,
        244, 245, 246, 248, 249,
        250, 251, 253, 254, 255,
        256, 257, 258, 259, 260,
        268-283, 455
Fuki-gumi. See *Fuki*
Fuki no Kyoku, 155
Fune no Yume, 16, 20
fushi-mawashi, 227, 246, 255, 256
Fuyu Nagauta, 5, 7
Fuyu no Kyoku, 17
gagaku, 3, 5-6, 50, 53, 58-60, 133,
        148-155, 258
    See also *Bairo*; *Etenraku*; imayō;
        koto: playing techniques, gakusō;
        netori; saibara; tomede
Gagaku-ryō, 3, 23, 468
gakusō, 3, 6, 23, 24, 58, 468, 472
    See also koto: playing techniques,
        gakusō
Garfias, Robert, 22, 23, 59, 468
gekyoku, 13
Genji Monogatari, 6, 148, 155
Genjo, 6, 7, 469

Gin no Shirabe, 218
Godan:
    in Japan, 12, 63-85, 94, 99, 103,
        104-107, 110-117, 119, 121,
        127, 128, 130, 133, 136, 139,
        140, 142, 144, 426-430, 454
    in Okinawa, 64
Godan-Ginuta, 16, 20
goku-hikyoku, 14, 39
Gulik, R.H. van, 22
Gyosei no Kyoku, 20
Hachidan, 10, 48, 49, 63-85, 94, 98,
        103-107, 110-114, 118, 119, 121,
        127, 128, 132, 133, 135, 136, 139-
        143, 258, 454
Hagi no Tsuyu, 16
Hagiwara Seigin, 124, 265
Hagoromo, 182, 190, 195, 243, 245,
        250, 256, 455
haiku, 227
Hakata, 5
Hakke no Kyoku, 7
Hana no En:
    by Kenjun, 7, 11
    by Ishizuka Kengyō, 14, 186, 189,
        193, 199, 201, 245, 256, 456
han-hikiren. See koto: playing tech-
        niques, zokusō, right hand
hankake. See koto: playing techniques,
        zokusō, right hand
han-ryū. See koto: playing techniques,
        zokusō, right hand
Harich-Schneider, Eta, 468
Harukaze, 7
Haru no Kyoku, 17
Haru no Miya (Mitsu no Shirabe), 14
        38, 39, 186, 195, 200, 215, 218,
        256, 358-371, 456, 462, 464, 476
Hasetomi Kengyō, 18, 261
Hashihime, 186, 194, 195, 201, 240,
        456
Hatsune no Kyoku, 18, 19, 188-190,
        196, 197, 200, 204, 207-209, 246,
        386-399, 456, 476
Hatsusegawa, 17
hauta, 470
hayagaki. See koto: playing techniques,
        gakusō, right hand

hayakake. See koto: playing techniques, zokusō, right hand
Hayashi Kenzō, 23, 471, 472
Heian sōkyoku, 4, 5
Heike Monogatari, 6, 148
heikyoku, 18
Hida, 25
Hien no Kyoku, 14, 218, 219, 221, 246, 255, 342-357, 456, 460, 472
hikiren. See koto: playing techniques, zokusō, right hand
hikisute. See koto: playing techniques, zokusō, right hand
Hikoyamagongen shrine, 4
hikyoku, 7, 14, 39, 194, 200, 214, 217-219, 225, 469
Hirano Kenji and Kishibe Shigeo, 469
Hisamura Kengyō, 14, 194, 197, 200, 201, 203, 205-208, 227, 234, 456, 466
hitsu (no koto), 22
hogaku, 21
Hōkasō, 16
hon-chirashi, 15
hon-chōshi, 42
honte, 16, 65
Hood, Mantle, 472
Hosui, 7, 11, 18, 469
Hototogisu no Kyoku, 20
hyenkeum. See komunko
hyōjō. See tuning, in gagaku
Ichidan, 5, 64
Ichiura Kengyō, 16
Ikuta Kengyō, 12, 13, 14, 38, 258, 261, 454, 456, 466, 474
Ikuta koto, 24
Ikuta-ryū, 6, 12-14, 18, 19, 24, 47, 50, 56, 124, 133, 154
Imakomachi, 16
imayō, 3, 148
Ingyō, Emperor, 3
Inoue Mina, 7
in-sen, 33, 34, 35, 151, 213
Ishikawa Iroko, 4
Ishikawa Kōtō, 16
Ishimura Kengyō, 9
Ishizuka Kengyō, 14, 39, 190, 195, 197-201, 203, 205, 206, 218, 234, 255, 261, 456, 466, 476
Isochidori, 16

Isshi no Kyoku, 7
Itchūbushi, 18
Jichō, 13, 15, 183, 198, 201, 203, 209, 210, 245, 252, 255, 456
Jinchi Yōroku, 59
jiuta, 9, 12-13, 470
jo, 15, 218, 472
    See also makura; zensō
jo-ha-kyū, 13, 107-108, 173-174, 193, 211, 222, 227, 258, 470, 475
Johide, 7
joruri-mono, 19
Jūdan, 63
    See also *Midare*
Junidan, 63
    See also *Midare*
jun-sōkyoku, 466
jūshichi-gen-kin, 23
kabuki-uta, 9
kadozume: See tsume
kaete, 16, 64, 474
kaete-shiki sōkyoku, 16, 474
Kagami no Kyoku, 12, 219, 456
Kagawa Kengyō, 12
Kaikyū no Kyoku, 7
Kaji Makura, 16
kakezume. See koto: playing techniques, zokusō, right hand
kakite. See koto: playing techniques, zokusō, right hand
kakuzume. See tsume
Kamakura Hakkei, 16
Kambun Ōtsu no Kyoku, 155, 176, 202, 457
Kamejima Kengyō, 12
Kamigata-uta, 12
    See also jiuta
Kamigata nagauta, 13
Kaminaga Kengyō, 7
kandō, 65-67, 115, 117, 124, 133, 258
Kan no Kyoku, 14, 215, 218, 220, 221, 457, 461
Kansai district, 18, 19, 25, 26
Kantō district, 18, 19, 25
Kanya no Kyoku, 7
Karagoromo, 17
Karakami, 7
Kara Kinuta, 21
Kasumi no Kyoku, 14, 220, 221, 457, 461

katarimono, 18, 470

Katōbushi, 18, 19

kayakeum, 22, 23, 50

kayako. See kayakeum

Keene, Donald, 476

Kengyō, 11, 12, 469

Kenjun, 5, 6, 58, 147, 148, 151, 153, 155, 468, 469

Keshi no Hana, 16

Kigan no Kyoku, 6, 7

Kikkawa Eishi, 9, 20, 64, 147, 469

Kikudaka Kengyō, 20

Kikuike Kengyō, 14

Kikuike-ryū, 14

Kikuoka Kengyō, 16, 20

Kikuyoshi Kengyō, 20

Kikuzaka Kengyō, 20

Kikuzuki, Shūei, 476

kin (no koto), 22

Kin no Shirabe, 218

Kinki area, 5

Kinkyoku Shifu, 22, 45, 64, 158, 473

Kiritsubo, 10, 11, 148, 179, 190, 195, 236, 245, 249, 255, 256, 455

Kisegawa Kōtō, 10

Kitajima Kengyō, 10, 12-14, 38, 190-198, 200, 201, 203, 205-207, 210, 211, 234, 259, 455-456, 466, 469, 470

Kō Dōjōji, 16

Kofukuji, 148

Kō Genji, 14, 217, 218, 221, 457, 463

Kogō no Kyoku, 19, 466, 473

Kogō no Tsubone, 6

Kojiki, 22

Kokingumi, 17, 466

Kokinshū, 17

Kokoro Zukushi, 10, 11, 148, 177, 195, 197, 199, 201-203, 214, 231, 235, 239, 240, 247, 248, 252, 254, 455

Kokuli, 3

kokyoku, 466

kokyū, 18

Koma. See Kokuli

Komiya Toyotaka, 20

komunko, 22

komusō, 18

Kondō Soetsu, 18

Kongōseki, 20

Konkai, 16

Korea, 3, 22, 23

    See also   Kokuli; Paikche; Silla

Koryū Shiki Genji, 218, 219, 457, 471

kō-shinkyoku, 466

koto:

    acoustical properties, 29, 30

    Ikuta koto, 26, 27, 28

    instrument, 6, 19, 24-29

    manufacture, 25-27

    origin, 3, 4, 22-23

    parts, 25-29

    Yamada koto, 26, 27, 28

    playing position. 50, 473

    playing techniques, gakusō, right hand:

        hayagaki, 58

        kaeshizume, 59

        kozume, 58, 473

        musubite, 59

        ren, 59

        sawaru, 58

        shizugaki, 58

        sugagaki, 58

        tsumubite, 59

    playing techniques, gakusō, left hand:

        nidooshihanashi, 60

        oshihanashi, 60

        oshiiri, 60

        toriyuru, 60

    playing techniques, zokusō, right hand:

        general, 137-144, 148-156, 172, 202-211, 221

        awasezume, 51

        chirashizume (chirashi, san), 52

        han-hikiren, 51

        hankake, 53, 54-55

        han-ryū, 52

        hayakake, 53, 55-56

        hikiren (shan-ren), 51

        hikisute, 52

        kakezume, 53-54

        kakite, 51

        mukōhan (kake), 54-55

        nagashizume (ryū, kararin), 52

        namigaeshi, 52

        oshiawase, 51

        sukuizume, 51

        surizume, 52

        tanhan (kake), 54-55

488　INDEX

uchizume, 51
uraren (ren, sararin), 51
waren, 52
warizume, 52-53
yokozume, 56
playing techniques, zokusō, left hand:
general, 20, 48, 57, 60, 173, 211
chitsu (tsuki-iro), 57
en (ato-oshi), 57
ichijū-oshi, 57
ju (hiki-iro), 57
kasaneoshi, 57
keshizume (soede, soe-iro), 57
kō (oshide), 57
left hand plucking, 20
nijū-oshi, 57
oshihanashi, 57
sanjū-oshi, 57
Yamada koto, 26, 27, 28
yōgin (yuri-iro), 57, 473
See also gakusō, Ikuta koto,
jūshichi-gen-kin, shinsō,
tansō, tsukusō, Yamada
koto, zokusō
Kōtō, 11, 469
kouta, 5, 9, 10, 12
kuchi-jamisen, 41-45, 472
See also shōfu
Kudan, 63, 65-85, 94, 99, 103-107,
110-115, 117, 119-121, 127-129,
135, 136, 138, 141, 142, 143,
454, 474
Kudara. See Paikche
Kudara-goto. See Kugo
Kugo, 22
kumikyoku, 473
kumiuta:
Ikuta-ryū, 7-19
shamisen kumiuta, 9-10, 12
Tsukushi-goto, 5, 10, 11
Yamada-ryū, 18, 19
Kumiuta Zenshū, 44, 155, 264, 466, 471
Kumoi Kudan, 63-85, 94, 100, 103-107,
110-113, 115, 116, 118-121, 127,
128, 131, 135, 136, 139, 140, 142,
143, 431-439, 454, 474
Kumoi no Kyoku, 8, 10, 11, 214, 215,
217, 218, 229, 221, 241, 245, 265,
284-300, 455, 459

Kumoi Rōsai, 8, 10, 12, 455, 469
Kumo no Ue, 11, 179, 189, 193, 195,
197, 210, 236, 241, 249, 251, 252, 254,
255, 455
Kurahashi Kengyō, 12, 38, 456, 466
Kuroda-bushi (Chikuzen-imayō), 475
Kurume, 5, 147
Kyōgoku, 20, 50
Kyōmono, 16, 20
Kyōto, 3, 4, 5, 7, 12, 14, 16, 17, 18, 20,
44, 51, 124, 261
Kyūshū, 4, 5, 7, 147
mae-biki, 15, 155, 156
mae-uta, 15
Makino Kengyō, 38, 195-198, 200, 201,
203, 205-207, 234, 455, 466
Makita Unshō, 16
makura (jo), 15
Makura no Sōshi, 148
Malm, William P., 41, 228, 229, 468,
470, 472, 475
Mamiya Michio, 21
Matsu no Ha, 470
Matsuura Kengyō, 16
Matsuzaka Harue, 17
Meiji shinkyoku, 20
Meiji Sho-Chiku-Bai, 20
Meng Tien. See Mōten
Midare, 10, 43, 63-65, 94, 102, 103,
108-114, 119, 121, 127-132, 135, 136,
138, 141-144, 258, 440-451, 454, 473,
474, 475
Midare Rinzetsu, 64
See also *Midare*
Mikuni no Homare, 20, 466
Minezaki Kōtō, 15
Mingaku, 6
Mitsuhashi Kengyō, 13, 14, 18, 38, 39, 55,
56, 189-194, 196-198, 200-203, 205-207,
211, 214, 227, 234, 259, 454, 456, 466,
474
Mitsuhashi Kōtō, 15
Mitsuzaki Kengyō, 16-17, 222, 224, 456
Mitsu no Keshiki, 20
Mitsu no Shirabe. See *Haru no Miya*
Miyagi Michio, 21, 23
Miyako no Haru, 19, 466
Miyama Jishi, 16
Miya no Uguisu, 13, 182, 201, 216, 226,

237, 248, 255, 456, 462
Mizu no Hentai, 21
modality:
    Chinese, 31
    in gagaku, 32-34
    in Tsukushi-goto, 33
    in zokusō, 20, 33, 115-124, 171,
        198-199, 213, 217
    See also in-sen
modulation, 38, 39, 119, 121, 171, 196,
    199-202, 211, 220, 221, 224, 260
Morton, David, 472
Mōten (Meng Tien), 23
Motoori Nobunaga, 17
mukōhan. See koto: playing techniques,
    zokusō, right hand
Murai Reiko, 7
Murasaki Shikibu, 6
    See also *Genji Monogatari*
Mutamagawa, 13, 184, 196-198, 201,
    204, 207, 456
Nagara no Haru, 16
nagashizume. See koto: playing techniques,
    zokusō, right hand
nagauta, 12, 13, 470
Nagoya, 17, 44
Naikyobu shrine, 4
naka-chirashi, 15
Nakamura Sōzan, 50
    See also *Shichiku Shoshinshū*
naka-uta, 15
Nakayama Yukinaga, 6
    See also *Heike Monogatari*
naka-yurushi, 13, 39
    See also classification; Ikuta-ryū
namigaeshi. See koto: playing techniques,
    zokusō, right hand
Nanakomachi, 16
Nara, 23
Natsu no Kyoku, 17
Nebiki no Matsu, 15
netori, 58
Nidan, 63
nō, 146
Noda Chōshō, 6
Nogawa Kengyō, 9
Nogawa-ryū, 9
nokorigaku, 3, 148, 151
notation, 41-49, 472

See also shōfu
Obata Jūichi and Sugita Eizi, 29-30, 40
odori-uta, 5, 9
ōgi, 6, 7
    See also classification; Tsukushi-goto
Ōgi no Kyoku, 10, 11, 180, 189, 197, 199,
    241, 249, 251, 252, 255, 455
Ogura no Kyoku, 5, 7
Okayama prefecture, 5
Okinawa, 5
Okinawan koto, 5, 64, 68, 468
Omoigawa, 12, 220, 221, 256, 456, 459
omotegumi. See classification; Ikuta-ryū
ornamentation, 67, 71, 73, 74, 76, 78,
    80, 82, 121-132, 173, 246-256
    See also koto, playing techniques,
    left hand
Ōsaka, 5, 12, 14, 15, 16, 20, 51
oshiawase. See koto: playing techniques,
    zokusō, right hand
Osuma, 14
Otome no Kyoku, 5, 7
Ōtsu no Kumi, 222, 457, 465
Ōtsu no Kyoku, 14, 176, 188, 194, 200,
    201, 203, 207, 208, 216, 264, 373-385,
    457, 463
Ōuchi Yoshitaka, 147, 148
Paikche (Kudara), 3
performance practice, 227
Péri, Noël, 242
playing position. See koto: playing position
playing techniques. See koto: playing
    techniques, right hand, and playing
    techniques, left hand
Rankyoku, 7, 11
Reinhard, Kurt, 23
Reischauer, Edwin O, and John K. Fair-
    bank, 468
ren. See koto: playing techniques, zokusō,
    right hand, "uraren"
Rengi, 16
rhythm:
    in danmono, 133-137
    in kumiuta, 159, 161, 164, 166, 168, 170,
        171, 211, 229-234, 239, 257, 260
    meter, 8, 47
    syncopation, 70, 73, 74, 76, 78, 80,
        133-137, 171, 260
Rinzetsu:

in *Shichiku Shoshinshū*, 5, 65, 473, 474

in Tsukushi-goto, 5, 64

ritsu, 33, 35

Rōei, 5, 7

Rokudan, 10, 17, 44, 45, 47, 48, 63-95, 103-107, 110, 111, 113, 117-129, 131, 132, 134-136, 138, 140, 141, 143, 144, 258, 260, 265, 402-413, 454, 468

Rokudan Sugagaki, 64, 468

Rōsai, 469

ryō, 33

ryū. See koto. playing techniques zokusō, right hand, "nagashizume"

Ryūkyūs, 5, 9

　　See also Okinawa; Okinawan koto

Saga clan, 6

saibara, 3

Saikiku, 7

Sakakiba, 16, 187, 194, 227, 456

Sake. See *Sasa no Tsuyu*

Sakuragawa, 16

saku-uta, 19, 470

Sampōin, 11, 148

san. See koto: playing techniques, zokusō, right hand, "chirashizume"

Sanada Shin, 12, 470

Sandan, 64

Sandan-Jishi, 15

sankyoku, 18, 65

Sansom, George B., 468

sararin. See koto: playing techniques, zokusō, right hand, "uraren"

Sarashi, 15

Sasa no Tsuyu, 16

Sato Showa, 16, 44, 155, 466, 471

　　See also *Kumiuta Zenshū*

Sayama Kengyō, 15

scales. See modality

se, 22, 23

secondary dominant, 119-120, 171, 199, 220, 221, 223, 260

secondary subdominant, 119-120, 200-201

Sesshu, 145

Setsugekka, 13, 183, 196, 198, 201, 202, 253, 456

shakuhachi, 18, 65

shamisen, 9-10, 12-14, 18, 65

shan-ren. See koto: playing techniques, zokusō, right hand, "uraren"

Shiba Sukehiro, 58, 59, 468, 475

Shichidan, 63-85, 94, 96, 103-107, 110-114, 118-121, 127-130, 135, 136, 138, 140, 141, 143, 144, 454, 468

Shichidan Sugagaki, 64, 468

shichi-gen-kin, 6

　　See also   kin

Shichiku Shoshinshū, 5, 45, 64, 154, 473, 474

　　See also   Nakamura Sōzan

Shidan, 64

Shigedayu-mono, 470

Shigemoto Fusakuchi, 19

Shiki, 7, 11

Shiki no Fuji, 13, 38, 183, 196, 203, 220, 227, 250, 254, 456, 460

Shiki no Koi, 13, 185, 196, 201, 202, 220, 221, 227, 250, 331-341, 456, 462

Shiki no Kumi, 227

Shiki no Kyoku, 11, 180, 189, 190, 193, 196, 197, 200, 203, 209, 227, 228, 231, 235, 255, 455

Shiki no Midare, 7

Shiki no Nagame, 16

Shiki no Tomo, 14, 185, 194, 199, 227, 236, 249, 456

Shin Ikuta-ryū, 14

Shin Kinkyokushū, 10

Shin-kokingumi, 17

Shin-kumiuta, 17

Shin Kumoi Rōsai, 10, 12, 456

shinkyoku, 20, 40, 50, 466

shin Nihon Ongaku, 21

shin saku-uta, 19

shinsō, 23

Shin-sō, 23

Shinsōgochō, 11

shinsōkyoku, 19

Shin Ukifune, 16

Shinya no Tsuki, 16

Shin Yatsuhashi Kengyō, 14, 190, 195, 197-201, 205-207, 218, 234, 457

Shin Yatsuhashi-ryū, 14

shirabe, 219

shirabemono, 10, 473

Shiragi. See Silla

Shiragi-koto. See kayakeum

Sho-Chiku-Bai, 15, 466

shōfu, 41-46, 51-53, 57, 472

shōka, 41

Shoku-yashiki, 11-12, 14, 20, 261

Shōmu, Emperor, 23

shōmyō, 107

Shōsōin, 23, 471

Shūfū no Ji, 7

Shūka no Kyoku, 7, 11

Silla (Shiragi), 3

sō. See koto

Sōfukoi, 6

Sōfuren, 6

Sō-Kengyō, 14

Sōkyoku Taiishō, 18, 45, 46, 47, 48,
    53, 55, 56, 64, 133, 147, 156,
    213, 218, 226, 227, 471, 472,
    473, 475

    See also   Yamada Shōkoku

Structure:
    danmono, 65-144, 474
    jiuta, 13
    koto kumiuta, 6, 8, 9, 11, 155-
        175, 217-218
    shamisen kumiuta, 9, 10
    tegotomono, 15

Sue no Chigiri, 16

Sue no Matsu, 12, 181, 195, 199,
    200, 201, 203, 204, 241, 242,
    243, 249, 251, 253, 302-315,
    455

Sugagaki, 5, 68, 473, 474

Sugawara no Michizane, 5

sukuizume. See koto: playing techniques,
    zokusō, right hand

Suma, 11, 180, 189, 190, 197-199,
    207, 209, 234, 237, 241, 245,
    250, 252, 254, 255, 455

Sumiyama Kengyō, 14

Sumiyama-ryū, 14

Suō, 147

Suribachi, 16

surizume. See koto: playing techniques,
    zokusō, right hand

sūsō, 23

Suzuki Koson, 20

Tachibana, 16, 187, 194, 227, 235, 245,
    456

Taira no Kiyomori, 5

Takano Tatsuyuki, 11, 473, 474

Takiochi. See *Otome no Kyoku*

Takiotoshi Sugagaki.   See *Ichidan*

Tamagawa, 16

Tamakazura, 13, 38, 184, 194, 196, 198,
    201, 204, 207, 220, 243, 246, 316-329,
    456, 460

Tama no Utena, 16

Tanabata, 16, 187, 190, 194, 227, 245,
    456

Tanabe Hisao, 5, 7, 10-11, 468, 469, 475

tanhan. See koto: playing techniques,
    zokusō, right hand

tanka, 227

tansō, 23, 24

Tateyama Noboru, 20

teaching:
    method, 41
    limitations, 6, 466

tegoto, 15, 17, 19

tegoto-mono, 15, 19, 21, 466

Teikajō, 6

Temmon, Emperor, 147

tempo:
    general, 48
    in danmono, 65
    in jiuta, 13
    in kumiuta, 155, 159
    in tegoto-mono, 15

Tenka Taihei, 11, 178, 189-191, 195, 196, 209,
    231, 232, 233, 234, 245, 251, 252, 256, 455

text:
    in jiuta, 13
    in koto kumiuta, 8, 9, 10, 11, 226, 227
    in shamisen kumiuta, 9, 10
    treatment, 228, 229

Tobiume, 14, 188, 189, 190, 195, 200,
    201, 207, 234, 235, 236, 245, 457

Tōdaiji, 23

Tōgaku, 32

Toko no shirabe, 469

Tōkyo, 18, 19, 20, 44

    See also   Edo

tomede, 58

Tomimoto-bushi, 18, 19

Tomo Chidori, 14, 185, 190, 193, 195,

199, 207, 236, 240, 245, 456
Tone system:
    in China, 31
    in Japan, 31
Torazawa Kengyō, 9
Tōryū Shiki Genji, 218, 219, 221, 222,
    457, 465
Tōsō, 471
Toyoichi, 18
Tran Van Khe, 471
Tsuda Seikan, 12, 471
Tsugiyama Kengyō, 14, 39, 194, 197,
    200, 201, 203, 205-208, 218, 457
Tsugiyama-ryū, 14
Tsukimi, 16
Tsukushi-ei, 7
    See also classification;
    Tsukushi-goto
Tsukushi-goto, 4, 5-7, 8, 10, 11, 12,
    18, 50, 58, 147-155, 227, 258,
    468, 470, 473
Tsukushi-hiei, 7
    See also classification; Tsukushi-
    goto
Tsukushi-ryū. See Tsukushi-goto
tsukusō, 6, 23, 24
tsume:
    gakusō, 6, 28, 50
    Ikuta-ryū, 13, 28, 50
    kakuzume, 13, 28
    maruzume, 28
    Tsukushi-goto, 6, 50
    Yamada-ryū, 19, 50
tsunagi, 15
Tsunoda Ryusaku, William Theodore
    De Bary, and Donald Keene, 468
tuning:
    general, 6, 31, 34-40
    in gagaku:
        hyōjō, 58, 153, 155
        banshiki-chō, 153
        ichikotsu-chō, 153, 154
    in Tsukushi-goto:
        ichikotsu-chō, 153, 154
        ōshiki-chō, 153, 469
    in zokusō:
        akebono-chōshi, 14, 34, 35, 37,
            38, 39, 470
        akemi-chōshi, 37

Akikaze-chōshi, 17, 35, 37
han-kumoi-jōshi, 14, 35, 36, 38, 39, 65
han-nakazora-chōshi, 14, 35, 37, 38, 39
hira-jōshi (Toko no shirabe), 34, 35,
    36, 38, 39, 40, 42, 48, 53, 54
hon-kumoi-jōshi, 8, 34, 35, 36, 38,
    39, 54, 115, 471, 472
karigane-chōshi, 35, 37, 38
kin-uwa-jōshi, 35, 36, 38
kokin-chōshi, 17
kumoi-jōshi, 6, 35, 36
nakazora-chōshi, 14, 34, 35, 37, 38, 39
shimo-chidori-chōshi, 35, 36, 38
ura-chidori-chōshi, 35, 37, 38, 471
    in Okinawa, 64
    method of tuning, 39-40, 115
    change of tuning, 14
uchiawase, 16
uchiawase-mono, 16
uchizume. See koto: playing techniques,
    zokusō, right hand
Uda, Emperor, 4
Uji Meguri, 16
Ukifune, 13, 184, 193, 194, 226, 235,
    249, 254, 456
Ukigomo, 7
Umegae:
    by Kenjun, 7, 11
    by Yatsuhashi, 11, 148, 154, 177, 189,
        191, 195, 199, 203, 210, 214, 231,
        232, 233, 236, 239, 240, 243, 245,
        248, 250, 455
uragumi, 13, 39
    See also classification;
    Ikuta-ryū
uraren. See koto: playing techniques,
    zokusō, right hand
Usugoromo, 10, 179, 190, 193, 196, 201,
    231, 236, 252, 455
Usuyuki, 11, 148, 178, 189, 191, 195, 196,
    208, 215, 241, 248, 252, 253, 256, 455
uta-mono, 466, 470
Utsusemi, 12, 181, 189, 190, 197, 198,
    234, 235, 236, 243, 245, 251, 255, 455
Uya no Kyoku, 7
vocal part, 226-257
voice quality, 226, 227
wagon, 22
Wakaba, 39, 182, 196, 197, 200, 220,

455, 459
Wakana:
    kumiuta, 16, 187, 195, 208, 209,
      227, 245, 456
    kyōmono, 16
Wakan Rōei Shū, 155
Waley, Arthur, 6
waren. See koto: playing techniques,
    zokusō, right hand
warizume. See koto: playing techniques,
    zokusō, right hand
Yachiyo-Jishi, 16
Yaegaki, 14, 217, 218, 243, 457, 463
Yaegoromo, 16, 466
Yaezaki Kengyō, 16, 20, 227, 471
Yamada Kengyō, 16, 18, 19, 190, 196-
    198, 200, 201, 203, 205-208, 219,
    456, 466, 473
Yamada koto, 23
Yamada-ryū Koto no Kagami, 44, 55,
    56, 156
Yamada-ryū, repertoire, 19
Yamada Shōkoku, 18, 22, 226, 227
    See also *Sōkyoku Taiishō*
Yamada Takao, 468
Yamaguchi, 147
Yamakazura, 17
Yamaki Kengyō, 19
Yamase Kengyō, 19
Yamase Shōin, 19
Yamato-goto. See wagon
Yamato Kengyō, 19
Yamazumi Kōtō, 7, 11
Yanagawa Kengyō, 9
Yanagawa-ryū, 9
Yasumura Kengyō, 14, 15, 18, 210,
    212, 218, 258, 261, 456, 472
Yatsuhashi Kengyō, 5, 7-13, 33,

34, 35, 38, 148, 151, 153, 154, 155,
190-198, 200, 201, 203, 205-211, 214,
218, 227, 230, 234, 256, 258, 259, 261,
455, 466, 469, 470, 471
Yatsuhashi no jūsan-gumi, 11
Yatsuhashi no sankyoku, 11, 470
Yatsuhashi-ryū, 12, 18, 50, 219
Yōgaku, 21
Yokan no Kyoku, 6, 7
Yokozuchi, 16
yokozume. See koto: playing techniques,
    zokusō, right hand
yōkyoku, 18
yōkyoku-mono, 26, 470
Yondan, 64
Yoshida Itchō, 18
Yoshino Shizuka, 20
Yoshizawa Kengyō, 17
yotsumono, 19
Yotsu no Tami, 16
Yoyo no Hoshi, 16
Yūgao, 16
Yuki no Ashita, 10, 178, 189, 210, 236,
    239, 248, 256, 455
yuri, 473
    See also. koto: playing techniques,
    zokusō, left hand, "yōgin"
Yuwate, 25
Yuya, 19
Zangetsu, 15
Zatō, 11
Zeami, 107
Zendōji, 5, 147, 148
Zendōjigaku, 6
zensō, 218
zokkyoku, 5, 64, 468, 474
zokusō, 23, 469